Woolley of Ur

By the same author

Captain Shakespear
Gertrude Bell
The Illicit Adventure
Leachman: OC Desert
The Diaries of Parker Pasha
Uncovering the Ancient World
Royal Copenhagen Porcelain

(with Zahara Freeth)
Kuwait: Prospect and Reality
Explorers of Arabia

(with Gerald de Gaury)
The Spirit of the East
The Road to Kabul

WOOLLEY OF UR

The Life of Sir Leonard Woolley

H. V. F. WINSTONE

SECKER & WARBURG
LONDON

First published in England 1990
by Martin Secker & Warburg Limited
Michelin House, 81 Fulham Road sw3 6rb
Copyright © 1990 by H. V. F. Winstone

A CIP catalogue for this book is available
from the British Library

ISBN 0 436 57790 9

Set in Linotron 11/13pt Sabon
Printed in Great Britain
by St Edmundsbury Press,
Bury St Edmunds, Suffolk

For Dominique

Contents

List of Illustrations

Woolley was an experienced excavator, sharp-eyed, intuitive and skilled at technical improvisations. Above all he had the imagination to be an excellent writer, well able to rouse public enthusiasm – and therefore the disapproval of the more high-and-dry type of academic scholar.

JACQUETTA HAWKES in introduction to *World of the Past*, 1963

For his work at Ur alone our debt to Woolley is immeasurable. In three things he excelled. First, his recognition of how much a knowledge of architectural development can contribute to our understanding of ancient society. Next I think comes his incomparable sense of craftsmanship, for which he had a genuine love . . . Whenever he found something produced by human hands he tried to visualize the process of creating it, and to share the aspirations of its maker. Lastly, he was a most gifted writer with a fluency of style which has entranced a multitude of readers the world over.

Sir MAX MALLOWAN, Memorial in *Iraq*, Vol xxii, 1960

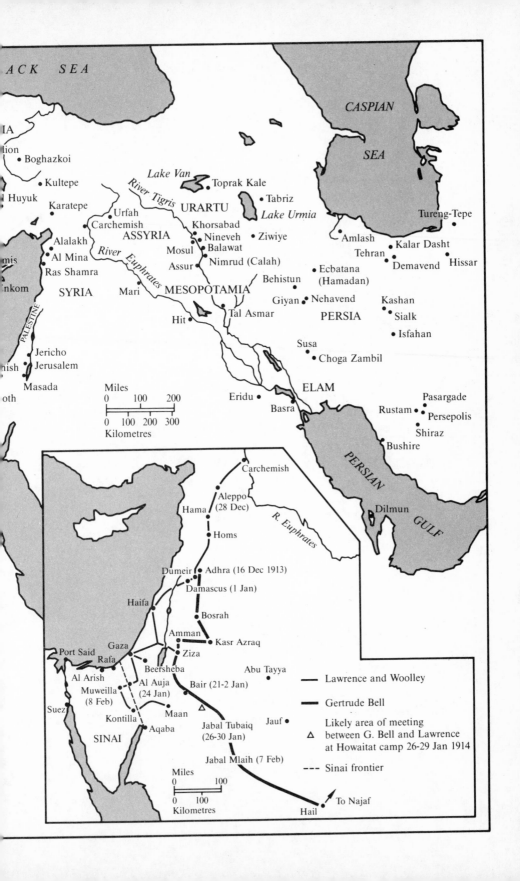

BLACK SEA

CASPIAN

SEA

lion
• Boghazkoi
• Kultepe
Huyuk
Karatepe
Urfah
Carchemish
ASSYRIA
Alalakh
Al Mina
Ras Shamra
mis
nkom
SYRIA
Mari

Lake Van
• Toprak Kale
River Tigris
URARTU
Khorsabad
• Nineveh
Mosul • Balawat
Assur • Nimrud (Calah)
MESOPOTAMIA

• Tabriz
Lake Urmia
• Ziwiye
Tureng-Tepe
• Amlash
• Kalar Dasht
Tehran
• Demavend • Hissar
• Ecbatana
(Hamadan)
• Behistun
Giyan • Nehavend
• Kashan
• Sialk

River Euphrates
Hit •
• Tal Asmar
PERSIA
• Isfahan

PALESTINE

• Jericho
• Jerusalem
Masada
oth
hish

Miles
0   100   200
0 100 200 300
Kilometres

Eridu •
Basra

Susa •
• Choga Zambil
ELAM

Rustam
Pasargade
• Persepolis
Shiraz
• Bushire

PERSIAN
GULF

Carchemish
Aleppo
Hama (28 Dec)
Homs •
Dumeir • Adhra (16 Dec 1913)
Damascus (1 Jan)
Haifa
Bosrah •
Amman • Kasr Azraq
Ziza
Gaza
Beersheba
Abu Tayya
Port Said
Rafa
Al Arish
Al Auja
Bair (21-2 Jan)
Muweilla
(24 Jan)
(8 Feb)
Maan
Jauf •
Kontilla
Aqaba
SINAI
Jabal Tubaiq
(26-30 Jan)
Jabal Mlaih (7 Feb)

Suez

Dilmun

R. Euphrates

—— Lawrence and Woolley

—— Gertrude Bell

△ Likely area of meeting
    between G. Bell and Lawrence
    at Howaitat camp 26-29 Jan 1914

--- Sinai frontier

Miles
0   100
0   100
Kilometres

Hail
To Najaf

Preface and Acknowledgements

And Terah took Abram his son, and Lot the son of
Haran, his son's son, and Sarai his daughter-in-law, his
son Abram's wife; and they went forth with them from
Ur of the Chaldees, to go into the land of Canaan; and
they came unto Haran, and dwelt there.

Genesis 12.4–5

'The like of this prodigy we shall never see again.' The words
belonged to Sir Max Mallowan, written in his *Memoirs* in 1977,
fifty-two years after he first went to Ur of the Chaldees in the ancient
land of Sumer as an apprentice to Leonard Woolley, the prodigal
archaeologist. And it was there that Mallowan met a woman writer
who was destined to fall in love with antiquity and with him –
Agatha Christie.

If future generations were bound to lose sight of the magnificence
of Woolley's professional achievements, they would at least find
reminders of his existence in the works of Miss Christie, who made
dramatic use of the 'celebrated archaeologist' and his wife Katharine
in one of her best-known detective stories, *Murder in Mesopotamia*.

Perhaps it is in the nature of things that a chance meeting between
the already successful novelist and the scholarly Mallowan at a
remote excavation site on the banks of the river Euphrates ensured
the everlasting renown of Woolley as the homicidal husband of a
domineering woman in a popular 'thriller'. Oblique literary recognition must not, however, be allowed to cloud the man's first claim
to immortality: the unveiling of one of the world's first urban
communities, Ur of the 3rd millennium BC, supposed birthplace of
the patriarch Abraham; and the elegant, painstaking reconstruction
of the earliest of civilizations.

Among British archaeologists of the twentieth century, Woolley stood beside Sir Arthur Evans, Sir Flinders Petrie and Howard Carter. Until very recently none of that imposing quartet had excited the slightest literary interest, and up to the publication of this work only Petrie can lay claim to full biographical treatment. Woolley would probably have preferred it to remain so. He was never conscious of greatness or given to self-importance. He liked to think of himself as an ordinary man with a God-given opportunity to do an extraordinary job of work. If his origins were not exactly humble, neither were they exalted. Like the rest of his large family, he relied on scholarship places at school and university to further his ends in life.

His work has contemporary glamour. He dug up a site of primary religious importance, Ur of the Chaldees, according to Genesis the birthplace of the patriarch Abraham. In the new age of religious revivalism, he has a particular appeal. Had he dug at Nippur, or Kish, or Ugarit, or even Karnak, it might have been a different story. The great American, British, German and French archaeologists who excavated such places, and who translated the languages of the cuneiform and hieroglyphic scripts, gave to the modern world an unparalleled treasury of knowledge. They gave us the earliest recorded history of mankind, unearthed immense libraries, and drew ever more precisely the thin line which divides history from pre-history. Most remain anonymous to all but the expert.

Even among the great men of his day, Woolley was exceptional in at least one important respect. He was the communicator extraordinary. He attracted public attention as no other archaeologist before him (though his friend and protégé Mortimer Wheeler was to lift the art of publicity to even greater heights after him), and so entranced the world-famous writer Agatha Christie with his accounts of the tombs and palaces of southern Mesopotamia that she promptly caught the Orient Express and went off post-haste to Ur. The substance of Woolley's appeal might have been very different. Ironically, he began digging at Ur at almost the same moment that Howard Carter unearthed the hidden stairway which led to the tomb of Tutankhamen. Some years earlier, Woolley had turned down an invitation from Lord Carnarvon, Carter's patron, to join him in Egypt. Had he taken up his lordship's offer, the story of modern archaeology, and the burden of this biography, might have been very different.

Woolley cultivated popular interest, often with brazen resort to propaganda methods which he perfected as an officer of military

intelligence in two world wars. He became an unrepentant popular-
izer of archaeology, and in an academic world which, on the whole,
likes its sons and daughters to conform to some recognizable stamp,
he was an outsider. In the sense that he joined few organizations,
espoused hardly any causes, seldom supped with the mighty, and
spent most of his working life in distant places and in secret military
activity, he was something of an unknown quantity, even in his
lifetime. When he wrote of his personal, as opposed to his professional activities, he covered up more than he revealed. The
biographical web has had to be woven rather than unravelled.

I have received so much co-operation from so many people that I
am forced to pay most of my debts with a scanty list of acknowledgements. But there must be a few exceptions. First, Dr Duncan
Noble, who began to write the life story of Sir Leonard Woolley
before I came on the scene. As an academic archaeologist, he was
admirably qualified to take on the task and he had done a good
deal of research. Even so, when he found that I had embarked on
the same task he most generously left the field to me and
subsequently handed me the fruits of his investigations. This book
could not have been written at all without the splendid help of Mrs
Margaret Witton, Woolley's niece and godchild, who was unstint-
ing in her efforts to provide and to verify family records, letters
and photographs. Her brother, Mr Warren Laxton, helped too in
important areas of family research. On the professional side, I
cannot neglect an opportunity to express my gratitude to the British
Museum and its neighbour the British Library. To the trustees and
directors of those remarkable institutions I offer my sincere thanks.
It is to the generosity of the Museum's academic staff – particularly
in the Western Asiatic Department – that I am most indebted. I
must put on record my particular thanks to the Keeper of the
Western Asiatic Department, Dr John Curtis, and his colleagues Dr
Julian Reade, Dr Irving Finkel, and by no means least, Dr
Dominique Collon. Also to Mr Terence Mitchell. If the errors of
archaeological treatment are mine, any virtues are largely theirs.
The other museum with which Woolley was associated for much of
his life, the Philadelphia Museum of the University of Pennsylvania,
was just as willing to provide information and photographs from its
Near East (Ur) Archive. I would like in particular to thank the
Reference Archivist, Mr Alessandro Pezzati, for his generous help. I
must also make special acknowledgement of the help of Dr Roger

Moorey, Keeper in the Department of Antiquities of the Ashmolean Museum, whose edited version of Woolley's *Ur of the Chaldees* is the standard work, and of his colleague Mrs Ann Browne. My thanks also to Professor W. G. Lambert of Birmingham University, whose recollections and advice were invaluable. The librarians of the Bodleian and New College, Oxford, and their assistants, made light work of a short but frantic period of research. Ms Caroline Dalton, Assistant Archivist at the New College Library, and Mr Steven Tomlinson, Assistant Librarian of the Bodleian, were especially helpful, as was Dr D. S. Porter, sometime Senior Assistant Librarian of that institution. Miss Pauline Adams, Librarian and Archivist of Somerville College, provided important information with regard to Lady Woolley. The Headmaster of St John's School, Leatherhead, and Mr M. E. C. Comer, teacher at the school and Secretary of the Old Johnian Society, provided me with indispensable background to my subject's school life. The Royal Geographical Society, as ever, was an invaluable source of books, papers and information, and my thanks go to the Director, Dr John Hemming, the Librarian, Mr David Wileman, and the Archivist, Mrs Christine Kelly. At a personal level, I am greatly indebted to Lady Mallowan (Barbara Parker-Mallowan) who guided me to her late husband's family and friends, particularly his stepdaughter (and Agatha Christie's daughter) Mrs Anthony (Rosalind) Hicks. And to Mr Sinclair Hood, Mr William C. Brice and Professor Seton Lloyd, to whom I am indebted for valuable recollections and anecdotes. Most importantly in terms of personal knowledge and observation, Mr and Mrs Alfred Waters, who looked after Leonard Woolley in the last ten years of his life; without their help this picture of the man would have lacked vital substance.

As for the rest, I can make only the sketchiest of acknowledgements to the many to whom I owe varying debts of gratitude: The Rev. H. F. N. Ball; Mr M. V. Carey of solicitors Tweedie and Prideaux in connection with the T. E. Lawrence correspondence in the Bodleian Library; Mr Michael Diamond, Director of Birmingham City Council Museums and Art Gallery, and in particular Mr Richard Lockett, the Assistant Director; Mrs Margaret Drower whose personal generosity and excellent biography of Sir Flinders Petrie I have battened on equally; Mr Tony Innes, Hon Secretary of the Shaftesbury and District Historical Society; Mr Michael Hughes, present owner of Sedgehill Manor; Mrs Gillian Grant of the Middle East Centre, St Antony's College Oxford; the Rev. J. C. Hibberd of the London Diocesan Fund; Mr Geoffrey Herridge; Mr George Tod; Mr Michael Rice; Mr Luke Herrmann, art historian, who directed my attention to the disposal of some of Woolley's Mesopotamian and Greek objects; Ms Honor Clerk, Research Assistant in the National Portrait Gallery; Mr Dimitri Anson of the Otago Museum, Dunedin; Mrs Henrietta McCall; Mr Peter Scott, FRCS; Mr and Mrs J. M. Mallowan; Mr S. M. Andrews, Headmaster of Clifton College; Mrs Angela Downey, present occupant of 'Uplands', the old Woolley home at Bath; Mrs Ailsa Corbett Winder; Mrs Glyn Daniel; Lady Wheeler; Rice University, Houston, Texas, and Mrs Nancy L. Boothe, Director of the University's Woodson Research Center; Messrs Christie's; Mrs Judith Nugee; Mr Rowan Laxton; Mrs Jill Sturgeon; Mrs Janet Raikes; Professor Edith Porada; Mr Tony Benn MP, who corrected me on small but vital matters concerning wartime operations in the Mediterranean in which his father, the first Viscount Stansgate, was involved; Mr Julian Wiltshire, custodian of Bateman's and the Kipling archive there; the publishers and authors of the many studies of Agatha Christie to which I have made particular reference; my wife Joan and daughter Ruth whose unceasing burden of reading, correcting, conveying and copying is almost insupportable.

Note on transliteration: I can offer the reader no sensible explanation for inconsistencies in the spelling of Arabic words in direct and reported speech. Despite many efforts to establish a common approach, some choose to translate from the spoken word, others from the written: thus *Tel, Tell, Tal*, meaning mound, though why the capital letter in a language which has no capitals it is hard to imagine; thus also, *Amir, Emir, Ameer, Jubail, Jubeyl, Shaikh, Sheik, Sheyukh*, etc, etc. I can only say that the fault is not mine.

HVFW, November 1989

Inheritance

Charles Leonard Woolley was born on 17 April 1880 at 13 Southwold Road, in the London borough of Hackney. His father, the Rev. George Herbert Woolley, was vicar of the nearby parish of St Matthew's in Upper Clapton.

The Rev. Woolley and his wife Sarah brought up a family of eleven children in an atmosphere charged with learning and almost devoid of emotion, and with precious little money to spare. Leonard (his first name was never used) was the third in order of birth. Sarah Louise, or Sadie, was the eldest, followed by George Cathcart who was always known by his second, and his mother's maiden, name.

After Leonard there came a procession of three boys and five girls, mostly known by their second names – Alice Mary, Herbert Martin (Bertie), Edith Pearce, Amy Kathleen, Frances Rachel, Marjory Maude, Geoffrey Harold, and Alfred Boyle (who died in infancy).

Leonard seems to have maintained his middle station in family life with the kind of *sang froid* for which, as an adult, he became renowned. A factor which may have contributed to a confidence and gift of leadership apparent even in raw youth was the gap of nearly four years between his own birth and that of the next boy, Bertie. The last surviving son, Geoffrey Harold, made his appearance in 1892. Cathcart, the elder brother, was a retiring youngster so that during his most impressionable years Leonard held centre stage in a family life which was at once intellectually stimulating and morally censorious.

The girls went to a local school. For the boys, tuition began at home and was centred chiefly on the Bible and classical studies. The peremptory manner of their strict father-teacher caused Leonard and his brothers little inconvenience. On the whole they were studious, keen to learn and indifferent to the sports and pastimes which occupied the minds and set the ambitions of most schoolboys at a time that is remembered more for the leg-glances of Dr W. G. Grace than for the wisdom of philosophers and politicians.

Before the question of formal schooling arose there was a change of living for Woolley senior. He was appointed Vicar of the busy parish of St Peter with St Thomas in Bethnal Green, not many miles from his Clapton living. The vicarage which became the new Woolley home was built of brick in an economical square fashion, situated to the east of the tree-lined, iron-fenced, Victorian-Saxon-style church. Bethnal Green, now a traffic-congested nightmare of a place memorable only for its austere blocks of council housing, was a quiet backwater in the early years of the century, with elegant Victorian houses and plentiful gardens. Near the vicarage was a Tudor-style building which was the church school, of which the Rev. Woolley was governor. It was there that the Woolley children began their formal educations, though the boys left as they reached the 'senior' stage to attend Parmiter's School, a brisk walk from the vicarage. In their first real contact with the rough-and-tumble world of schoolboys in the mass, they were embarrassed by constant allusions to 'Woolly sheep'. Leonard, already regarded as the historian of the family, rescued his brothers from the taunt by announcing that the name Woolley was 'a corruption of Wolf's Lea', and that they were, in reality, wolves in sheep's clothing.

In fact, the family tree could be traced back as far as John Wolleius, who made the patriotic journey from Lincolnshire to Tilbury to help resist the Armada and who was buried in the crypt of St Paul's Cathedral in 1595. Some descendants were prominent in the Merchant Taylors Company. Several took the cloth and combined business with devotion. The Rev. Woolley's branch were successful wine merchants. One member of the family, Thomas, emigrated to America in the early 1800s and formed a Woolley association there. Other relatives found their way to Australia.

Sarah Woolley had the more distinguished parental pedigree, with three earldoms, several bishoprics and two generals in direct line. Born in 1852, the daughter of a bank official, Charles Cathcart, she was the granddaughter of Sir George Cathcart, distinguished soldier of the Napoleonic wars who served at Russian HQ, attended the Congress of Vienna, was present at Quatre Bras and Waterloo as ADC to Wellington, became Governor and C-in-C of the Cape Colony and, finally, second to Raglan in the Crimea where he fell in the battle of Inkerman. He married Georgina Greville, and through her Sarah was related to the Earls of Warwick and Mansfield. Her great-grandfather, William Shaw Cathcart the first Earl, was Commander-in-Chief Ireland and was in charge of the expedition to Copenhagen, which city surrendered to him in 1807. After fighting alongside his son with the Russians against Napoleon he returned to St Petersburg as ambassador and military commissioner. Father and son were amply rewarded by a grateful nation, and Sarah took a very respectable dowry into marriage.

Woolley Senior was not from the first destined for the church. Indeed, Sarah was under the impression at the time of their marriage that she was entering into prosperous union with a successful businessman, senior director of a company of wine merchants which had thrived from the time of his maternal great-grandmother's marriage to the founder, John Barton of Tower Street in the City of London, in the last decade of the 18th century.

The long unbroken record of professional and financial aggrandisement on all sides of the Woolley family seems to have made little impression on Leonard's father. Within a year of his marriage the wine business was on the verge of bankruptcy, despite an infusion of £1046 from Sarah's inheritance. The trustees of his wife's estate were reluctant to agree to the loan, a large sum in those days and not, in their view, a sound investment, but according to the terms of the arrangement it was to be interest-free and repayable only at Sarah's written request. The first child, Sadie, had been born in 1875, when George was twenty-nine, within a year of the marriage. In the following year George's health broke down and Sarah was pregnant with their second child. A year's rest was prescribed for the father, and so the family rented a home in North Wales, where Cathcart was born. When they returned to London in 1877, the wine business was in ruins. Somewhat pathetically, George Woolley told his children in later years 'I never saw any accounts; indeed, I was quite unfit to take up business life again.' The trustees of Sarah's estate adamantly refused to allow any further gift or loan, suspecting that it would be 'good money after bad'. All the same, family and friends decided they must summon resources enough to set the penniless George on some kind of career. He opted for Holy Orders and King's College, Cambridge, where he took a good 'first' in only eighteen months, having been permitted by Bishop Jackson to cut short his studentship by six months for lack of funds.

The circumstances of George Woolley's early life were unusual, and subsequent follies were legion. Their effect on a large and growing family must have been daunting. Yet from Leonard's point of view, paternal eccentricity proved a disguised blessing. The Rev. Woolley could have been forgiven had he acquired a taste for wine in the course of a young life spent among the finest vintages, and he would not have been unique in his calling had he taken to gambling or some other sinful extravagance. But his weakness was of no such mundane kind. He had a passion for beautiful things.

He was, all told, a forbidding man. The severity of his demeanour was emphasized by brooding dark eyes, sensuous lips and a burgeoning black beard; the kind of man who, in appearance and manner, might have lurked in the imagination of a Dostoyevsky or a Strindberg. The fearsome exterior concealed a wilful head in dangerous tandem with a sensitive soul. He was devoted to painting, engraving, and that most seductive of the applied arts, pottery. What was more, his judgement was good. He could not resist the temptation of a fine work of art in whatever medium, and having acquired it he could not bring himself to part with it. He was a fine pianist, an expert on Beethoven, whose music he played and studied with great devotion. Leonard and his brothers and sisters grew up in a veritable gallery, where music and all the arts were venerated, but where money for the essentials of life was always in short supply.

As soon as he left university, George Woolley took up a travelling job in the church, inspecting parochial arrangements for the care of waifs and strays. It was at that time that he fell into the extravagant ways of the ragged-trousered connoisseur, as he admitted in an intimate account written for posthumous consumption by his children, telling them how their relative poverty came about. The essay was hidden away and was not rediscovered until 1966, forty years after his own death and after the deaths of most of his children, when his daughter Edith found it concealed in an old family Bible.

'Often,' he wrote revealingly, 'have your mother and I talked and laughed together about the account we could write some day for you children, of how and why we made our collections of pictures, china and old furniture . . .'

When he came to declare his prodigality, Sarah was long since dead, though he often spoke of her in the present tense. 'I little thought that I should have to write it alone. – We, I say; for those who sharply criticized me for waste of money and time, did not understand that there was a definite purpose in our purchases and that your Mother was greatly interested both in them and the object we aimed at.' The apology struck a disingenuous note: 'We had a few pretty things when we married, but not many . . . I think it was while I was travelling for the Waifs and Strays that my love for Pottery & Porcelain woke up. I saw very fine Oriental ware in some of the houses I visited and I went over several factories in the Potteries, and bought some nice pieces of Minton and Copeland – and then I was introduced to Bingham, the Castle Hedingham potter, whom I helped with money to buy fine clays and who made some beautiful things for me.' He described purchases of furniture during his curateship at St Michael's in London Fields. He met a dealer from whom he bought furniture and paintings – 'St Peter (school of Murillo), a small Teniers, English copies of Hals and Vandervelde ... the portrait of the French Abbé & the old Spanish landscape.' There were more purchases at Bethnal Green, 'but for several years there was not much money to spare – there were so many children.' After his wife's death he was financially dependent on his sons.

He listed his acquisitions for the benefit of the family that maintained him in his old age while he enjoyed the works of art and craft that surrounded him. It made impressive reading. The ceramic wares were valued at £600, no mean sum in those days. Hundreds of engravings were said to be worth thousands of pounds. Represented in passing, almost as subsidiary items among those engravings, were 'the Old Masters, the Rembrandts and Bartolozzis and the great series of Turner'. There was a library of more then three thousand books, including sets of first editions of Ruskin, Carlyle, Dickens, Kipling, Stevenson, Tennyson, Browning and Kingsley. And there was a blue 'Boccaro' or Yi-hsing teapot of the Ming period the like of which the British Museum had not seen before. 'I think you will see that our great hope is accomplished and that you, our children, will inherit a full equivalent of the money I lost so many years ago.' That was to prove a pious hope. 'Ah, I daresay, your Mother would hardly like me to put it thus – she always wished the loss to be utterly forgotten but she knew I could not forget & that it was a joy to me to hope it could be replaced. It has not been without effort – & she bore more than her share of that; in living very quietly, in dressing very plainly, yes, often shabbily, – & above all in bearing hard words about our folly.'

There was more than a suggestion of self-justification in his concern for a dead wife and a dispersed family. All his life, from early manhood to the day of his death, George Woolley took cold baths. In winter he would fill the bath and washbasin the night before, so that in the morning he could break the ice in order to take the plunge. The psychoanalyst might see a too tempestuous nature cooling itself before the lid blew off, and there was something of the kind in his intimate scribblings. 'What will become of all the various things, is not our affair – you children may divide them, sell them as you think best – we have enjoyed them, used them, seen that they helped in your comfort & education, & rejoiced in the hope that their value may cancel the past ... I feel that by your Mother's courage & loyal help I am handing to you in full your Mother's inheritance – she joyed most, I think, in my joy.'

The folly had not run its course. In the end, the children would see little of the proceeds of their father's collection. But if Leonard and his brothers and sisters were not to be surrounded by affluence, they at least had an early introduction to the glories of art.

For Leonard, the move to Bethnal Green had one specially fortunate aspect. Round the corner from the vicarage, amid impoverished homes and shops, was the Whitechapel Art Gallery. It gave the boy his first encounter with a truly cosmopolitan view of high art. Progressive in policy, the gallery was bedecked with contemporary works and lesser known items from the past, as well as some fine old masters. Almost daily visits nourished an inherited enthusiasm and infused Leonard with a sense of the true breadth of art and craftsmanship. It also reinforced a mania for collecting paintings and *objets d'art* that must have come to him at an early age and remained with him to the very end.

Life in Bethnal Green also had a less cultural aspect. Drunkenness and street brawls were rife and soon after moving to his new living the Rev. Woolley was attacked in public and left bleeding from a wound in the throat. The Woolley daughters, who went to school near their old home at Stamford Hill, were told on one occasion to take an alternative route as a shooting had taken place on their customary way. Poverty was the inevitable bedfellow of ruffian behaviour, and Mrs Woolley, a small, physically frail but purposeful lady, made it her business to alleviate some of the local distress. Countless children went without proper food and she took over the main room of the church school across the road to institute the first penny dinners in London for school boys and girls. Each day a hundred or more children sat down to a meal of meat stew and vegetables, usually followed by treacle pudding, and all the available Woolleys were mustered to serve at table. There were moments of studied amusement, as when the Rev. Woolley allowed the Liberal candidate Sir Charles Russell to use the vicarage garden for a meeting at the Hackney election of 1886, where his opponent was Mr Justice Darling. Next day a wit scribbled on the wall:

> Oh, pity poor Russell!
> His case is a hard'un;
> He has to hold meetings
> In Woolley's back garden.

Presently another verse appeared:

> Oh, pity poor Darling,
> His case is more hard:
> His hopes of election
> Lie in the churchyard.

In 1891, when Leonard was eleven, learning began in earnest with a scholarship place at St John's School at Leatherhead in Surrey, an establishment founded forty years before in North London for the education of sons of the clergy. The school had moved to Leatherhead in 1872 and in time it broadened its scope by taking in the sons of the laity. It was widely esteemed in church and lay circles for its all-round academic excellence. For the new boy, progress was rapid. By his fourteenth birthday he had won distinctions in scripture, Latin and additional maths in the Lower Oxford and Cambridge Board exams. In the Upper School he recorded his first and only sporting achievement, a 350 yards swimming certificate. His ability in the water could hardly be regarded as exceptional, but it would eventually save his life in the course of events as yet unsuspected by a generation made prosperous and secure by the *Pax Britannica*.

School holidays were almost always spent at Kingsdown, near Walmer Sands in Kent, no great distance from London. There was insufficient money for the grand holidays of the rich in Italy or France, but the Woolleys went in style to their south-east coast resort, conveyed by two horse-drawn carriages and accompanied by a nurse or two when there were infants to be cared for. Occasionally, mother and father would slip over to the Continent for a few days but more often than not such journeys were connected with George's latest acquisitions – 'I bought the green inkstand with the goat on the lid at a Jew's old clothes shop in Whitechapel; it is by Jean Petit of Paris about 1800,' he noted on one occasion, and later, 'when your Mother & I were in Paris we went to Sèvres and in the Museum there saw the lamp and candlesticks which are part of the same set.' His father's obsession with decorative art, particularly with pottery, had a profound influence on Leonard who, even before he went away to school, could distinguish between hand decoration and the 'bat' prints on the blue china of the day, could recognize porcelain, stone and earthen clays and evaluate the varied glazes appropriate to them. The archaeologist's chief dating instrument, pottery, was already familiar to him.

Leonard was smallish in stature as boy and man. At school he was lithe rather than sturdy, awkward at games, studious and articulate in the classroom. There were plentiful signs of later prowess. He was good in debate and at the age of sixteen took part in an Essay Society discussion on 'Greek drama compared with the Modern'. Many academic prizes came his way. In December 1898 he won an open scholarship to New College, Oxford. By then he was head monitor and pride of the school.

It was an altogether satisfactory academic record which pleased his parents as much as the headmaster of the day, Mr A. F. Rutty. At the Old Johnian's annual dinner in 1898 the head told the gathering proudly, 'Woolley the head monitor has gained one of those coveted scholarships at Oxford which so seldom fall to the lot of a school.' Overcome perhaps by a sense of academic priority, he added that the prize of a keenly contested scholarship at New College was a distinction 'only inferior, if at all, to one gained at Balliol.'

In the months of marking time before going up to Oxford at the end of 1899, Woolley devoted himself to the debating and dramatic societies. He opposed the motion 'This House congratulates Lord Kitchener of Khartoum,' pursuing a vigorous argument against the victor of Omdurman and white hope of the Boer War on the grounds that his policies were 'converting peaceful agriculturalists into blood-thirsty veterans'. A few days later he made an impressive speech from the floor in support of the motion 'This House approves the Czar's manifesto'. When speech day came round on 1 August 1899, the head told the assembled school, 'Woolley . . . has doubtless a great career before him (*applause*), and you will watch, I am sure, with great interest and great hope, and I think without disappointment, the next four years during which he is at Oxford.' After the young lion had received his parting prizes, nine in all, his father rose to offer his grateful thanks for the great lift the school had given his son. 'I only hope that in his future life my son will never forget the lessons, the highest and best lessons, he has learnt at St John's,' said the Rev. Woolley. To cap his last day at the school, Leonard quick-changed for a succession of dramatic roles in *The Knights* of

Aristophanes, Molière's *Le Médecin malgré lui*, and Sheridan's *The Rivals*. His performance as Mrs Malaprop in Sheridan's comedy won the approval of the critic of the school magazine, the *Johnian*, and the same journal was soon carrying cryptic commentaries on Woolley's progress at Oxford where the student found himself under the sympathetic spell of New College's famous warden, the Rev. W. A. Spooner.

Theology was the obvious path to the 'brilliant' future foreshadowed by his headmaster, though classical study remained an important ingredient of his academic life. In 1901 he took a second in Moderations and a year later won an exhibition. Finals in 1903 brought a second-class degree. He had done well enough to gain the confidence and admiration of his tutors, including the kindly, diminutive warden. But the expectations of his school years were not quite realized. He had confidently expected a first. When the results came through he wrote to his tutor, the Rev. Dr Hastings Rashdall.

> Dear Dr Rashdall,
> I am very much disappointed by the result of Greats: apparently my history, especially the Greek, which I had thought my strongest point, proved the weakest, and the philosophy was not quite good enough to make up for it . . . I am not exactly surprised at the general result, but am naturally very sorry indeed for it: still I hope not to give up the idea of reading for the Theological School. I can't settle in a hurry . . .

Forlornly he told Dr Rashdall that he hoped for a Magdalen fellowship. The Warden of Keble had already offered him a place. He continued:

> I'm afraid that a double second is a very poor return for a four year's scholarship, and I am grieved for that as for the loss to myself.

In 1904 he took his theology finals: again a second.

Dr Spooner considered the results and decided that theology would not offer Woolley suitable challenges or rewards. Some sixteen years after the event Woolley recalled the interview with the man whose name would enter the English language for a verbal eccentricity which, according to many who knew him, was apocryphal:

Towards the end of my last year at New College I was honoured
with an invitation to wait upon the Warden in his lodgings at
10 AM. Wondering which of a good many things might be the
reason, and hoping it was not most of them, I duly presented
myself in as non-committal a frame of mind as I could assume;
but I was not at all prepared for the turn the conversation took.

'Ah, Mr Woolley,' began the Warden. 'Quite so. I think that
when you came up to Oxford you had every intention of taking
Holy Orders?'

I murmured something unintelligible and waited.

'And I am afraid that you have quite abandoned the idea.'

'Oh, rather,' I said hurriedly; 'yes, quite Mr Warden, quite
given it up.'

'And what do you propose to do?'

'Well,' I answered, 'I want to be a schoolmaster; I've done a
little at odd times and I like it awfully, so I think of going for it
permanently.'

'Oh, yes; a schoolmaster, really; well, Mr Woolley, I have
decided that you shall be an archaeologist.'

There was, as Woolley observed, no more to be said. The little
albino who presided over academic life at New College was a man
of renowned concern for his students and few were bold enough to
ignore his well-meant advice. In Woolley's case that advice squared
with his own conviction that he was not cut out for the church.

As soon as he had finished his finals he went off on a European
holiday to exercise his modern languages, particularly French and
German, living rough for most of the time. His younger brother
Harold had succeeded him at St John's where he too became head
monitor, and won distinction at games as well as studies, gaining his
colours at fives. Their father, still suffering the poverty attendant on
his taste for art in the depressingly poor surroundings of London's
East End, had no money to spare. There was, however, promise of a
paid job when Leonard returned to Oxford. Father was doubtless
glad to know that one more financial burden was about to be lifted.

The 'Oxford Letter' in the St John's magazine kept the next
generation of pupils informed of the distinguished old boy's progress
at university. There were enigmatic observations, such as a reference
to the old boy 'of the 29 per cent and the brilliant future', and
'Woolley lunches on Sundays'. Again, 'Woolley has not been sent
down up to the time of writing.'

Incomplete as they were, such remarks suggested something of an Oxford life that went on beyond, or perhaps beneath, the eyes of most dons. Woolley's Sunday lunch parties were not extravagant or waggish affairs. They were usually witty, always erudite. At the centre of them was the small, goatee-bearded David Hogarth, tutor at Magdalen since 1886, a man of wide learning, unbending patriotism and weighty intellect. Hogarth's father, like Woolley's, was a minister of the Church of England and it is not impossible that the two parents knew each other and thus brought their offspring together. It is more likely, though, that they met first at the Ashmolean Museum of which Sir Arthur Evans was keeper and Hogarth the keeper elect. Woolley became an assistant keeper within a year of his finals, in 1905.

While working under Hogarth's attentive eye, he made a bold if rather obscure entrance to the literary stage. He had introduced himself to Mr Martine Ronaldson, an artist whom he had seen wandering with sketch-pad in hand in the corridors and gardens of New College. Ronaldson was producing a book of line drawings of the college, much in the scraper-board style common to advertisements of the time, and Woolley expressed a knowledgable appreciation of the artist's work. Duly flattered, Ronaldson asked him if he would write an introduction. Woolley's first public essay appeared in old-English type, often referred to as 'Gothic', and it struck an editorial note not far removed from its typographic affectation:

> To those whom this book will interest most the history of New College should be already not unfamiliar . . . More familiar yet must be the scenes whose illustration is the book's sole reason; but just as Mr Ronaldson's work draws further merit from remembrance, so perhaps I too may plead that the barest chronicle of our College history can never wholly pall . . . etc.

He had been at the Ashmolean for just over a year when, in 1907, he went off on his first 'dig' to Corbridge, ancient *Corstopitum* in Northumbria, where work was beginning on the excavation of several buildings of some size and importance facing the old Roman thoroughfare. The leading authority on Roman Britain at Oxford was Professor Haverfield with whom Woolley had struck up an acquaintanceship based on a common interest in Robert Burton, the Elizabethan writer who resided for most of his life at Christ Church and whose best-known work was *The Anatomy of Melancholy*. While biding his time at the end of 1906 he had helped Haverfield to catalogue Burton's publications in the Christ Church library, and the professor recommended the young assistant keeper as site manager after consulting Sir Arthur Evans. Woolley admitted that he had no knowledge of archaeological methods. There were no books on the subject and he had no field experience. All the same, he took charge enthusiastically, helped by an experienced architect W. H. Knowles, and visited once a week by Professor Haverfield who was interested only in finds and never ventured a word of criticism regarding the crude excavation methods used. Still, Woolley gained there his first brief experience of digging and he was grateful for the opportunity. Before he returned to Oxford at the end of the summer dig he made his first important discovery and enjoyed a brief taste of publicity. Chancing on the great cistern one Saturday morning as he returned from the bank with the men's wages, he saw a group of workmen crowded together and talking animatedly. Beside them was the statue of a lion grinning over a fallen stag. The men had removed the stone group from the cistern, and the workman who had made the discovery was beside himself with excitement.

'Did *you* find that?' asked Woolley. The man stammered, 'Yes, sir, and you'll never believe me but it's God's own truth, when I first saw that there lion he had a blooming orange in 'is mouth.'

The orange was never explained but Woolley liked the anecdotal approach to archaeology, as his later writings would show. Hexham Abbey nearby boasted a Roman tombstone with a representation of a Roman cavalryman, which had been looted from Corbridge many years before, to the alleged irritation of the local populace. Now they had their own lion and Woolley was credited with its discovery. *The Times* carried a detailed report on 12 August 1907. Woolley read his own words in a newspaper for the first time and experienced the common first thrill of public acknowledgement. The same newspaper followed up with a further report on 9 September. The young archaeologist read such reports carefully. He began to sense that his kind of work, involving the great expense of dozens and sometimes hundreds of field workers, needed public support if it was to attract the necessary funds from governments and wealthy institutions, and that newspaper publicity was the key.

It was gratifying to see his name and his small dig in print, but it was the time of some of Evans' most spectacular discoveries at Crete and the Lion of Corbridge could not compete in national or international terms with the Bull of Minos.

Back at Oxford, early success was put in perspective by one of the dons, H. E. Craster, who later became Bodley's librarian. Woolley boasted of the Corbridge dig. 'Yes,' said Craster, 'a very successful dig. I don't think anyone would now write a really detailed history of Roman Britain without putting in a footnote to the effect that there was also a Roman station at Corbridge.'

If Dr Spooner had reinforced the young man's enthusiasm for antiquity, it was Hogarth who convinced him of the opportunities offered by field work, of digging up the past in derelict regions which, until the second half of the 19th century, had represented no more than the backwash of classical literature, the supposed scenes of ancient legends which were themselves often the recapitulations of even more ancient tales.

First there was need of experience, however, and the aspiring digger could hardly have been in better hands than those of Evans. 'Ashmole's Keeper' had begun in 1899 to excavate a piece of land purchased from his own pocket on the island of Crete. In March 1900 Evans was joined by Hogarth who had been digging on and off for twelve years past in Cyprus and Crete for the British School at Athens. The unearthing of the site of Knossos had begun. When Woolley arrived at the Ashmolean, that famous museum was already the repository of some of the rarest gems of antiquity.

There was another side to Hogarth. That pedantic fellow of Magdalen moved not only among scholars in the course of his travels. It was through clerical friendships within the family that he came into contact with Captain William Hall RN, the navy's first director of intelligence. Another contact in a very different field was the director of the foreign department of *The Times*, Valentine Chirol, who had been employed by the Foreign Office from 1872 until he took up journalism in 1899. Chirol knew the great and the aspiring of many nations but was sickly and accident-prone and often in trouble with his employers in Whitehall and Printing House Square. All the same, he had been useful to Hogarth during the latter's travels in Asia Minor and had secured for him an appointment as *The Times*' correspondent in Crete in 1897 when the Powers were acting to expel the Turks and Hogarth, fortuitously, was digging there.

Hogarth was to succeed Evans as keeper of the Ashmolean in 1909. In the interval he became head of the British School in Athens, dug at Ephesus and Knossos, and commuted to Oxford. His sister Janet had gone up to Lady Margaret Hall in 1886 and had introduced her brother to her closest and 'most brilliant' friend,

Gertrude Bell. Two decades later, in 1905, another exceptional scholar introduced himself to Hogarth and Woolley at the Ashmolean, 'a shy schoolboy' named Thomas Edward Lawrence, later to become an exhibitioner at Jesus College. He took to the museum bits of medieval pottery found by workmen digging house foundations in Oxford. Woolley was certainly interested in the visitor's potsherds; and he was attracted by the young man's keen intelligence and bright, razor-sharp manner. A tradition in the Woolley household has it that the boys' parents knew each other, and that Mr Lawrence approached George Woolley to see if Leonard could find an opening for his 'awkward' son. There is no support for the story, however, in Woolley's writings or those of Hogarth, who knew the circumstances of their meeting better than anyone. And Lawrence could never have been described as 'awkward'. Shy perhaps, but even as a youth he was, if anything, precociously self-confident.

Others along the way joined an academic circle which combined urbanity and a desire to work in the world's open spaces with an assured, often didactic approach to every subject under the sun; notable among them was the Scot Dr R. Campbell Thompson, fellow of Merton, who translated the ancient legends of Babylon and earlier civilizations in verse which lay somewhat between Burns and McGonagall.

Before he left Oxford, the cast of Woolley's life drama had more or less assembled and he had stated the creed that would see him through to the end. Contemplating the Warden's words – 'one did not lightly play with the Warden's decisions' – he was not altogether happy. 'For me, and I think for the Warden too, archaeology meant a life spent inside a museum, whereas I preferred the open air and was more interested in my fellow men than in dead-and-gone things.'

In 1908, after only two years at the Ashmolean as junior assistant keeper, he decided to leave for an active job in archaeology. He was offered a place with the University Museum of Pennsylvania's team which was digging in the Nubian desert at the cataracts of the Nile, following an earlier expedition led by E. W. Budge of the British Museum. Oxford's distinguished museum was in a mess. Evans was on the point of resigning, and the official report for the year 1907 announced, 'The resignation at Midsummer of Mr C. Leonard Woolley, the Junior Assistant Keeper of the Ashmolean, who had done much good work in the Egypto–Roman and other sections, has been a great personal loss to the Museum.' The report went on to speak of a 'prolonged state of uncertainty' which had greatly hampered the normal running of the institution. Woolley was succeeded by Thurlow Leeds, a young man of farming stock from the Fen country and a Cambridge scholar. Leeds would eventually become Ashmole's Keeper and was destined to have a good deal to do with Woolley and Lawrence in the years ahead.

In the Sudan, Woolley joined a brilliant young American archaeologist, Dr Randall MacIver, in excavating at Karanog, where they uncovered the first major Meroitic necropolis. Woolley described the region as the 'Dodekaschoinos of Greek and Roman Egypt'.

He quickly discovered the importance of tact, and perhaps more to the point, of *bakhsheesh* in oriental archaeology. The reputation of Sir Flinders Petrie, MacIver's old master, now working at sites in Lower Egypt, also brought home useful lessons of method and management.

There were some important finds, including bronze vessels of Greek origin, but the burial sites of the dark-skinned Sudanese people who occupied the ancient city on the east bank of the Nile in Upper Egypt, with its two hundred or more derelict pyramids, left Woolley unmoved. He decided that the whole Meroitic civilization was 'but a backwater, remarkable as an isolated phenomenon in African history, but contributing nothing to the general stream of culture and art.' It was the kind of verdict, emphatic and deriving chiefly from an interest in art rather than antiquity, that would characterize his reports and essays henceforth. But there was early indication of humility too. He admitted that he could not read the hieroglyphic inscriptions of Egypt and that without that ability neither he nor anyone else should attempt to reconstruct the country's past.

He and MacIver dug up several other 'non-Egyptian' sites, as the Meroitic graveyards were designated, but the creative urge of the apprentice archaeologist was not satisfied. He conceded that he had learnt valuable lessons from his companion whose immaculate methods, learnt from Petrie, the most prodigious of Egyptologists, marked a turning point in archaeological fieldwork. He had gained much knowledge, too, in unearthing artifacts which ranged in date from early dynastic times of the third millennium BC down to Roman occupation. 'I must confess that when we began finding tombs of the same sort at Halfa, a year later, our enthusiasm was not so keen, and when I dug some hundreds more of the same type at Faras in 1911 it was difficult to pump up any pleasurable emotion.'

He was to contemplate his first brief encounter with Egyptology a few years hence. He remembered looking down from the hills of Korosko to the plateau which still, thirty years after, bore the ruts of wheelmarks and guns where Hicks Pasha and all his men went to their deaths. He recalled that when the sun of the great Ramessids went down, there rose to independence in the far south an Ethiopian power 'whose swarthy kings of the XXVth Dynasty overran and for a time ruled Egypt as Pharaohs.' Then Egypt fell under Persian rule, and then the Greeks came in the shape of the Seleucids, Alexander's successors. After them, the Romans: Cleopatra, last of the Ptolemies, was minded to seek asylum among the people of Meroë. Then came the advance of Christianity and Islam, and though Diocletian had guaranteed the rights of the Isis-worshippers at Philae, neither Christian nor Moslem could suffer such paganism. And coming almost up to date in a few pages of cleverly condensed history in a little book called *Dead Towns and Living Men* dedicated to the Warden of New College, Woolley recorded a singular event in the modern history of Egypt. It was the tale of the pursuit by the Turkish Viceroy of Egypt, Muhammad Ali, of the Mameluks, the Circassian bodyguard whose massacre he had ordered, to the same southern outpost, wiping out the soldiers who had secured his power and leaving Meroë to its final ruin and decay.

MacIver soon went off to a new site which he fancied, Buhen in the Wadi Halfa near Abu Simbel, leaving Woolley alone at the Meroitic cemetery to control the Egyptian workforce, make notes of finds, draw plans of the excavation, and photograph everything in sight. He was glad when his first season came to a close. On the strength of a few months' digging he had completed his first part-work, a book written jointly with MacIver and with a chapter on the Meroitic inscriptions by one of the outstanding Egyptologists of the day, F. Llewellyn Griffith, and a foreword by Eckley B. Coxe, the Philadelphian in whose name the expedition was sponsored. Published by the University Press, the book dealt with many objects of the reign of Tothmes III, the Meroitic inscriptions and the cemeteries at Gezira and Amada. Perhaps its most interesting chapter, contributed by Woolley, dealt with the history of the First Cataract of the Nile, by then effaced by the Aswan dam, and the Negro element that had contributed much to its history in the vassalage of its northern reaches, which began under Menes, King of the First Dynasty, and in the independence of the black kingdom of the south. Woolley also wrote about the painted pottery of the region and its 'eclectic range' of ornamentation.

He was committed to visiting Philadelphia in the autumn. Meanwhile, looking for more congenial pastures than he had so far found in Egypt, he travelled home in April 1910 by way of Italy.

In Italy he found a tutor in Italian, 'a dear old Professor Zaccardi', who taught rhetoric in the University of Florence. When not learning the language, Woolley spent a few weeks digging at the ancient baths of Teano on a Sabine hilltop. He greatly admired the attitude of the Italian government and people to archaeology, contrasting it with the indifference of the British to the distant past.

He made the first of many protests at the niggardly philistinism of fellow countrymen. 'The [Italian] Government, comparatively poor though it be, spends yearly upon excavations and upon the upkeep of national monuments an amount of money which the British public would grudge in a decade.'

There were plans to dig at the surviving Roman circus of Lepcis Magna in Libya, but the Turco-Italian war defeated the scheme. Other developments were afoot in the much more ancient lands of Mesopotamia, and already Woolley's name was under consideration by the Ashmolean and British museums.

In the first decade of the 20th century, a school that was to revolutionize field archaeology, the Deutsche Orient Gesellschaft, began digging at the Mesopotamian sites of ancient Babylon and Assur on the Euphrates and Tigris rivers, and German railway engineers began the construction of the Berlin–Baghdad rail route. Hogarth set out in 1910 to dig at Carchemish by the village of Jerablus on the Euphrates, where Britain had acquired a lease from the Ottoman Turks through the embassy of Sir Henry Layard. Hogarth took Campbell Thompson and T. E. Lawrence as his assistants. He stayed for less than a year at Carchemish before accepting Evans' Ashmolean job and leaving Thompson in charge of the dig. Meanwhile, Woolley made his first very rushed journey to America where he spent little more than a fortnight working on the Egyptian finds at the University Museum of Pennsylvania. On his return to England in 1911, Hogarth asked him to assume the leadership of the Carchemish team, a job less grand than the offer suggested, for by then the team in its entirety consisted of Woolley and Lawrence.

The formative years had passed quickly. Leonard Woolley was past his thirtieth year and archaeology had claimed his heart and mind. He was in no doubt that the discerning Dr Spooner was right. He was not suited to the pastoral life, and he found a certain relief in the fact that his younger brother Geoffrey was about to take his degree with a view to Holy Orders, and that family honour would thus be saved.

Mrs Woolley, never a robust woman, had died while he was away in 1909. Some years later, one of her granddaughters was allowed to wear her wedding dress to a fancy dress party. Its waist measured nineteen inches.

An amiable task awaited Woolley in London. Dr Aurel Stein, the Budpest-born Orientalist whose travels in Chinese Turkestan, Kashmir and Afghanistan Woolley had followed closely, was based temporarily at Merton College, Oxford, and he sought someone who could put his 'finds' in order at the British Museum. Woolley had been recommended to him. On 16 February 1911, Woolley wrote from the family home to assure Stein that it would be 'a great pleasure' to work over his artifacts. On 3 June he confirmed that he had completed the task. He had left behind suggestions for illustrating and captioning the material, and an inventory of the sites represented by Dr Stein's discoveries: 'I have catalogued the tray of objects previously uncatalogued . . . I have left a note on the Crimean fabrics, on the Coptic textiles.' He was stuck for suitable precedents when it came to cataloguing other Coptic remains – 'the spirit is there all right, but precise parallels are not easy to find.' He hoped to see Dr Stein in Oxford. But stomach pains had suggested appendicitis and he had been advised to attend the London Hospital for an operation. 'Hope to see you when I have gotten over my operation,' he wrote, using the American tense he had picked up in Philadelphia. Stein was impressed by his work and tried to talk him into a further period of 'classifying' work: 'I should find your help very useful.' Woolley had undergone his operation and was recuperating at Highclere, the country home of Lord Carnarvon, who was also interested in his services. He told Stein that he would much like to carry on working for him at the British Museum, but that there was an obstacle: Lord Carnarvon wanted Woolley to work for him in Egypt in August. If that work was successful, it might go on into the following year. He was not certain that he would take up his lordship's offer, 'but I have to bear it in mind when undertaking anything else.' In the end, he decided to accept Hogarth's offer and work at Carchemish.

In 1911, when Leonard started to make a respectable living, he joined with his elder brother Cathcart in buying a house for their father, whose resources permitted continued investment in art but not in property. It was a delightful William and Mary mansion with Queen Anne additions called Old Riffhams, at Danbury in Essex, a pleasant place indeed for retirement and for sons and daughters to return to. Gardener, cook and parlourmaid were employed and casual hands taken on to till the land. Several horses were stabled, and a governess cart provided shopping transport to the nearest town, Chelmsford. George Woolley was able to enjoy the last years of his life surrounded by favourite possessions, in a landscape very different from the one he had known for most of his working days. Cathcart and Leonard seemed to accept cheerfully their father's rather quaint view of parental responsibility, and as their incomes increased they contributed not only to the comforts of his retirement but also to the education of their brothers and sisters.

Leonard Woolley was set on his life's course – to dig up the past in remote regions where entire civilizations had grown up and faded into oblivion, leaving behind tantalizing traces of communities which could be identified and described only by the most patient and painstaking scholarship, helped in his case by a quality of quiet command which made him an ideal field leader.

And almost imperceptibly, he was being prepared for a secondary career in another and most dangerous calling.

'Mound of many riddles'

Woolley reached Aleppo from Egypt, where he had been working out his 'Nubia' contract with the Philadelphia Museum, in February 1912, a year after Hogarth had set up camp there with Campbell Thompson and T. E. Lawrence.

It was characteristic of Hogarth digs that no expedition house had been built in the interval and that the question of the ownership of the site remained in doubt.

At the end of the 1911 season Campbell Thompson ('C. T.' to all who knew him) had returned home to Scotland to marry, dashing off an article for *The Times* before he left in which he described Carchemish as 'a mound of many riddles'. In the hope of solving some of those riddles he and Lawrence had, said C. T., gratefully taken up clues 'which D. G. Hogarth had left behind'. Lawrence had taken himself off to Egypt for a short period of digging with 'the master', Flinders Petrie. He returned late to Carchemish with a poor opinion of the matriarchal regime obtaining under the master's omnipresent wife, observing wryly that 'tinned kidneys mingle with mummy-corpses and amulets in the soup.'

Thus when Woolley arrived at Aleppo in February 1912 (the 'season' in the Near East usually ran from September to April) he discovered that he had nowhere to sleep and no assistant. When Lawrence eventually turned up it was agreed that they would have to make do with a temporary hut while a proper house was constructed.

Carchemish, thought to have been the ancient capital city of the Hittites, was a messy archaeological site, a collection of earthworks and trenches, scattered stones and tattered remains, with a mauled and scarred acropolis dominating the scene. A. E. Henderson, an architect who had dug with Hogarth at Ephesus in 1904, was the first of its excavators, working there on behalf of the British Museum from 1878 to 1881 while he was Consul at Aleppo. Six years before

Henderson's appearance, in 1872, George Smith, the British Museum's famous self-taught epigraphist who first translated the Babylonian version of the antediluvian 'Flood' story, visited the site and reported a fine Hittite sculpture.

When Hogarth arrived at the Syrian mound he roundly condemned Henderson for the mess he had made thirty years before. It cannot be said that, in their few months of digging at Carchemish, the latest British Museum team had done much better. Indeed, all Hogarth's expeditions were notable for their confusion, for squabbles among the site workers and a paucity of finds. At the Dictaean Cave and Zakro in Crete he had found little of note and at the latter site he failed to discover the palace area which yielded his successors such spectacular results. He was confident all the same of his field abilities. Before leaving his apprentices at Carchemish he told them: 'When excavations are successful there is never a moment to spare.' The Jerablus dig hardly lived up to any such sense of urgency.

On 13 March 1911, Hogarth had reported to the British Museum the visit to the site that day of the Turkish 'Commissaire', who inspected the deeds of a local claimant to the land. It seemed that Henderson in 1878 had purchased a third share in the land, at the instance of Sir Henry Layard in Constantinople, while the local shaikh had acquired two-thirds. The Turkish official scrutinized the deed or *tapu* of the Arab claimant and declared it worthless. Then another complication arose. When Hogarth made a preliminary visit to the site in 1908, the Turkish governor of Biajik, the nearest township of any size, had laid claim to what had become a wasteland after Henderson's withdrawal. The interest of these local worthies in an apparently worthless piece of ground was perhaps explained by the decision of Germany to build the Berlin-Baghdad railway, necessitating a bridge across the Euphrates at Jerablus. That circumstance also went a long way towards explaining the presence of the British archaeological team.

The first task, archaeologically speaking, was to rationalize the earlier excavations which had exposed the oldest, early Hittite level. Priority had to be given to making their own habitat comfortable, however, and to other matters which had no obvious academic significance.

Though nominally carried out for the British Museum, the Hogarth expedition was financed by 'a well wisher'. It has never been established who it was who so generously financed for four years a minor dig in Turkish Syria while Petrie in Egypt and Evans in Crete, among other notable claimants, were so short of money. Hogarth, through whom the funds were paid to the British Museum, never divulged the source, but the fact that the financing of the Carchemish dig was *ad hoc* gave rise to constant friction between Woolley and his employers. Up to the moment, Hogarth had done little digging at Jerablus but had written a long essay for the Museum in which he announced that he was handing over to Campbell Thompson, disputed the common association of Carchemish with Europus (Oropus) of the Romans, 'which is a place some 15 miles south', and told the director that he spent £700 in his first year.

In the same report to the director of the British Museum, Sir Frederic Kenyon, Hogarth mentioned a meeting with Sir Edwin Pears and Gerald Fitzmaurice in Constantinople, the latter chief dragoman of the British embassy, and closely linked to the secret service organization established in the Mediterranean by Admiral Lord Fisher through 'the patriotism of several magnificent Englishmen'. Copies of the report went to Pears, Fitzmaurice, and the archaeologist and historian Professor Ramsay. The British Museum's role seems at best to have been one of giving respectability to an archaeological expedition which had shadowy undertones. Sir Frederic was a man of great renown, respected throughout the academic world for his discovery and publication of Aristotle's Constitution of Athens, and for his critical writings on the poetry of the Brownings. He had been director and principal librarian of the British Museum since 1902 and had many friends in high political places.

Foreman of the Carchemish expedition at the start was Gregorios Antoniou, always known as 'Gregori', a Cypriot who had worked in Crete for Evans and Hogarth. He was getting too old for the task and was there only to train the local candidate, Hamoudi. 'Hoja' Hamoudi was a tall, thin Arab with a sandy beard and powerful arms. When work was on hand or discoveries were coming to light, said Woolley, 'his eyes blazed, the skin was drawn tight over the face-bones, his teeth bared, and the man laboured like a fury and looked like a devil.' He had been largely responsible for saving the life of Lawrence during the first year of the dig, nursing the Englishman to health after a bout of typhoid which brought him to death's door.

Hamoudi had spent five years as an outlaw, pursued by up to sixty Turkish soldiers, but he had a well-armed gang at his elbow and he was never captured. He was the mainstay of Woolley's team. Another member of the 'inner circle' was the Arab servant Hajji Wahid, 'a big brawny fellow,' said Woolley, 'handsome, vainglorious, a lover of finery, honest and faithful, a brave man for all his boasting.' He drank heavily and was in love with his gun. A female missionary who appeared at Jerablus heard of his antics and refused to be served at table by 'a cold-blooded murderer and worse'. He and Woolley enjoyed a long friendship. And there was Shaikh Ahmed, or Dahum, the camp photographer, young, handsome, fair-skinned and illiterate, soon to be immortalized by Lawrence who was devoted to him and taught him to read and write. He had travelled widely with Hamoudi the adventurer, charming their way to Beirut and Alexandria, and talking ships' captains into giving them free voyages, but neither had been civilized by travel. They shared a common dislike of Beirut. With irony that would take more than half a century to prove itself, they decided that it was a 'bad town . . . untouched by shot and shell'. Throughout the spring season of 1912, it was Lawrence who kept in touch with Hogarth, passing on both personal and professional titbits, often in the same breath – as on 10 April when he announced that he had bought a carpet for Hogarth which was being shipped through Mme Koch, well known as a German agent in the Levant, and then: 'Woolley says tell you 3 more large reliefs making 5 this month . . . Gregori arrived unexpectedly 5 days ago . . . Woolley's love to Bell.' Bell was senior assistant at the Ashmolean and Woolley's immediate senior at the museum. They struck up an easy accord in their two years together under Evans, but the term 'love' should not be misconstrued. Lawrence sent love to and from everyone. When he passed Hogarth's love to Hamoudi, the Arab roared with laughter and said that the chief 'must have got his words mixed up'.

Woolley decribed progress so far. In fifty feet of vertical digging the great mound of Carchemish had revealed the huts of recent Arab generations and, proceeding down, Armenian, Byzantine, Roman and Greek ruins. Beyond and below lay Carchemish of the Hittites, at the most recent level revealing the fort rebuilt by Sargon of Assyria after capturing the city in 717 BC, the prize of protracted years of war. Then came the strata of even earlier Hittite communities, still with human remains and the ever-present vehicle of community life, pottery, to remind the archaeologist of four millennia of war and peace. Campbell Thompson had aroused public interest and some speculation in academic quarters with his article in The Times. Much

of it was devoted to the evidence of the burial rites of the early
settlers. The bodies were first cut into small pieces and then placed
in urns. As in the early Egptian tombs, food was placed alongside
the vessels to accompany the dead on their voyage to the nether
world. There was no trace of cannibalism or of burning, wrote
C. T. Pottery was crude and there were few bronze or steatite
articles. Mud and stones were used in their buildings, and stones
provided the wherewithal of the most important industry, corn
grinding. After these first inhabitants had established themselves,
stronger Hittite hordes swept down from Anatolia and the locals
absorbed the savage invaders. Campbell Thompson paid homage
to his assistant, and the newspaper's typesetters got the initials
wrong. Much of the detailed evidence was attributed to 'Mr J. E.
Lawrence, the pottery expert of the expedition . . .' A large number
of horses modelled in clay were found. C. T., bluff, hearty and
careless of detail, gave the reader no clue as to the dates of
habitation of the site.

In contrast to the small and relatively frail figures of Woolley and
Lawrence, C. T. was a hulk of a man, a keen wrestler, a good shot,
devoted to the early cinema, and by report mean with money. At the
conclusion of his work at Carchemish, he accounted to the British
Museum for his expenses and balanced the account by sending them
a postage stamp for two pence.

Woolley would compensate in full for C. T.'s omissions, providing
the public with colourful and easily assimilated essays on the history
and topography of Carchemish. He often went to the top of the
mound to look across at the Great River of the Bible and feel the
surge of history that crowded in from north and south. Northward,
fields stretched along the right bank, with villages 'half seen in the
folds'. Looking south, Woolley described the rich plains where the
Pharaoh Necho, three years after defeating Josiah and the Israelites
at Megiddo in 608 BC, fought his great battle with Nebuchadnezzar
and the army of the Chaldaeans. Closer to the city walls, the new
railway, built by German engineers under the dispensation of the
Sultan of Turkey, was about to cross the Euphrates by an imposing
bridge then under construction. And on the edge of limestone hills
sweeping towards the river, was Tal Amarna, another Hittite fortress
mound, and across the river almost to the horizon, Tal Ahmar, the
Red Hill which gave Shalmaneser I of Assyria mastery of the region.
Looking down on the old fortress, Woolley's eye was engaged by the
scattered remains of Roman Europus, which, despite Hogarth's

assertion to the contrary, Woolley did equate with Jerablus and its surroundings. From the southern gateway, a long straight street of typically Roman construction ran almost to the foot of the acropolis, and broken shafts of a great colonnade marked its course. On the adjacent side-walk, shop fronts had been revealed with narrow grooves into which shutters were let down at nightfall. And a curved wall betrayed fragments of a moulded architrave with the titles of Caesar boldly displayed. The Romans had used massive Hittite sculptures as in-fill for their concrete foundations. Henderson had had to fight his way through these thick concrete layers to reach the Hittite levels.

Hogarth, Thompson and Lawrence had applied pick-axe and shovel to the task. Now Woolley and Lawrence, with Hamoudi as their charge-hand, took up the challenge. Getting rid of the broken stone was their most troublesome task, for it quickly brought them into conflict with the German railway engineers who lived alongside them.

Woolley was to become the finest of all popularizers of archaeology, his deft, fluent style of writing conveying great knowledge and reducing immense complexity of subject matter to an easy intelligibility which concealed painstaking effort. His ability to explain his discoveries in simple language came to light as he jotted down his first chapters at Nubia and at Carchemish in the alternating spring and autumn seasons that he spent between one and the other. He envisaged the great buildings which once stood where the debris of thousands of years now lay. '. . . certainly when the wall stood with its towers and battlements complete and the water glistened in the moat below, this was a barrier that may well have defied the hosts of Assyria throughout forty years of siege.'

On the western front of the wall they came to a gate approached by a causeway of rock, with three pairs of folding doors with guard chambers between. Towers of stone and brick flanked the entrance.

Here was the vulnerable point in the defences, and here we found signs of tragedy. The outer gateways with their buttresses had been razed to the ground, and athwart the jambs of the inner door a solid mass of brickwork had been built to close the entrance. The slipshod style of the brickwork spoke of haste, and bones and fragments of armour found in the rubbish piled in front of it would seem to show that the barrier was thrown

up under the stress of war; a signet engraved in the very latest
Hittite style was also found here, and we may well see in this
rough blocking of the road a desperate shift employed when
Sargon's army was encamped on the level ground beyond the
walls, and his rams had breached the gate, and the end of the
long war hung imminent over Carchemish.

It was not on this desolate stretch of the Euphrates but a thousand
miles away in Egypt that the story was told of the earlier destruction
of Hittite Carchemish.

In the mortuary temple of Ramesses III, stone tablets inscribed in
relief, of the kind common to the Mesopotamian civilizations but
uncommon in Egypt, offered a permanent record of the march of a
sea-borne force across Asia Minor and the eastern Mediterranean, a
force which burnt and destroyed everything in sight as it made its
way from city to city, until it reached the end of the Sinai coast road
and came to the Delta gateway of Egypt. One tablet read:

> No country has been able to withstand their might. The land of
> the Hittites, Kode [Cilicia], Carchemish ... and Cyprus have
> been destroyed ... They march against Egypt.

The marauders were called the Sea Peoples, and they finally met
their match in Egypt where the Pharaoh's swift chariots inflicted
decisive defeats on them. Neither the contemporary chroniclers of
Egypt nor later historians have been able to say precisely where this
will-o'-the-wisp army came from, but the tablets of Ramesses III (c.
1195–1164) indicate when and how the ancient Hittite capital of
Carchemish met its doom. Beyond those ruins, Woolley could speak
only of evidence in the sides of the trenches, below the lowest Hittite
level, of mud-brick walls and floors of beaten earth; and under the
floors 'the graves of those who once lived there, skeletons laid out at
length in stone cists crowded with clay vessels of offerings, and
farther down broken bones in jars, types of burial differing with the
ages'; and still the walls went down and down, revealing more
rubbish, flint instruments and brightly painted neolithic pottery,
back perhaps to 2,500 BC and beyond. 'But here, thirty or fifty feet
down, we can speak no more of dates nor calculate the lapse of
time; the workers of the Stone Age who first held the fort on the
rocky promontory came before the beginnings of history.'

Woolley, now entering the fourth decade of his life, was still
involved in two excavations; and he was responsible to two separate

masters. He could keep only a transient eye on his assistant as he travelled between the Nubian desert and Carchemish while they sifted through Henderson's debris, crated up the best of the stone gods, idols and statues, the pottery and tools of the ancient world, and carried on with some rudimentary digging. Between times, the two Englishmen waged battles with their workers and servants, and with their German neighbours and Turkish hosts, which each of them recounted amusingly, and none too consistently, in diaries, letters and books.

The tales of Carchemish told by these richly informed and articulate young men who tolerated each other without ever approaching closeness or friendship, constitute an epic of irrelevance. Woolley's version of events is no more reliable than Lawrence's. Perhaps each of them was hiding behind a curtain of humour while working on and off at the dig and engaging in other activities the true nature of which would emerge in time from the shadows of letters and abstruse essays.

It was many years hence that Woolley's work was subjected to critical appraisal, and by then he was one of the world's most renowned archaeologists. Lawrence's career in the same discipline was short-lived and Woolley said of him, 'In the actual work he was curiously erratic.' It all depended, he said, on the extent of his assistant's interest, 'and not everything in field archaeology did interest him or appeal to his sense of values.'

During the first season's digging, while Woolley was in Nubia and Campbell Thompson was in nominal charge, Gertrude Bell had called at the site. By that time, the woman who came to be known to the Arabs of Syria and Iraq as *Al Khatun*, The Lady, had achieved wide fame for her two books *The Desert and the Sown* and *Amurath to Amurath*, the latter containing a dedicatory epistle to Lord Cromer in Egypt in which she remarked 'The banks of the Euphrates echo with ghostly alarms; the Mesopotamian deserts are full of the rumour of phantom armies; you will not blame me if I passed among them *trattando l'ombre come cose salde*.'

She was a woman much after the hearts of Lawrence and C. T. But there was a moment of tension when Gertrude, fresh from an admiring visit to the German archaeologists Koldewey at Babylon and Andrae at Assur, accused her compatriates of 'prehistoric methods'. C. T. was not amused and Lawrence, not given to humility in such matters, told Hogarth that they had 'crushed her with a show of erudition.' All the same, Gerty had been 'a success, and a brave one.' Gertrude wrote home to her stepmother on 18 May 1911 to tell her '. . . the Kaimakam came over to call on me and told me that Mr Hogarth had left but that Mr Thompson was still at Carchemish. Accordingly I went there – it was only five hours' ride – and found Mr Thompson and a young man called Lawrence (he is going to make a traveller) who had for some time been expecting that I would appear. They showed me their diggings and their finds and I spent a pleasant day with them.' Soon after Gertrude Bell came the Rev. A. H. Sayce, Professor of Assyriology at Oxford, a man profoundly convinced that the work then going on in Syria, Meso-potamia and Egypt demonstrated over and over again the literal truth of the Old Testament.

Thompson had been responsible on arrival at the site for the appointment of the irrepressible Hajji Wahid as camp cook and general factotum. Hajji had just been released from jail. He had been frustrated in his attempt to woo a local girl by the refusal of her brothers to permit the liaison. Hajji had taken matters into his own hands, attacking the brothers and several kinsmen and killing four of them. A local official, speaking for the kaimakam (provincial governor) observed that one murder, or even two, might have been overlooked, but 'four was too much of a good thing'. Campbell Thompson thought him the ideal candidate as camp provider and protector.

Hajji Wahid had made it his business to stay at C. T.'s side, always armed with a gun, even in the kitchen. When Woolley took over as expedition leader, Hajji became his personal bodyguard. When he was alone on one occasion he held the chief German engineer on the rail bridge project at gunpoint rather than let him remove much needed earth from the archaeological site. Anyone who ventured on to the site without authority took his or her life in their hands.

Jerablus and its associated archaeological remains came within the administrative competence of the Kaimakam of Birajik, a place 25 miles upstream and famous for a flock of black glossy ibis which, though unknown in the rest of Syria, returned with unfailing regularity to Birajik and nested on a horizontal ledge of the castle wall. While looking for materials for the expedition house that Lawrence was supposed to have built before Woolley's arrival, the archaeologists were led to a fine piece of mosaic floor of about the fifth century AD. On it was a representation of the glossy ibis, showing that even in Roman times that rare bird, which winters in the Sudan and returns unfailingly to its Euphrates nesting place, attracted attention. It proved an omen of some kind, leading the two Englishmen on a crazily irresponsible expedition.

The local Arab whom Hogarth had referred to when he tried to sort out the ownership of the Carchemish site, was one Ali Agha. It was he who had claimed a title to the excavation area before Henderson started digging there in 1878. It was not his in truth, but other Arabs who lived on the site were not anxious to proclaim themselves landlords to the Imperial Government and thus incur land taxes. The perspicacious Ali Agha refused the attempt of Britain to buy the land but said that he had no objection to their digging. For his pains he was arrested by the Turks and sent to jail, whereupon the conscience-stricken British consul pleaded for his release. In consequence, the grateful Arab agreed to Britain purchasing a share in the estate, which was duly registered in the land court of Birajik. By the time Woolley arrived on the scene, Ali's son Hassan, himself an old man by then, had succeeded to his father's majority share.

Finding the local population antagonistic and the Turkish military presence unhelpful, Woolley and Lawrence armed themselves with revolvers, mounted their horses, and went off with Hajji Wahid to present their compliments to the Kaimakam. The local governor was unwelcoming but the two Englishmen made themselves comfortable on his divan while Hajji Wahid stood by the door and interpreted for them. The Kaimakam kicked off by refusing to acknowledge their *firman*, made out to Hogarth, acting for the British Museum, and signed in the name of the Sultan of the Ottoman Empire. After looking closely at the document, the Kaimakam said 'It is made out in the name of Mr Hogarth whom I know. Your name, so you tell me, is Woolley.' Woolley had already hired 120 workmen and was in no mood to be told at that stage that he must cease digging.

'I *shall* start tomorrow,' said Woolley.

The governor said that if he did, troops would be sent to stop his workmen. The interview became tense.

'You shall *not* do any work,' said the Kaimakam.

'I made up my mind that he was not a man who would call a bluff,' Woolley decided, as the Kaimakam turned a cold shoulder on his guests.

Taking my revolver out of its holster I got up and walking to the side of his chair put the muzzle against his left ear. 'On the contrary,' I said, 'I shall shoot you here and now unless you give me permission to start work tomorrow.'

The Turk leant back in his chair, his hands flat on the desk before him, his lips 'twisted into a wintry smile'. He could see no reason why work should not commence on the morrow.

The revolver was removed from the Kaimakam's ear, coffee and cigarettes were handed round, and the Carchemish party rode off to the accompaniment of Hajji Wahid's pistol fire as he announced the news of his employer's success. 'In a moment there was pandemonium: a hundred men were blazing away all the cartridges they had, and we rode in through a lane of dancing Arabs, shouting and shooting in honour of the victory.'

It was not the last the Englishmen would hear of the Kaimakam of Birajik.

Woolley appeared on the scene at a critical juncture of the Balkan Wars. With the advent of the Young Turks, Britain and France viewed a possible Turco-German alliance with growing paranoia, and spying activity in the Ottoman dominions was at fever point. But whatever part Woolley and Lawrence played in a drama that was to lead to world war, they showed little sign of sharing the anxiety of politicians back home. Their relations with their Turkish and German neighbours had the air of a Boy's Own escapade. Money, or shortage of it, was Woolley's main preoccupation. On 19 October he wrote to Hogarth from Carchemish to tell him that 200 men were by then at work on the mound, double the force used before his arrival, and that he was 'absolutely out of funds'. He had been forced to borrow from Aleppine moneylenders to keep his men at work. Lawrence needed money in order to travel home for Christmas, and he too wanted to winter at home. Three days later he acknowledged a letter from Hogarth that had crossed in the post with his. 'I must say that the contents rather dismayed me as I had hoped the £200 you had sent was over and above the £1000 which I know you had already deposited with the BM. I had already written to you on money matters on this supposition.' He went on to list current expenses:

Salaries – self and TEL for season £225
Gregori – travel & salary £35
Living allowance £25
Travel – self and TEL £100

He concluded: 'I write to you to send out in any case the remainder of the £1200 and I greatly hope that you may see your way to increasing the season's allowance beyond that figure.' Otherwise, he said, he would have to go back to the moneylenders. Little more than a month later the two men arrived in England.

Kenyon was clearly worried about their safety. More than that, he was concerned about the possible international repercussions of their presence in a volatile province of the Turkish Empire. In December when Woolley and Lawrence were at their respective homes spending Christmas with their families, the director of the Museum wrote to Hogarth:

> I have seen both Woolley and Lawrence. The latter seems very confident that, if trouble comes, they would, at the worst, be able to get away to the coast, and I have tried to impress on him that it is very desirable to avoid serious risk, not merely for their own sakes, but in the interest of the museum, and indeed of the political situation generally. What I am most afraid of is an attack on the Germans, which would give an excuse for German intervention, or compel the Turks to come down in force in order to avert such intervention. However, we can only wait and see what the next six weeks produce, before it is time for Woolley to start . . .

The burden of Kenyon's meeting with Woolley was clear from his last paragraph.

> As for Woolley's accounts, we must try to get things straightened out before he starts. He appears to go on the principle that if any sum has been mentioned to him, any sum that is subsequently sent or mentioned is an addition to the original figure, not a part of it. At the same time, I see no objection to the work being done rapidly, if it can be done efficiently.

Lawrence went on ahead for the start of the 1913 season. Woolley had been invited to spend a few days in January with Carnarvon at Highclere. Lord Carnarvon's attempt to excavate at Thebes in 1906 had led the French director of the Egyptian Antiquities Department, Sir Gaston Maspero, to suggest a collaborator. As a result, he had gone into partnership a year later with a brilliant but aggressive, sometimes violent, young man by the name of Howard Carter who, like anyone who was anyone in Egyptology, had worked for Petrie.

The paths of the digging fraternities of Egypt, Syria and Mesopotamia all crossed at some time in Constantinople, where Carnarvon's myopic half-brother, Aubrey Herbert, was an honorary attaché. Many came to know each other through that extraordinary, erratic young man.

On 5 January 1913 Woolley wrote to Lawrence from Highclere, just before his assistant was due to sail from Southampton, to tell him about information he had received concerning the interception by a certain Bagdoyan in Aleppo of two large inscribed Assyrian relief figures which the German excavators in Mesopotamia were shipping to the Berlin Museum via Mme Koch. They were, said Woolley, 'standing draped figures, winged, very big, and said to be good work'. Whoever had 'intercepted' them wanted £800–£1000 for the pair. It was proposed that Lawrence should call on Dr Wallis Budge, Keeper of the Egyptian and Assyrian Department of the British Museum and ask him if he wished to buy them. If so, he (Lawrence) should proceed to the place where they were hidden 'two days' journey' from Aleppo, and conclude the deal.

By early February 1913 Lawrence was aboard the British naval vessel HMS *Tewfiq*, writing to Hogarth to tell him that nineteen boxes of 'goodies' were on their way, '13 Kenyon to 6 of yours.' He had written to Kenyon to suggest that in view of the split with the Ashmolean, the British Museum should stand his expenses in the ratio 13/16. If the arithmetic was not good, the intention was clear. Whether the draped figures stolen from the Germans were included is not apparent. Woolley had sketched an impression of them from his informant's description but they were not easily identified. In any case, the Assyrian figures were a small part of what, by the standards of Carchemish, was a small conspiracy.

Woolley, at home with his family in Essex while Ned Lawrence conspired at Aleppo, wrote to Hogarth on 8 February to inform him of the political news passed on by his assistant. Khalil ibn Ibrahim, son of the Kurdish leader Ibrahim Pasha, of whom the Englishmen had seen a good deal during their travels on the other side of the Euphrates, was reported by Lawrence to be in Constantinople and 'very disgusted with his treatment'. The Kurds were quiet and had no intention of doing anything 'unless matters get bad in Stamboul'. Rich Armenians at Aintab and Aleppo were leaving, fearing an outbreak of the Turkish violence which they had experienced on and off since the purges under the Sultan Abdal Hamid in the last century.

Woolley quoted Lawrence as saying that despite the rising political temperature, further digging was quite possible 'if Constantinople holds straight'. All the same, the latest information was not good according to Ned: 'Latest news here is the fall of the [Turkish] cabinet: how and why is not known; it sounds to me like war and the Young Turk party on top again: if so matters will hum.' Lawrence's political education had begun and the inside view of Near Eastern politics which would inform his later literary work was beginning to form in his mind's eye. Before leaving for Carchemish at the end of February, Woolley wrote to Budge from Old Riffhams, telling him that five pots acquired in Syria were on their way. Conspiracy seemed to be entering into every transaction. 'I am sending them up to you in my brother's name as you wished,' he wrote. This season he would look out for Babylonian seals etc., but he mistrusted his own judgement in that specialist field and thought he might be forced by his ignorance to pay high prices.

In March he assured Hogarth that his, or the Ashmolean's, artifacts would be packed quite separately from the British Museum's and would, as usual, be addressed to Thurlow Leeds. There was a pervasive air of mystery. Leeds had started to keep a diary as soon as he succeeded Woolley at the Ashmolean, and in November 1909 he recorded in his journal the 'amazing endurance' of Lawrence who had recently returned from a thousand-mile journey in Syria in search of Crusader defences for his finals thesis. In November 1913, Woolley listed several Hittite seals that Lawrence had purchased, remarking that they would 'form a link with Hogarth'. When at a later date suggestions were made that Hogarth was at this time working for the secret service, Leeds expressed doubt. Secrecy about the financing of the Carchemish expedition and the subsequent activities of Lawrence and Woolley suggest a certain innocence on the part of Hogarth's young assistant keeper.

Woolley had set Lawrence to work at the South Gate of the old city of Carchemish. The Roman gateway had been cleared and below it they had uncovered a gate of the late Hittite period 'fairly well preserved'. By mid April bronzes, pots, beads, figures and seals were being recovered in growing numbers from the Hittite tombs. Lawrence was limping from a sprained toe, otherwise life was uneventful at the site. Mr Fontana, the Consul at Aleppo, and his wife, Winifred, came to stay with them. Lawrence reported back to Hogarth 'Both seem very fit and well . . . pleased with results of the dig to date . . . Everybody and every race seem heartily sick of the Turks and their miserable rotten rule.'

By the end of April, Lawrence was pleading directly to Hogarth for money. He needed £20, having spent out heavily on cylinders. 'Look out for our report this month,' he added almost by way of inducement. 'We have just found the largest inscription, and the fine prettiest (*sic*) sculpture of the dig.' Many of the best Syrian and Mesopotamian artifacts were to be found in the bazaars now that the Arab traders were aware of the willingness of museums to pay good prices for them. No security efforts on the part of the excavators could ever prevent a leakage, though Woolley's reputation, at Carchemish and after, was one of mutual trust with his foreman and workers. He could usually be relied on to pay good enough *bakhsheesh* to make robbery unnecessary.

In May, Hogarth reversed the general trend of correspondence, making placatory noises about money. 'With regard to money,' he wrote on 9 May, 'I have passed over to Kenyon a further sum of £200 to be placed to your credit at the Bank of England by the Trustees, and Kenyon has promised that this will be done at once. Don't draw it if you can help it; at the same time, there it is available.'

Then came a significant admission.

> If also you have been forestalling a certain amount on account of purchases for us, the BM and yourself, get that replaced as soon as ever you can in the Summer, for the using of these excavation funds for purchases is a practise open to obvious objection, and if my benefactor were to make any inquiries or demand to see interim accounts it might be awkward.

At the same time, Hogarth wanted to reassure Woolley. 'We do want you and Lawrence to use the full opportunity for acquiring things.' There was also the hope that the monthly report would be encouraging to Kenyon and would contain photographs of the latest sculptures. Was there any sign of a palace at the head of the staircase they had uncovered? Woolley replied on 27 May. 'But the purchase of antiquities, whether for the BM, for you or for myself does not appear in my accounts & does not really come out of excavation funds; so it could not cause any embarrassment if eg. your benefactor wanted to look into things.'

Work at Carchemish was vastly complicated by political matters. Relations between Britain and its old ally Turkey had been upset in 1906 when Turkish patrols stepped over Cromer's arbitary Sinai frontier and Britain reacted as though a foreign army had landed at

Dover, threatening to bombard the Dardanelles in retaliation. The Young Turks' rebellion of 1908 had caused some of the brasher elements in Constantinople to look to the German Emperor. The European concert which in 1911–13 presided over the destruction of the Ottoman Empire in Europe had not sweetened the atmosphere. The British Foreign Office, which had always held the security of the Ottoman Empire to be essential to the safety of the Indian Empire and to British commercial interests in the Near East, began to make plans to fill the vacuum which the disintegration of Asiatic Turkey would cause. Now Britain was negotiating with the Prime Minister elect of Turkey, Hakki Pasha, to form a new alliance and hopefully to prop up the liberal old guard in opposition to the Young Turks.

The conflicts of interest between the European powers spilled over to the distant provinces of the Ottoman Empire. In the *vilayets* of Beirut and Aleppo, Hogarth's men had become involved in the Royal Navy intelligence department's effort to acquaint itself with all the native chiefs and all potential enemies in the region. Carchemish fitted nicely, and with academic respectability, into the official plan of 'listen and observe'.

On the other side, a German archaeologist and member of a distinguished banking family who was to become the Reich's chief of Middle East intelligence, Baron Max von Oppenheim, was currently digging at another north Syrian site, Tal Halaf, where distinctive pottery would eventually reveal a Syro-Mesopotamian culture of the 5th millennium BC.

Archaeology had become inseparable from patriotic duty and the diggers of Carchemish played their part with panache and an instinctive sense of being actors in a farcical stage play. In the process, tit-for-tat battles with their German neighbours became dangerous almost to the point of bearing out Kenyon's worst fears.

The expedition's house was built eventually and Lawrence carved a 'Hittite' alabaster relief sculpture and fixed it over the doorway to the confusion of all but the most wary of visitors. More pointedly, Woolley and Lawrence were able to use the house to observe the comings and goings of the Germans through their Zeiss binoculars. They were also able to photograph them with the aid of a telephoto lens attached to their camera, something of a rarity in those days.

At this time, Woolley was looking for somewhere to dispose of the site rubbish, particularly the broken stone and concrete of the Roman level. The Germans, busily building houses, hospitals and

schools for their site workers, needed the rubbish for their foundations. And so a deal was struck. The Germans would sift and take
away the debris at their own expense. Hassan had been paid a
modest sum by Hogarth at the beginning of the excavation, but the
small print excluded the need for further payments for use of the
land. The Germans also refused to pay the unfortunate landlord.
Hassan, whose wife had drowned herself in the river and who
needed money for a second marriage, argued that the material being
given to the Germans was rightfully his. Could the Germans not be
forced to pay for it? The chief engineer of the railway refused to do
so, and Hassan Ali Agha then went to plead with the Kaimakam of
Birajik who, anxious to repay the arrogant English, decided to plot
his revenge.

Lawrence was presented with a summons to appear at the Birajik
court. He was charged with stealing property, to wit stones, belonging to the plaintiff Hassan Ali Agha, and having sold them to the
German rail engineers at Jerablus for thirty pounds Turkish. As it
happened, the Capitulations which the European powers had forced
on the Ottoman Empire as a penalty for its international debt,
forbade the trial of any British subject in a Turkish court except
when a British consul was on the bench. Worse, the court before
which Lawrence was ordered to appear was a Shari, or Koranic,
tribunal and its rules applied strictly to Moslems. Woolley decided
that for the sake of appearances his assistant should, none the less,
appear. Lawrence took his place in the dock, protested that the court
had no proper jurisdiction, denied the charge and produced documents to show that he had no part in the affair, with affidavits
showing that Woolley was responsible for the British side's actions
and that the Germans had not paid and would not pay a penny for
the stones. He also produced an agreement signed by Hassan
relinquishing his rights in the area from which the stones came. The
prosecuting counsel then asked that the court impound Lawrence's
documents and stated that the prosecution would call at least sixteen
witnesses who would say that the stones had been sold to the
Germans, and that the conversations between them and Lawrence
(in French!) had been overheard. Before Lawrence could protest the
court was adjourned. The Kaimakam issued immediate orders that
no further stones should be sold, and told his *yuzbashi* (subaltern)
at Jerablus to station troops at the Carchemish gate to ensure that
his orders were obeyed. Woolley, by now practised in Eastern ways,
came to an arrangement whereby the Germans gave him the money

they were paying to their donkey-gangs so that he, Woolley, transported the material for the Germans and paid the men their wages. The *yuzbashi* was given a suitable cut, cigarettes were smoked and peace prevailed. The farce continued in court when the trial resumed at Birajik. This time Woolley accompanied Lawrence and as soon as the case opened he objected that a charge could only be brought against him, not against Lawrence, since he was responsible for the excavations. Counsel for the prosecution promptly asked for a week's remand. Then there was a row over the papers which the court had impounded at Lawrence's first appearance. A fight ensued which pleased Hajji Wahid no end. Woolley ordered his *major domo* to leave the court. The Hajji refused point-blank to desert his employer at such a propitious moment. He had armed himself with two revolvers which he brandished threateningly. Woolley held the Cadi, the judge, at gunpoint. Lawrence bolted to an adjoining room where he held up the Kaimakam. 'You will not leave the room alive . . . unless I get those papers,' Woolley told the Cadi. Lawrence found the papers on the Kaimakam's person and returned to court with them. Woolley paid for a penny stamp to be affixed to a copy of the Hassan Agha contract which was then lodged with the court. Woolley pocketed the original papers, and the Cadi pronounced the case closed.

When the three musketeers appeared outside the Serai, Hajji Wahid swaggering in the van and twisting his moustache imperiously, the assembled troops stood stiffly to attention and saluted.

A month after the event, Hogarth arrived from Oxford to see how things were progressing. Woolley told him the story and he went off to Birajik to make sure the Kaimakam had cooled off. The governor assured him that the whole thing had been a regrettable mistake and that there were no ill feelings.

The same to and fro of archaeology and horse-play marked the next two seasons. There were journeys home between times, and visits to friends and contacts in Aleppo, Jubail and Beirut. At the American Mission School in Jubail, Lawrence had come to know most of the women teachers, particularly Fareedah al Akle who taught Arabic there and helped the Englishmen in their onslaught on the language. One family that always waited expectantly for a call from Lawrence and Woolley as they passed their way were the Elroy Fleckers. James Elroy Flecker was then Vice-Consul at Beirut, observing the east with an acute sence of loneliness and isolation. At Beirut Woolley and Lawrence spent a good deal of time at the American University where the antiquities collection was in such a mess that an ox-head from a decorative tin-opener posed as 'Hittite sculpture'. They subsequently labelled the exhibits for the classics professor who looked after them. At Safed they sometimes called on the London-based Mission to the Jews run by Dr Anderson and his assistant Nora Harrison. And at Tiberias on Lake Galilee they met the man to whom all travellers in Palestine and Syria gravitated, Dr Torrance, a Scot who espoused Christian Zionism, believing that the Jewish reoccupation of Palestine would be the harbinger of the second coming of Christ. So many, in fact, were their contacts in the Levant that the two men often devoted their furloughs to visiting them rather than return to England and their families. The East had taken its traditional hold, and thoughts of home did not often trouble them.

Still, there were brief visits to England. They went home again in June 1913 after closing the site amid scenes of brotherly love and tribal warfare. In April, eighteen Kurds, representative of tribal shaikhs who had been at war for forty years, had descended on the camp and were induced by the English to enter into a pact of friendship. They fell into each other's arms and kissed, and peace broke out in northern Syria. Later there was a fight between rival tribes among the workforce. The men separated into two armed camps and refused to eat or work together. With Hamoudi's muscular help, the rival factions were locked in the photographic dark room until blood money was paid over and a peace pact made.

That matter settled, Woolley and Lawrence packed their bags and left for England accompanied by Hamoudi and Dahum. Woolley stayed with his family in Essex while Lawrence took the Arabs to Oxford where they were lodged in a small bungalow at the end of Mrs Lawrence's garden. Lawrence took them to the Ashmolean to see the 'chief', Hogarth, to the 'scandalization of Oxford', and to Harpenden in Hertfordshire where their friend Mrs Rieder of the American Mission had taken up a teaching appointment. Towards the end of their stay the Arabs were taken to meet the Woolleys, where they were received urbanely. Leonard and 'Ned' took them to a show at Earl's Court. Hamoudi in particular was entranced; his young companion was taciturn and not so easily pleased. The Arabs' brief stay – about which they boasted for ever after – was marred at the end by a free fight with an Egyptian student friend of Ned's brother Will. Before leaving, Woolley asked Hamoudi what he would like to take home with him. 'A tap,' replied Hamoudi. 'You see, I can then have water all the time in my tent.'

Lawrence's close relationship with Dahum was to cause much future speculation. Woolley, who observed the friendship from the outset and watched it develop, was to describe the affair years later when Lawrence was famous. Dahum was 'beautifully built and remarkably handsome,' he wrote, and Lawrence was 'devoted to him'.

Lawrence took the Arabs back to Jerablus in August while Woolley went to Egypt on unspecified business.

There was speculation on the part of local Arabs and visitors to the site when it was discovered that Lawrence had set up house with the Arab boy, especially when Dahum was seen to pose as a model for a crouching figure which Lawrence carved in limestone. It was the 'Assyrian' slab which Lawrence placed over the door of the site house. In the eyes of locals, to make an image was bad enough, 'a naked figure was proof of some sort of evil.' Woolley was the first to dismiss suggestions of homosexuality. 'Lawrence had in his make-up a very strong vein of sentiment,' he wrote, 'but he was in no sense a pervert.' He added: 'Greek homosexuality interested him, but in a detached way, and the interest was not morbid but perfectly serious.'

Woolley arrived back at Carchemish in October. One day he heard Hamoudi telling an enthralled audience about Oxford. 'There is a big public park,' he told them, 'with little metal chains to keep people off the grass. They could easily step over the chains, but they don't. It was the most wonderful thing I saw.'

Already Lawrence – who had scouted the region since he first arrived as a student in 1909 in search of crusader fortresses – had begun to photograph and make detailed notes on the Arab tribal leaders and their Turkish accomplices and enemies. While he was at home at the end of 1912, he had purchased a Canadian canoe which he shipped to Beirut and thence to Carchemish, where he fitted it with an outboard motor. Woolley was later to describe the long trips his colleague made on the Euphrates. On their return to Syria in February 1913, both men spent some time in Beirut where, according to Lawrence, they engaged in gun smuggling with the assistance of the British consul and his wife, Mr and Mrs 'Raff' Fontana. The guns were intended for the Consulate-General at Aleppo where Woolley and Lawrence believed the Kurds were intent on an attack. Winifred Fontana persuaded the German Consul at Beirut, who had come to learn of the escapade, that T. E. and

Woolley were romantic boys whose legs had been pulled by their Kurdish friends. 'What I really feared was that T. E. and Woolley were pulling their consul's leg.' Mrs Fontana wrote subsequently that 'T. E. was certainly in touch with the Kurds. It is quite likely that he knew of a smouldering project on the part of the Kurds to sack Aleppo . . .' Nearly a quarter of a century later, when Lawrence's letters were published, his editor David Garnett remarked that in a letter he was not allowed to publish, dated 'the end of February (1913)', Lawrence had mentioned 'gun-running and also rifle-practice'. Two years earlier, when the Fontanas first met the archaeologists from Carchemish, Winifred, who was a keen amateur painter, had noted that all three (she included Hogarth) would have made 'beautiful models'. It was Lawrence who attracted her attention and most appealed to her. But a Syrian guest at the consular house, when he overheard Mrs Fontana's praise, thought otherwise. 'What an unhappy contrast *ce jeune Laurens* makes with Monsieur Woolley, who is so much a man of the world, and a *parfait gentilhomme.*'

Lawrence had been less than open in his dealings with Woolley. In January 1913 he had told Hogarth in a letter from Port Said, 'You will understand that when Woolley is here I can't buy anything.' On 15 October he wrote to the chief to tell him of the progress of the German railway – Jerablus station was under construction with twenty-four stone buildings and was scheduled for completion a year hence – and remarking that he and Woolley had been to Aleppo and Damascus to buy a number of cylinders and 'little bronzes'. 'Nothing stupendous,' he said, 'but all quite nice. The prices of seals in Aleppo are rising very fast . . .' Woolley relied greatly on his foreman Hamoudi for whom he had the utmost liking. Lawrence, after the return from England, took a sudden dislike to the Arab and asked Hogarth to send out his old Cretan foreman, Gregori, 'the poacher turned gamekeeper' as Woolley had described him. After instructing Hamoudi in the duties of site foreman at the start of the Carchemish dig he had returned to Evans in Crete. In October 1913 he was back working at Carchemish, 'deadly jealous of the two who went to England'. He helped prepare the site for the winter which the Englishmen had decided to spend *in situ*. Lawrence told Hogarth, 'I gave your love to Gregori.' The Cypriot 'seemed amused'. The Englishmen and Dahum shared a beautiful white snow leopard as a companion and were amused at the Arabs' fear of it.

By the end of the year, Woolley was able to report to Hogarth and the British Mueum the discovery of some interesting artifacts. Most significant were the limestone and basalt relief panels secured to the Processional Wall of Carchemish. The relief slabs had fallen from their place four feet up on the wall and lay among the foundations of the Roman buildings. Woolley replaced them as best he could, restoring the cracked and broken friezes of warriors, of foot soldiers marching in pairs behind chariots whose horses trampled on the defeated enemy. On the last of the slabs was the figure of the goddess Ishtar, naked and holding her breasts, symbol of the temple to which the Hittite army returned in triumph from one of its many victories. The slab was inscribed with the story of the battle, but it could not be read. It was a German team digging far to the north-west in Turkish Anatolia, at the site of Boghazkoi, which was unveiling the true centre of the Hittite empire, ancient Hattusas. It was there that Professors Winckler and Puchstein dug up thousands of inscriptions on sculpture and tablets, and the tell-tale cylinder seals that reveal so much of ancient history. One such inscription gave the name of the Hittite or Hatti king Mursili, which many scholars were to relate to one of Pelops' charioteers, Myrtilos, thus suggesting a link between Trojans and Hittites, and strengthening the widely held theory that Greece of the 14th century BC was dominated by a Hatti ruling dynasty. In 1915 the Czech scholar Hrozny revealed that the language of the Hittites was not, as generally supposed, Semitic but Indo-European in origin, though, to complicate the picture, the cuneiform texts embraced eight different languages, one of which was Akkadian, the earliest of the Semitic tongues. Winckler's team at Boghazkoi unearthed more than ten thousand inscribed tablets, a vast addition to the store of man's knowledge of the ancient world. Woolley's two years of work could boast nothing like that, but if Carchemish was shown to be nothing but an outpost of the empire, its haul of monuments, especially its robustly sculpted lions, bearded gods and sphinxes, and the pottery and seals found in the vast necropolis beyond the city walls, was impressive in view of all the diversions faced by the Hogarth-Woolley expedition.

In December 1913 a message from Kenyon requested Woolley to leave Carchemish and go down to Palestine with Lawrence on an important mission. Perhaps the purpose and nature of this strange journey, which has always intrigued the biographers of Lawrence and exponents of 'intelligence' matters, was discussed between Woolley and Kenyon during the former's visit to London in the summer. If so, no record of their conversation remains. Only Woolley's published words and Lawrence's letters are there to guide us.

The Egypt Exploration Society, Woolley said, 'wanted some archaeologists to follow in the footsteps of Moses'. But it was the Palestine Exploration Fund for whom the diggers of Carchemish ostensibly acted when they took the train from Aleppo to Damascus, bound for Sinai.

In the Footsteps of Moses

And Moses sent them to spy out the land of Canaan,
and said unto them, Get you up this way by the South,
and go up into the mountains; And see the land, what
it is; and the people that dwelleth therein, whether they
be strong or weak, whether they be few or many.

Numbers 13. 1–17, 18

Among the last visitors to the Carchemish site in the late summer of
1913 was Captain Hubert Young of the 116th Mahrattas on his
way through the Ottoman dominions to Karachi, on special duty.
He found Lawrence there alone with Dahum and the Arab servants.
Writing from memory of that visit, Young said:

> I never quite fathomed why Lawrence was still at Carchemish
> when the 'digs' were closed down, but I gathered that it was
> partly from choice and partly from economy. He used to spend
> his time wandering about in Arab dress, sometimes for days at
> a time, storing his phenomenal memory with scraps of local
> knowledge which came in very useful later on. When he was
> not doing this he was trying to puzzle out the Hittite inscriptions
> or target-shooting with a long Mauser pistol.

The Indian army officer, later to find employment as an official of
the Foreign and Colonial offices, competed with the 22-year-old
Lawrence in target shooting but had to admit defeat. 'Lawrence was
a wonderful shot,' he conceded, adding that the natives of Jerablus
'loved him'.

Frederic Kenyon recalled that at the time he was asked 'whether
the services of both scholars could be made available for an
archaeological survey which the Palestine Exploration Fund desired
to undertake in southern Palestine.' The museum, he said, ensured

that the men remained at Carchemish rather than 'going off on their own devices', and at the end of the year they left to join Captain S. F. Newcombe, who was 'in general charge of the survey'.

Captain Newcombe RE, known as 'Skinface' because he was so much in the searing desert sun that his face was permanently peeled, was carrying out a military survey of Sinai and Transjordan ostensibly for the Palestine Exploration Fund. There was little apparent need. Lord Kitchener when a young sapper lieutenant had carried out a trigonometric survey of 8,000 square miles of the region with his friend Lieutenant Claude Conder, completing the exercise in 1878. Before and since, a host of visitors to the Christian Holy Land had filled in missing detail, not the least of them the French scholar-priests Jaussen and Savinac, and the Austrian Professor Musil. More importantly, the Military Governor of Sinai from 1906 to 1912 was Colonel 'Wallier' Parker, Kitchener's nephew, and he and two assistants, the brothers Alwyn and Jennings Bramly, had mapped the peninsula thoroughly and secured a network of agents there. Now, Field Marshal Lord Kitchener was British Resident and Consul-General in Cairo and it was under his aegis, though on the orders of the Director of Military Intelligence, Colonel Oliver Stack, that Newcombe was in the Palestinian desert, ostensibly looking for biblical landmarks, in fact seeking out disaffected tribesmen who, it was hoped, would act as 'news agents' for Britain in the event of trouble with their masters the Turks.

Woolley had closed the Carchemish site on 7 December 1913. He and Lawrence left on the 20th bound for Jaffa by way of the Ottoman rail road from Aleppo to Deraa on the Hijaz line. Lawrence had written to Mrs Rieder the day before, announcing that they were off to 'survey Arabia Petraea', and referring to 'horrible political complots'.

Woolley wrote most of the account of their journey for the records of the Palestine Exploration Fund. It was a description full of archaeological, geographical and botanical information, with an entire section on early churches, but in terms of places and details of terrain it contained nothing that was not already on record.

Dahum was with them and they hurried south by rail from Aleppo to join Captain Newcombe who awaited them at Beersheba. They reached Gaza on the Palestinian side of the border with Sinai, in the first week of January 1914, where they were greeted by the missionary Dr Sterling, head of the Christian Mission School, whose fee for medical treatment or consultation was a compulsory Bible reading, and Mr Knesevich the British consul and his son Emil. From there they went to Beersheba through an undulating, treeless plain, its villages strewn with Byzantine pottery, olive presses and broken cisterns. 'At Beersheba we spent three days, and then, on January 11th, moved to Khalasa.' That was all Woolley had to say of their meeting place and the long-awaited rendezvous with Captain Newcombe.

They passed through barren hills and along dangerous ridges in a desolate region that had seen days of better husbandry. They stayed at Khalasa for four days before moving camp to Esbaita – 'It is clear that Esbaita came to a violent end' – by way of sand drifts whose ridges rose from forty to fifty feet, over limestone hills and flinty plains until the ground fell away and they stood over the Wadi Migrih, the walls of Esbaita and Mishrafa – which some scholars believed to be Zephath of the Amorites – rising to west and east. The travelling scholars of 1914 insisted that neither place predated the Christian era. 'The planning of the ruins and a visit to Mishrafa occupied us until January 24th, when we shifted camp to Al Auja.' It was there that they picked up Yusuf Canaan, a long-serving field foreman with the PEF. They were still inside Turkish territory, as they had been from the outset, east of the border which Cromer had drawn in 1906 from Rafa to Aqaba.

It was not the legal frontier, which in the centuries of Ottoman occupation of Egypt and Syria had been drawn only across the north-west corner of the peninsula from Suez to Rafa, the rest of the region popularly called Sinai being administered as part of the Sanjuk of Jerusalem (which was more or less ancient Palestine). But it was the frontier which Britain insisted on, and military action one way or the other would depend a great deal on a knowledge of water supplies. If there was a serious purpose to the journey, it was probably that consideration as much as any which caused Cairo to send the diggers of Carchemish on a 'red-herring' mission to take attention away from Captain Newcombe.

Ain Kadeis, the watering place to which they went next, was just over the frontier in Cromer's Sinai. They were at biblical Kadesh, on the route of the Israelite Spies. The camels had taken off for better pasture in the night and their owners had to scramble on foot over barren mountainous roads. On 27 January 1914 they completed the day's march skirting the foothills of the Kadesh plain to the Egyptian government station at Kossaima, camping in the valley of Ain Guderat. Woolley's commentary explained, 'On February 8th we separated, Mr Lawrence to go south to Aqaba and thence up the Wadi Araba, I to return north.'

Woolley's journey from here on was punctuated by archaeological detail which said much for his powers of observation and description, for many famous journeys had been made that way; but few, if any, of the travellers, had noticed the same landmarks or, if they had, described them so well. Of the Wadi Ramliya, for example:

> Though broken terraces spoke of former cultivation, the soil was practically pure sand, through which the torrent waters had cut a deep bed. It was curious to see here, reproduced on a small scale, the phenomenon remarked by Sir Aurel Stein in Chinese Turkestan: many fragments of walls are left standing on isolated tongues of islands of sand some six feet high, while around them the light soil, not solidified by any superimposed weight, has all been carried away by the flood. At one point on the west bank stood the ruins of a large farmhouse with caves behind it cut in the lofty cliff: fragments of Syrian *terra sigillata* showed that the building dated back fairly early in the Roman period.

Only three years before he had corresponded with Stein about the orientalist's travels in Central Asia and his discoveries in Turkestan. Apart from the coincidence of their observations on two similar but far removed desert regions, Woolley contented himself with the Byzantine pottery and ruined buildings on the road to Wadi al Sidd. The road swept eastward 'in a great curve under the high southern hills up to Tel Kurnub, when it breaks through them by a precipitous gorge, and runs on to the Dead Sea.' On 22 February he struck north to Gaza.

When they parted a fortnight before, Lawrence had gone south, striking for Aqaba along the Darb al Shur, a winding desert road via the new frontier post of Kuntilla. This was Bedouin country, wild and flinty, its road surface polished by the hoofs of countless camels. The north-eastern region which they and Newcombe had traversed was almost certainly the route an invading army would take if it set out to attack Egypt's lifeline at Suez. To the south lay Jabal Tih and the Mount of Moses, on the route taken by the Israelites to the Promised Land.

No dates are given by either man for this stage of the reconnaissance. On 6 February, two days before he parted from Woolley, Lawrence wrote to an anonymous friend from 'The Wilderness of

Sin, An Oasis.' He probably posted the letter at the armed post of Kuntilla. The rest of the journey took him, according to Woolley's account, along the Wadi Araba to the hills of Harun and Wadi al Musa. He is said to have gone thence to Petra where he met Lady Evelyn Cobbold and a friend who were sightseeing. They told Fareedah al Akle in Dasmascus that they had found Lawrence in a half-starved state. Lawrence told his brother that they had given him money to make the return journey from Maan to Damascus on the Hijaz railway. Whatever the truth of his movements at that time, Gertrude Bell was close to his route for almost the whole of January and the first week of February. She was on her way to Hail, the capital of the rulers of northern Arabia, the Ibn Rashid, where a power struggle was taking place between pro- and anti-Saudi factions of that royal house; a struggle in which Britain, France and Turkey took a keen interest. On her way, 'The Lady' took photographs of the women of the Howaitat tribe, and among them is a remarkable likeness of Lawrence in female desert garb. A few weeks after Gertrude Bell's departure, the British consul in Kuwait, Captain Shakespear, arrived at the gates of Hail on his way to Kuntilla and Egypt after an epic journey across Arabia. While he waited in the desert the pro-Saudi regent of Hail was murdered nearby and the boy-prince Saud ibn Rashid became the ruler of the northern region of Najd (central Arabia). The division of central Arabia, which suited the Turks and Britain too, was assured.

By then Woolley was back at Carchemish waiting for Lawrence, who had arrived in Damascus on or about 28 February. On that date he wrote another letter to his anonymous friend in which he told of being 'Alone in Arabia!' and said that the Kaimakam of Aqaba (which was just outside the British zone and administered as part of the Turkish Hijaz) was 'a bad man' who 'had (or said he had) no news of us and our little games', and refused to allow Newcombe to 'map' and himself, Lawrence, to 'photograph or archaeologize'. The two men were together again at Carchemish by the end of March.

It was a suspect journey. Woolley's own reflective words about the Egypt Exploration Society's wish for 'some archaeologists' to follow in the footsteps of Moses, has about it the ring of half-truth, especially when looked at in the light of his following words: '. . . Moses' footsteps, of course, led us outside the Egyptian frontier into the Turkish part of Sinai, and the expedition we were joining was headed by a sapper officer who, with his assistant, was making a military map of Turkish Sinai.' Kenyon, who gave permission for the enterprise to take place, said nothing of the Egypt Exploration Society, and nothing of map-making in describing its provenance. In any case, Sinai was not the end of the affair.

Woolley explained: '. . . at the end of it all I talked to our senior officer, Stewart Newcombe, who was an extraordinarily nice fellow, and said "Look, when you have done your job (he had to go to Cairo and work up his report), come along to Carchemish and stop with us."'

The 'senior officer', an unusual term for civilian archaeologists searching for antiquities to employ, told Woolley that Kitchener would not hear of it. Woolley replied that they were only a stone's throw from the German rail engineers, and that he, Newcombe, could 'pick up a whole lot of useful military information'.

Newcombe duly appeared at Carchemish in April, his journey authorized by the Sirdar of the Egyptian army, General Wingate, and presumably by Kitchener. In making the trip Captain Newcombe missed the famous Cairo Ball, Kitchener's last peace-time fling. France had just withdrawn from the Baghdad Rail Consortium, in which Britain was also represented though Germany was the senior partner, and in return the Quai d'Orsay had won vital concessions from the Powers including preferential rights in Syria and other parts of Asiatic Turkey. An Anglo-Turkish Convention was being negotiated in London. About a month earlier, in January, a joint War Office and Admiralty plan for the transport of a British Expeditionary Force had been formulated. Talk of war was widespread and the stability of the Middle East, the source of oil for Britain's warships and the buffer of the Indian Empire, was threatened. Doubtless Newcombe's journey to Carchemish and thence across the Taurus range by way of Adana to Constantinople, was a small part of a complex intelligence jigsaw. As it happened, Newcombe was apparently unable to collect the military information required by the War Office. 'So would we, when we had finished our work, follow in his steps and see what we could do?'

Woolley thought it would be 'great fun'. The entire Carchemish enterprise was infused with a sense of fun, almost of frivolity. With Lawrence, he went to Aleppo to call on the chief German engineer, Meissner Pasha, the man who had built the Hijaz railroad and was now in charge of the Baghdad line and rushing to complete a task that had been dogged by unsuspected problems of terrain and climate.

Another small drama was enacted. Woolley's anecdotal versions of events then and later somehow portray the nature of the man better than his sparse letters. His autobiographical meanderings and chatty style are uniquely revealing.

'We are going home in a day or two and want to go over your construction road.'

'Why?'

'Because I understand you get the most lovely views.'

'Well, you are not going. Who put you up to this? You couldn't go because the construction road has been destroyed.'

'What a pity. A lamentable thing.'

'Your friend who suggested that you should take that route, he went that way, didn't he?'

'Yes.'

'Your friend who?'

'Mr Newcombe.'

'You mean Captain Newcombe of the Royal Engineers.'

'Well, he might be of the Royal Engineers, yes, but he is a friend of mine and he told me to go and look at the view.'

'Exactly. You are not going.'

'I assure you Herr Meissner that we are going that way.'

'I promise you that you won't.'

The English decided that Meissner was not going to relent and so in early May they went to Alexandretta and travelled part of the way by road before boarding a train at the construction terminus. As the train was about to depart, their compartment door was opened by a fat elderly German loaded with baskets. The baskets were full of plants and the breathless fellow traveller explained that he was working for the Horticultural Society of Berlin.

'That's a very nice job, getting your expenses paid and travelling all round the place, and that sort of thing.'

'Oh yes, but it isn't my only job. I'm also employed by the Kaiser Friedrich Museum to collect photographs of antiquities, and I've got a very fine collection . . . one day I'm going to try to get down to Carchemish . . . where the English are digging.'

Lawrence and Woolley both spoke German passably and they assured their companion that he would be most welcome.

The conversation took on an increasingly disingenuous air.

'What are you doing now?' the German asked.

'We are going home . . . what we wanted to do was go over the construction road of the Baghdad railway.'

'Oh but you must. It's magnificent!'

'So I've heard say,' said Woolley. 'But do you know the Chief Engineer in Aleppo? He's forbidden us . . . He seems to think we're spying.'

'A great shame,' said the German, 'I wish I could help you.'

'Possibly you can. Do you know any of the German engineers in the mountain area?'

'I know them all very well.'

'Do give us letters of introduction.'

'Certainly.'

'Will you make them out to Mr Jones and Mr Robinson.'

As the train puffed towards Adana, the German wrote three letters to engineers on the route in the assumed names of the Englishmen.

The first of the engineers turned out to be an Italian who was in a raging temper. He had just been dismissed by the Germans for overspending his budget.

'It's because I'm Italian and not German that they are turning me out,' he told the visitors. The Englishmen realized that they had found an ally and told him confidentially that though they were archaeologists they happened, in point of fact, to be doing a job for the British War Office.

'Good heavens! Can I help?'

Lawrence and Woolley began to share the questioning.

'We want to know exactly how this line is planned, what progress it is making, what its prospects are, and so on.'

By the next day the Italian had furnished them with a pile of documents, 'the whole of the information the War Office could have hoped for.'

Woolley and Lawrence were making their way back to Adana with their baggage and two muleteers when they ran into a party of Turkish soldiers with a German NCO, who told them they had no right to be where they were. 'Clear out', the NCO said.

'No, we'll do nothing of the sort.'

'We know all about you and I've got my orders. We know that two British spies, Woolley and Lawrence are coming this way.'

'Ah, dear me. Now who gave you this order.'

'The Engineer.'

'Interesting, I've got a letter of introduction to him. Here it is. Our names are Jones and Robinson.'

The German apologized and saluted. 'I suppose they are further along the road.'

'Possibly they are.'

It was, said Woolley, the only piece of spying he did before the war.

The puckish facial expressions, the laughing blue eyes and the slurred r's which gave a slight but distinctive lisp to his speech, seep through Woolley's accounts of early adventures, essentially true but doubtless much embroidered in the telling. In later years, as his archaeological fame spread, he was to become a sought-after dinner guest and one of the finest speakers and lecturers in the English-speaking world, addressing the studious and the mighty in much the same semi-humorous and often irreverent vein.

Carchemish had set the two archaeologists on their way to a promising career which was about to be rudely interrupted. Before leaving at the end of April, Lawrence had written to their friend James Elroy Flecker, by then dying in a Swiss sanatorium, to give the poet a last vivid account of a fight between Arabs, Kurds, Turks and Circassian gendarmes, in which Woolley was shot at and the archaeological workforce acquitted itself well. Before Flecker's last illness, Lawrence had written to Hogarth to ask him if he could find a billet for the poet at Oxford.

Hogarth had decided to make a flying visit to the site in May 1914 but before the date of departure he changed his mind. Lawrence wrote to his friend Thurlow Leeds at the Ashmolean.

> O Leeds!
> Now what is there to tell you? of D.G.H. you say that he may not come out, if we are not at work . . . but O Leeds that shows a fundamental and basic ignorance of Woolley and myself: it is when we are not at work that we are most charming . . . then the flowery smiles, the companionable talk . . . then too the hunt for seals & carpets . . .

Then he gave another account of recent fighting between Kurds and Circassians at the site.

> Last week there was a battle here. Kurds started out to scupper the Circassians of the Baghdad Railway, & went on to consider the engineers: 'Let us look one another in the face' . . . We were

at peace in the house – contemplating a letter to you, and lo and behold, the sound of rapid firing & bullets dropping about the house . . .

He went on to describe how he and Woolley grabbed their rifles and joined in. Although Lawrence did not say so, it must be assumed that Hajji Wahid was in the thick of the battle. Kurdish women were howling at their menfolk to redouble their efforts. Warring factions fought for two hours, using the site house as a demarcation zone. It was all over in two hours. Several contestants were injured but only one man died. There was a suggestion of anti-climax in Lawrence's report of the affair.

Hogarth made the promised journey eventually, and the three men fought over a copy of Flecker's novel *The King of Alsander*.

They had packed up the most important finds and sent them to Aleppo where the Consul arranged for them to be sent to England and the British Museum. Others were sent to Beirut, where they were to be transported by warship according to the instructions of the Consul at Damascus. Most were put aboard ship before war was declared. Others were left behind on the quay and were eventually taken to Constantinople, and from there to Ankara where some of the best of the Hittite sculptures found a permanent resting place.

Secret Service

Woolley approached his 35th year at Old Riffhams, resting from eastern travail and awaiting the call of King and Country. He enjoyed a small but growing reputation as an archaeologist and he had accustomed himself to a life style based on an income of £250 a year from the British Museum (in fact, the museum only distributed the sum since it was derived from Hogarth's 'well-wisher'), as the leader of its expedition. It was no mean income at the time, but he and Cathcart still maintained their father and two sisters at the Danbury house, and had only recently been relieved of the need to contribute to the educations of the last in a long line of younger brothers and sisters. Lawrence had made do on an Oxford demyship of £80, which Hogarth had arranged so that his protégé could join the dig, with the addition of about £100 from the Carchemish fund.

According to Lawrence, Newcombe had told the War Office about his Sinai companions and recommended them for intelligence duties. But in September 1914 the British army was slow to mobilize and was certainly no match for its Prussian opponent when it came to putting an army in the field. Turkey had not yet entered the war, though its alliance with Germany was *de facto*.

Woolley and Lawrence waited impatiently with thousands of other young men in daily expectation of a call to serve. Woolley joined the Territorial Army on 23 September, his unit being embodied in the Inns of Court Officers Training Corps.

Newcombe, being a regular officer, went to France with one of the first sapper contingents. The archaeologists he left behind worked on the 'Wilderness of Zin' for the Palestine Exploration Fund, an account of the Sinai journey insisted upon by Kitchener, 'the only begetter of the survey'. Much of the work was done at the Royal Geographical Society where Arthur Hincks, the Society's secretary, and Douglas Carruthers, honorary head of the map room, worked with Dr H. N. Dickson of Captain Hall's Admiralty intelligence department in an attempt to catch up with the urgent need of the High Command for maps of land and sea. They also worked closely with MO4, the cartographic division of army intelligence under Colonel Coote Hedley.

As the involvement of the newly empowered Young Turks with Germany became ever closer, the need for a Sinai map became urgent. The first threat was likely to be an attack on Suez. Woolley and Lawrence took 'digs' in London so that they could help with vital map work (still without the most essential element, a guide to water sources) and complete their joint essay – each editing the other's contribution – which Kitchener was demanding as 'archaeo-logical whitewash'. They had finished those tasks by the end of September, dedicating their book to Newcombe, 'Who showed them *the way wherein they must walk*, and *the work they must do*.' The italics were theirs.

Woolley could contain himself no longer. He successfully applied for a commission in the Royal Field Artillery (effective from 14 October 1914) and, as he put it, was 'shoved into the Intelligence'. Lawrence hung around the RGS in Kensington Gore and Hedley's department in Whitehall and was rewarded with a job in MO4 (Section 4, Military Operations; the actual designation 'MI', or Military Intelligence, was not used until 1916).

Woolley spent as much of the interval as he could with his father and sisters at Old Riffhams. Brother Harold was also living at home while waiting for his call to military service. Their sister Alice had died in Belgium less than a year before from scarlet fever, caught from her baby daughter, Sylvia. The daughter survived and was sent to Danbury where Edith looked after her. Two older girls remained with their father in Belgium and were involved in a dramatic escape along iced-up canals when their home town near Antwerp was overrun by the Germans. Of the other Woolleys, most were now living away from home, several of them abroad. The two sisters living at the Essex home, Edith and Marjory, ministered not only to Mary's child and their ageing father, but also to a detachment of the Gloucester Regiment that was billeted at the house. Edith married one of the officer 'lodgers', Matthew (Harry) Laxton, and Marjory emigrated to New Zealand later in the war.

Harold had not changed his mind about holy orders but seeing young men at Oxford standing at street corners in dog-collars did not encourage haste. He considered becoming a coal miner or soldier in order to gain experience of life before ordination. War decided the matter and he took a commission in Queen Victoria's Rifles. He and his elder brother had seen little of each other since childhood, and they had only a few weeks together before Harold said his goodbyes to the family in November.

By then Turkey had entered into military alliance with the Central Powers and the need for troops and a reinforced British administration in the east had become urgent. Egypt under the British Protectorate was the obvious point of focus. Lawrence was transferred from Whitehall Place, where the map makers worked in overcrowded corridors, to Cairo. Woolley was ordered there too. Newcombe, back from France and already with a DSO to his name, was sent with them. So were George Lloyd, an up and coming figure in politics, and Aubrey Herbert, by now a familiar figure to Woolley, with his astigmatic vision, bedraggled appearance, kindly wit and open Turcophilia.

Hogarth was in Athens on an unexplained mission when Woolley and his companions left from Southampton in the second week of December. He was almost certainly working on plans for the organization of a Middle East Intelligence service on behalf of Captain W. Reginald 'Blinker' Hall RN (the 'D.I.D.', Director of the Intelligence Division), effectively the supreme head of Britain's wartime secret service. Among Hogarth's companions in Greece were a number of Oxonians whose paths would cross Woolley's in the months and years ahead, notable among them the writer Compton Mackenzie, the archaeologist A. J. B. Wace and the redoubtable John Linton Myres, whose piratical role in Mediterranean intelligence (Mackenzie said he looked like 'Assur-Nazir-Pal with more than a suggestion of the pirate Teach') contrasted markedly with his exalted *alter ego* as Wykeham Professor of Ancient History and Fellow and Librarian of New College.

Lawrence had delivered the final manuscript of *The Wilderness of Zin* to W. J. Crace, secretary of the PEF, a few days before their departure, explaining that he had only received it the day before (2 December) from Woolley who had worked on it while receiving his initiation in the Intelligence Corps. Woolley went by P&O from Southampton two days after Newcombe and Lawrence, on the 12th, accompanied by Lloyd and Herbert. Fellow passengers included the architect Edwin Lutyens and the painter William Nicholson, who proved 'delightful' companions. They arrived in Cairo just in time for Christmas.

Staff offices were in the Savoy Hotel, next door to the dormitory, the Grand Continental. There to greet the new recruits were the new C-in-C, General Maxwell, and his senior staff officer Colonel Neill Malcolm, and the Sirdar of the Egyptian army, General Wingate. Lt-Col. Gilbert 'Bertie' Clayton, chief of civil and military intelligence under Wingate's pre-war regime, was also waiting to present his compliments. They were later joined by Ronald Storrs, Oriental Secretary to the Resident, Colonel Sir Henry McMahon, and Philip Graves, *The Times*' man in Constantinople before the war.

It was a brilliant assembly, and Woolley found the company much to his liking. But the telling of what went on in Egypt and elsewhere was left to others. Woolley was a spasmodic letter writer, always too busy with work to keep family or friends informed of his activities, and his published testimony was often deliberately misleading. All military letters were, of course, censored but Lawrence's correspondence with his brother mostly passed through the diplomatic bag and was not to see the light of day until after his death. When it came into the open it provided a unique record of military chaos and mercurial relationships.

The hurried departure from Carchemish the year before was revealed in a letter from Lawrence to Mrs Fontana, who was still at Aleppo, written from MO4 in London before he left for Egypt. 'I hope the men will carry off everything from the house before any Turk can sack it. I would grieve if any Turk shot me with my own revolver. However I asked Haj Wahid & Dahoum to see to them. Woolley goes E. with me . . .' He wondered also what had happened to the Aleppo consulate. 'It has been searched I know, but apparently the rifles etc. were not found . . .'

By Monday 20 December, Lawrence was writing confidentially to Hogarth, who was in touch with Admiralty Intelligence in London, preparing to join his old team in Cairo: 'Newcombe and I got here last Tuesday, and Woolley with one Lloyd and Aubrey Herbert turned up on Friday. There wasn't an Intelligence department it seemed, and they thought all was well without it; – till it dawned on them that nobody in Egypt knew about Syria.' Then there was a surprising revelation about Woolley. 'It seems Woolley did want to stick to the Army permanently, & coming out here cuts that out: which is just as well.'

Perhaps conversations at home with his brother Harold, who

entertained thoughts of a permanent commission, had caused Woolley to reconsider his future as an archaeologist. Lawrence must have had good reason for telling the man who had been the superior of both men in archaeology, and was about to become their immediate chief in Cairo Intelligence, about Woolley's intention, but there is no mention in any of the subject's writings or surviving letters of an intention to take up the army as a career. The same letter announced that a young man they had come to know at Carchemish, Lt Harry Pirie-Gordon of the Royal Navy, had arrived in Egypt aboard one of HM ships. He was remembered by Woolley and others from Oxford days in the first years of the century. Compton Mackenzie had flung one of Pirie-Gordon's brogues from a Christ Church window and it hit a policeman on the head. It had fallen to Linton Myres, then Junior Proctor of the University, to impose a fine on Pirie-Gordon as the owner of the offending weapon, though Mackenzie paid his share. In 1911–12, Pirie-Gordon and an RE officer, Captain Smith, had been conducting a survey of the Syrian coastline around Alexandretta for the Admiralty and a number of high officials, including Kitchener, had been attracted to the idea of an invasion of Syria by way of Alexandretta as an alternative to the widely canvassed notion of an invasion of Turkey through the Dardanelles. Lawrence and Woolley had used Pirie-Gordon's detailed map when travelling in the Kurdish area above Carchemish.

Lawrence worked disconsolately in the cartographic division and a grand scheme began to form in his mind for saving the Turkish Empire for Britain and keeping the French out of Syria. The others laboured at more mundane tasks. 'Woolley sits all day doing precis, & writing windy concealers of truth for the press . . . Newcombe runs a gang of most offensive spies, & talks to the General [Maxwell, the C-in-C] . . . Aubrey Herbert, who is a joke, but a very nice one: he is too short-sighted to read or recognize anyone . . . unearths futile conspiracies.' Herbert had his say too, writing in his diary: 'Newcombe, captain and head, a vain ambitious inarticulate man; Leonard Woolley, a good sort, archaeologist. Lawrence, an odd gnome, half cad – with a touch of genius.'

On 24 December, Lawrence had written to Leeds at the Ashmolean, outlining his own and other roles in the intelligence office: 'Woolley looks after personnel . . . is sweet to callers in many tongues, & keeps lists of persons useful and objectionable.'

Early in March 1915, Lawrence was in touch with Leeds again. 'So you see I'm bored, & Woolley's bored & Woolley wants to go home, & I want to go anywhere where there are no politics – only peace. I think that is probably heaven.'

That short letter gave rise to a reflective note by Leeds long after the events to which it referred, and after Lawrence's death, about Hogarth's involvement in the military intelligence department which he, Leeds, was destined to join in 1917. 'Some of Lawrence's biographers have suggested that Hogarth had a working relationship with British Intelligence before the First World War. The facts of his career during the first year of the war belie this theory,' he wrote. He went on to quote Compton Mackenzie, 'a well-known intelligence agent in the Piraeus in war days', who said that Hogarth travelled to Athens early in the war in search of an intelligence job, and being unable to find one went to Cairo. Leeds' view was ingenuous. If he did not know of Hogarth's secretive financial arrangements at Carchemish, of his close links with the Admiralty through Admiral Fisher, whose brother H. A. L. Fisher was Warden of New College, he must surely have known that as soon as Hogarth reached London early in 1915 he was closeted with 'Blinker' Hall in the famous Room 40 in Whitehall, preparing the ground for a joint naval and army intelligence office within the Cairo General Staff which, in the event, became the Arab Bureau. Hogarth arrived to take charge of that organization early in 1916.

Lawrence felt that his talents were being wasted and he turned more and more to political conspiracy, 'letting fly' to Hogarth in March with an embryo plan for the invasion of Syria by way of Alexandretta and a suggestion that he, Hogarth, should get word to Winston [Churchill], the chief protagonist of the Dardanelles venture, that there were rich pickings in Syria of oil and iron which would make armed intervention worthwhile. The covert correspondence went on throughout March 1915, culminating in a plan of action, to 'roll up Syria by way of the Hedjaz in the name of the Sharif [of Mecca].'

In a later reflection, Woolley was to examine his young colleague's personality, and his suspected xenophobia. Of the clashes with Turks and Germans at Carchemish, which both men found exhilarating, Woolley said of Lawrence, 'He had indeed a cool indomitable courage . . . he did not mind the risk, and the bluff appealed to him immensely.' Of the Arabs, on whom Lawrence's reputation was to rest: 'Though he had an actual liking for few Arabs he was already [in 1915] an enthusiast for the Arabs as a whole'. Then:

But it would be truer to say that he was an enthusiast for Syria; the country appealed to him more than did its inhabitants and, while he really disliked the Syrian townsman, for Syria he had a passion. This went far to explain his attitude to the Germans and the French. For the Germans . . . he had nothing but contempt . . . he thought them idle and incompetent and corrupt, and loved to score off them and hold them up to ridicule . . . he would rail at their meticulous scholarship and lack of imagination . . . With the French it was quite otherwise . . . But especially after a long stay in the Lebanon, he felt a profound jealousy of the part they played or wished to play in Syria. That French politicians should aim at a control of the country he had come to love infuriated him. He hated the Turks because they were masters of Syria and treated the Arabs as inferiors . . . Lawrence was an enemy of France in the Levant, and that sentiment was the key to many of his later acts.

In April Woolley left the 'press desk' in the political hothouse of Cairo to take up new duties with the Port Said intelligence office, where he had charge of eastern Mediterranean spy ships of the British and French navies. 'Woolley is in Port Said, controlling the French Navy, & taking prize ships,' Lawrence told Hogarth on 29 March. The Mediterranean Expeditionary Force destined for the Dardanelles and Salonika had just arrived in Egypt. An Arab Bureau was being formed as part of the Intelligence office in Cairo and Hogarth was on his way from London to take charge. Before leaving he and the chief, Captain Hall, had called Gertrude Bell from France where she was running an office for tracing missing servicemen. Her knowledge of the Arab tribes was needed in Cairo. She was met at Port Said by Woolley on 28 November and they spent the evening talking of Oxford and Carchemish, and he saw her on to the train next day. She reported to her stepmother, 'Captain Woolley, ex-digger at Carchemish and head of the Intelligence Department at P. Said came on board to meet me.' The Oxford group that had criss-crossed its way through Asia Minor in the first fourteen years of the century was reunited in wartime Egypt.

As he arrived at Port Said, Woolley opened a newspaper to read a sensational piece of family news. Headlines told of a battle on the Western Front and the name Woolley stared at him in bold type. His young brother Harold had been awarded the Victoria Cross for conspicuous bravery at a place called 'Hill 60'.

It was not until some time after the event that Woolley heard the full story from his brother of an action at Ypres, then the slaughter-house of the Western Front, that would enter the annals of wartime valour and win the ultimate accolade of glory; a battle ever to be remembered by a prosaic number on the military map.

It was a stirring story, and Leonard took obvious pride in his brother's heroic achievement, but his own job was demanding, and not without danger. He had no time to rest on family laurels.

Port Said was the seedy centre of intrigue and counter-espionage in Egypt, the base for the sea-planes which dropped messages and spies across the water in Syria, search point for ships as they made their way through the canal to and from Suez carrying illicit cargoes and personnel, the relay station for wireless traffic passing between GHQ at Ismailiya and the regional headquarters of British intelligence at Piraeus in Greece. Woolley was an ideal intelligence officer. He was discreet and, unlike his colleague Lawrence in Cairo, he committed little to paper. Throughout his life he kept the secrets of his work intact, giving mainly anecdotal accounts long after the event, and only once revealing an agent's name. His work at this time has to be pieced together from other people's revelations, and from such official records as tell the bare facts. Much of the story is confused by the legend that grew up in the wake of Lawrence's adventures, by invented and exaggerated tales which for half a century after the Arab Revolt turned the desert war into a reckless and improbable saga. Confusion is not lessened either by Woolley's own inclination to lace his activities with colourful inventions. But one long confidential letter of the time to his father was retained by his sister Edith who was keeping house at Old Riffhams when it arrived, probably in August 1915. It described one of his first Intelligence commands, aboard the French schooner *La Belle Alliance* between 30 June and 10 July. The main objective was to drop an important agent, Dabrouge, close to Beirut. Other tasks were to intercept contraband and Arab dhows trading with the Turks off the Syrian coast. Since the schooner relied on sail and a rickety 20hp motor which produced a maximum combined speed of six knots, the journey was slow and hazardous. And since their cargo consisted of a vital agent and several radio receiving and transmitting sets, together with ciphers and code books, capture must be avoided at all costs. The pilot, Ibrahim abu Gosh, proved incapable of recognizing any of the Palestinian landmarks as they proceeded along the coast. The agent was seasick for the entire duration of the voyage and Woolley himself was seized by an attack of the gripes. All in all it was ideal material for Woolley's irrepressible sense of humour. For the most part, however, the letter to his father was down to earth, though at times a lively sense of the ridiculous showed through.

Log of Schooner 'La Belle Alliance' June 30–July 10, 1915

> *Crew*
> C. L. Woolley
> Quartermaster Boeduc
> Quartermaster Le Geaster
> Gunner Fauque
> Signalman Cornec
> Engineer Machifaux
> Pilot Ibrahim abu Gosh

My dear father
This is intended to be a sort of diary of the good ship La Belle Alliance: whether it will be worth reading or not is another matter. I must try to get you a photo of the ship, but you must picture her as with difficulty holding her crew of five French sailors, myself, a Syrian pilot, and another Syrian who got left behind with the parent ship so had to come with me. The little aft cabin is mostly taken up with stores etc. as I sleep on deck, the men in the hold. We mount a small French gun forward, a maxim aft, & we have rifles all round, so we are a dangerous lot to meet!

They set sail from Port Said at 8.30 in the evening of 30 June. The motor stalled as they left the harbour and took five minutes to revive.

July 1st. At dawn saw to the south a line of fairly high sandhills which I knew must be Al Gaess, though the pilot at first assured us it was Al Arish. Lay down all day and ate hardly anything . . .

Two days out they were ordered to join up with the French armed merchantman *Rabenfils* which had hydroplanes aboard and would take then on tow when they neared Beirut. The larger vessel would conceal the departure of the agent by dinghy.

July 2nd. At midnight saw shore ahead . . . then saw sand dunes & a few palms. The pilot said we were at Gaza – I could not recognize it . . . As the rendezvous with *Rabenfils* was for just south of Gaza I cursed him and ordered the men to sail south . . . About 4 PM we came abreast some palm trees which the pilot had long declared to be Gaza; now on seeing them he admitted he was wrong & said we had been just south of Gaza in the early morning . . . cursed him again and then turned north, now having the better of the wind . . . but the strong wind made it impossible to use the stove for cooking so, probably because I was hungry, I suddenly felt rather giddy & rotten . . . so went to bed . . . I discovered when I woke up after a very good night's rest, that we had gone somewhere off between Rafa and Al Arish.

No one, least of all our pilot, knew where we were.

July 3rd . . . It was 4 AM and I gave the order to start the motor . . . & while I drank some badly burnt coffee & ate gooseberry jam with my stale bread we were running merrily NE. Of course the great question is, shall we find the *Rabenfils*? For there was a message from Admiral Dartige saying he might want her north of Beirut on the night of July 3–4: if he has ordered her up there she is lost to us. 7.30 AM motor stopped suddenly – no blame to it, poor thing, as they'd forgotten to feed it with petrol . . . I gave the men instructions on the English .303 which differs in some respects from what they're used to . . . 10.15 AM. Ship ahoy! there really is a steamer just visible on the N horizon . . . 11.20 She must be the *Rabenfils* – she should see us now – so we hoist the White Ensign (to which we have no right at all!). We now come opposite Gaza, which I can recognize . . . got on board *Rabenfils* about midday . . . she started towing us towards Jaffa where she hoped to make a flight in the morning. Anchored in the evening S of Jaffa, *Belle Alliance* still in tow.

July 4th. Went aboard in the morning & had a bathe (water was lovely) & then returned to the *Rabenfils* which had towed us all day at slow speed.

July 5th. Came aboard at 7 AM . . . Arranged that *Rabenfils* puts into St George's Bay to try & get in a flight over Beirut . . . while we steer for Cape Yunis and then turn north along the coast to Jebail looking for a good spot to land Dabrouge tonight . . . I made a rather frugal supper of cocoa & bread & jam & went rather early to sleep. It is no use pretending to keep watches when there's nothing on but managing the ship – for that I can't do, & I've really no great desire to learn! Those jobs are better left to people who really understand them; so I go to sleep & leave the ship in charge of the sailors with a clear conscience.

There was a description of the crew. 'We now look awful pirates, rigged out in as varied a kit as we can manage, all wearing red kabuches & white skull caps – rifles have been served out & the forward gun is masked with a spare awning.' It was intended that they should be taken for Arab pirates if they were spotted from the shore. Just before the agent was landed the *Rabenfils* would stage an arrest of the contraband sailing vessel.

July 6th. Finding on waking up that we were 10 miles off land (Cape Shukah) & going out to sea, I ordered to about ship. As we came closer there was an alarm of a sailing-ship making South close in to shore ... we put a bit more South than we were so as to get a chance at her if she proved to be a ship. [When they closed it turned out to be an abandoned sailing craft.]

Another purpose became clear. They hoped that some hardy Syrian vessels might try to run the British blockade, so that they could take prisoners and find out if any German submarines had yet got through. So far there had been false alarms but no real sightings.

The captain of the *Rabenfils* insisted that the weather was too rough that day to put the agent ashore.

The Captain (Jenkins) was rather upset at our being so far north (40 miles N of Beirut) but I told him that this was convenient rather than otherwise for landing an agent as I had spotted near Batrun a better place than any near Nahr al Ibrahim. So after talking to Dabrouge, who had quite recovered from his seasickness, I made my plans with Captain Jenkins ... At 7 PM I went off to the Belle Alliance taking with me Dabrouge & three of my Syrians, & swapping my tiny little dinghy for a decent size rowing boat which was to serve for the embarcation.

The main purpose of the voyage was realized on the night of the 6–7 July.

It was dusk when we cast off from the *Rabenfils* – the whole thing had been so arranged that from the shore it looked as if the *Rabenfils* had taken us prisoner, & no one could see us leaving her . . . We sailed NE in the dark. I took a rest, giving orders that I was to be called when we were off Batrun. 10.45 PM . . . roused the unlucky Dabrouge who had become again violently seasick and was now in the cabin feeling very sorry for himself. However, we got him & his wireless apparatus & his luggage into the boat with the 4 Arabs who were to put him ashore & they pushed off. It was very dark . . . The boat was away for a long time – twice we thought we saw them wave the lantern as the agreed signal . . . We had waited for over an hour & I was quite anxious when a light flashed to the N & then our signal was cheered – two minutes later the boat came alongside & there tumbled aboard the fat brothers Khazel, stark naked & roaring with laughter.

When the Arabs returned to the *Belle Alliance*, they announced that poor Dabrouge had stepped straight into a rock pool with his luggage as they put him ashore. The Arabs, the Khazel brothers, had stepped out of the boat to assist him only to find that they too were up to their necks. Dabrouge was pulled out of the hole, dried off and given the Arabs' clothes. They then returned in their dinghy, naked, to the *Belle Alliance*. The radio equipment in waterproof bags had to be concealed in water-holes and weighted down so that Dabrouge could return for them when the coast was clear.

By the time the Arabs were ready to row back to the schooner, Woolley was convinced that they had been captured and all was lost. In his anxiety he had failed to notice that the ship was drifting south away from the rendezvous point. The correct position was restored and the dinghy crew returned. Next day radio contact was established by the *Rabenfils* with the Beirut agent, and two of the sea-plane pilots, De Saissons and Ledger, flew over Beirut to drop Woolley's propaganda pamphlets. On 8 July Woolley's crew on *La Belle Alliance* were taking things easy in a calm sea north of Jaffa when their lookout spotted a single sentry high up on a sand bank. As they went closer in-shore, the sentry was seen to wave and then lay down.

I saw on the beach a trench containing 5 men, & two more further South each with a tall black wigwam in it which I took to be a brushwood shelter. Soldiers could be seen in the middle . . . and N trench. Just as we passed they opened fire with rifles – we promptly got our .037 into action & fired 9 shells at the middle shelter, one of which seemed to hit it . . . After our 2nd shot the enemy replied with two small field guns — two shells burst about us, making several big holes in the mainsail and slightly wounding Quartermaster Geaster in the right shoulder. I was scratched on both forearms: another shell hit the water about 20 feet in front of our bows . . .

As soon as he was able to rendezvous with the *Rabenfils*, Woolley called up the French flagship *D'Entrecasteaux* with Admiral Danviers aboard. Later in the day he sailed with the French ship to guide the Admiral to the spot. From 3000 metres off-shore, the French warship shelled the gun emplacement; 'about 20 shells were fired . . . shooting was poor (light bad) & no direct hit was made. I saw one man leave the emplacement & return but no harm was done.' Quartermaster Geaster, with a shrapnel wound two inches deep in his shoulder, was left aboard the *D'Entrecasteaux*. Woolley went back to the depleted crew of the *Belle Alliance* and was taken in tow by the parent ship *Rabenfils* off Jaffa. On 9 July they were fired on by shore batteries off Nakhl Yunis. They cast off from the *Rabenfils* in the early morning of 10 July, and reached Port Said at 7 AM Woolley's initiation in clandestine naval warfare had been eventful and he had acquitted himself well.

Another of the surveillance vessels, or 'spy ships', under Woolley's control was HMY *Zaida*. She had been Lord Rosebery's yacht in peacetime and its new owner turned it into a very civilized conveyance for its crew, himself, and its secret human cargoes. He encouraged the chef to produce sumptuous meals in the belief that each journey might easily be the last, and extremely dangerous trips to enemy territory during and after the Dardanelles campaign were enlivened by animated conversation around a good table.

Woolley had a fund of good stories to do with intelligence blunders. One of them concerned a French armed trawler captain who reported seeing signalling from ashore in an area where German submarines were believed to be loitering. Some time later an English sea captain reported a similar sighting in the same area. He thought the signals came from a block of flats on the sea front, at the end of a breakwater along the coast. A signals officer and two NCOs were posted at the far end of the breakwater. As darkness fell lights went on in a block of flats and a morse signal began to emerge from one of the windows. They made notes of the ensuing message.

'What did it say?' asked Woolley.

'The thing's in code,' said the officer, 'I can give you the letters, but they don't mean anything to me.'

The officer thought it was perfectly sound morse, but done clumsily by someone who was not used to signalling. Woolley ordered an investigation and agents came up with the information that the offending flat was occupied by a German subject who was a Suez pilot. 'You couldn't have anything better than that,' said Woolley. He was surely an enemy spy. 'We'll strike!'

'We'll raid the place when the signalling is going on,' he said. Signals officers returned to the scene and a small army force was concealed in beach bathing huts. They waited, breathless, for the signalling to start. Duly at eight o'clock the morse began to issue from the window. An officer gave the order and troops rushed to the house to guard every exit and entrance while intelligence officers went to the door of the offending flat. An Egyptian servant opened the door.

'Where's your master?' Woolley demanded.

'He's out with his wife.'

He was, it appeared, in another flat in the same building, being entertained by a British canal pilot. The intelligence men ran down the stairs and hammered on the door. A servant refused them entry on the grounds that his master was entertaining friends. Meanwhile Woolley had decided to investigate the first flat. He pushed past the servant and rushed into the room facing the shore. In the middle of the room was a bath with a baby in it, and a terrified nurse stood against the wall. When she was reassured the nurse told them that she bathed the baby every night promptly at eight o'clock. The portable lamp used in the room was placed behind her and whenever she moved she blotted out or released a beam of light, thus giving rise to a kind of morse code gibberish.

A more serious side of the work concerned communication with, and the protection of, agents in Syria and along the Turkish coastline, at a time when the war was going badly for the Entente. Syria was by 1915 in the grip of Jamal Pasha, who had already put to death many Arabs who were working against the Turco-German alliance and had been exposed by the French who left behind incriminating documents when they evacuated their consulates. By November 1915 Churchill's Dardanelles baby was dying in its father's arms. The grand strategy of the 'easterners' had given rise to a spectacular defeat in Mesopotamia where the British army was enduring its longest-ever siege at Kut-al-Amara on the river Tigris.

Life at the Port Said intelligence office was, as usual, described by Woolley only in conversation-pieces which gave little away. A young officer who came after him, however, had much to say in his letters home. He was John de Vere Loder, later Lord Wakehurst, who told his parents:

> Life is really quite like a page out of a novel . . . The air vibrates with hushed whispers, the stairs leading to the office resound with the stealthy tread of stage villains, corpulent Egyptians with tarbooshes, down-at-heel Greeks, Syrian refugees, and terrified enemy aliens. Rifles, revolvers and ammunition pass in and out disguised as rations; in the office we keep invisible ink, secret drawers and insoluble ciphers. Letters arrive by special messengers enclosed in two or three envelopes covered with mystical seals, while the least member of the organization is known by a number and the greatest by a single letter.

The great men with single-letter designations were mostly in Cairo and Alexandria. Woolley and his colleagues, whose designations changed at irregular intervals, were simply staff officers to the outside world; GSOs, grades 2 and 3, to their own kind. Much of their time was spent at desks by day and in restaurants and bars at night, shadowing suspected enemy informants in an international community where anyone could be taken for a spy, and most were. Woolley told of agents within his own organization whose identities could never be established; Lebanese Arabs who had lived in the Spanish sector of Tangiers, wandering musicians who carried their messages in crotchets and quavers. A Papal dispensation had to be obtained to interrogate two Trappist monks on the detailed geography of the Antioch region at a time when a landing was contemplated north of Syria, and two dear old men of 78 and 85 with long white beards eventually appeared at Port Said.

Much of the work of the office was carried out under the aegis of Special Intelligence, which in World War I (from January 1916) was an amalgam of certain sections of MI 1 and MI 6. In the very secret tasks often involved, Woolley was joined by two experienced staff officers, Captain C. M. Firth who had worked with the Egyptian Antiquities Service, and Major Ian Smith, the officer who had helped Pirie-Gordon to map the coastline of Ayas Bay near Alexandretta in 1906.

Seaplane pilots attached to Port Said were the most intrepid of all the men Woolley worked with. His signals officer, Captain L. B. Weldon, had been working with Lawrence in the map room at Cairo before joining a captured German tramp ship, the *Anne Rickmers*, as miliary CO, responsible for planting some of the first wartime agents along the Syrian and Red Sea coasts. He also had responsibility for the seaplane missions of the French pilots Grall and de l'Escaille, and their British observers Captains Herbert and Todd.

Woolley made the Irishman Weldon his chief signals officer, working at different times aboard the *Zaida*, the Fleet Auxiliary *Ben-my-Chree*, and other small ships in the charge of the Intelligence office. In a truly British wartime dispensation, the spy ships were actually registered with the Ports and Lights Administration in Cairo since the Royal Navy would have nothing to do with such a motley assortment of marine itinerants.

The ever-present dangers attached to the work of the seaplanes (and the land-based craft which operated from Ismailiya) seemed to attract a particular breed. The aircraft were mostly French Nieuports and Henri Farmans, though there were a few Shorts and Sopwiths and one BE2a from India. Any craft which was forced down in the desert faced natural as well as man-made hazards. Death from a merciless sun was just as likely as capture and torture by the enemy. In January 1915 the Frenchman Lt Grall and Captain Stirling, transferred from the Dublin Fuseliers to the RFC, were forced down in the Wadi Araba. Weldon sent a Marines search party out only to find that Grall had died from heat exhaustion though Stirling had survived and was rescued on the verge of death.

Three remarkable men, destined for famous roles as political radicals, were attached to the Port Said planes. They were Captains William Wedgwood Benn (later Viscount Stansgate), Erskine Childers whose life was to end in a tragic triangle of feuding Irish Republicans and the British army, and C. l'Estrange Malone who became a prominent revolutionary socialist after the Russian revolution. Planes towed by the *Ben-my-Chree*, designed for the Liverpool – Isle of Man run and flagship of this 'intelligence' fleet, made many sorties over Palestine before the 'carrier' was sunk by enemy shore guns. On one mission ten aircraft took to the air at the same time to bomb the Turkish rail junction at Al-Afuleh. The young Loder described Wedgwood Benn, already an MP, as 'very brave and keen as mustard, but dreadfully rash and impetuous'.

For his part, Benn wrote with pride of the achievements of his fellow airmen and with scepticism of the political compacts which were already taking shape in the Middle East. It was Wedgwood Benn who provided the best brief description of the base. 'Our habitat was a portion of one of the sand islands which had been created by the dredging of the harbour ... We lived in the usual military huts and had our workshop, intelligence office, photographic department, hangars and slipways all within a camp of about an acre in extent.'

The men of the *Ben-my-Chree* had a small musical group which was the pride and joy of Woolley and the other army men at Port Said who sometimes wanted to cock a snook at the senior service. Made up of stewards, stokers and a Greek cook who was later to wind up with Woolley in captivity, the band always played the ship out of harbour, even when taking part in secret missions. It helped to give an air of innocence to its voyages. One Royal Naval vessel which it passed in the harbour had never taken to sea since hostilities commenced, and whenever the *Ben-my-Chree* went by its band played 'Keep the Home Fires Burning'. The navy was not amused.

On one occasion in March 1916, Benn and Woolley found themselves together in an effort to prevent the illicit trade carried out by dhows along the Syrian coast. Woolley had persuaded the French to give him a 45ft schooner which they had captured from the Turks. Benn was invited to act as navigator on the projected mission. Their very oriental craft with its two small lateen sails, its high poop deck and low bow and richly carved taffrail, would excite no great interest on the part of the Arab pirates, and their French three-pounder was well concealed. Woolley and Benn were to dress the part, wearing jackboots and sombreros and wielding cutlasses. It was Woolley's brainchild but Benn was more than happy to take part in what he regarded as a romantic adventure. He was the more experienced small-craft sailor and he suggested that rather than rely on sails as was Woolley's intention they should fit an engine. A Swedish single-cylinder contraption was found but it took the adventurers, working in their spare time, several weeks to find out how to start it.

Eventually the workshops made them a special starting handle. When they did start up, the hull was shaken to its keel by the violent splutter and throb of the engine, and rivets could be heard popping from the timbers. Then the vessel started, but it went backwards and forwards unaccountably. Benn, ever the political animal, said it was like a coalition, 'no one could say which of its constituent tendencies

it would at any moment satisfy.' Came the day of the test – it was a
Sunday – they took to the water to the cheers and jeers of almost the
entire Port Said military establishment. They reached the de Lesseps
monument under sail, then turned the handle and the engine burst
into life. A few moments later the temperamental power unit grunted
and shuddered to a stop. The two men sailed disconsolately back
into port. The sailors of the French warship *Jeanne d'Arc* lined up
amidships to cheer them into harbour. Every spy in the town knew
that the crazy British were up to something and Woolley's scheme
for attacking the dhow traders was abandoned.

One of Woolley's most productive agents was a shy young
Christian Arab in Haifa, Charles Boutagy. Post-war hysteria would
have it that he was an agent trained personally by Lawrence, though
in fact Lawrence never had any part in the briefing or training of
agents. Boutagy had been appointed by Newcombe, or one of his
regional controllers, before the war. His father had been assistant
British consul at the port of Haifa in pre-war days. Charles had fled
Palestine as soon as war broke out to offer his services to the British.
After interrogation in Cairo he went to Port Said and Woolley
arranged for him to be taken back on the *Zaida*. Agents were
dropped at night out of sight of coastal lookouts and rowed ashore.
When the young man returned to Haifa he found that his father had
been jailed for 'suspicious behaviour'. The charge was not proved
and he was released. Charles Boutagy survived the war to become
the popular owner of the Windsor Hotel at Haifa, where Woolley
sometimes would meet old friends and enemies.

From the military point of view, a much more significant duty for
Woolley and the *Zaida* was to keep in touch with a Jewish spy ring
based a little way down the coast from Haifa at a place called
Zichron Yakov and known by the acronym NILI.

The leader of NILI was the remarkable Aaron Aaronsohn, an
outstanding agronomist who was credited with the rediscovery of
wild wheat. He had been to America before the war where his
understanding of world affairs and his commanding personality
brought him support and recognition in political and scientific
quarters. Funds were placed at his disposal for the development of
an agricultural centre at Athlit near Zichron Yakov which was to be
the precursor of a land revolution in Palestine. When he returned
home, he and his friend Avshalom Feinberg began to establish a
close-knit pro-British circle designed to free Palestine from the
stultifying rule of the Turks and bring about a Jewish-led national

revival in co-operation with Moslem and Christian Arabs. Aaron-sohn saw the victory of the British empire over the Turks and Germans as the key to progress. By the time Woolley arrived at Port Said, an effective spy network was in place. Aaronsohn was in Damascus as agricultural adviser to the Turkish Governor of Syria, Jamal Pasha, and Feinberg was waiting at the Casino Hotel, which was staff HQ, Port Said.

Captain Weldon worked out a cipher with Feinberg which could be used in different ways, one of which was the arrangement of washing on the line at the Aaronsohn's home at Athlit. Clothes were to be so positioned as to give a clear view from the ocean, using white and coloured garments to make up coded messages.

Aaronsohn's younger brother Alex, who had served in the Turkish army, was sent to America with their sister Rivka, after being interviewed by Woolley and by Colonel Deedes in Cairo. Woolley was not happy about him and thought he might be an enemy agent. Another sister, Sarah, had been called from Constantinople where she had been living with her husband, to help in intelligence gathering. Before Alex left home, Aaron told him 'We can't even be sure that they [the British] will have confidence in us. Nobody is more conservative in this respect than the English ... They may think us capable of betraying them as we are betraying the Turks.' While working under the very eyes of Jamal in Damascus, he told his brother to tell the British in Egypt, 'We do it because we hope we are serving our cause.'

Alex Aaronsohn and the British did not hit it off at first, but when he returned from America he became a regular officer in the British army and one of the longest serving officers of military intelligence. It was a family as remarkable for its looks as for its activities. All the Aaronsohns were fair-haired and blue-eyed. For the moment, though, it was their brave young friend Avshalom who took charge. Before leaving Port Said he wrote to Henrietta Szold, secretary of the American Zionist Committee, 'The die is cast.' He added:

Our fate is more and more linked with the Allied cause ... If there is a nation whose attitude towards us is even finer than that of America, which is above all praise, it is that of the English. For if America offered its bread and its gold to friends who had need of it, England let this bread and this gold into an enemy country; sent it, almost. And with what delicacy, what discretion.

Here was barely concealed proof of the secret preparations that had been made after Newcombe's Palestinian excursion to create a reliable Allied intelligence source at the heart of the Ottoman empire. Feinberg and Aaronsohn had traversed the Syrian and Palestinian deserts for ten years past, accumulating a vast knowledge of the terrain and the water sources on which an Allied invasion from Egypt would depend vitally, and when the offensive eventually took place a year hence Aaronsohn would find himself at Allenby's headquarters as the linchpin of field intelligence.

Woolley took Avshalom back to Athlit on 4 November 1915. The young Jew immediately sent a message to his friend Raphael Aboulafia who was serving with Captain Trumpledor's famous Zion Mule Corps in Egypt, trundling back and forth to the Dardanelles. It said simply 'Long live the King, and long live our country! I shall be returning in six to eight weeks. You know my address, c/o Lt C. L. Woolley Esq, HQ Port Said.'

In December, as the hopelessness of the Dardanelles campaign became increasingly apparent, Eastern Group intelligence centred at Piraeus began to report defections among Arab officers in the Turkish army. A plan was hatched to encourage an Arab revolt in Syria. But Cairo told Piraeus that such a scheme was undesirable as it would 'give rise to savage reprisals on the part of the Turks'. There was a report, too, this time from Russia, that Jamal Pasha was disenchanted with his German allies, whose commander in the Dardanelles had called his chief Enver Pasha, the Turkish War Minister, 'a military buffoon'. Jamal, it was said, wanted to lead a rebellion and come over to the Allies on certain terms. All such plans were countered by the plans of Hogarth and Lawrence and their Cairo cabal for a revolt of the Arabs in the holy cities of Mecca and Madina. The high politics which Lawrence had espoused from the beginning took over, and the Foreign Office and High Command stood by helplessly while power and decision-making were taken from their hands by relatively junior officers who were allowed to run amok by weak army commanders. Woolley, aware of what was going on and of Kitchener's complicity in their aims and methods, concentrated on the everyday tasks of nursing his Syrian agents and collecting their intelligence.

For the next twelve months, the *Zaida* kept up its surveillance and contact duties along the Syrian coastline, operating out of Cyprus and Port Said, collecting and delivering Arab and Jewish agents at Haifa and Athlit. Washing-line signals told of Turco-German troop movements and conveyed the gossip of Fast's Hotel where officers under the command of General Kress von Kressenstein talked of their sporadic attacks on Suez. Weldon and his signals colleagues sent semaphore or morse messages ashore only rarely, when agents were on the point of discovery and had to be rescued urgently. At Athlit, in particular, there was an ever-present danger of detection, since the agricultural estate created by Aaronsohn attracted German and Turkish visitors. The Anglophile Aaronsohns were opposed by the majority of indigenous Jews, the Yishuv, and by the Jewish home guard, Ha-Shomer; sooner or later they were sure to betray the spy ring to Jamal's police. Sooner or later too, the messages to Sarah from Woolley's ship were sure to be noticed. Indeed, a month after NILI's recognition by the British secret service, there was evidence of Weldon's cipher having been broken and Woolley ordered it to be changed. It was at that stage that Feinberg decided to make an overland trip to Port Said to find out from Woolley what was going wrong. He was within sight of Suez when a Turkish patrol caught up with him and he was imprisoned at Beersheba. One of Aaronsohn's men working within Ha-Shomer bribed the guards and Feinberg escaped. In the meantime Woolley had put an agent ashore with a new code.

Exactly a year later, in December 1916, Feinberg decided to make another overland journey to Egypt. The *Zaida* was by then being watched closely and it was too dangerous to send a landing party for him. He decided to go overland, coincidentally along Woolley's Sinai route, and was murdered on the way.

After Avshalom Feinberg's death, Sarah Aaronsohn took over the local leadership of the group, and her brother wrote to Henrietta Szold: 'Avshalom is dead. Upon a young woman close to me has devolved the difficult and dangerous role of first lieutenant. I dare not write her name'. Woolley himself had met with disaster by then.

By June 1916, the *Zaida*'s activities were well known to the Turco-German staff. Further visits to Haifa and Athlit would endanger agents in those places. Aaronsohn was planning to make his way to England to contact the chiefs of naval and military intelligence. His sister and colleagues were left in grave danger. *Zaida* paid a last call to Athlit. The code had been broken once more and Woolley sent a written message ashore: 'In three weeks' time to the day, we will return.' But *Zaida* did not return. It was never seen again in the shadow of Athlit's brooding Crusader castle. Sarah Aaronsohn's washing line went on signalling, but in vain.

Zaida had been taken out of service temporarily, and Clayton had suggested to Woolley that he take a holiday. Woolley, unimpressed by warnings that the Turks or Germans would blow them out of the water given half a chance, decided to take 'a luxury sea voyage' to Alexandretta aboard the yacht. It is much more likely that Woolley was taking the vessel on another 'intelligence' task. On 3 July he wrote that he intended to do 'a few jobs and then put into the Gulf of Alexandretta'. On 17 August the crew were enjoying breakfast in the calm waters of Ayas Bay, planning the evening meal, when disaster struck. They hit a mine. There was a mighty explosion and Lord Rosebery's yacht went down in 28 seconds. Woolley and the rest of the crew had no time to act deliberately. He was simply tipped into the water and found himself next to a drowning chef whose lifebelt had become entangled with his legs so that he hung in the water upside down. Woolley's single sporting accomplishment stood him in good stead. He righted the cook, who lamented bitterly that his goose stuffed with dried peaches and pistachio nuts had been ruined, and the two men clung to a wooden raft.

Rescue came after nearly four hours. A Turkish vessel picked them up and they were transported to Stamboul.

Prisoner of War

There's Cockneys here from Mile End Road
    And artists from Soho;
There's jockeys from the famous Downs
    And gentlemen from the Row;
There's Lancashire lads from Blackburn
    And valets from the Square;
There's two from far Killarney's Lakes
    And some from God knows where.
    Refrain
But one and all their toast shall be
God save our King and our Country.

From 'Soldiers All', Song of the captives of
Kastamuni.

Three of Woolley's fellow officers rescued at Ayas Bay were taken into custody with him – Lt Dunlop, Lt Nicholson, and Commander Crabtree, the *Zaida's* skipper. Crabtree, injured by the explosion and older than the others, could not cope with the long journey from Constantinople to prison camp and died soon after arrival.

Kastamuni, the Turkish prisoner of war base to which they were sent, was about 110 miles north-east of Ankara and about fifty miles from the Black Sea. Situated 2,750 ft above sea level, and bisected by a stream which watered the cornfields and orchards shimmering in the valley below, it presented an amiable face to the prisoners as they trudged the last weary steps of their long march. Few Britons had made a mark on the town in the long centuries of its existence, but in the year 1101 some five thousand Crusaders, mostly British, were massacred there while trying, under the command of Raymond of Toulouse, to escape to the Black Sea. To their twentieth-century successors, Kastamuni seemed not too bad a place as penitentiaries go.

The men from Ayas arrived there on 29 September 1916. Other less fortunate officers had turned up three months earlier from Mesopotamia, modern Iraq. They were survivors of the British garrison at Kut-al-Amara on the river Tigris which at the end of April had surrendered to Khalil Pasha, after being holed up for five months at the small township to which it had retreated. It had withstood what was, to that date, the longest siege in the history of the British army, but starvation and the terrible losses sustained by relief forces had compelled its commander, General Townshend, to surrender. At the last, Lawrence and Aubrey Herbert were sent down by the General Staff in Cairo to negotiate with Khalil, to offer the Turco-German command a million pounds for the release of the men, plus an exchange of Turkish prisoners. The misery of a courageous garrison was compounded by that shameful offer, and most of the generals and political officers on the spot refused to be associated with it. The Turks, in any case, turned it down with contumely. They said, simply, that as 'gentlemen' they could not entertain it. Woolley, who was to spend the next two years alongside the tragic survivors of the battle, never ever referred to Lawrence's and Herbert's attempt to bribe their captors. When they did meet again after the war, earlier camaraderie had cooled drastically.

On the day of the surrender at Kut, 2,800 British officers and servicemen and 7,200 men of the Indian army were sent down river to the Turkish base camp at Shumran. On arrival, a thousand of the troops were too sick to go on and were exchanged for healthy Turkish soldiers. The Turkish general staff at Shumran insisted that troops should make the onward journey to prison camps in Turkey by foot. Officers would be transported as far as Baghdad by river paddle steamers. General Townshend had already gone on ahead of his men to comfortable confinement on the island of Prinkipo in the Sea of Marmara. The men were given three dry biscuits each, their ration for three days, and thus began the long march to captivity in Turkish Anatolia.

Woolley, hearing the story of the men of Kut from officers who had ended up at Kastamuni, told of their fate:

There was tragedy enough in Turkey, but it was rather for the men than the officers. The Turk, who cares little for his own men, cared nothing for ours, and from sickness and neglect, hunger and brutality, three-quarters of them miserably died.

In fact, many of the men died on the way to Turkey, their boots and few belongings taken from their bodies by marauding Arabs and Kurds. Of those who survived, most were put to work on the famous railroad that was to have connected Berlin with the Persian Gulf but which still had great gaps in its zig-zag length; others were sent to coal and salt mines.

Self-contained and effortlessly superior, Woolley inspired something akin to awe in the prison guards. He became a law unto himself in captivity. The Ottoman Turks, who had shown themselves at Gallipoli and in Mesopotamia (and in the Crimea long before) to be among the finest hand-to-hand fighters in the world, were just as patently among the world's most supercilious rulers. His colleague back at Port Said, Wedgwood Benn, had noted that the Turk divided the world not into nations but into social strata, and as the squire of his part of the world he viewed Greeks, Armenians, Kurds and Arabs as 'vermin'. He viewed other ranks in much the same light, while for the British officer class he showed a respect that was often reciprocated. It is doubtful whether Woolley, who frequently exchanged good-humoured banter with his radical colleagues at Port Said, ever quite shared 'Wedgie' Benn's growing conviction that the world was divided irreconcilably into 'gentlemen' and 'players'. But he saw clearly enough that there was a tendency on the part of many British and Turkish politicians and senior officers to treat each other as though they were members of the same club.

Because of the absurd intervention of Aubrey Herbert, an impenitent Turcophile, and Lawrence at Kut-al-Amara, the enemy command and its principals in Constantinople had been seen to stand *rectu in curia*. From his new standpoint as a prisoner of war, Woolley found the mutual sympathy which existed between his captors and some of his fellow countrymen anything but congenial. The Turks, for their part, found him unfathomable; clearly a gentleman, but one who seemed to take an impish delight in making light of everything, and to think that work was a virtue to be pursued as actively by the privileged classes as by those who were supposed to serve them.

The officer prisoners were in a fairly demoralized state when Woolley turned up. Most had arrived by forced march from Ankara (then known as Angora) in July. Hunger and cold had reduced them to a bedraggled state. Despite favoured treatment, many died on the way from Baghdad and other gathering places. A few died soon after arrival at Kastamuni. Some, including the 30th Brigade from Kut, were housed in a Greek school on a hill, others – chiefly Gurkhas, Rajputs and Punjabis – were sent to a group of unoccupied houses in the lower part of the town. Woolley's contingent joined the former and brought the total complement to just over one hundred officers. The school house was crowded, with eight or nine to a dormitory. Furnishing, as Woolley remarked, was scarcely luxury, 'but all we wanted for the time being was to get into the clean beds and sleep.' The Commandant, 'a moth-eaten dugout Kaimakam' – Woolley's description again – said that he hoped the newcomers would be happy, and at first they were. Disillusion soon set in, however. The Commandant announced that pay for the officers would be seven liras a month and that contractors had been engaged to feed them for six liras a month per man. There would be a charge for furnishings of three liras. Thus, inescapable costs exceeded the prisoners' pay by two lira before washing, soldier servants and tobacco were taken into account. Woolley was particularly incensed since he had become a regular, though not heavy, smoker of Turkish cigarettes. When the senior officer, Colonel Annesley, protested, he was told that if the prisoners did not like the arrangement they could go into barracks. The Kut men, who had seen Turkish barracks in Ankara, decided that anything was preferable to that fate. An arrangement was made eventually between the British and Turkish War Offices, through the Dutch envoy, whereby colonels received fifteen liras (or Turkish pounds) a month, lt-colonels ten, majors eight, and others seven. The mess contractors also graded their charges, though everyone received the same food and treatment. Money sent by the officers' relatives, if and when it arrived, was seized by the contractors who made up any deficit before handing the balance to the owner. The commandant, Tewfiq Bey, turned out to be ill-tempered and unwashed. He smelled to high heaven, and even the Turkish inspector of prison camps, Colonel Zia Bey, was constrained to say that he was not fit to sit at table with British officers. It transpired also that he was a drunkard and dishonest. His second in command, a *bimbashi* by the name of Nuri Bey, also gave off a nasty body odour and was generally avoided. A third Turkish cavalry officer, Sherif Bey, joined them shortly after Woolley's appearance, a handsome man with erect, military bearing who had accompanied the Kut contingent along part of the road to Kastumani. Sherif Bey insisted that he was an unashamed Anglophile.

By September there had been several deaths. The Kut men, so near starvation when they surrendered, and forced to walk for hundreds of miles since, were a sickly bunch. A British medical officer had arrived a month before, along with a chaplain, but some of the men were beyond medical if not spiritual help by then. For the living, food – for so long denied to them – was a constant preoccupation and there was soon trouble with the contractors. Woolley and another officer, Major H. H. Syer, were appointed to run the mess and control the caterers. As soon as money from home began to arrive through the American embassy there was a mighty squabble over the right of inmates to do their own shopping in the town for such items as tobacco. The contractors, who sold such goods at 50 per cent above the market price, protested that walks into town should be forbidden. Woolley led a protest and one walk a week was permitted, though only orderlies could do the shopping and shops were made out of bounds to them. Threats to protest to the War Minister Enver Pasha through the Americans finally won the day. Then a group of officers tried to buy furnishings locally and to return the contractors' rickety hired chairs and beds. That led to Commandant Tewfiq threatening to have Major Saunders, one of the offenders, flogged. More outraged protests led to alternative punishment. It had not taken the British long to adopt the public school formula and nominate their quarters 'School House' and 'Lower House' at the Greek school. The Turks were convinced that 'Lower' meant inferior. Saunders was ordered to share accommodation with Colonel Pocock, while two other officers, Channer and Sweet, were banished from 'School' to 'Lower'. At a subsequent interview Tewfiq told them, 'At the beginning of the war you stole two of our battleships'.

Channer: 'I didn't'.

'And now you have seized most of Egypt, and lately you have been cold to me, have not invited me to dinner or drinks. I will break up your home. You will get your mess back when the British Government returns the two battleships.'

The condition was never fulfilled.

Most of the houses of the town were of wooden construction. Streets were narrow and cobbled. Only the Turkish baths and mosques, and the quintuple calls of the muezzin summoning the faithful to prayer, suggested that this was an oriental rather than some kind of recrudescent English scene. When a minor fire broke out near the town quarters of the officers, the lower houses, the fire brigade turned out with handpumps and a Greek waiter used a carafe of water to supplement their efforts. Major Stewart burst out laughing and the Commandant sentenced him to 15 days confinement.

Running the mess and coping with Turkish paranoia was the least of Woolley's voluntary activities. Before very long he was involved in a busy programme of lectures on ancient history. That entailed making rough maps of the ancient world. A sketch map of Asia Minor in the second millennium BC illustrating a lecture on the Hittite Empire was confiscated as having a direct bearing on the current conflict. The lectures proved extremely popular, demonstrating an ability for which he would become famous in the world at large in future years. He followed up with 'Roman Frontier Problems', and a course of talks on 'The Evolution of Religion in the Old Testament'. If the title suggested dry subject matter, the crowded audiences, which included Turkish guards and British orderlies, thought otherwise. Woolley's talks competed successfully with Motoring, The Horse, Gallipoli, Gold Mining, Sketching, Astronomy, and many other popular subjects. He also took a class in Italian, while other officers with specialist language qualifications took Russian, Arabic, modern Greek, Tamil, Burmese and Turkish.

As autumn gave way to winter the need for warm clothing became desperate. Just in time, a large consignment came from the American embassy and each man was able to have an extra sweater and a greatcoat. Summer suits had arrived only a month earlier from the Red Crescent – white striped cotton suits and floppy khaki hats with mauve and pale green linings. The new outfits were just in time to lend an air of farce to an order from the Commandant to the effect that prisoners should, when attending his office, 'wear official hats, not have cigarettes or pipes, keep the place clean and not throw pieces of paper on the floor, or spit.'

The first Christmas in captivity was held under a cloud of separatism. It was no good trying to tell the Turks that Christmas was the one time when the British dropped class barriers. An Ottoman army circular announced that 'prisoner officers and privates will not be allowed to come together in the same place for the services which are to be held on Christmas Day.' The Padre, Spooner, had to hold separate services throughout the day, and troops and officers somehow contrived to lay their tables with turkey (about which the customary jokes were made), and even mince pies and improvised Christmas pudding. Celebrations were overlain by some dismal statistics produced by the Turks a few days before the feast. Of all the troops taken prisoner at Kut, several thousand in all including Indians, only 600 remained alive. Of 41 orderlies whom the officers had taken with them as far as Ankara, 23 had died in the interval, most working on the mountain railroads to the north or in the mines.

The most spectacular of all the prison improvisations came into being on 13 January 1917. It was the first rehearsal date of the camp band, with the imposing title of the Kastamuni Orchestral Society. It was born out of the remarkable craft skills of Lieutenant Munroe. He had worked for several months at making banjos out of spare pieces of wood and wire, and other officers had observed his labours without comment. He produced the instruments at Christmas time and a few would-be musicians plucked away at them. Then he made a cello, and the decision was taken to form an orchestra. A violin, a flute and two clarinets were purchased in the town. More violins and mandolins were conjured, it seemed, from thin air. The first rehearsal was conducted by Munroe, but he preferred an instrumental role and opted for clarinet. Lt R. G. Parsons, a professional musician, took over as conductor. There was a piano in School House and Woolley showed himself to be a passable pianist but he had nothing like his father's ability, and failed to earn himself a place in the orchestra. The band's repertoire was restricted by the absence of sheet music, at least until the end of May when the blacksmith in the Kastamuni bazaar produced copies of 'Donauwellen'. Woolley helped with the organization of the camp's intensive musical life from then on, but apart from minor vocal roles his chief contribution was in scenery and costume design.

March 1917 was a critical month. It was the bitterly cold end of an icy winter, and without warning the bread ration was cut from a loaf a week to half a loaf. A new commandant arrived, Fatteh Bey, who made a startling contrast with Tewfiq. He was a tubby little man who had spent some years in Berlin and married a German woman. He was civilized and surprisingly easy-going. His friendly manner had the unfortunate effect, however, of goading Sherif Bey into a state of jealousy, and into childish acts of reprisal. Prisoners from different houses were forbidden to congregate for music, long walks were banned, and other petty restrictions came into force. As it happened, Fatteh was devoted to music and soon cancelled Sherif's order. Then, in the middle of March, twenty-four new orderlies arrived from Ankara. They carried terrible stories of mortality among the diminishing ranks of the ordinary soldiers captured in Mesopotamia. They had worked through the winter on railway

construction and, with scanty food and bad treatment, had been
made to march to Kastamuni to serve their own officers. Many were
too weak to complete a journey that would have taxed perfectly fit
men. They were segregated in the Turkish hospital when they
arrived, but three of them – Martin, Thirkell and Maddocks – died,
the latter after being released from hospital. One of the men gave
vent to his feelings in verse:

> Far away in Anatolia
>   A dying captive lay,
> And the wind among the forest pines
>   Whisper'd and seemed to say:
> 'I would I were in the homeland
>   Where mother and sweetheart pray,
> To ease their anxious suff'ring hours
>   In this my long last day.'

There was another influx at the same time. A regular winter
migration took place of Armenians, Greeks, Jews and other Ottoman
minorities to Kastamuni. In 1917, the number was swelled by the
appearance of sixty exiles from Smyrna, mostly Levantine Jews who
were technically French or British subjects. They had left their homes
without baggage or belongings of any kind. Like the soldiers, they
had been made to walk the hundred odd miles from Ankara. Local
officials on the way refused to feed them and the Turkish soldiers
who accompanied them robbed them of what little money they had.
One bedraggled exile accosted a group of British officers who had
been for a Turkish bath, escorted by a guard or *poster*. He begged
for help in an educated English voice, but before he finished a
sentence the *poster* hit him in the face and knocked him down. The
British officers present, including Woolley, promptly laid into the
Turk with walking canes. The matter came before the new Commandant. Fatteh simply could not understand why officers should take
the slightest interest in the fate of a mere refugee civilian. All the
same, he pardoned the officers and allowed the padre to visit the
exiles. The officers raised 140 liras to distribute among the refugees
before they went off to work in surrounding fields. They were never
seen again.

In March too, a house magazine was launched, called *Mastik*,
edited by Lieutenants Elton and Jones. Bound in a leather cover by
Major Rybot, an amateur artist of exceptional ability, it was hand
written and the single copy was passed from one inmate to another.

It contained a good deal of satirical verse, some excellent drawings (mostly by Rybot, a few by Lt Colonel Cramer-Roberts of the Norfolks and Woolley), together with letters to the editor, fake advertisements, an 'agony column', apocryphal interviews and a fortnightly column entitled 'In Kastamuni – Now'. Woolley's usually anonymous input was considerable.

A good many of the officers, deprived of home comforts, had eyed local girls, especially the Greek maidens, with more than ordinary interest. Woolley, hitherto, had known few such delights and seems not to have sought them. He was much taken by a song, though, which appeared in the men's camp magazine *Ekmek*, containing the memorable verse:

> Jewesses all over the earth I've loved,
>   And a beautiful Eskimo,
> I told them the same, I'd return again
>   When the stormy winds do blow.

One gallant captain in School House was so love-sick that he spent most of each day leaning out of a window in the hope of catching a smile from a passing girl of eight. Usually the girl responded with a provocative wiggle and ran away.

Another, 'Red Heels', was startingly mature though perhaps only fourteen and the captives of Lower House suffered stoically as she made her provocative way past them each morning. A verse in *Mastik* lamented:

> Little Red Heels, iridescent and charming,
> Red as the lips that I humbly adore,
> Breaker of hearts at a rate most alarming,
> Surely you know that you've broken one more.

Throughout the first year of captivity escape plans had been under discussion. A few sympathetic inhabitants of Kastamuni had been approached with a view to their providing shelter if need be, and in some cases relatively large sums of money had been handed over. It was a foolish move. Three naval officers had escaped from the prison camp of Afion Karahissar in the Spring of 1916, and had been recaptured within a few miles of the sea in a state of complete exhaustion. They had since been confined in a filthy prison in Constantinople awaiting trial by court-martial. To impress on other prisoners the folly of escape, all the fellow-prisoners of the naval officers had been incarcerated in a cold, disused church. Such warnings are seldom heeded by determined escapers and on 8 August, the day after a large fire broke out in the town, four of the Kut men – Keeling, Sweet, Tipton, and Bishop – saw their chance. Sweet was a last-minute inclusion. One man dropped out at the last moment, after a heated discussion in the dressing room of the Turkish bath, and Sweet was invited to take his place. Woolley considered the plan hopeless and declined a place in the escape party, as did almost all the other officers. The idea was to make for the Black Sea where a boat arranged by a native of Kastamuni was to take them to a Russian occupied zone. Unfortunately, the Russians were in retreat at the time and no one knew where their lines were. The men left at 10 PM on the 8th. The alarm was raised in minutes when a returning orderly who had accompanied the officers to help with their luggage, which included a large sail for their boat, awakened a guard. The French-speaking Captain of the guard addressed the men in bed in the Gurkha house, where Sweet's bed was found to be occupied by a dummy: 'Où sont les officiers? Il n'y a pas quatre camarades!' All prisoners were put under close confinement, with orders from Constantinople to keep them under lock and key. On 17 September Sweet, the only Turkish-speaker in the party, reappeared under guard and was paraded through the town by his captors. Sweet was the bravest of men. At Kut, Townshend had recommended him for the VC but he was awarded the DSO. During the escape, he had become separated from his comrades and was chased from a wood close to a German signals station at Sinope. He escaped his pursuers and took cover on the Black Sea coast. He went for a bathe one night and a waiting party of soldiers arrested him as he left the water. When brought back to Kastamuni he shouted to the prisoners who came out to greet him that escaping was 'easy as falling off a log'. He was taken away and not heard of again, except in an official report which said that he was sent for trial at Ankara and then removed to the notorious Yuzgad camp where he died of influenza. The other three men, aided by brigands in the mountains around the Black Sea, escaped to tell their story. They made their way to the Crimea and then across Russia to Sweden, Norway and England.

The harsh regime which followed the escape brought a new commandant, Sami Bey, in place of the unfortunate Fatteh who had left on 1 August before the escape but was held to blame because of his lax regime. They were difficult days and, to make matters worse, cholera broke out in the town. The officers' teeth began to cause trouble because of the poor diet and the ever-rising cost of food, and they were at the mercy of a Turkish dentist who was willing to perform any operation, however complex, with a few dirty instruments. As another winter approached they were heartily glad to learn that they were to be transferred to another camp, Changri (or Tschangri), half way between Kastamuni and Ankara.

The move took place on 27 September, each prisoner taking his belongings on a donkey cart, 500 Turkish soldiers, sent down from Ankara, flanking them as they went. The barracks where they were to be housed were a mile outside the town. The big two-storey building was filthy beyond description and though Colonel Annesley was alloted a small stone room of his own the rest of the officers were crowded into a single bare room with an allowance of one foot between beds. The courtyard was deep in horse-dung. The kitchen was ankle-deep in muddy water and the latrines were, in Woolley's words, 'not for publication'. A single standpipe in the yard represented the only washing facility for nearly a hundred men, the complement having shrunk from its original number by death and escape. Annesley protested vigorously about the conditions to Osman Bey, Commander of the Army Corps at Ankara. On 15 October a letter from War Minister Enver Pasha was posted on the notice board, telling the prisoners that they had been moved from Kastamuni because of the escape of three British officers, and that 'should any others make a like attempt' they would be shifted again, 'to a remote village in the middle of Anatolia'. The generalissimo promised that officers who signed a declaration that they would make no attempt to escape would be transferred to 'more suitable camps'. But escape fever had taken hold of the officers and even their own senior officer, concerned for the health of some of the men, could not extract a promise that would satisfy the Turks. The GOC Ankara understood the message. By November he had decided to move the group to a safer camp at Kedos (Geddos), on the rail line from Afion to Smyrna. Escape plans would have to be held in abeyance. Meanwhile the English and Scots in the party had to finish their ritual football contest, which had started up at Kastamuni the previous winter. It was a matter of some importance since a thriving betting business had grown up around the league, which embraced officer and orderly teams. The final twice resulted in a tie and it was necessary to play the deciding match only hours before the departure for Kedos. Most of the officers preferred hockey and though Woolley took no part in these or any other sports he was caught up in the general enthusiasm. A poster advertising a 'University Hockey Match' between Oxford and Cambridge men, held on Saturday 6 April 1917, had advertised 'Bully-Off 4PM: Woolley Off at about 4.45 PM'. A legend on the poster, illustrating a discussion about a small ball on the field seen through a lanky pair of legs, ran:

> *Prof. Stapiens*: My dear Woollibus, this is obviously a unique specimen of Gediobokienosaurus, although somewhat the worse for wear, you must admire the markings –
> *Prof. Woollibus*: My dear Stapiens, don't be absurd, it is clearly tangible evidence that the Ancient Greeks played golf in these parts –
> *Voice from Aloft*: When you fellows have quite finished with the ball, we'll get on with the match.

'Stapiens' probably referred to Lt Staples, a keen naturalist and member of the Field Society. There was no such frivolity when it came to rugby football. The game was foreign to the Turks at that time, and Sherif Bey, Captain of the Guard, asked if he could borrow a ball so as to teach his men the game. Another Turk exclaimed at the end of a match: 'I am a *bimbashi* who (Allah be praised!) has been in many wars and seen much bloodshed. But *never* have I seen a more desperate battle than that which you call football. The officers have indeed fought well. Are there any wounded?'

The prisoners struggled over the last few muddy miles to Kedos on 31 December 1917. The Commandant, Habib Nuri, was much as they expected, obstinate, ill-tempered and unprepossessing. He quickly became known as 'Dippy Dick'. He spoke an incomprehensible language of his own, derived from French and Turkish, and since his orders were never understood they were seldom obeyed. A few officers from the Palestine and Baghdad fronts had been at the camp since April and were able to greet the newcomers with a welcome hot meal. Fortunately, Dippy's departure was announced after four months, a new Commandant arrived, and life at Kedos took on a new optimism. As the war neared its close and the Turks began to realize that their once powerful empire was about to fall, the officer prisoners found a new lease of life under Commandant Adhem Bey.

Even allowing for Dippy's inefficient regime, Kedos seemed like paradise after the privations of Kastamuni and Changri. With the advent of Adhem Bey, the officers were able to leave the crowded barracks in which they were first accommodated and rent their own houses in the town. The Gurkhas took a large private house to share, others formed small units each with a senior officer as head monitor, as it were, in a dispensation that was still based on the pubic school system. A large hall in the old barracks served as lecture room, chapel and mess; bedrooms and sitting rooms in the private dwellings were furnished anew. And the surrounding countryside – with deep valleys, fertile stretches of orchard and vineyard, pinewoods, stony hills, and scrub-dense moors – was made 'within bounds'. Artists and field biologists were in their element, and soon the countryside was dotted with men at easels and floppy-hatted officers armed with butterfly nets. There was only one cloud on the horizon, shortage of money. The long trek from Changri had exhausted the meagre savings of the prisoners; every snack and service had to be paid for exorbitantly. The new Commandant solved even that problem. He was, said Woolley, *rara avis*; a good Turk, civilized and understanding. He issued rations at correct prices and loaned money to the senior officers for distribution to those in need, and was soon reprimanded by Stamboul for his pains. 'A gentleman,' *Mastik* called him.

The summer of 1918, though many of the men had become bitterly resigned to an eternity of homesickness, especially when they heard of new German offensives on the Western Front, was memorable for all the captives. For Woolley it was to be the perfect finale to an episode in his life that he had from the outset treated as no more than an unfortunate setback.

'It is not recorded, I believe, that Robinson Crusoe indulged in private theatricals with Man Friday on their island, but I have little doubt something of the sort occurred,' he wrote. Praise for bringing drama to the prison camp belonged to another, however. 'To Munroe, remains the glory of providing initial impulse to that first Kastamuni, as to the later more sublime Kedos, effort.' The Kastamuni effort had been modest indeed. A Pierrot troupe known as the Kusty Minstrels was formed in December 1916 under the direction of Colonel Neufville Taylor of the 2/7 Gurkha Rifles. Its first and only performance was given on Christmas night before a riotous assembly of prisoners and in the presence of the Turkish Commandant and his guests. The camp interpreter, known as 'Napoleon', gave the uncomprehending Turks a running commentary on such perennials as 'Hold Your Hand Out', 'Tipperary', 'Dixie', 'Roamin' in the Gloamin''', 'Love's Old Sweet Song', and 'Oh, You Beautiful Doll'. There were carols of course, and the entertainment ended with a brief sketch. *Mastik* proclaimed it a 'not-to-be-forgotten experience', and the dispersing audience was said to have 'completely forgotten captivity'. Not until May 1918 was the enterprise resurrected in the shape of the Kedos Amateur Dramatic Company. *Twelfth Night* was the first production, fostered by Captains Elton and Brickman who had formed a short-lived Shakespeare reading society. Colonel Taylor again produced and Woolley took the part of Maria, Olivia's maid. Captain Spackman of the Indian Medical Service, now the camp medical officer, sacrificed his proudest possession, a bushy moustache, in order to play Olivia. The programmed noted also: 'Dresses designed by C. L. Woolley.' There were grave misgivings about offering Shakespeare to the officer prisoners. In the event the show was received with rapturous applause. *Mastik* under Elton's energetic editorship was fulsome in its praise of 'Our Woolley':

'The dresses were a triumph for Woolley. Seen from the audience they seemed worthy of any conventional London theatre. No detail lacked. And the things they were made of! Scarcely anything was bought – how could they be bought in Kedos? – and the strangest fragments of costume metamorphosed themselves into rich Illyrian silks and satins – Viola's delightful green, white and mauve costume was crowned with a jaunty jewelled silk green cap and feather, which behind scenes she would turn inside out into the gauntest of gift caps, wearable in broad daylight without a trace of the theatre about it.' It was a prophetic tribute to Woolley's imaginative skills in recreating period costume. A few years hence, novice archaeologists under his command would sit in a distant desert and express their astonishment as he reconstructed the headdresses and costumes of queens and princesses who had gone to their ritual deaths in girlhood some three thousand years before Christ.

After the tributes which greeted *Twelfth Night*, Woolley was able to find his true metier in captivity. Others could kick balls and play their off drives and leg glances to their heart's desire, he had reverted to those far off days at St John's when he would sometimes play three separate parts in a production and show off those talents for gesticulation and poetic expression which would yet make him a lecturer who was capable of using outrageous thespian tricks, and un-academic flights of imagination, to grip the attention of audiences in several languages in many parts of the world.

In August, the Kedos prisoners had their first visit from a neutral embassy, the Dutchman Menten. He had no sooner departed than there was an outbreak of 'Spanish grippe', which most of the officers thought the unsuspecting visitor had brought with him. It was inconvenient, for a performance of the play *Theodore & Co.* was in full swing.

The men sensed that they were approaching the end of their captivity and there was a heightened sense of camaraderie. Several officers from the Kut contingent who were still not fully fit were told to prepare to go home. On 9 September the Freemasons of the camp held a farewell dinner for one of their number, Captain Cummins, who was summoned to Constantinople where freemasonry thrived at the highest levels of Moslem, Christian and Jewish society.

There was yet time for a further theatrical success at Kedos – a musical review 'concocted by Munroe and spiced by Colonel Taylor', with dresses and wigs by 'C. L. Woolley & Co'. Sonia, a drag-figure played by Lt Lacy, wore a dress of such magnificence that its creator kept a colour drawing of it and the programme detail, which began: 'Toque of imitation astrakhan (the collar of a "British warm"), crown of claret-coloured silk (handkerchief), osprey of grass-flower, buckle purchased in bazaar . . .'

Spackman, a leading light of the drama society, was told to prepare for repatriation, and he gave a fancy dress ball to mark the good news. *Theodore & Co.* finally made the stage on the 27th. Ten days before, the Pierrots had come to life again, 'positively the first (and last) appearance in Kedos'. It called itself the 'Dottyville Pierrot Troupe' and the programme announced the event in true vaudeville manner:

> Their songs are amongst the rarest relics of the past, even in a country so full of 'istorical hinterest as Asia Minor. No less an authority than Prof. W. OLLEY states that some of them originated long before the Babylonian era. The persistency with which his youngest daughter practised one of them upon her lyre is the authentic reason for Noah's taking to drink. The flight of the Israelites from Egypt is now known to have been a desperate attempt to escape from some of the others.

The show ended with the farce *Packing Up*. But there was more real-life drama to come before the prison show came to its conclusion.

As the curtain went up on the third act of *Theodore & Co.* on the

27th, the call echoed through the audience *Fire*! The town of Kedos was in flames. Several of the officers who lived in town were unaccounted for, since they were not at the play. The conflagration started in a house near the Khan, the caravan park, when a woman cooking in her kitchen accidentally set fire to some fat. The local fire-engine with its hand pumps was on the scene but its attempt to stem the blaze was hopeless. British orderlies who rushed to the scene confiscated the engine and used it for localized dousing while others began to demolish wooden buildings to stem the fire. The blaze was spreading too rapidly, however, and it became necessary to pull down a mosque near the cemetery. When Colonel Cummins asked the Commandant for permission to demolish the holy building, he replied 'The English are in command.' Women of the town were rushing round in circles, screaming and lamenting, and cursing their menfolk who stood by and watched the British fight the fire. In two hours, 2,000 or so houses of a total of 2,300 had been reduced to ashes. The fight was hopeless and all the soldiers could do was rescue as much as possible from the charred remains. When it was over, after midnight, some of the Turks decided that the English must have started the fire and began to stone a party under Lt Munroe.

The official report sent to Constantinople remarked that 'whatever was saved of the town was saved by the efforts of the British officers and men.' At the moment of the departure of those men, Kedos ceased to exist, though mercifully there had been few casualties. Many of the officers in the town had lost everything they possessed. Sadly, Lt Elton's file copies of *Mastik* went up in flames. Woolley had saved copies of his contributions, but a unique record of an exceptional group of prisoners of war was lost. When the fire was out and the town lay a charred ruin surrounded by cherry orchards, news came through that General Townshend was about to sign the instrument of peace with Turkey. On 26 September two German officers appeared at the barracks. They refused the invitation of British officers to join them at breakfast and treated the Turks curtly. When news came that Lille and Ostend had fallen and the German army was about to capitulate, the two officers mounted their horses and went off disconsolately into the wilds of Anatolia.

The invalids had gone home first. It was not quite the end for Woolley and his fit comrades. They were sent to the transit camp at Ouchak in the Smyrna region. Then they were despatched to Smyrna itself, modern Izmir. On the rail platform at Ouchak they bade goodbye to the Commandant, Adhem Bey. He shook hands with every prisoner present and the British cheered him and sang 'For he's a jolly good fellow'.

'He may not have realized', wrote Woolley later, 'just how great a compliment it was . . . we for our part were indeed grateful to a man who was a gentleman himself, and treated us as such and we felt that he thoroughly deserved both his musical honours and the piece of plate for which we subscribed.'

When the officers reached the city of Smyrna they found that the entire pre-war colony of French and British had survived the conflict, and all were at the quayside to wave them off. A cartoon in the local Smyrna newspaper, five days before the armistice, had carried a cartoon showing a British soldier under the banner 'Welcome'.

Woolley was to gather the impressions of his fellow inmates when he reached home little more than a month later and Basil Blackwell, book-seller extraordinary, and friend of the Woolley family through two generations, offered to publish them in a limited volume entitled *From Kastamuni to Kedos*. It was, according to its title page, *'written by many hands and edited by C. L. Woolley, Capt. RFA'*. He saved a piece of verse that had been used in *Mastik*, entitled 'Mounds', and he ended the story with it in tribute to fallen comrades.

> Nebuchadnezzar, the king of the East,
> Stamped his bricks with the sign of the beast,
> And his wives were a hundred dames at least,
> With a thousand slaves to mind them.
> Now slaves are a perilous seed to sow,
> And mounds are a curious crop, I know,
> But mounds are all that the soil will grow,
> Whoever does the sowing.
> We, too, have sowed the desert ground,
> Blood of our blood we sowed; and found
> Its only fruit the cross and mound,
> *And still the fruit is growing*

Return to Archaeology

Of Hogarth's original quartet, Lawrence and Woolley had returned home at the armistice; the former covered in the glory of his exploits with the Hashemite princes of Mecca, the latter to enjoy the quiet and brief respite due to a man who had performed unsung feats of enterprise as a staff officer (the French awarded him the Croix de Guerre), been dumped in the sea and spent two years as a prisoner of war. Hogarth himself returned to the peaceful life of Oxford. Gertude Bell had served as an intelligence officer and then as a political officer in Mesopotamia under the chief civil administrator Sir Percy Cox before becoming his Oriental Secretary during the military occupation. Campbell Thompson, who had served throughout the war in the military intelligence office at Basra, resumed his archaeological work as soon the armistice was signed, digging principally at Abu Shahrain (ancient Eridu). He went to Tal al-Muqayyar, the Mound of Pitch, with a party of Turkish prisoners to make soundings at the site which had been identified as the Sumerian city of Ur. After a week's work he returned to England to seek the support of his old employer the British Museum and his pre-war colleague Dr Leonard King for a full-scale expedition. Dr King fell ill, however, and the plan failed to materialize. In his stead, Dr H. R. Hall of the Museum staff went out to Tal al-Ubaid where he unearthed the First Dynasty Temple of A-anni-padda which had a close bearing on the dating of the stratified remains of Ur. He also dug at Eridu, and briefly at Ur itself, where he began the excavation of a palace that he was able to identify as that of King Ur-Nammu of the Third Dynasty of Ur. Hall's work was exploratory, however. Ur remained more or less intact for another three years.

At home on leave, Woolley found small respite in the company of his ageing father in Essex. The old man had become testy and difficult, spending much of his time sitting bolt upright while a girl servant brushed and combed his long silver mane and beard, or playing the piano with utter dedication. There were occasional contacts with brothers and sisters in England, but most were still abroad, and mostly serving religious denominations of one kind and another. Bertie, the younger brother who had followed Cathcart to Borneo before the war to take up rubber planting, had been killed on the Somme in 1917. His sister Edith and her husband had moved after the armistice to Midsomer Norton in Somerset with their one-year-old daughter Margaret, so that cross-country contact with them was rare. All the same, Leonard was able to attend the child's christening and to take on the welcome duty of godfather. Sylvia Eyskens, sister Alice's daughter who had been given sanctuary at Old Riffhams during the war, had gone home to her father but died soon afterwards from the consumption that had afflicted her since infancy. Harold returned from the conflict to enjoy the fame and glory of a VC, and more than ever determined to take holy orders.

Only a few months after returning home from prison camp, Captain Leonard Woolley was ordered back to Syria, then under Field Marshal Allenby's command and joint Anglo-French occupation, as a Political Officer with the temporary rank of Major. Military duties were not allowed to stand in the way of digging, however.

In June 1919 he arrived back at Carchemish after five years' absence, having purchased *en route* a bronze of Athena and a terracotta of Apollo for the British Museum. The part of the world he and Lawrence had roamed before the war was now disputed territory and the Peace Conference in Paris was trying to make up its mind whether the Cilician region which had once spilled across the old Ottoman districts of Aleppo and Adana was to be administered by the French, within their Syrian domain, or by the defeated Turks, as part of Anatolia.

Whatever the outcome of those discussions, the French were in possession of Jerablus when Major Woolley arrived there in mid-summer. To escape the financial uncertainties inherent in Hogarth's Carchemish 'arrangement', made worse by the post-war political climate, Woolley had appointed an agent in Manchester, Mr F. Poche, who had close connections with the French in Damascus and Aleppo. As soon as he arrived, he found there were bills to pay. Hamoudi, Hajji Wahid and Dahum had all been keeping an eye on the site since 1916, and all had been summoned to resume their various tasks. Expenses, 'ordered by Mr Woolley' came to £T56. In addition, workmen had been taken on at a fixed rate of 300 piastres a month each (about £3). Digging resumed in conditions of guerrilla warfare.

Open conflict had returned to Syria and the Cilician plain by the end of 1919, with the French now in *de facto* control by virtue of the Sykes–Picot agreement which allotted the region to France. Another secret agreement had, however, allocated the same region to Arabs under the banner of the Sharif of Mecca, and they were noisily engaged in the creation of a royal Arab household with the Sharif's third son Faisal on the throne in Damascus – though he was absent at the time in Paris where he and the 'Hashemite' lobby, with Lawrence much in evidence, were pursuing their cause in the inner sanctums.

Kurds, who recognized none of the wartime compacts, contested the claims of both France and the Arabs and were running riot at Carchemish when Woolley arrived there. The French military authorities had turned the old expedition house into their local HQ. Woolley decided to make the best of a bad situation and tried bravely to resume the examination of the acropolis which had been left exposed but virtually undisturbed in 1914.

Woolley's official role was that of political officer charged with liaison duties with the French military occupiers of Syria. Because he was still in uniform, he felt entitled to claim the C-in-C's protection when the private war between the French and the Kurds became too obtrusive and cut across his archaeological work.

By 1 September he was able to write to Kenyon to express his relief at hearing that £500 had been paid to Poche in Manchester, thus enabling him to draw funds in Aleppo. He told Kenyon that he had written to a young Scottish architect, Philip Guy, whom he was trying to persuade to join him as assistant in place of Lawrence. Meanwhile, he told Kenyon, he had discovered a continuation of the late Hittite cemetery he had been digging in 1914, with many promising graves to be investigated. For the moment, all looked plain sailing. The French commandant, Lt-Col Capitrel, underwent a sudden change of mood, however, telling Woolley on 23 October that he was 'unaware of any authority' by which 'Mon cher Major' proposed to carry out excavations. Woolley protested vigorously that he had every right, but thought better of an open quarrel. He decided he had better go to Cairo to see the High Commissioner and C-in-C, Field-Marshal Allenby, convinced that only the approval of the highest British authority would guarantee his freedom from French intervention. He left for Egypt on 11 November and booked in to his old haunt, the Grand Continental, on the 26th. From there he wrote to Kenyon, revealing an interesting aspect of Lawrence's post-war career that was to go unnoticed for seventy years. It was clear from Woolley's correspondence with Kenyon that Lawrence wanted to return to Carchemish and that the British Museum wanted him to do so. Equally, Woolley was quite unwilling to have him. Before he left Jerablus, he wrote to the Museum's director to tell him that Guy was on his way from England, and to say that Hogarth had asked him to send 'a small sum' to Gregori in Cyprus, adding 'he is too old for excavations'. As for his erstwhile assistant:

> As regards Mr Lawrence, I hope that he still has the intention, expressed last winter, of continuing work as my assistant. But in the present state of affairs in Syria, and until there is a final settlement of that country with a permanent form of government constituted and functioning, it will not do for him to come out. I shall be working to some extent on sufferance of the French and I cannot afford to have with me anyone whose presence would be sure to cause friction. I regret this, but the political situation makes it unavoidable.

Allenby composed a note to the French High Commissioner in Syria, General Gouraud. 'M. *Woolley retourne actuellement pour étudier ses découvertes et pour reprendre . . . dans les ruines de Carchemish.*' Having observed the diplomatic nicety of a French opening he ended abruptly: 'Please accord him all necessary facilities.'

On 6 December Kenyon wrote to Woolley explaining that several letters addressed to Carchemish had been returned to sender. He confirmed, however, that P. L. O. Guy had been approved as his assistant. He acknowledged Woolley's assurance that the French were happy with a reciprocal arrangement whereby their archaeologists could work in the British occupied territories of Palestine and Mesopotamia while the British could dig in French-occupied territory in Syria. Kenyon explained, though, that both Hogarth and Lawrence had expressed doubt about digging being possible in the forthcoming spring season. 'But you must judge,' he told Woolley. He added: 'I think it is pretty plain that it will be inexpedient for Lawrence to go out at present; but I hope the atmosphere of political suspicion will blow over in time, and thus he will be able to return to archaeology, as he desires, without affecting any susceptibilities.'

Woolley returned from Cairo to his old mound with renewed confidence. Guy had contacted him directly to say he was on the

way and they met at Port Said on 9 December, going off together to
Beirut where they saw General Gouraud. They were at Jerablus by
21 December. This time, the French Commandant was there to greet
them, and to propose an Anglo-French Christmas. Woolley found
him 'friendly and irritating'. In Beirut, he had struck up a much
more promising relationship with the French Directeur du Service
des Beaux Arts, M. Brosse, who addressed him as 'esteemed colleague' and invited him to call on his help at any time. But for the
moment, the problems confronting the Englishman were military
rather than archaeological. Woolley's irritation was not lessened by
the discovery that while he had been away an Armenian soldier
under French command had attacked the exposed relief sculptures
on the King's Gate. The top of an inscription, the head of the Queen
and the upper parts of three royal children had been broken. The
damage to one of the finest of all the Carchemish sculptures was
considerable.

Woolley had told Kenyon in November that he would like his
contract with the Museum to begin on 1 December 1919, by which
date his demobilization should be effected. By the end of the year he
was officially a civilian again, though posted to the Emergency
Reserve. He continued to use military rank on the spot, since the
Turks were more inclined to respect army titles than civilian status.

Through January to March 1920, when digging was to resume,
the battle of accountancy which had marked the Carchemish excavations from the outset, started up again. A revised arrangement had
been struck between Woolley and Hogarth whereby he and his
assistant were paid by the day. Guy received one pound and Woolley
one pound and ten shillings. The report to the British Museum for
1919–20 contained some unusual financial items, such as '500
cigarettes for Mr Guy'. Apparently, £400.12.9 was due to Woolley
and he asked for an increase in pay 'in view of the general rise in all
values'. On the work front, Woolley was pessimistic. A small
museum he had established at Jerablus was in a deplorable state.
French troops, increasingly under attack from the well organized if
illegal army of Turkey's war hero Mustafa Kemal, had dug trenches
and machine gun emplacements along the old city walls. 'It is not
without interest,' he told Kenyon, 'that modern operations should
bear witness to the strategical value of the site chosen by the Hittites
for their defences.' Kenyon responded sympathetically as far as the
digging was concerned, expressing appreciation for Woolley's
remarkable efforts in the face of so many difficulties. As for a French

proposal to take over the local museum 'without any reference to us', it seemed to him 'rather wanting in international courtesy'. The director was less sympathetic about financial matters. He reminded Woolley that a 'considerable sum' was outstanding which was not covered by any accounts submitted'. Dealing as he was with excavations of a complex character while surrounded by warring armies and gun-happy guards, it was not surprising that Woolley neglected the site accounts. For a man who was obsessed with his work and seldom went to bed before he had noted and described every find of the day, usually about 2 AM, accounts were always the last straw. Only when the need for money compelled it did he try to provide details of past expenditure.

To compound the misery of Carchemish, thick snow came in February and there was a shortage of firewood. In March, French reinforcements arrived at Jerablus station and Woolley was immediately called on to protest at the treatment of his men, several of whom had been fired at. Colonel Capitrel's reply was 'not sympathetic'. Woolley retaliated by demanding reparation for the damage caused to the King's Gate sculptures. He had just resumed the excavation of the city wall looking for the north gate of the old city, ignoring French military guards as his men worked under their noses. Hajji Wahid had been disarmed by French troops and Woolley demanded a certificate from the Commander of the Gendarmerie enabling Hajji to carry arms at all times. Hajji without a gun was roughly the equivalent of a camel without a hump.

Hogarth had expressed a wish for the excavation work at the Yunis cemetery outside Carchemish to be resumed, but military conditions made it impossible for Woolley to comply. By April, in any case, all such debates were rendered academic. On the 12th of the month, the French garrison at Urfa across the Euphrates was massacred by a Turkish force. Fighting ensued over the entire region. The Turks refused Woolley any guarantee of safe conduct for himself or his men, and on 19 April he wrote to Kenyon to announce that he was abandoning Jerablus.

After a chaotic season, Woolley and his promising apprentice Guy summarized their finds and impressions: '. . . the papyrus that bore the cartouche of the Pharaoh Necho, the broken bronze shield decorated with rows of animals and a Gorgon's head in the Ionian style, the early graves on the Acropolis.' Woolley was able to write a characteristic epitaph:

Our house [one of the last he examined] dated to the very last
days of Carchemish, for the battle [in which the house had been
destroyed] had taken place in the year 604 BC when the prophet
Jeremiah thundered in triumph 'against Egypt, against the army
of Pharaoh Necho king of Egypt . . .'

The bronze shield, he observed, had belonged to one of the Greek
mercenaries 'who, as Herodotus tells us, served in the Egyptian army
and dedicated the spoils taken from Gaza in the temple of Apollo at
Branchidae in Ionia.' He, Woolley, had brought together a pharaoh,
the Hebrew prophet and the 'Father of History'. That, surely, was
enough. As for the excavations at the Neo-Hittite city of Carchemish,
they were 'fated never to be finished'.

Woolley returned home to find an invitation from the Egypt Exploration Society awaiting him, an invitation that was to lead him to
the verge of academic and popular renown.

He had decided to stay with his father in Essex at the end of June
1920, after firing a last broadside at General Gouraud on the first of
the month demanding compensation for the damage caused to the
relief sculptures at Carchemish. Summer and autumn were spent in
a torment of indecision about his future. He was loth to leave
Carchemish unfinished and he was not greatly drawn to the idea of
returning to Egypt. That ancient land had never attracted him as
much as Mesopotamia and Syria. The territories were very different
in their respective appeals to the excavator. Much of Egypt's past
was above ground, great pyramids and temples rising out of the
sands, or not far below the surface, inviting for thousands of years
the attention of the tomb robber. And though the records of Egypt
had miraculously survived the passage of time, they were made on
papyrus which could perish in wet or fire. Much had been lost for
ever. In the lands of the Tigris and Euphrates valleys it was different.
The cuneiform tablets and cylinders, the great relief inscriptions, had
preserved a uniquely detailed record of civilizations stretching intermittently over a period of three thousand years back to the time
when writing was invented in the Uruk (or Late Prehistoric) period.
Woolley, like many great field archaeologists, never had time to
master the ancient languages in which he dealt. Constant practice
is essential to facility in reading complex variations of pictograph
and ideogram, word and syllable, consonant and vowel inflexion,
which characterize the old languages of Mesopotamia, Anatolia

and Syria. Such specialization, he decided, was best left to the expert, the epigraphist. Equally, Woolley believed that the great cuneiform libraries which had been found at Nineveh, Babylon and Assur, were only the tip of a vast iceberg. Already clay tablets and reliefs weighing hundreds of tons had been shipped to the world's great museums, giving rise to a never-ending industry in translation.

If he had a choice in the matter, Woolley would prefer to return to excavating in Syria, whatever the dangers. Guy was ready to go with him. Meanwhile, he worked at Old Riffhams on his Carchemish reports which the Trustees were said to be demanding.

'Dear Budge, Could you very kindly arrange that your "formatore" should set his hand to the cuneiform tablets which I brought back from Carchemish?' The 'formatore' referred to in this request, dated 11 August 1920 and sent from the Royal Societies' Club in St James's, was the new philologist, Sidney Smith. Part 1 of the *Carchemish Report* had been published by the Museum in 1914. It consisted of an introduction to the subject written by Hogarth and prefaced by Kenyon. Part 2, 'The Town Defences', was written by Woolley and came out within a year of his starting to write up his notes, in 1921. The third part, again written by Woolley, with notes on the Hittite inscriptions by a new member of the Western Asiatic department's staff, R. D. Barnett, would take a further thirty years to materialize.

Of more immediate importance was the publication of Woolley's book *Dead Towns and Living Men* in July 1920, just as he arrived home. He had worked on and off since his first days at Carchemish before the war to produce what was, in effect, a saleable collection of essays. It was a popular success, with its mordant, throw-away anecdotes about his early digs. A broad public had begun to appreciate his simple, unacademic approach to a fascinating but difficult subject, and the reviewer in *The Times Literary Supplement* approved of the expert's 'common touch'.

Writing, lecturing and planning his future as a field archaeologist, were not the only tasks awaiting him while on leave in the late summer and autumn of 1920. The Rev Woolley still dominated the family from the Essex home he had turned into a minor museum and library. But he had begun to feel isolated there. Youthful memories of the West Country were revived and he decided that he would like to live in Bath, close to the home of his daughter Edith and her family. With his sons and other daughters either married or living abroad, he would have at least one ministering offspring nearby. Now 75 years old, with his thick cultivated mane of snowy white hair reaching down his back and his beard resting in his lap, George Herbert Woolley made an unforgettable impression on all who came into contact with him. His entire family was in awe of him still and the sons maintained him without protest. Leonard, who had saved a useful nest-egg while in prison camp during the war, and with a respectable income from his book, newspaper and British Museum fees, purchased for his father a house called 'Uplands' on Bathwick Hill in Bath. A receipt from his accountants, Meade-King & Company, shows that he paid £2,200 7s.3d. for the purchase of the house and grounds. The 'grounds' were important, for apart from his art collection, Woolley senior also had a rare collection of sub-tropical plants, bred from specimens he had brought back from a stay in the Azores many years before, and heated greenhouses were needed for their accommodation. He also required an orchard, since he had been accustomed to growing his own fruit and vegetables at Riffhams. It was, by middle-class standards of the time, a generous act on the sons' part. Cathcart doubtless made a contribution to the new home, but no records have survived to show the extent of his investment.

Another, if less taxing, family matter arose in 1920. Leonard's brother Harold, now an assistant master at Rugby School, was ordained at last on Sunday 19 December 1920 at Coventry Cathedral. The war had, of course, intervened to hold up his ordination, but now the family was able to show a rare unity in celebrating the event.

A letter written from Old Riffhams to an assistant keeper at the British Museum in September was to set in train Woolley's most uncomfortable academic relationship. It was addressed to Sidney Smith and asked him simply if he would be good enough to send a copy of a Carchemish tablet to Campbell Thompson at the latter's Oxford home. Smith was a clever epigraphist with an acknowledged future in the museum, but he was a difficult young man, abrasive and with a personality altogether inimical to Woolley's outgoing manner. He had returned to the museum immediately after the war, writing to Budge from France in pencil to ask if he could return to his old job, explaining that there was no ink at the front.

Almost the whole of the following year, 1921, was spent in the vain hope that the Turks and French would resolve their differences and that he could resume his work at Carchemish, or perhaps take on another site in Syria or Mesopotamia. Lawrence, back at Oxford for the time being, sent Woolley some Carchemish slides in January 1921. Woolley was in Beirut where he had promised to deliver two lectures. 'Thanks to Hogarth for helping to select them,' he wrote, 'but I wish you had included more on South Gate and the big house in the centre of the town.' He could not say what would happen in the spring. Kemal Ataturk was being 'very intransigent'.

John Garstang, who had learnt his digging from Petrie before going on to Woolley's first substantial stamping ground at Meroe in Lower Egypt, was working at Askalon in Palestine and Kenyon wanted Woolley to join him. 'The PEF will pay,' the director told Woolley in February 1921. Woolley had gone out to Beirut in the New Year and Garstang met him there and extended his own invitation. But Woolley had reverted temporarily to the archaeology – intelligence role he had performed before the war. 'Sorry,' he told Garstang, 'at the moment I am doing work for the FO and the French want me to undertake a small dig in the Lebanon.' The FO work was innocent enough, keeping the Office abreast of Franco-Turkish affairs, and testing the temperature for his own possible return to Jerablus. The French had just taken Aintab from the Turks and there was a momentary gleam of light. By March, depression had settled in again. 'Kemal has given strict orders that we may not enter Jerablus,' he told Kenyon, adding that an armistice had been agreed between the Kemalists and French and he thought a general peace settlement possible. He decided to write a personal note to the Turkish Commander who had taken over from the French at Jerablus. The letter, addressed from the Aleppo Consulate and dated 24 March 1921, was written in Turkish with a literal translation, and referred to previous correspondence.

Gentlemen

I had received a previous letter from you in which it was stated to me that, owing to the orders of Mustafa Kemal Pasha, I couldn't do any excavations on the site of Jerablus until hostilities have ceased. Now that there is armistice between the national forces and the French, I came here to continue my work. Consequently I send you this letter to get an immediate reply, whether there is any objection to you and to your government, of my coming, and if not please let me know . . .

Another young architect, F. G. Newton, had been recommended to
Woolley by the Royal Institute of British Architects and Woolley
was waiting on a decision about Carchemish before confirming his
appointment. Newton and Philip Guy got along famously and in
March they joined Woolley in Beirut. The Egypt Exploration Society
still wanted Woolley to dig for them at Tal al-Amarna and he
decided there and then to accept the job and let Carchemish take its
course. He stipulated that Guy should be his assistant and that
Newton should go with them. In the meantime, Guy and Newton
decided to embark on an overland tour of Asia Minor, as far as
Lake Van in Armenia. Woolley returned home to 'Uplands', the new
family home in Bath, to prepare for Egypt. A card from Guy
announced that his two assistants were in Constantinople on their
way home. In August Guy wrote from his home in Renfrewshire,
remarking on what an 'excellent fellow' Newton was, and finishing
'Lord what a screed! Best love old thing.' Woolley would, in time to
come, be accused of standing a little on his dignity in his relations
with assistants, but there was no sign of pomposity or reserve in his
dealings with his latest aides. He had a particular liking for architects, whom he found on the whole better prepared for field
archaeology than other candidates in what was still a relatively new
academic discipline, and he had close ties with the major architectural schools. E. Stanley Hall, the head of one of them, the
Architectural Association, contacted him in June to say that one of
his students had just won the coveted Prix de Rome, carrying an
annual scholarship of £250 for three years, and had expressed a
wish to join Woolley's Carchemish excavation as part of his scholarship work oversea. Woolley agreed to the young man – S. Rowland
Pierce – joining him, subject of course to a resumption of work at
Carchemish. That eventuality was to be hit on the head by the
continued Turkish occupation of Jerablus and the decision of the
Foreign Office to oppose a resumption of work. The official view
was conveyed to Kenyon in December. The director told Woolley:
'The FO say it would be most undesirable from a political point of
view to continue digging at Carchemish for the moment.' On 28
December Woolley scribbled a last word to Kenyon, expressing his
great disappointment that Carchemish was 'indefinitely postponed'.
The position was made hopeless by the refusal of the FO to recognize
'Ataturk'. At the same time he expressed keen interest in a proposed
joint expedition with Philadelphia. By then he was in Egypt, digging
at Tal al-Amarna with Professor Eric Peet, an Egyptologist whose

work had won wide fame. Perhaps the knowledge that he would have to abandon his Hittite excavation was made a trifle more acceptable by the decision of the Trustees, conveyed at the same time, that they had approved a grant of £100 for his authorship of Part 2 of the *Carchemish Report*.

It was almost exactly a hundred years since Shelley had written his famous lines on that 'shattered visage' which greeted the traveller in the Nile valley. The search had turned by 1920 to the 18th-dynasty predecessors of Shelley's enigmatic pharaoh, Ramesses II. The most famous of the kings and queens of that dynasty was the heretic Akhenaten who in the 14th century BC had introduced into Egypt the unique notion of a single god, and had built a city of his own, Akhetaten, at Tal al-Amarna, about 150 miles north of Thebes, where the new cult of monotheism based on sun-disc worship could be practised. From 1902 until the outbreak of war, the American Theodore Davis had dug in the valley where most of the royals of the 18th dynasty were buried, the Valley of the Tombs of the Kings, and had found there among others Thethmosis IV, Queen Hatshep-sut, and Yuya and Thuya, great grandfather and great grandmother of Ankhesenpaten, the child queen of the child pharaoh Tutankha-men. He had also found a vault containing the mummy and coffin of the heretic Akhenaten, a few remains of funerary equipment, and parts of the sepulchral shrine of the king's mother, Tiye. In 1914, Mr Davis decided that there was nothing further to be found in the Valley of the Kings, combed as it had been for thousands of years by tomb robbers. The concession was awarded by the Egyptian Antiqui-ties Department to the Englishman Lord Carnarvon, 'Porchy', and Mr Howard Carter was invited to assist him.

Woolley's visits to Carnarvon at Highclere Castle were now but a distant memory, but he and the man whose place he might have taken, Howard Carter, were dimly acquainted. They had met aboard ship and in Egypt before the war, and in the first year of war at the the Savoy Hotel in Cairo when Woolley was finding his feet at General Staff HQ. But even among fellow professionals Carter was an outsider, a difficult man with a short fuse, a brilliant archaeologist who lacked the customary background of such men, public school and university. His own training had been in art and draughtsman-ship, at his father's hands. One of the few men he could ever get on with was Lord Carnarvon, the honest-to-goodness aristocrat.

Carter and the civil and military powers soon parted company. He was given the title 'King's Messenger' but neither he nor anyone else ever discovered what it implied by way of war duties and General Allenby, when he took over the command in Egypt, sent him back to the Valley of the Kings where he had already spent some time working unofficially at His Majesty's expense. He would work patiently for another six years, searching and digging among Davis's 'exhausted' tombs, before the world was awakened to the most spectacular find in the vivid records of archaeological discovery, the furnished and undisturbed resting place of Akhenaten's successor Tutankhamen.

Woolley's role in the post-war Egyptian scene was comparatively mundane. He was concerned not with the burial places of kings but with the city of Akhenaten; or more accurately with the 'council estate' just outside the royal city, where the modest homes of the building workers of Tal al-Amarna were situated.

The first season closed down early, in mid January 1922. He returned home to disturbing news about the men he had left behind at Carchemish. Remarkably, by the time he left there was a surplus in the funds sent out via his Manchester agent, and he left the money at Aleppo so that Hamoudi, Hajji Wahid and the others could be looked after, while they in turn preserved the site as best they could. By February, Hajji and his family had been forced to flee. Hamoudi's whereabouts were not known, though he was to turn up safe and sound. The site house which was chiefly Lawrence's work had been sacked by Mustafa Kemal's troops. Priceless antiquities damaged by the French lay exposed at the site. The credit facility at the Aleppo bank had to be withdrawn.

Woolley returned to Tal al-Amarna in March 1922, and in May he reported progress in an article in the *Illustrated London News*:

Akhenaten, who as a boy ascended the throne of Egypt early in the fourteenth century before Christ, was a religious reformer who tried to impose a new-fangled monotheism upon a country where gods were even more plentiful than usual. Unable, at the old capital, Thebes, to avoid the painful sight of temples and monuments dedicated to the faith he had forsworn, he left it and built for himself a huge new capital on uncontaminated ground at Tell el-Amarna; and here, while the neglected empire went to rack and ruin, he devoted himself to the One God symbolized by the disc of the Sun ... Two miles behind Akhenaten's city, in the cliffs of the high desert, lie the half-finished rock tombs of his courtiers; and in a sandy valley, we found the compound where lived the workmen employed in excavating them.

Woolley, writing in the popular vein that was to captivate millions of readers in all parts of the world and turn archaeology in its heyday into a mass entertainment, was able to demonstrate a striking affinity between the 'model' township of working Egyptians more than three thousand years before and its English counterpart in the 20th century.

> It was not the normal Egyptian village, grown up haphazard by degrees, but a settlement built to order on the regular lines of a scheme of model dwellings for the working classes. We know from Theban records that the tomb-quarriers were a rough lot, given to riots and strikes, and so it was perhaps not merely for the convenience of having them close to their job that they were housed, not in Akhetaten itself, but out here in the barren desert, and that the settlement was walled all round and had but two small gates, and that there were sentry boxes along the road leading to the city. Yet these people, though under a certain discipline, were not slaves, but free Egyptian workmen, who lived with their wives and families, enjoying quite as much comfort as those of their class elsewhere . . .

The compound unearthed by Woolley and his assistants – mostly drawn from Sir Flinders Petrie's old team of Egypt Exploration Society workers – was an exact square divided unequally into two housing estates with straight roads running through and between them, and cross roads at either end. Here was an archetypal workers' estate, emulated by builders and town planners ever after. Every house was the same except, every now and again, for a larger and better finished residence, the foreman's. But the accommodation was more generous than was generally found necessary in modern times. Each house had four ground-floor rooms, a front hall, central living room, kitchen and bedroom. A staircase, usually found at the end of the front hall, led not to another storey but to a flat roof. In the heat of the Egyptian summer, then as since, most people preferred to sleep and live on the roof, and most owners erected some kind of shelter on it. One thoughtful husband had indulged his wife with a roof-house for the summer, gaily painted and adorned with religious texts. Workrooms on the ground floor were often found to contain looms at which wives worked while husbands were building the fine palaces and places of worship across the sandy divide at Akhenaten's new city. Bow-drills with bronze bits, wooden mallets, picks and adzes, suggested that the menfolk were hard at work making articles of metal and stone in their spare time. Fireplaces and kneading tables still contained the evidence of bread-making in the kitchens, and tethering-stones suggested that donkeys – every man possessed his own donkey – were brought indoors at night.

Such were the minutiae which Woolley assembled from the 3000-year-old remains of the workmen's village at Tal al-Amarna. He found unconfined delight in reassembling the past and in writing about it in the simple, graphic terms which the man in the street could understand. That desire, and that ability, had already won him a popular following. He was recognized by the world's leading universities and museums as an excavator of the first rank, and was one of archaeology's most popular advocates. He left Tal al-Amarna in May 1922 at the end of the first season, to the joyful news that he had been offered the directorship of the joint expedition of the British Museum and the University of Pennsylvania to Ur of the Chaldees. The offer came just in time. Sir Arthur Evans was about to publish an account of the magnificent 'Little Palace' at Crete with its bull's-head rhyton, 'as old as Akhenaten's city'; and news had come through that Howard Carter had opened the sealed door to Tutenkhamen's sanctuary and beheld 'wonderful things'.

Egypt had not quite done with Woolley. While he was sifting the remains of the workmen's homes at Tal al-Amarna, another part of his workforce was digging at Akhetaten itself and one of its first finds was the house of Akhenaten's 'Prime Minister'. Woolley gave a provisional account of the discovery of the house in the wealthier quarter of the city in December 1922. A month earlier *The Times* had revealed the discovery of the tomb of Tutankhamen. Thus, at almost the same moment, one of the most fascinating and historically most important dynasties in Egypt's long history was being uncovered from two sides; from the city of the heretic king – Amenhotep IV prior to the adoption of his apostate name, Amenophis IV of the Greek nomenclature – whose wife was the beautiful Nefertiti, and from the burial place of his obscure successor, the young king whose splendid death suit of gold and magnificent headdress had yet to be shown to the world. The press, working from 'hand-outs' from the Department of Antiquities in Cairo, began to see the limitless possibilities of this ancient royal story, of the boy successor who was perhaps a commoner but elevated to royal status by marrying the daughter of Akhenaten and Nefertiti, abandoning the sun-worship of his father-in-law before his untimely death and reversion to the ancient cult of Amen-Re. On 29 November, Tutankhamen's chamber in the Valley of the Kings was opened officially by the Earl of Carnarvon and Carter in the presence of Lady Allenby, wife of the British High Commissioner, and Lady Evelyn Herbert, the earl's ever-present daughter. American and European visitors were arriving by the boatload. The world's press rampaged and Carter, in a characteristic fit of anger, was soon to padlock the door to the sepulchral chamber and announce that work would cease henceforth.

Woolley gave historical flesh to the news sensation, with his account of political feuds at the birthplace of Tutankhamen. Nekht, it seemed, had been the overseer of Public Works in Akhenaten's government and was therefore responsible for building the royal palaces. When the chief minister fell from grace Akhenaten did not dismiss him, he simply invited Nekht to join the cabinet with precedence over all others, and a new title affirming his service to 'Aten, the One-God'. Thus Nekht became Nekht-Pa-Aten, and he began at once to excavate for himself a tomb alongside the other courtiers in the sacred valley where Carter was now at work. After Akhenaten's death, wrote Woolley, the new capital was abandoned and accursed. 'The Prime Minister was not one to stand out against a popular movement; work on his tomb stopped before the first chamber was fully dug, and his fine house was left to fall to ruin; he must have gone back to Thebes with the rest; and, as there was plenty of work to be done restoring the temples of the old religion, we may imagine him, with his name changed again, back at his old business and doing very well!'

By the time his words were published Woolley was in modern Iraq, at the start of one of the most important of all archaeological enterprises. But Akhenaten's successor, the boy king clad in a suit of gold, would dog Woolley's footsteps, as he dogged those of Evans, Petrie, Garstang, Wace, Blegen and the other great men of the day, drawing the public gaze irresistibly to the drama in the Valley of the Kings. Alone among the diggers of the ancient world, Woolley proved sufficient master of the publicity art to counter-attack.

Ur of the Chaldees

While Woolley fretted for two years about Carchemish in an understandable desire to complete the investigation of that much abused mound, the directors of the University Museum of Pennsylvania in Philadelphia and the British Museum, had been in regular contact about a new project.

Correspondence on the subject had begun in February 1920 when the director of the Pennsylvania University Museum, George Byron Gordon, wrote to Kenyon to remind him of a matter raised briefly between them when he, Gordon, had stopped off in London in June and October of the previous year on his way to and from Egypt and Palestine. He had broached the possibility of a joint dig in Mesopotamia, in particular at 'Ur of the Chaldees'. Now he wrote to ask if the settlement of political questions in Mesopotamia was sufficiently advanced to permit such a co-operative venture. Kenyon replied that the Secretary of State for India, 'in whose Department the civil administration of Mesopotamia is at present placed', would not hear of it until at the very least a peace treaty had been signed with Turkey and the mandate decided. There was also the matter of funds and the ability of the provisional goverment of Mesopotamia to afford such excavations. Nevertheless, the British Museum had recommended to the government that excavation work should begin as soon as possible 'under scientific control', to prevent inevitable illicit digging and smuggling. It had also been suggested that Mesopotamia should have its own department of antiquities and a museum, possibly in Baghdad. Kenyon was on the side of his American opposite number, suggesting that Pennsylvania University should make a formal application to the India Office in London: 'Some pressure may be necessary to secure what we want.' The correspondence was to go on, unabated, for two years, in which time the Colonial Office, under Churchill, took over from the India Office, the mandate (awarded in May 1920) was followed by an insurrection in which many young drafted soldiers of the Manchester Regiment were killed by tribesmen, and Sir Percy Cox was called back from Persia to preside over the selection of a king for the new State of Iraq, as ancient Mesopotamia was to become. Gertrude Bell, Sir Percy's right hand in war, became his Oriental Secretary, but much of her old authority had been dissipated by her insistence in conversations with the GOC, General Haldane, at the time of the rebellion that the tribes were well disposed and did not represent a problem. The General had foolishly believed her and after the event ungallantly allowed her to shoulder much of the blame.

Woolley came into the Anglo-American scheme at the beginning of 1921 when his name was mentioned as the prospective leader of a joint excavation. On 15 January he wrote from Beirut to Gordon in Philadelphia to explain that he was unable at the time to continue at Carchemish, and implying that he might be available for the proposed Ur dig. In March, Lawrence came into the picture. He was then one of Churchill's advisers on Middle East affairs at the Colonial Office. 'The person principally concerned,' Kenyon told Gordon, 'is Col. Lawrence, who was digging for us at Carchemish before the war . . . Unfortunately he has to go out with Mr Churchill to Egypt for a conference on the affairs of the East, and until he comes back no decision can be taken.' In August, Lawrence's protégé, the Prince Faisal ibn Hussain of Mecca, was proclaimed King of the new Iraq. Somewhat naively, Sir Percy Cox announced that 96 per cent of the people had voted for Faisal in a a plebiscite, neglecting to say that much of the population was illiterate.

The to and fro of transatlantic correspondence went on until the end of the year and beyond. In September Dr Gordon visited London where he spoke to Lawrence at the Colonial Office. In November Kenyon told the American that no progress could be made until a Director of Antquities could be found in Iraq. If Woolley could not go back to Carchemish he 'would be available for Mesopotamia after Christmas'. In his frustration, Gordon began to turn to the idea of an 'archaeological survey' of Iraq rather than continue the battle with a seemingly impenetrable British bureaucracy.

On 25 January 1922, Lawrence wrote to Gordon: 'Well, we have now appointed a provisional Director (the Education chief, who has worked at our School in Athens, and will look after Archaeology till the work gets too heavy). Consequently the Mesopotamian Government is in a position to consider applications for permits to excavate.' Lawrence went on to say that the British would be particular about who such licences were awarded to – 'Mesopotamia has suffered so much in the past from unscientific work (carried out under the auspices of the most distinguished bodies!)'. In future, permits would only be given to field experts who would record their finds and do the practical work, 'not a cuneiform expert: at least not necessarily . . . the Reisner or Petrie – or Woolley – of the business.' He foresaw no difficulty in the case of the University Museum, advising Gordon to apply to the Under Secretary of State in Downing Street, asking him to forward the application to Baghdad.

In March 1922, the inevitable question of money came up. Kenyon reminded Gordon that the British Museum's funds were for the acquisition of objects. He found the idea of an archaeological survey interesting, but the Museum's funds could not be used for the purpose. Gordon replied that his Museum had already put aside $25,000 towards the cost of a first season's work. Then: 'It is my thought that arrangements might be made to begin work in the field as soon as the climate permits . . . Concerning the Director of Excavations, Mr C. Leonard Woolley is one who would be satisfactory to the University Museum and in case he should be your choice we would be glad if he were available to take charge of a joint expedition.' Gordon wrote to Lawrence at the same time, stressing that adequate funds were available and that Woolley was his preferred director of excavations. By May, the idea of excavating a particular site was agreed upon and the survey proposal was dropped. The Americans wanted to continue work begun in former years at Nippur and other sites in Mesopotamia. Gordon was sympathetic to the post-war financial plight of Great Britain and its national museum. 'Working with the British Museum would be to us equivalent to a measure of insurance. On our part we might furnish most of the funds.' On the other hand, the field director's salary should, he thought, be split between the two museums. In June, it was announced that Gertrude Bell was to take over the responsibility for antiquities in Faisal's government, and not the 'Education Minister' (in fact, the man who had been first suggested was Lionel Smith, British Advisor to the Education Minister, who was Dean of Magdalen and tutor to Edward VIII before the war). Gertrude had already drafted an Antiquities Law and was convinced that the King would push it through; 'he's perfectly sound on archaeology, having been trained by T. E. Lawrence.'

In August, Gordon arrived in London to discuss the details of the proposed expedition, in particular the division of finds. The Iraqis were unlikely to claim much 'but legally they are entitled to claim a good representative selection'. On 24 October, Gertrude Bell wrote that she had been appointed honorary Director of Antiquities, working within the Iraq Ministry of Public Works under her friend Sabih Bey and with the support of Major J. M. Wilson, an architect trained by Lutyens. There had been a change of Government in England, with the short-lived Conservative administration of 1922 taking office along with the sleepiest of all Colonial Secretaries, the Duke of Devonshire. Gertrude knew the Duke, however, and was 'enchanted'.

The actual site was hardly mentioned by either museum in the final months of negotiation. It was assumed that Ur was the chosen place. Woolley was formally offered – and accepted – the appointment of director of the excavation, and the High Commissioner for Iraq, Sir Percy Cox, wrote to Kenyon in September making it clear that 'it was highly desirable that the expedition should go out.' Woolley left home at Bath at the end of the month. On 26 October he cabled both Gordon and Kenyon from Basra, 'Expedition starting out.'

On 1 November Gertrude Bell wrote to her father, the iron-master Sir Hugh Bell, from Baghdad, telling him that Woolley – whom she 'had met briefly' at Carchemish before the war – had arrived there on the way to Ur. Her mother, who edited her letters for publication, cut out the first clause of a sentence which actually read: 'He's a tiresome little man but a first class digger and archaeologist after my own heart – ie. he entirely backs me up in the way I'm conducting the Department.'

It was an extraordinary statement. Gertrude Bell was not given to deception or dissimulation. Yet her earlier correspondence with her parents made it perfectly clear that Woolley was away – in Egypt – at the time of her visit to Carchemish in May 1911. She neglected, or forgot, her pleasure at being welcomed to Port Said by Woolley, 'ex-digger at Carchemish', in November 1915, their first meeting. Her tune soon changed.

There have been several places called *Ur* in the once fertile region which the world knew as Mesopotamia, the land between the two rivers, from Greek times until the 1920s when, under British occupation, it resumed the ancient name of Iraq.

Present-day Ur lies about six miles to the west of the existing course of the Euphrates, about 250 kilometres as the crow flies from

Babylon, about 300 kilometres from Baghdad and 160 from Basra. Before the arrival of the Woolley expedition in October 1922, the true history of this place, so important in biblical legend, was at best sketchy. Admittedly the British surveyor and naturalist W. Kennett Loftus had in 1849 visited the group of mounds (or 'tell' or 'tal') west of the river, the highest of which Arabs called Tal al-Muqayyar, the Mound of Pitch, and had tried to trace the canal of Pallacopas, shown on many old maps, which Alexander the Great had cut between the river and the ancient city nearby. But neither the Greek conqueror nor Loftus suspected that he was at ancient Ur. However, Loftus's book *Travels and Researches in Chaldaea and Susiana* was largely responsible for a burst of Anglo-American enthusiasm for excavation in the lower region of Mesopotamia in the second half of the nineteenth century.

In 1854 the British consul at Basra, Mr John G. Taylor, was asked by the British Museum to visit some of the mounds at the southern reaches of the Euphrates. He went to Tal al-Muqayyar, hired a labour force of hundreds, and dug for about four weeks. He unearthed inscriptions in the ancient cuneiform script which showed that this was indeed the site of Ur, or Urim to its original inhabitants, one of the oldest cities in the world. More importantly perhaps, he observed an arrangement of bricks at ascending levels in the main mound which he said was 'probably a flight of steps'. He had unearthed the beginnings of a great stepped, flat-topped pyramid known technically as a *ziggurat*, stairway to the high temple of the gods. And in each corner of the stairway he found a chamber, a *khazna*, within the foundations of the building, containing inscribed cylinders whose translation showed that they had been put there by Nabonidus, the last king of the neo-Babylonian dynasty (555–539 BC).

At the end of the nineteenth century an expedition was despatched by the University of Pennsylvania, Woolley's intermittent employers, but the results of their investigation were never made public and there the matter had been allowed to rest until the conclusion of the war. Dr Hall's four months' excavation in 1919 had led to the important discovery of E-Khursag, the palace of King Ur-Nammu of the Third Dynasty of Ur, who reigned in about 2100 BC. The name E-Khursag, meaning 'The House of the Mountain', was written not in the familiar language of the early cuneiform inscriptions, Akkadian (the prototype of the Semitic languages), but in an even more ancient pictographic form, the language of a people of unknown origin who first inhabited the city states of the region from the end of the fourth millennium BC and perhaps beyond. Records showed only that these people called their region 'Sumer', and unaccountably called themselves the 'black-headed', and that in about 2300 BC, they were united by Sargon the Great with the alien culture of Akkad, before their joint destruction at the hands of tribal invaders from the east. It was Ur-Nammu who revived the fortunes of the old city states and assembled them in cultural and administrative unity. The language of Akkad, translated in the mid-nineteenth century from the cuneiform inscriptions on the memorials of Persia and clay tablets of Babylon and Assyria, was both syllabic and ideographic. Its signs were capable of representing whole words or parts of words which could be combined variably. Linguistic scholarship had labelled the language 'Semitic', a definition based on the employment of stable consonants and vowels of variable weight and value. The earlier language of Sumer, originally pictographic, was thought at first to be related to the Scythian or Turanian languages. Others thought it came close to Manchu or Mongol; then again, affinity with the Turkish-Finnish-Hungarian group was thought probable. It was not until the first years of the twentieth century that the rules of Sumerian grammar were formulated and tentative translations made by comparison with the Akkadian in bilingual inscriptions. Even to the present day, however, neither the people of Sumer nor the language they spoke have ever been traced to convincing origins.

From the standpoint of the two museums, linguistics had given new impetus to excavation among the city states of Sumer. The challenge remained when Woolley arrived with his first assistants, the architect F. G. Newton and A. W. Lawrence, 'Will', younger brother of Ned. His *Seven Pillars of Wisdom* still in preparation, and his re-entry to archaeology baulked three years before, Ned had decided on the anonymity of a place in the infant Royal Air Force, as Aircraftsman Ross.

The three men travelled up from Basra by the single-line railway built in wartime, and disembarked at the stopping place named Ur Junction, on Sunday 29 October 1922. Woolley promptly left his colleagues to set up their tents while he went on to Baghdad to meet officials of the new Iraq.

While in Baghdad, Woolley had been promised by Gertrude Bell that the proposed Antiquity Law would go before the cabinet on the morrow and that he would therefore be able to take a full permit with him. In fact, Faisal's cabinet never agreed anything as speedily, and Woolley had to take with him a temporary permit issued by the Ministry of Public Works. Reporting the matter to Gordon, Woolley said, 'in Miss Bell we shall of course have a most sympathetic director'. Gertrude had told her father that the visiting expedition was 'prepared to put in two years' work'.

Miss Bell made it clear that she intended to establish a museum in Baghdad to house the nation's antiquities and she insisted to her guest that all the finds at Ur and other sites belonged to the new kingdom of Iraq. She would divide the spoils fairly. She must ensure that the best artifacts remained in Iraq but Woolley would have a fair selection for his client museums in London and Philadelphia. It seemed a reasonable attitude, for all sites of the Near East had been denuded of their finest treasures in the past and in an atmosphere of resurgent nationalism Gertrude saw her primary duty as that of preserving Iraq's heritage rather than enriching Europe's or America's. Woolley saw the point and raised no complaint, though, like any other archaeologist, he was apt to protest when his best finds were taken from him.

For the moment, though, he was content to be at the fount of biblical history, away from the over-dug and over-publicized sites of ancient Egypt. He was embarked on the greatest of all unveiling tasks, the revealing of the earliest recorded events in human history, events which had been imprinted on his mind indelibly in his first conscious years.

Hamoudi, the faithful foreman of bygone days, was there to take command of a workforce which would soon be more than 200 strong, composed of the usual argumentative factions. Hamoudi's two sons, Yahia and Ibrahim, had come along to reinforce the team. They were soon needed. On 7–8 November, just a week after Woolley's arrival, the camp was invaded by armed robbers. One of the guards was shot dead, and most of the personal belongings of Woolley's team were stolen. Turkish gold coinage valued at £30 was included among the items taken. Reporting the incident to Gordon and Kenyon on 16 November, Woolley made it clear that the robbers had been arrested, though the money had not been recovered. Perhaps recalling the constant money problems at Carchemish, he decided however to make the theft an opportunity to establish at the outset some financial precepts. 'I trust that you will agree that this loss should be borne by the Expedition and not laid to the charge of the members of the staff concerned.' He had considered increasing the size of the guard but that would have entailed a serious outlay in wages. He was anxious to stress his prudence in the stewardship of Pennsylvania's money.

On the journey out he and Newton had drawn up plans for an expedition house. It would have fourteen rooms and an attached guard house. They had budgeted £150. In Baghdad, they were told the price was more likely to approach £750. On arrival at Ur they found that prices had escalated on news of their coming but, Woolley assured Gordon, he had talked a local builder into doing the job for £200, though, 'as I supply the bricks (taken from the ruins) the actual price will be something above this.' The house was ready for occupation within twenty days of starting to build, on 22 November. At least tents could be dispensed with and the first Christmas at Ur spent under permanent cover. On the 18th Woolley had reported: 'It is not an ideal country to dig in; hopelessly ignorant workmen, lots of trouble with local sheikhs, etc., the discomfort of tent life, and general insecurity; but the site is a fine one and should yield very good stuff'. If the year ended on a despondent note there was at least the promise of a satisfactory return for the paymaster

Will Lawrence went home at the end of the first season, never to return. The need by that time was for an epigraphist – a cuneiformist, as the Americans called such experts. Sidney Smith, the quarrelsome Assistant Keeper of the British Museum, was sent out to begin the analysis and translation of the inscribed cylinders, bricks and tablets of Ur.

The first two seasons were spent in clearing the great ziggurat of Ur and in digging at Eridu to the south and al-Ubaid to the north-west, where vital evidence relating to Ur itself had been partly revealed by Dr Hall three years earlier. The expedition soon made its first important discoveries; flint instruments and painted pottery common to both sites which were recognized as 'prehistoric', and a First Dynasty temple at Ubaid revealed an island of river silt which originally rose above the surrounding plain and was seized upon by the first immigrants for building their reed huts. In the topmost layer of ruins they found a mud-brick wall contemporary with the First Dynasty temple nearby. The wall was separated from older remains beneath by an unknown time gap. It was all grist to Woolley's unshakeable belief that he had begun to unearth urban communities much older than those of Egypt which he had until recently helped to popularize. The pottery of Ubaid and Eridu spoke of a civilization which did not use metal (at Ubaid, at any rate) which was yet shown by the skilful decoration of its clay vessels to be advanced, even sophisticated.

While dating from pottery sherds from surrounding sites was in progress, a large gang was at work at Ur itself, where the ziggurat was being traced inch by inch in its upward flight. At the start of the 1923 season, Gertrude Bell turned up in a a model-T Ford driven by J. M. Wilson, the architectural adviser in Baghdad. They were there to examine Woolley's 'booty'; to divide the finds between 'the diggers and the Iraq'. Woolley told Gordon that the debate on the Antiquities Law in the Baghdad Chamber had been 'acrimonious' and that he expected 'some worry' over the details of the division of finds. The first disputed object was a headless statue in carved diorite. Woolley wrote again to Gordon on 26 February: 'The Iraq Government has in its share of the objects taken the diorite statue of Enannatum [King of Lagash c.2400BC]. Apart from this loss the Expedition comes out well on the division . . . all inscribed objects are being brought home for study including the share of the Iraq Government.' By March, Miss Bell was singing Woolley's praises. 'It took us the whole day to do the division but it was extremely interesting and Mr Woolley was an angel. We had to claim the best things for ourselves but we did our best to make it up to him and I don't think he was very much dissatisfied. We, for our part, were well pleased. The best object is a hideous Sumerian statue of a King of Lagash, about three feet high but headless. It has a long inscription across the shoulder . . .' The King in question was Entemena, son of Enannatum of Lagash, and not the father as was at first thought.

By the beginning of the 1924–25 season, Woolley was able to address a world already reeling from Carter's description a few months earlier of the sargophagus of Tutankhamen, and to offer it the first lifelike reconstruction of a 'tower of Babel':

> The Ziggurat of Babylon has been made famous to us by the Biblical story of the Tower of Babel and the confusion of tongues; and it was only one of many, for every great city of ancient Babylonia possessed a similar staged tower, and to-day the ruins of these are the most conspicuous features of the flat Euphrates valley.

He described the great rectangular tower built by imposing small cube upon larger, 'so as to give something of the effect of a stepped pyramid'. And finally, the little shrine on the flat top of the topmost stage, 'dedicated to the Moon God Nannar' – the core of mudbrick, its outer walls of kiln-burnt bricks laid in pitch, 'the *slime* of the writer in Genesis'. Proof, indeed, of the engineering skill which here, as in Egypt, marked the constructional wonders of the first civilizations. But for Bible scholars and the faithful of Judaean, Christian and Islamic traditions, there was much more. The first tower of Ur-Engur 'was built in about 2300 BC, some three hundred years before Abraham lived here'. The home city of the patriarch was being reconstructed, though Woolley's date was two centuries too early.

If events in the Valley of the Kings stirred the hearts and minds of millions of men and women the world over, news from Ur fed the insatiable urge of the faithful for confirmation of holy writ. Day in and day out, by 1924, archaeology took on a universal fascination, occupying the headlines of the press with a seemingly endless drama of discovery. Woolley, ever conscious of the competition of Egypt and Howard Carter, used all his talent for popularization to broadcast the historical and chronological significance of ancient Sumer, which, he insisted, predated the First Dynasty of Egypt. He was not the first academic to take the path of exaggeration in such matters, or the last. Sir Arthur Evans was doing it in Crete, where Minoan dating always had to keep pace with Egyptian chronology, which Sir Flinders Petrie, foremost among Egyptologists, had in turn placed more than a thousand years earlier than its actual time. The battle for priority in time between the three great centres of civilization of the Mediterranean and the Near East would continue even after the deaths of the archaeologists who, at that moment, stood in the spotlight.

Woolley's finds were beginning to justify the publicity claims. He was still a casual letter writer and it was left to others to describe events at Ur. In January 1924, Gertrude Bell recorded: 'Mr Woolley at Ur has been making wonderful finds and has written urgently to me to go down. So I'm going next Sunday, taking Kish *en route*.' Kish was close to Babylon, well to the north of Ur, and an Anglo-American team under Professor Stephen Langdon of Oxford was digging there. Evidence was beginning to come from Kish, as also from Eridu, of a devastating flood recorded on the clay tablets of royal libraries in epics such as that of *Gilgamesh*. A Sumerian king-list gave the rulers of the region from earliest times to about 1800 BC, and recorded: 'The Flood came. After the Flood came, kingship again was sent down from on high.' An antediluvian section shows the kings of the first capital, Kish, then of a new capital, Uruk (biblical Erech), then of the First Dynasty of Ur. Thus, Kish and Uruk were probably the oldest of the city states of Sumer, and Ur third in chronological order. But Ur had more to offer the questing archaelogist, though Woolley as yet had no idea of the full extent of its riches.

Miss Bell arrived at Ur in the bitter cold of a January morning and met Woolley on his way from early morning excavations. They took breakfast together and they went on to al-Ubaid 'which gave me the greatest sensation, I think, which in archaeology I have ever experienced,' she wrote. She was shown a reconstruction of the ziggurat, drawn by Woolley's architectural assistant F. G. Newton for public consumption and about to be sent off to the press with a brief description (have corrected in some details).

> When one realizes that the lower stage alone (Ur-Nammu's work) is a solid mass of brickwork nearly 200 feet long by 150 feet broad and about 50 feet high, and that this is only one of many such towers that dotted all the land, one may well ask whatever induced people to go to all this labour? The explanation seems to be this. The Sumerians, who are the authors of the ziggurats, came into Mesopotamia from somewhere in the north-east, a mountainous country where, like all mountain folk, they had worshipped mountain gods and had built their temples on the hill-tops. When they moved down to the rich newly-formed plains of the river country, they must have been terribly upset to find that there was no hill whereon a temple could be built – and what was the use of a temple on level ground? God would never be at home in a house built on the flat. So they set piously to work and built artificial mountains of brick where God might have his seat as of old on the holy hills ... yet it remains a hill, as the name 'House of the Mountain' clearly shows. And if, as certain inscriptions seem to imply, trees were planted round it, and even set in tubs on the terraces, the man-made ziggurat could not fail to recall to the Sumerian the highlands where once his fathers lived and the true nature of the gods he worshipped, bidding him lift up his eyes to the hills from which came his help.

So too, the British Museum had, under his guidance, reconstructed the interior of the dimunitive temple at Tal al-Ubaid. 'The little temple at Tell el Obaid [Woolley's spelling of the Arabic words is phonetic, but as good as any] does not really exist ... To attempt to reconstruct the original appearance of a structure so hopelessly destroyed might well seem rash, fanciful and unscientific. Yet I claim a very fair degree of truth,' he wrote. It was not the language of the academic, whose reports for his employers were being prepared at the same time in the matter-of-fact language appropriate to matters which remained conjectural. But Woolley was addressing a wider audience. Of the temple at Ubaid, he concluded:

> What makes this temple and everything found in connection with it of quite extraordinary interest is its great age. From the foundation tablet we learn that it was built in honour of the goddess Nin-Khursag by A-an-ni-pad-da, who was the second king of the First Dynasty of Ur, a dynasty which, until the material proof of its existence came to light, was commonly regarded as mythical . . . the most conservative estimate would assign to our temple an antiquity of some 5,400 years.

On 4 March 1924, Gertrude Bell and Wilson were back again, marvelling at the great stairway whose last royal users in antiquity were Nebuchadnezzar and Nabonidus, and sharing out the spoils. 'Before 9 we started the division (it began by my winning the gold scarab on the toss of a rupee) and we carried on till 12.30, when I struck . . . We sat with our catalogues and ticked the things off. But the really agonizing part was after lunch when I had to tell them that I must take the milking scene. I can't do otherwise. It's unique and it depicts the life of the country at a very early date. In my capacity as Director of Antiquities I'm an Iraqi official and bound by the terms on which we gave the permit to excavate. J. M. [Wilson] backed me but it broke Mr Woolley's heart, though he expected the decision.'

As the 1924 season progressed, a limestone slab, beautifully carved in relief emerged from the rubble beneath the courtyard of Ur-Nammu's *dublal-makh* shrine, a holy monument only slightly less imposing than the shrine of the great ziggurat itself. It had been cleared down to the pavements laid by Kurigalzu the king of Babylon in about 1400 BC. The slab or stela was 15 feet high and five feet across and bore the portrait of the ziggurat's builder, receiving from the moon god the order to build, the god holding out to him the rod and line of the architect; that very measuring reed and flaxen line 'with which Ezekiel, an exile by the waters of Babylon, saw planned out the city and temple of his dreams'. There were scenes too of music and sacrifice, and of Ur-Nammu carrying the tools of the mason in obedience to his god. Woolley was quick to send by post to London an account of the find and a photograph which gave the public a clear and dramatic image of a ruler of the Third Dynasty of Ur in about 2100 BC, one of the oldest and finest examples of third-millennium art yet to come from Mesopotamia. Gertrude Bell and Wilson were there to see it. By then other dramatic archaeological news had made the world's headlines. This time it was from India, where Sir John Marshall, Surveyor General and Director of Antiquities, had found cylindrical seals in the Indus Valley identical to those which Woolley was finding at Ur, and their discovery led to the excavation of Mohenjo-Daro and Harappa. Yet more early civilizations, a thousand miles away beyond the Persian Gulf and across the Indian Ocean were, it seemed, trading with ancient Sumer. Gertrude told Woolley that she had written to Marshall for impressions of his seals. 'Kish and Ur are opening,' she wrote at the beginning of the new season, 'and we are all frightfully thrilled by the discovery in India.'

Another essay from Woolley's pen told of the worship of the moon-god at Ur, revising previous estimates of age and listing the functionaries of the temple – priests and ministers of state, choir-master, controller of the household, master of the harem, directors of livestock, dairies, fishing, donkey-transport; and women employees engaged in weaving. 'It is immensely old . . . By the time of Ur-Nammu (2100 BC) the temple had been completely rebuilt several times, and the building with which Abraham was familiar was perhaps the fifth to occupy the site.'

Treasures of Mesopotamia

'At the beginning,' Woolley said, the workmen at Ur were 'completely ignorant, had no idea what good workmanship was, were reckless, and of course dishonest.' It was a frank and accurate catalogue of the shortcomings of his men in the early stages of the dig. Woolley's strength was his ability, shared by few other field archaeologists of his time, to turn incompetent and undisciplined labourers into an effective and loyal workforce by example and perseverance. He bided his time at Ur, holding up the excavation of some of the most promising areas, such as the royal cemetery and the principal palaces and temples, until he was satisfied that his men had reached a sufficient level of competence. He was lucky, none the less, to have in his foreman, Hamoudi, a philosopher and disciplinarian who could win the loyalty and affection of men with a mixture of good humour and iron resolve. 'Work,' he was heard to say, 'was sent by Allah to prevent men from thinking.'

The disparate Anglo-American academics who made up his professional team were no less given to abuse and in-fighting. Again, example was his weapon. 'If ever conditions were bad, in sandstorm or rainstorm, Woolley was out on the job, *pour encourager les autres*,' said Max Mallowan, an assistant who arrived later, in the third season, to find at Ur the high-point of a working lifetime in archaeology. The same assistant was told off for not being on site at 5 AM on one occasion, a good half hour's walk from the staff residence. 'If you cannot get up in the morning you should go to bed earlier.'

Woolley was in some ways secretive, often enigmatic in his dealings, but he did not mince his words or show bias in his relations with workmen or professional assistants. He controlled them all with the ease of a leader whose sense of humour, conscientious approach to his own work, and confidence in his own abilities combined to defuse anger and imbue achievement with a sense of communal pride. He was resolute and determined but he never lost his temper. His unruffled approach to every problem, like his offhand manner of speaking of his own accomplishments, was balanced by a perfect willingness to admit to error. He understood fallibility in others because he recognized it in himself.

The two years he promised Gertrude Bell he would spend at Ur had already become three, and the real tasks – and the most remarkable finds – were still hidden from sight. So were troubles as yet unheralded.

The Peace Treaty between the victorious powers and Turkey, signed at Lausanne in July 1923 after five years of haggling, resolved at least some of the frontier disputes that had dogged Woolley at Carchemish. But the treaty gave rise to newly constituted nations in the Middle East, such as Iraq, with alien monarchies and untried politicians to determine the conduct of everyday life, including archaeological work. Woolley was sensitive enough to realize that he must play up to the new-found nationalist urges of his hosts. When Gertrude Bell invited him to Baghdad in May 1924 to give a lecture before a select audience of Arab notables and high-ranking officers of the British High Commission, he jumped at the opportunity. He had given talks before when passing through Baghdad, but this, at the moment of drafting Iraq's new constitution, was by far the most important. He spoke in English and Arabic, detailing the ancient history of the land that had gained its independence after four hundred years of Ottoman rule. Gertrude Bell had arranged an exhibition of Ur finds from her museum to accompany the talk, given on 10 July in the serai of the old pashas of the 'Beloved City'.

'Mr Woolley was as good as ever', Gertrude wrote afterwards. His enthusiasm, conveyed in a a torrent of English and Arabic, left his audience spellbound. Even he was pleased. 'The effect of the exhibition and lecture was distinctly good,' he told Gordon. He added a note to his American sponsor which would have increasing relevance as the excavation of Ur proceeded:

> I thought it politic to make as much as possible of the advantage gained by the Iraq Gov't in the partition of the spoil, so as to make the ministers and others understand the wisdom of letting the excavators have a share – and therefore excavate – so that the country gets a great deal for nothing. Actually, in the division we did very well and have no cause for complaint – though I would not say so to Miss Bell.

The museum established by Gertrude was the glory of Baghdad in its first years of independence. 'I burst with pride when I show people over the Museum,' she told her stepmother in a a letter. Even so, her policy of letting the diggers have the tablets which only they and their museums could translate, along with the less spectacular pottery and bronzes, while the most magnificent artifacts went to Baghdad, still caused some resentment. Professor Langdon at Kish was beginning to share some of Woolley's concern. He was so annoyed on one occasion that he threatened to close his site. Gertrude wrote: 'I, unknowing, while eating a scrap of lunch, explained that my object was to leave, as far as possible, the tablets to them for they should be at the disposition of students. On the other hand, they would have to make up by parting with some other fine objects.'

'Who decides if we disagree?' asked Langdon. 'I replied that I did, but he needn't be afraid for he would find me eager to oblige.' Characteristically, she told him: 'Come on, Professor, you'll see how it works out.' Langdon went along with her. A few days later, writing to her father, Gertrude exclaimed: 'And isn't it fantastic to be selecting pots and things four to six thousand years old! I got a marvellous stone inlay of a Sumerian king leading captives and not being at all nice to them, and a mother-of-pearl inlay of a king and his wives – inscribed with his name. The Professor got what he longed for, a mother of pearl inlay representing a milking scene – you see I have my milking scene in the great plaque from Ur.'

There was many a fight between Woolley and al Khatun (the name – 'The Lady of the Court' – given by the Arabs to Gertrude Bell). A particularly fierce dispute arose over a diorite statue of the goddess Bau. Lionel Smith had gone to Ur with Gertrude. She turned to him for support, but when, to her surprise, he spoke up for Woolley she overrode his plea. On the way to Ur Junction to catch the train back to Baghdad – the statue tucked safely in her satchel and Smith walking behind her at a discreet distance as though she were the Queen – she muttered in a a voice loud enough for all to hear, 'The traitor! The traitor!'

The other Smith, Sidney, returned to London after the 1922–3 season at Ur. Their relationship had been strained from the beginning, and Woolley had asked Hall at the British Museum to send him a more congenial epigraphist. Cyril John Gadd, 30 years old, slim with ill-fitting clothes and pleasant manner, was sent out, to Woolley's great delight. Smith's voice was heard from a distance, however. He was in touch with the RAF who had taken over the military supervision of the Arab lands following Churchill's Cairo Conference two years before. The Air Command had also taken over the responsibility for transporting the more important Ur antiquities to London. On 29 February 1924 Woolley received a cable from RAF HQ Baghdad, addressed to 'L. C. N. Woolley', referring to the transport of 'certain tangible results of your work at Ur'. The 'tangible results' were to be despatched by him 'carriage paid', to the Kidbrooke (London) depot of the Royal Air Force. The message concluded 'All charges to be borne by him.' Smith's approach to Woolley usually smacked of insolence. He was soon at work on Dr Hall, who had just succeeded Wallis Budge as head of the Egyptian and Assyrian Department. In March, Hall cabled Woolley to express his concern about the division of spoils. 'Don't worry,' Woolley replied. 'Baghdad is not going to do us down over this deal.' In the same letter Woolley referred to Smith's 'smirk' over a reference he had made to pottery kilns, presumably in the pre-historic period before the kiln came into general use and the open fire or hole in the ground was the common baking device. 'I never worry about having made a mistake as long as I can correct it,' said Woolley, determined not to be visibly angered by Smith's provoca-tions. Worse, he had described a seal found at Ur as 'scaraboid'. It was loose description in a note probably scribbled in the late hours of the night. Smith had poured scorn on the use of the word. 'Well, that is the shape of it . . . and if it raises the hair of the Egyptologist, it's my turn to smirk.' Then a postscript: 'Gadd, by the way, is obviously very good, and also a most delightful person to have about the house. He has enjoyed his time here, likes the people and has got fatter and better in health . . .' Smith's term as Woolley's epigraphist had lasted long enough for the Arabs he prodded and hectored to nickname him al Khanzir. Mallowan translated the term generously as 'wild boar', but in common parlance it is simply 'pig'.

Gadd's term as epigraphist was also brief, ending in the summer of 1924, along with that of a 'voluntary' helper, G. M. FitzGerald. The two assistants were present for long enough to witness the surprise arrival of a European lady at the site in the spring of 1924. She was tall, slender and cultured and showed a keen interest in all that was happening. She also demonstrated some skill as an artist, working alongside Woolley and drawing many of the objects he selected from the palaces, houses, courtyards and cemeteries of Ur.

Mrs Katharine Elizabeth Keeling was a widow with emphatic ideas conveyed by precisely articulated words. She was attractive in appearance and, at first acquaintance, in manner, and soon had the young men of the expedition in the palm of her hand. She dressed smartly, almost always in her favourite shade, *vieux rose*, with shoes and gloves to match, and was given to sudden headaches which necessitated retirement to a darkened room where she would lie in apparent agony for hours on end. Woolley's assistants said nothing of the visitor, but outsiders visiting the site began to talk and it was not long before Gordon in Philadelphia was apprised of her presence.

Kenyon told each of the British assistants before they left London: 'You will hear many things but keep your thoughts to yourself.' The young men obeyed the director's edict, but they had eyes and ears. Mrs Keeling was, they decided, in her mid thirties and something of a female Jekyll and Hyde, changing her mood without warning from enchanting liveliness to black depression. It was said that she had attended Somerville College, Oxford, and had been widowed for some four years. What was not generally known or suspected was that she came of a central European, German-speaking family and that her 'perfect' English was an acquired tongue. Her maiden name was Menke, and though the family's origins remain uncertain they probably arrived in England in the late nineteenth century from the eastern region of Prussia. Carl Theodore Menke and his family settled at Kings Norton in the Midlands where he became a successful merchant and where Katharine Elizabeth was born in June 1888. They can have spoken little English in the home because when Katharine sat her entrance examination at Somerville in 1910, in her twenty-second year, she did so in German. She entered the Modern History School and remained for two years without sitting a single examination. She was, even then, subject to constant ill-health.

At the end of the 1914–18 war she had returned to central Europe, to the town of Strzalkovo on the old Russo-German border, where a large army of Ukranians was imprisoned. Her work in the prison camps there was rewarded by an illuminated testimonial. More significantly, she met her first husband while working there, an army staff officer with a distinguished record, Lt-Col B. E. F. Keeling. The couple married at St Martins-in-the-Fields, London, on 3 March 1919, and a fortnight afterwards went to Baghdad and on to Egypt for their honeymoon. Before leaving London on 18 March, Keeling made out a brief, uncomplicated Last Will and Testament in which he left all his worldly possessions to Katharine and appointed her his executrix. On 29 April, General Allenby, the new High Commissioner in Egypt, appointed Keeling Director-General of the Survey of Egypt and President of the country's Cotton Research Board. On 23 September 1919, *The Times* reported that three days earlier, on 20 September, 'Lt Colonel Bertram Keeling ... died suddenly ...' That singular report went on: 'Great regret is felt everywhere. Much was expected of him in his new posts, and his death is a great loss to the country.' Death added to the mystery of a man whose life had been spent in the shadows. The General Registry of the United Kingdom records the death as having occurred on 'Twentieth September 1919'. The certificate was signed by the Acting Consul in Cairo, Edgar Gout, and gave the place of death as Gezira, Cairo. The War Office records department would issue no details of the Colonel's death but a certified entry under 'War deaths 1914–1921', issued under the Registration 'Special Provisions Act' of 1957, records that he died on '29th September' but gives no cause. Whatever the real date or cause of his demise, it marked a dramatic end to a very brief marriage. But there may have been more to the Colonel's death than the shock of discovering that he had married a demanding and uncompromising woman. He had been engaged in intelligence work of a very secret nature at the time of the Bolshevik revolution and at a vital juncture of German, Polish and Russian military activities which led to the settlement of Brest Litovsk. Few newspapers reported the event. Those that did, like *The Times*, appeared to exhibit no curiosity about the fact that a 39-year-old British officer, holding a high official position in the Egyptian administration, simply died, without cause. More than forty years later, Max Mallowan passed on the version which Woolley gave to him, a version which smacked a little of some of the teller's 'secret service' yarns. According to Mallowan, the distraught sapper Colonel shot himself at the foot of the Great Pyramid of Cheops. Whether the deed was in affirmation of his devotion to archaeology, or of his grievous error in marriage, nobody who knew the circumstances has ever been willing to say. But there was almost certainly more to the matter than Mallowan knew, or at any rate was prepared to tell.

Woolley and Mrs Keeling returned to England together at the end of the 1924 season. It was a busy time. He was lecturing and writing articles throughout the summer. He visited Katharine at Gerrard's Cross in Buckinghamshire where she was staying, but there was little time to pursue the friendship. She was certainly much in his thoughts, none the less, as he laboured with long articles on Ur for the *Antiquaries' Journal*, travelled between the family home at Bath and the British Museum, and visited one city and university after another to give lantern-slide talks.

While in London in July he met the American scholar-priest who was to become his next epigraphist, Dr Leon Legrain. The Philadelphia Museum had wanted Legrain to join Woolley at the outset, but it was considered wasteful to send out an accomplished cuneiform scholar when the greater need was for all-round dogsbodies. Legrain found London, and the British Museum in particular, beyond understanding. Hall introduced him to Woolley and to Smith, and the canny American quickly assessed the temperature. He wrote to his chief, Dr Gordon:

> The collections were scattered in five or six different locales of the British Museum, partly unpacked, partly under repair, partly in the showcases of a temporary exhibition that was to open the following week . . . Division of the material – I mentioned your intentions to Mr Woolley, but as Head of the Joint Expedition, Mr Woolley thought that the division was not incumbent to him – Mr Hall listened to the request, but leaving for his vacation the next few days, he referred me to Mr S. Smith. Mr S. Smith thought the proper man to do the division would be Mr Gadd, who had been in the field and knew the material. Mr Gadd being on his vacation . . .

And so the letter went on, recording the phlegmatic British in contemplation of their holidays, unable to come to terms with the simplest request. Legrain returned a few days later and had limited success in passing on Gordon's wishes. 'This was the best I was able to do under rather difficult circumstances,' the Jesuit Father concluded. 'I must add that every official of the British Museum was as polite as possible and Sir Fr. Kenyon particularly gracious.'

Gordon had told Legrain of his appointment in September 1924. In mid-October Woolley joined up with his epigraphist at Beirut. They went on to Aleppo together, where Woolley wanted to trace some missing Carchemish 'stones', allegedly sent to London. They also picked up Hamoudi there. The remarkable foreman, still living with his large family at Jerablus between seasons, had brought with him a steatite tablet found at the site of the outer town of Carchemish which Woolley had excavated in part in 1920. Hamoudi had

purchased the tablet from the man who found it, and was rewarded
by Woolley. Woolley sent it on to the museum complete with
Hamoudi's drawing of the anthropomorphic scene, made in case the
tablet was lost or its owner had refused to part with it. It showed a
leopard-headed figure standing on a horse, holding a snake in either
hand while being attacked by a wild boar. The quick but accurate
sketch said much for Hamoudi's powers of observation, and no less
for his loyalty to Woolley.

The new general assistant, Linnell, also joined them at Aleppo.
When the foursome arrived at Ur a few days later they discovered a
catastrophic mishap. Woolley explained to Hall:

> A disaster occurred during my absence from here. White ants
> got into my study and ate a number of books and papers,
> including your reports on Ur and Tell-Ubaid (they even man-
> aged to swallow the original plan of Building B!) . . . Please send
> duplicate copies.

He told Hall that he was delighted with Legrain, 'so excellent, he's
never tired of working over the inscribed material . . . and he's a
most charming companion . . . I'm sorry I can't have him out every
year.'

Legrain was obviously enjoying himself. In January 1925 he wrote
to Gordon: 'I beg you would believe we drank your health in good
style on Xmas and New Year's Eve. Despite the distance the desert
and the strenuous work we omitted none of the rites: turkey, plum
pudding and real Scotch Whiskey. That is some help to archaeology.
I am up every day at half past six and go to bed at half past ten.'

Cold and lack of firewood combined to make winter at Ur
extremely uncomfortable. They had to use bitumen left behind three
thousand years before to keep the fires going. 'We have to thank
King Nabonidus for the invaluable and unexpensive way of warming
up at Ur of the Chaldees,' wrote Legrain.

For the moment, Ur basked in amity and winter sunlight, though
the even tenor of life was disturbed in February by news of the death
of Newton in England. Woolley's architect assistant had stayed
behind in London to work on his drawings of the ziggurat, feeling
unwell but working industriously. Woolley wrote of his 'great
distress' at the death of an assistant he greatly admired and looked
on as a friend.

The season's main discovery was made in the courtyard of E-
dublah-mah and the chamber which led to it. 'Here there were

scattered over the pavement quantities of limestone fragments, large and small, which proved to be parts of one, or possibly two, huge stelae measuring five feet across and perhaps fifteen feet high, covered on both sides with finely executed reliefs.' What they had discovered was only a fraction of the whole imposing memorial, but it was enough to engender great excitement at Ur and in London and Philadelphia. A minor fragment revealed the name of the king whose activities in providing canals for his subjects and piously building the ziggurat, were commemorated; Ur-Nammu, founder of the Third Dynasty of Ur.

Woolley wrote immediately to Kenyon and Gordon. To the latter: 'This great stela is far the most important object yet found at Ur . . . To you, Sir, I need not insist upon its value, which fully repays all the cost of your Expedition up to date, but I should like to say, in view of its fragmentary state, that I by no means despair of recovering more of it.' He added, to the relief of both museum heads, that Miss Bell had accepted his argument that the great stone tablet must be left to the expedition. On 4 March, Gertrude Bell noted that the division carried out a few days earlier had been difficult but fair. 'I hope Mr Woolley feels the same.' Then: 'I left the great piece to them – it is a huge stele with amazingly interesting reliefs, but . . . I thought it was in the interest of science to let it go to some big museum . . .' But which museum? Philadelphia was anxious that it should not become the exclusive property of the British Museum now that it had been snatched from Baghdad's grasp. It was, said Gordon, 'worth much more than all the rest put together'. That was to prove an exaggeration, but up to the moment it was true. An equal division was clearly impossible. Gordon proposed to Kenyon that the division of the year's finds should be postponed for twelve months so that they could be assessed along with the following year's. The stela should be treated separately, unless a counterbalancing find came up. It was an inspired suggestion and Kenyon agreed to it.

The return to Ur after the summer break, in October 1925, was marked by the arrival of two new assistants, Max Mallowan and A. S. (Archie) Whitburn. Mallowan, like Woolley himself a graduate of New College, was another of Hogarth's discoveries. When Woolley let it be known that he was looking for a good all-round general assistant, Hogarth immediately put him forward.

It was the famous Spooner's successor as Warden of New College,

H. A. L. Fisher, brother of the First Sea Lord, who had commended archaeology to Mallowan. That fact apart, the young man seemed to have little in common with Woolley. He was fond of claret and cricket (penchants which Woolley looked on as vices rather than virtues) and he was first drawn to his new chief by the thought that he might by some happy chance be connected with his sporting hero Frank Woolley, the cricketer. His background was as cosmopolitan as Woolley's was insular. His mother was a Parisienne Christian Scientist, his father an Austrian immigrant. At Lancing he had resisted the advances of high-church theology and joined with Evelyn Waugh in opposing conscription into the Army class. Mallowan had attended lectures by the Wykeham Professor of Ancient History at Oxford, Percy Gardner, otherwise his only contact with the subject or with his employer was a visit to the British Museum where he had picked up a leaflet advertising one of the many Ur exhibitions of the period. In the summer of 1925 he was invited to an interview with Woolley. He was surprised to find that the questions put to him over tea and scones came not from his prospective employer but from a lady at his side who turned out to be Mrs Keeling. All the same, he was delighted to learn that he had been accepted for the job of general assistant.

Mallowan was twenty-five when he arrived at Ur, a short burly figure with a temperament which nicely complemented Woolley's. Whitburn, an impecunious young man, was recommended by the Royal Institute of British Architects as Newton's successor.

'Mr Woolley came towing two young men,' Gertrude Bell wrote from Baghdad. The faithful Hamoudi was there too, to accompany the party on the Pullman-style train to Ur. From then on Mallowan would chronicle people and events at Ur with intimate insight, filling the human-interest gaps which Woolley all too often left blank as a result of his preoccupation with the detailed records of the dig. The 25-year-old assistant, setting out on his first archaeological task, missed nothing and it was he who described the journey by Cadillac ('imported by the Nairn transport company') from Ur-Junction to the site, listening intently to the chief who was full of 'charm' and 'amusing anecdotes', observing as they arrived the busy scene as Hamoudi's men dug and hacked their way through the rubbish and habitations of five thousand years. He and Whitburn were on the best of terms by the time they arrived at Ur, and they quickly took the older and more experienced Legrain into their confidence.

Legrain had begun to build up an impressive library from the inscriptions of ancient Ur, depicting the lives of peoples who lived in Sumer and Akkad between four and five thousand years before. Mallowan observed him closely, like Woolley admiring the man's diligence. But he seemed to see an entirely different person from the one Woolley had described so glowingly. According to Mallowan, Dr Legrain looked on life with innate cynicism. His response to an unjust and often unfriendly world found expression not in religion – he was, said Mallowan, often mistaken for an agnostic, despite his priest's habit – but in ribaldry. He was amusing, irreverent and liable to offend what Mallowan was to describe in later years as 'the priggish side of Woolley'. He described the Sunday morning trek to worship at Nasiriya, Legrain like some Chaucerian friar singing and jollying the assembly along the ten-mile route with his constant jokes and ogling of Bedouin women – 'a pursuit not without risk; he sometimes met with a mincing response to his innocuous approaches.' Woolley became more sensitive to his crew's male-oriented merriment when Mrs Keeling came on the scene. According to Mallowan, he was particularly enraged by a coarse remark made on one occasion by Legrain to a drunken member of the expedition's domestic staff.

Both Legrain and Mallowan warmed to the youthful Whitburn, a war veteran with a limp and absolutely no resources beyond his meagre wage. He had an inexhaustible fund of Cockney stories to supplement Legrain's quips and the three young men often went off on short joyful holidays together, travelling steerage on river boats and Gulf steamers. Mrs Keeling did not share their sense of humour, however, and Legrain's days were numbered. After completing a second season he went back to Philadelphia never to return to Ur, though he continued to work on the cuneiform inscriptions. He was replaced by the Jesuit Father Burrows from Campion Hall, a man of wide learning who had the utmost difficulty in using any of the several languages he commanded even to order a jug of water or ask the time of day. Often when Woolley or one of his assistants was showing visitors round the excavations, Burrows was to be spotted squatting on the open-air closet, wearing his priestly habit and an unworldly demeanour.

It was in July 1926 that the subject of Mrs Keeling's presence, which had so far been ventilated only in private correspondence between Woolley and the heads of his sponsoring museums, came to a head.

On 8 July 1926, Gordon wrote to Woolley: 'This is personal and confidential. In your letter of Nov 30th last, written from Ur, you mentioned the name of Mrs Keeling as having been a visitor to the Expedition at Ur the year before and as having returned as a volunteer assistant. As you have not had occasion to mention Mrs Keeling again, and as Dr Legrain has not mentioned her presence in the camp, it is unlikely that the subject should have occurred to me had it not begun to give rise to some slight and inconsequential comment on the part of people entirely outside of the archaeological interests and outside of our acquaintance.'

Gordon went on to explain that the Ur expedition and everyone concerned with it had become subjects of public interest and discussion 'from Baghdad to Philadelphia' and that tourists and others made 'it' an important part of their recollections, 'though most of them know it only from hearsay.'

The presence of a lone woman with four men in camp made 'a more interesting figure for some of them than the outline of ziggurats', Dr Gordon suggested. He was concerned that a woman in that position might become the butt of 'inconsiderate remarks'. Without wishing to detract from Mrs Keeling's usefulness as an assistant, he doubted the wisdom of having volunteer assistants on site, male or female. He concluded: 'With every good wish and with entire confidence that I can as usual, count upon your excellent judgement.'

Mrs Keeling had been present at Ur during one of Gertrude Bell's visits and the two women had taken an instant dislike to each other. Four days after Gordon had sent off his letter to Woolley, al Khatun died, just before her 58th birthday, from an overdose of sleeping pills which many who knew her thought she had taken deliberately, disillusioned by her loss of influence and power in the Kingdom of Faisal I which she had been largely instrumental in establishing. Her death diverted Gordon and Kenyon temporarily from their concern about Mrs Keeling. Gordon was concerned that Miss Bell's successor might not be as intelligent or as sympathetic in the distribution of Mesopotamian artifacts. 'Her death will be a great loss to all of us,' he wrote.

Woolley had met Miss Bell for the last time in March, on the way home with Mrs Keeling. That 'dangerous woman' as Gertrude called her, kept her distance while Woolley and The Lady worked in the Baghdad Museum. 'Mr Woolley and I (chiefly Mr Woolley) have standardized wall cases and table cases so that one drawing does for all . . . We sat each on a Sumerian gate socket and drew up a scheme for numbering . . . in the downstairs rooms where all the big, heavy stone objects, too heavy to carry upstairs, will stand – a Babylonian room, an Assyrian room and an Arab room . . .' Woolley lectured to a crowded audience of Iraqis and British expatriates, 'admirably as usual', said Gertrude. They took tea with Harold Nicolson's wife, Vita Sackville West, on her way from Tehran to England. Gertrude had seemed in good spirit. Mallowan and Whitburn called on her a month later, and found her dispirited and lonely. Woolley was to write a postscript to earlier impressions, finding her, as she had come to find him, worthier than either thought at first sight. Her little brick museum, he said, was to serve for twenty years as Iraq's only repository of antiquities. It was eventually succeeded by a magnificent modern building which paid homage to Gertrude Bell as its founder, housing what he described as one of the richest collections of Sumerian and Mesopotamian antiquities in existence.

Gertrude left £6,000 to the British Museum for the founding of a School of Archaeology in Iraq. The school became known as the 'Gertrude Bell Memorial'.

With her death, Woolley's protective shield had gone in the fierce Iraqi summer of 1926. He was now without shelter from the determined nationalism of men who had lately served the Turkish rulers of their land, versed in Oriental ways of doing business.

Marriage, Pu-abi and the Flood

Woolley arrived home in 1926 not only to garner the news of Gertrude's death and to learn of his employers' concern about Mrs Keeling, but also to reap an archaeological whirlwind. Sensational news from Egypt had been added to in terms of press coverage and public interest by antiquarian gales blowing from as far afield as India, America and eastern Europe.

He had kept a press cutting of the year before, headlining Howard Carter's angry exchanges with officials following the revelation of the sarcophagus of Tutenkhamen. Even in the face of the gold-clad boy king of Egypt, the astonishing prehistoric wall paintings of Lascaux (discovered in 1925), the wonders of Crete and the Indus Valley, Woolley's uncovering of Abraham's birthplace held its niche in the public interest, but the competition was growing.

There was, too, a related development which caused great public excitement. At this moment of monentous discovery in all the great centres of ancient civilization, broadcasting had become a reality. The 'wireless' had a particular appeal for Leonard Woolley. Such by now was his achievement at Ur, even though its most spectacular artifacts were still to be recovered, and such was his reputation as a speaker, that he was seized on by the new broadcasters who had set up the first radio station at Savoy Hill in London. He was asked to prepare a series of six programmes.

On 22 May 1925 he had delivered a popular lecture to a crowded meeting of the Royal United Services Institution in a London. Inevitably, there was a growing demand for illustrated talks on 'Abraham's City' from clubs, institutions and universities at home and abroad. His first major article on the work at Ur had appeared in *The Times* of 14 May 1923, detailing the treasures of the Moon God Temple, and there had been subsequent articles and reports in the same newspaper throughout the next three years, the latest appearing on 28 April 1926, soon after his arrival in England.

Pennsylvania University, which was meeting the ever-growing costs of the Ur expedition, naturally wanted its pound of flesh. And there were other pressing calls on his time and energies.

During his summer leave, his father died at the home in Bath which he and Cathcart had bought for him. The Rev Woolley in his eightieth year still took his daily cold bath and sat in state at the head of the family dining table, his pure white head of hair still reaching down to his buttocks and the long beard resting on his lap. Grandchildren recalled visits to him in his last years, when they curtsied or bowed politely as they entered the room. Edith's daughter Margaret recalled the feeling of aversion as she was called on to kiss grandpa, negotiating the straggling beard and encountering the thick sensuous lips. The Rev. Woolley went on collecting until his last days, and still entertained friends and family by playing Beethoven on one of the two grand pianos in the drawing room at Uplands. 'Lovely runny music,' was Margaret's childish description. In his will, the selfish old man had specified that his art collection and furnishings should be auctioned. 'What will become of all the various things is not our affair – you children may divide them,' he had written years before. In the event, he willed that there should be no family squabbles over the things he had spent his wife's fortune on. His children could not prevent their disposal through a firm of auctioneers who allowed a magnificent collection of etchings and engravings of old masters, of rare ceramics, glass and furnishings to be sold at give-away prices. Shortly after his death, Turner engravings could be bought for a few shillings in the Bath and other West Country markets. Of the sons and daughters, only Leonard, Edith and Harold were in England when he died, and although they were able to buy back some drawings and furnishings, most were lost in the sale.

There were other matters to distract Woolley from the pressing demands of archaeology in that year. He was caught up in the dismal saga of the General Strike. Travel was difficult between London and Bath, and most of his time was spent at the family home. Harold entered the political fray with a letter to *The Times* demanding that Parliament should pass a law making it illegal for striking workmen to victimize those who continued to work. The familiar terms of industrial dispute were used in the abusive follow-up. Preoccupied as he was with the evolving woman-on-the-site saga, with never-ending demands for articles, books and talks, the problems of travel and the industrial dispute which gave rise to them, were the last straw.

On 8 August 1926, just a month before returning to Ur for the start of his sixth season of digging, Woolley wrote to Gordon from Uplands, responding to his remarks about Mrs Keeling's 'voluntary' role.

The letter had been addressed to him at his London club, the Royal Societies. 'Its first effect on me was to make me regret once more the fact that I can't see you: I'm always feeling what a loss it is, when I'm working under you, to be always at such a distance.' Since he could not get over to the States at that time, and Gordon could not find the time to come to London, he (Woolley) would have to answer in writing. There was a long apologia concerning voluntary workers in archaeology – 'Petrie in Egypt almost lives on them' – and he could not understand the objection. 'But when I got your letter I felt obliged to see Kenyon at once, because I don't for a moment want to set up my opinion against yours, or against his, and of course if a line of policy is laid down for me I am prepared to act on it.' Kenyon, it seemed, did not share Gordon's objection to volunteers. Sailing dangerously close to the wind, since the funding of the expedition now depended very largely on Pennsylvania's good will, he added that he trusted the American 'may incline to share' Kenyon's view.

> Kenyon said that as regards the particular question of how far Mrs Keeling helps the expedition he was prepared to leave that to my judgement (and I'd like to say, Gordon, how very much I appreciate the reliance which both you and he have placed in me and the freedom of action which you have allowed: that has always been a great comfort) – but it is only fair to you at a distance that I should say something to you on the point.

Mrs Keeling's work in the 1925–6 season had consisted of making drawings of finds for the catalogue and for use in the press. Not enough, he conceded, for a regular paid assistant, but in the absence of Mrs Keeling, and without an architect or draughtsman assistant, he would have to do the work himself. Mallowan, who had been given the job of writing the catalogue entries, could not draw. There followed tributes to Katharine's work in showing visitors round, helping to keep the site house decent and comfortable, and other tasks which she undertook 'from the goodness of her heart'.

'Lastly, I do think that the presence of a lady has a good moral effect on the younger fellows in the camp and keeps them up to standard.' Woolley went on at unaccustomed length to portray the indebtedness of the expedition to Mrs Keeling, their almost universal regret were she to decide not to go out again for the 1926–7 season. Indeed, Mrs Keeling had proposed to go to India during the forthcoming season, and Woolley had talked her into 'very generously' reversing her decision only because her going would have compelled him to send Mallowan for drawing lessons, a fate which even Mrs Mallowan, 'who takes a keen interest in her son's work', felt it necessary to resist. To tell Mrs Keeling after all her kindness and generosity that she could not now go out to Ur would, he insisted, be an act of rudeness, 'which I should hate'.

Then, with lamentable casuistry, he took up the question of Mrs Keeling's honour. He said that he had delayed a reply on this score until going to Oxford at the end of July to address the British Association there. She, Katharine, was also in Oxford by coincidence, staying nearby with an old friend of hers, 'a trustee of the British Museum'. She was hurt to think that her name could be so talked about. For people such as she, engaged in work in which they are keenly interested, in a 'scientific atmosphere', it almost exceeded her, and his, powers of comprehension that such gossip should exist. Perhaps it was the price women still had to pay for taking part in serious scientific work. In a small community like theirs, discussion always centred on personalities. Nevertheless, it was all wrong.

> Since I am discussing a lady confidentially, I might go further
> and say that Mrs Keeling is nearly 40 and has been a widow for
> over 7 years and, as all her friends recognize, has no intention
> of re-marrying!

There was more special pleading, more protestations about the unsubstantiated word of American tourists, many of whom had not even visited Ur, all set against the inestimable worth of Mrs Keeling to the expedition. And then a postscript.

> Reading over the above I'm not sure that I have made it clear
> how distressed Mrs Keeling was to learn of these rumours. But
> I assured her, as I knew you'd wish me to do, that your letter
> (which of course she has not seen) was written by you in her

interest entirely and that apart from her interest you would not have paid any attention to such tales.

Although he was sometimes closer to allegory than literal truth in relating stories of his pre-war and wartime adventures, Woolley was no liar. His letter to Gordon was out of character and contained several untruths, not the least of them the suggestion that Gerturude Bell, who would have nothing to do with Mrs Keeling, approved of her presence at Ur. It is hard to resist the thought that Mrs Keeling was standing over him when he wrote it.

Other less personal concerns had to be dealt with before the new season's digging began. Dr Hall had asked him to revise proofs of a German obituary of Gertrude Bell, sent to the British Museum for checking. Was Miss Bell not responsible for the wartime seizure of the German antiquities from Samarra, left behind in Iraq when British troops invaded, the German writer asked, and was it not she who, after the war, made handsome reparation by inviting Dr Herzfeld to London to take a reasonable share back to Germany? Indeed, Gertrude had been involved in the matter, but it was her chief Sir Percy Cox who had insisted on sending the Samarra wares to London, and it was his successor A. T. Wilson who had brought Herzfeld, the great expert on Persian history, to London to take his pick. Woolley had lunched with the German professor and Wilson at Britannic House, the London headquarters of the Anglo-Persian Oil Company. But less than a year before, Lawrence, then in the RAF, had been asked by Kenyon to make recommendations about the disposal of the Samarra pottery, and he advised that the British Museum and the Victoria and Albert should share it between them. Neither museum was greatly enamoured of the haul it finally received. The best pieces went to Berlin. 'I wish I had seen Lawrence,' Woolley wrote to Hall, 'I haven't heard from him for a long time.' The two men would never meet again.

On 19 October 1926 Woolley was back in Iraq. He wrote to Gordon on arrival: 'Mallowan comes again as general assistant . . . Mrs Keeling, as I have already told you, comes out again an unpaid assistant.'

A letter on its way to him from Gordon, dated 5 October, read: 'I note that you have made your decision concerning the matter about which I wrote you in private and that you acted, as you believe, entirely in the interest of the Expedition. That interest is, of course, my only concern in the matter'. He went on to discuss the position of 'qualified' women on such expeditions. When suitably qualified he saw no reason why they should not be employed on the same terms as men.

As the new team began to settle in, Mallowan and Whitburn were given the pedestrian tasks reserved for junior assistants, such as showing visitors round the site. They quickly discovered that Woolley's strong sense of public relations had turned Ur into a tourist centre for the devout. The chief had, said Mallowan, chosen to 'bring to life the Old Testament'. There were, after all, still a lot of Bible readers in the world, and on the whole they were the ones who followed up Woolley's publicity efforts with expensive journeys to Ur-junction. Woolley perhaps carried things too far when he took charge of visitors and assured them as they made their way along neatly labelled New Street or Gay Street or Quiet Street, that 'these were the houses in which Abraham's family resided'. One such visitor was the wealthy British industrialist and fundamentalist Sir Charles Marston who gave lectures in his native Birmingham on the discoveries of Ur, citing Woolley on the proofs of Biblical history demonstrated by the excavations, and proudly displaying to the audience a small clay figure the archaeologist had given him. Ten years after going to Ur, Marston published his book *The Bible Comes Alive* in which he expressed his gratitude to Woolley for 'his wonderful work at Ur of the Chaldees'.

There were visitors from as far afield as Japan and Chile. King Albert of the Belgians appeared and breakfasted with the staff, to be taken round afterwards by Woolley who had already done several hours' work. Mallowan was to look back on his time with Woolley at the high-point of the excavation, when Hamoudi controlled hundreds of men from his hilltop eyrie, when all the world wanted to visit the site and see its splendours at first hand. Those who were there were never likely to forget the experience, he said. 'To him, Ur was no longer a deserted ruin, but alive and thronged with its former citizens. Woolley saw in his mind's eye every building, not as a derelict stump, but complete to the roof up, and in his imagination it was once again refurbished ... "Now take a look at that roof," he would say, as we stared up at the empty sky, "I know you can't see it, but we know everything about it that matters ..."' He was a persuasive money-raiser, and doubtless many such visitors made contributions to the digging fund.

In four years' intensive digging, sifting and translating from the cuneiform, a considerable body of evidence had been accumulated. If it did not exactly prove Biblical legend, it did nothing to disprove the notion that this might well have been the place from which Abraham and his family set forth for Canaan. What it did show most graphically was that the Sumerians had lived much the same lives as their Arab successors of the present day. They kept the same kinds of domestic animals, cooked and ate their food in much the same way, slept on similar beds and shopped in much the same sort of market place. Life had changed remarkably little in 5,000 years. But there was one dramatic difference. The Sumerians retained their graveyards for ceremonial burial. They buried the common dead under the floors of their homes. There was evidence that many were forced to move to new abodes when their basements became too crowded with the bodies of generations of their families. Terracotta pipes revealed the earliest, but far from primitive, drainage and domestic plumbing arrangements. The picture of Ur as a thriving city of the earliest historical period, bustling with creative and commercial activity, had become familiar to millions of newspaper and magazine readers the world over.

There was a moment of self-awareness, when Dr Walter Andrae, the German archaeologist of Assur, the old capital city of Assyria, paid a visit to Ur. Astonished by the scene of frantic activity which greeted him, he flung out his arms and exclaimed, 'This is anarchy! This is Bolshevism!' Woolley wrote to Hall to tell him of the visit: 'Venit, vidit, vici!' The visitor was soon in Woolley's favour. He saw how 'wrong it was to visit a new site with one's head full of prejudices'. Andrae later wrote Woolley a letter of praise, 'more than appreciative and very friendly'.

At the moment of world-wide public awareness of Ur of the Chaldees, Woolley decided that marriage was, after all, consonant with his devotion to field archaeology. He had apparently forgotten that only a year before he had told Dr Gordon that Mrs Keeling had no intention of re-marrying.

It was soon after Colonel Keeling's death that Woolley met Katharine for the first time and invited her to join him in Iraq. She had cut herself off from her own family, the Menkes. Indeed, when she married the Colonel the entry on her wedding certificate and in the official register read 'Meuke'.

Woolley's upbringing had conferred on him not the slightest ability to deal with women on any basis save one of distant

Above left: Rev. George Herbert Woolley and his wife Sarah with the younger children of the family, about 1896 (*Courtesy Mrs Margaret Witton*)

Above right: Leonard's younger brother, Lt G. Harold Woolley, VC, 1915 (*Courtesy Mr Warren Laxton*)

Woolley and T. E. Lawrence with relief sculpture at Carchemish, 1912 (*British Museum*)

Above left: Progenitor of the Carchemish dig, D. G. Hogarth,
Keeper of the Ashmolean

Above right: Carchemish: Haj Wahid at the site house doorway,
with Lawrence's "Assyrian" sculpture overhead (*British Museum*)

Work in progress on Nebuchadnezzar's Wall (*c* 600 BC), over Bur-Sin's palace
(*c* 1895 BC) (*Courtesy Mr Warren Laxton*)

Above left: Woolley at work before the Ur expedition
(*Courtesy Mr Warren Laxton*)

Above right: Katharine Woolley drawn by Kapp soon after her marriage to Woolley, 1928
(*Somerville College, Oxford*)

The Woolleys back-to-back at Ur, 1928
(*Courtesy Mr Warren Laxton*)

Carchemish 1912: *left to right* Dahoum, Abdal Salaam, foreman Gregori
and assistant foreman Hamoudi (*British Museum*)

Woolley in action at Ur, with Rev. Eric Burrows (*far left*)
unidentified assistant, Katharine and Hamoudi (*British Museum*)

Above left: Sidney Smith, Woolley's epigraphist-assistant 1922–3
(*British Museum*)

Above right: Woolley shows visitors the golden bull's head
from royal grave of Ur (*Courtesy Mrs Corbett Winder*)

Archaeologists and civil administrators on a river excursion:
standing, far left, Dr Legrain; with umbrella, Mrs Drower, wife of the British
legal adviser; seated, Miss Hunter, Katharine Keeling, Woolley
and Colonel Gore (*Courtesy Mrs Corbett Winder*)

F. G. Newton's reconstruction of the Ziggurat of Ur
(*British Museum*)

Isometric projection of the Ziggurat of Ur
(*British Museum*)

Max Mallowan and Agatha (Christie) with Woolley at Al Mina, 1947–8
(*Courtesy Mr John Mallowan and Collins Publishers*)

Above left: Hamoudi at the centre of the workforce at Alalakh (Atchana),
1947–8 (*Courtesy Mr Sinclair Hood*)

Above right: Harold Woolley and Edith Laxton visiting Leonard Woolley
at Sedgehill Manor, July 1957 (*Courtesy Mr Warren Laxton*)

Above: Leonard Woolley
examining a display
of jewellery from the
royal graves of Ur
at Philadelphia Museum,
University of Pennsylvania

Right: Woolley striding
from the British Museum,
1950s (*British Museum*)

enchantment. Several of his brothers and sisters were confirmed spinsters or bachelors, and those who married demonstrated a family incapacity for any kind of warmth or understanding in their relationships. The omens for marriage were not good, on his side or hers. Katharine Keeling, 37, attractive and, when the mood took her, vivacious, was also determined to the point of ruthlessness and incapable of physical intimacy. The inexperienced Woolley, at 46 years, was taken by storm. At moments when Mrs Keeling decided to exhibit charm and a very misleading sexuality, the most worldly men would eat from her hand. But it did not take the majority long to discover that she was calculating, mischievous and self-interested. Many men had been entranced by her and had drawn back just in time, or had been cast aside.

From the moment they went to Ur together in 1924, she dominated his life. Max Mallowan was to come to know her as well as anyone, and to say of her in retrospect, 'She had the power of entrancing those associated with her when she was in the mood, or on the contrary of creating a charged poisonous atmosphere; to live with her was to walk on a tightrope.'

As Woolley made the most fateful decision of his life, everything seemed to conspire to bring honour and fame his way. His broadcasts, which began at the end of the year, were an immediate success and gave a new dimension to the popularity of archaeology among the general public. His articles in *The Times* and *Illustrated London News* reinforced that popularity and his own renown. He vied with the great men of his profession, with Flinders Petrie and Arthur Evans, for public and academic attention. Several universities offered him appointments but he was always reluctant to tie himself to an employer. He liked the freelance role.

Ur was about to underscore all previous accomplishment. Before leaving for home and marriage in January he sent identical cables to Kenyon and Gordon. They said simply, 'Found prehistoric cemetery very rich in gold etc.' All was set for the most successful period of his professional life, and for the nadir of his personal existence.

They were married by Woolley's brother Harold at the village church of Monk Sherborne in the County of Hampshire on 11 April 1927. Harold, the VC priest, was by now as distinguished in his own way as his brother. The war was growing distant in the public mind but it was still close enough for military heroes to be accorded red-carpet treatment. After spells as a master at Rugby and chaplain at Harrow, Harold had taken the living of Monk Sherborne so that he could devote more time to his ailing wife and young family.

The gathering consisted almost entirely of Woolleys. Three nieces and a nephew accompanied the few adults who were in England at the time. There were no guests from Mrs Keeling's side. The marriage register was signed by Harold's wife Janet and Edith's husband, Matthew Laxton. From the moment of taking the marriage vows Katharine treated her new family with contumely. Harold's sermon was hardly over before she started to lay down to Leonard the conditions of their future life. As for the Woolley family, she told her husband they were not the kind of people with whom she intended to spend much time, and furthermore he would be well advised to keep them at arm's length. Leonard soon learnt that argument was of no avail. Katharine did not argue or discuss. She simply asserted her will and at the first suggestion of opposition she resorted to her life-long excuse for gaining her own way, a migraine attack. She would scream like an ill-behaved and dispossessed child until doctors were called and she was propped up in bed. Her husband would then have to massage her neck and shoulders for hours on end until sleep, or another tantrum, intervened. The couple spent their first night together at a London hotel, despite an invitation to stay at the rectory from Harold and his wife Janet Beatrix, an Orr-Ewing by birth and the widow of her husband's CO in the Somme battle, Captain George Culme-Seymour. On that first night of their marriage, Katharine made it clear that she would occupy a separate bedroom. He protested, naturally, and she responded by locking him in the bathroom where he remained for several hours while she hysterically extracted a promise that he would sleep in another room. It was a strange start to married life and Leonard's sister Edith, to whom he confided the details of his plight, was not hopeful of the success of the marriage. Within weeks there was talk of divorce, but it was quickly decided by a family that came together rarely but with considerable zeal when moral issues were at stake, that such a course was out of the question. His career would almost certainly be destroyed. More to the point, the family's moral standing would be endangered.

The gods of ancient Sumer seemed to speak with a thunderous voice at this time. Twelve days before the wedding Woolley had received a call from Kenyon telling him of the death of Dr Gordon. 'I know well that this Expedition, which to me seems all-important, is but a minor issue in the total of Dr Gordon's work for the

University Museum', Woolley wrote in a tribute sent to the Museum's new director. In fact, Ur meant more to Gordon than any other dig undertaken by that famous institution and it was ironic that he died only weeks before Woolley was able to realize the promise of his telegram by revealing some of the richest finds in the history of archaeology.

There was little time for reflection or regret, however. The wedding over, he had to return to Iraq. The journey out, by way of Cairo, would constitute the honeymoon, such as it was. He wired Baghdad, at Katharine's command, to tell Hamoudi to construct a new site house for their arrival. It was to be painted white, and Mrs Woolley's bedroom and bathroom suite were to adjoin her husband's room. Max Mallowan was put in charge of the arrangements, a swarm of workmen was appointed to the task, and the expedition at Ur awaited the arrival of the chief and his wife with bated breath.

The sixth season at Ur produced the most magnificent discoveries so far. The Arab workforce had become accomplished and reliable, 'altogether trustworthy', and Hamoudi and his two sons achieved remarkable feats of digging, removing and sifting hundreds of tons of earth.

'Our object was to get history,' Woolley wrote afterwards, 'not to fill museum cases with miscellaneous curios, and history could not be got unless both we and our men were duly trained.' Early on he had called a halt to digging in the area he called the 'golden trench' as his men were not equipped for the task. The early lessons he had learnt from MacIver in Egypt, of the need for patience and careful method, paid dividends. When he resumed work on the trench in 1927 spectacular finds of the most delicate workmanship were immediate.

Early trenching, designed to lead to the Temenos or sacred area within Nebuchadnezzar's walls, was laid down by guesswork. It turned out that for most of its length the trench lay within the Temenos. They had hoped to find late Babylonian structures which would have been built on top of older buildings. There were no such structures, however, and so Woolley deepened the trench where he thought they should have been. Rich finds of pottery, bronze and ceramic and stone beads began to appear. Hamoudi was told to reward his men well. *Bakhsheesh* was essential if important artifacts were not to disappear from the site. A harvest of gold beads demonstrated Woolley's good commercial sense. After a few days they realized that they were digging across a cemetery. Then it became apparent that there were, in fact, *two* cemeteries sectioned within the trench, one above the other. The upper graves, dated by cylinder seals found within, belonged to the period of Sargon of Akkad c.2100 BC. Those below them, dug into rubbish mounds which lay just outside the sacred precincts, were labelled 'Royal Cemetery', stretching back into the previous millennium. Burials were of two distinct kinds, graves of ordinary folk and tombs of rulers and princes. Of the former, two thousand were cleared; of the latter, sixteen were in reasonable preservation and were investigated. By the following year, Ur had become fixed in the public mind as 'Abraham's city', and its story had overtaken even the history and legends of the heretical pharaohs and the warrior peoples of Crete and Mycenae. At the end of the 1927 season, newspapers and magazines the world over were full of reports of 'miracles' of the goldsmith's art dating back 5500 years. Among the first was a dagger and sheath, 'the season's crowning reward' in all its colourful beauty. The hilt was of one piece, deep-blue lapis lazuli studded with gold, the blade burnished gold, the sheath solid gold, its front intricately carved in filigree. It was one of the oldest examples of its kind ever found, 'a marvel of design and workmanship', said Woolley. Then came the equally spectacular 'gold wig' of king Meskalamdug from one of the sixteen royal graves. Inevitably, Woolley's statements to the press compared it to the gold mask of Tutankhamen, and it was, after all, 'some two thousand years earlier'. Egypt, said his assistant Mallowan, was always his 'bugbear'. Still, the 'wig' stood in its own right, a headpiece of hammered and engraved gold, life-size and therefore meant to be worn, with holes round the rim for a lining. Perhaps it was a ceremonial headdress, perhaps a helmet. 'The workmanship is admirable and reflects the greatest credit on the goldsmiths of the fourth millennium BC,' said Woolley. He added characteristically: 'This technical skill at so early a date is far more important than the mere richness of the material.' The graves had begun to divulge untold riches. There was a perfect bowl of fluted gold from the same grave. Its decoration contrasted with the simplicity of further finds, drinking bowls, and a lamp found inside Meskalamdug's coffin. The drinking vessels all bore the name of the king, and the legend 'good hero of the land', echoing the god-king status of the heroes of the Gilgamesh epic and the antediluvian story of the Deluge, which came down from Sumer through Babylon and the Greeks. Perhaps the most delightful find of the season was a tiny gold figure of a monkey forming the head of a pin. It demonstrated the remarkable skills attained in metalwork at the dawn of civilization, and something of the fauna of the region. Beautifully moulded in solid gold it measured only five eighths of an inch in height. Woolley was able to give vent to that strong sense of design and craftsmanship which had developed in his youth when he spent endless hours in the Whitechapel Gallery, admiring the masters of his own country and learning from them. Yet it was in the bronze pieces found at this time that the greatest technical feats were apparent. Perfectly formed, they were clearly the products of 'lost wax' casting, that most complex of all metal casting processes, still in the 20th century AD the supreme method of making bronze figures, and seen at Ur to have been mastered in all its complexity by the first urban men.

The following season saw the culmination of the long, careful excavation of the royal graves. 'Unrecorded barbarities' at the royal burials of 3000 BC made headline news everywhere. Woolley's notes were calmly academic. The subsequent presentation of the finds in his own great book on Ur was balanced, if tending always to push a little further into unrecorded time than the evidence strictly speaking permitted. Provision made for the dead seemed to imply a belief in some kind of afterlife. But nothing was found to define such a belief scientifically. No figures of gods, no symbols or ornaments which could truthfully be said to have 'religious' significance. The dead took with them the things they thought might be needed on that journey to another place, but there was nothing to tell what or where the people of Ur imagined that place to be.

Then came adjoining tomb-chambers, one behind the other. The first was the king's chamber, the second the resting place of the queen, Pu-abi.

The evolution of the story which followed was carefully traced. First five bodies were found side by side in a trench. The mere fact of their being present in such a number was unusual. Below them was matting, and tracing this along they came to another group of bodies, ten women arranged in rows, with headdresses of lapis lazuli, gold and carnelian, and elaborate necklaces. But no tomb furnishings appeared. At the end of the row of women a wonderful lyre was discovered: its woodwork was decayed but by careful restoration it was seen to consist of an upright wooden beam capped with gold, the strings secured by gold-headed nails, and a sounding-box edged with mosaic of redstone, lapis and white shell; from the front projected the head of a bull in wrought gold with eyes and beard of lapis. Across the lyre rested the skeleton of the musician who played it.

Queen Pu-abi (Shub-ad in Woolley's original notes), lay on a wooden bier at one end of the intact tomb. At the other end were piled offerings, covered with the fallen wreckage of the centuries. Her headdress, worn originally over a golden wig such as had been found in another grave, consisted of coil after coil of gold ribbon. Across the forehead was a frontispiece of lapis and carnelian beads from which hung rings of gold. Higher on the head was a wreath of mulberry leaves, and another of different leaves with large gold flowers between them, the petals inlaid with lapis and white shell. It was an incredible sight. Enormous gold earrings, a great gold comb, the cloak fixed to one shoulder with three gold pins with lapis heads, and amulets of gold and lapis fish, a reclining calf, two antelopes. By the side of the bier a second crown. And more ornaments, palmettes and flowers, ears of corn, clusters of pomegranates, stags and rams, antelopes and bearded bulls. There were more gold bowls, plain, fluted and engraved. There was a gold strainer, gold and silver cockleshells containing make-up paints, gold finger rings, a mass of copper objects – an Aladdin's Cave to compete with the tomb of Tutankhamen. It was, though, only the beginning of the discovery of the 1927–28 season.

They had been digging two adjacent pits, with the queen's tomb-chamber sunk below the level of her grave pit. They were able to follow now the ritual as well as the architecture of the royal tombs. The king had died first. The queen, wishing to be buried alongside him, had caused the grave-diggers to reopen the king's shaft and dig down to the chamber vault where the unimaginable riches of the king's burial furnishings lay. They then dug down from the back of the chamber to form a pit in which the queen's stone tomb was built. The queen had been buried with her court ladies and the riches of her tomb were great – but nothing like those of the king's chamber. The workmen broke through the arched brickwork which separated the vault from the chamber, carried off the royal treasures, and placed the enormous clothes-chest of the queen over the hole they had made to conceal their deed.

Gradually a picture dawned on the excavators of a death ritual so far unknown and unimagined. Reconstruction of bones and wood and metal demonstrated a scene of human and animal sacrifice accompanying the burial of the king.

'No less remarkable than the objects found last winter in the royal graves at Ur,' he wrote in June 1928, 'was the discovery of the rites of human sacrifice which accompanied the burial of a king. In all the literature of Babylonia there is no hint of any such custom as having been practised at any time ... But now we have definite proof that in the fourth millennium before Christ the Sumerian king went to his tomb in company with a whole following of soldiers, courtiers and women, who, like the vases of food and drink, the weapons and tools set in his grave, should minister to his needs and pleasures in another world.'

In 1929 he published a preliminary version of what was to become the most widely read book ever on an archaeological subject. *Ur of the Chaldees* went through eight impressions in its first six years; a mass-readership paperback was followed by a second expanded hardback edition, and that went into three impressions; then came a new and definitive version edited by a modern-day scholar of his old workplace the Ashmolean. The story deriving from the excavation of the royal death pits was to bring Woolley fame and wealth at a moment of disaster in his personal life.

His own words best describe the drama of the Sumerian royal burial:

Down into the open pit, with its mat-covered floor and mat-lined walls, empty and unfurnished, there comes a procession of people, the members of the dead ruler's court, soldiers, men-servants, and women, the latter in their finery of brightly coloured garments and head-dresses of carnelian and lapis lazuli, silver and gold, officers with the insignia of their rank, musicians bearing harps or lyres, and then, driven or backed down the slope, the chariots drawn by oxen, the drivers in the cars, the grooms holding the heads of the draught animals, and all take up their allotted places at the bottom of the shaft and finally a guard of soldiers forms up at the entrance. Each man and woman brought a little cup of clay or stone or metal, the equipment needed for the rite that was to follow. There would seem to have been some kind of service down there, at least it is certain that the musicians played up to the last, then each of them drank from their cups a potion that they had brought with them or found prepared for them on the spot – in one case we

found in the middle of the pit a great copper pot into which
they could have dipped – and they lay down and composed
themselves for death. Somebody came down and killed the
animals (we found their bones on top of those of the grooms,
so they must have died later) and perhaps saw to it that all was
decently in order – thus, in the king's grave the lyres had been
placed on the top of the bodies of the women players, leant
against the tomb wall – and when that was done, earth was
flung from above, over the unconscious victims, and the filling-
in of the grave-shaft was begun.

Gradually the vast site was dug through from the top strata of the
neo-Babylonian kings Nebuchadnezzar and Nabonidus to the ultimate level. As the drama of Ur unfolded, Katharine had become an
omnipresent member of the cast, demanding, unyielding, dictatorial.
Woolley deferred to her in almost every matter, professional and
personal, and because she was an accomplished artist she justified
her presence. She had filled her time at Ur with activities other than
drawing, however. She often retired to her room to write, though it
was generally assumed that she nursed a headache. At the start of
the 1928–9 season, she announced to the surprise of everyone at the
site that her first book was about to be published. It came out in the
following year, published by John Murray in London, and seeming
to owe a lot in inspiration and method to Agatha Christie. A
psychologist might make a substantial thesis out of a book written
by a gifted, sexless woman, with the inappropriate title *Adventure
Calls* (it contained no suggestion of adventure).

Perhaps there was biographical content, or perhaps nothing more
than the meanderings of a would-be imaginative writer, in a story
whose heroine (a girl named Colin) masquerades as a male and is
finally captured by romance.

> 'Look at me, Colin dearest. You are the most truthful woman
> in the world – tell me if there's any chance for me! I'll always
> love you, whatever your answer, but I must know if there's a
> glimmer of hope for me.'
> 'A glimmer of hope! Oh, Stanhope – can't you see all the
> stars in their courses shining down on you as on our last ride?'
> And her eyes were like stars as they filled with happy tears.

Dedicated unidentifiably to 'C and C and John in fulfilment of a
threat!', it was her first and last book. Whatever its merits, it offers

some evidence of an unspoken yearning – of a void created as much by her own nature as by the qualities of the men she married.

By 1929 Woolley had decided that the royal graves came before, but only just before, the First Dynasty of Ur. That would take them into the fourth millennium, to the pre-dynastic period known as Jamdat Nasr, or perhaps beyond that to Al-Ubaid, before the beginning of the Bronze Age; the 'Late Prehistoric'. He decided to dig deeper. A shaft about 5 feet square was dug below the level of the graves. Decomposed mudbrick, ashes, broken pottery – the usual deposits beneath ancient graves – came to the surface. Suddenly it all stopped. No more rubbish appeared. 'Only,' he wrote, 'clean water-laid mud.' Woolley was surprised. He had expected to find virgin soil, for he had assumed that Ur was built on a low mound rising just above the surrounding swampy land. 'I do not like having my theories upset by anything less than proof,' he noted. He told the workmen to go on digging through the soil. Suddenly, at eight feet, flint implements began to appear. Then fragments of painted al-Ubaid pottery. By the time he had written up his notes, Woolley was convinced of what he had discovered, but he dared not say the word. 'I brought up two of my staff and, after pointing out the facts, asked for their explanation. They did not know what to say. My wife came along and looked and was asked the same question, and she turned away remarking casually, "Well, of course, it's the Flood." That was the right answer.'

It was an answer that Woolley would make the best of as the world began to tire, temporarily at least, of the tombs of the Valley of the Kings, and to turn its full attention to Ur.

Another youngster arrived at the start of the 1930 season, soon to make his mark as man and archaeologist. He was the gentle, self-effacing Scot, John Rose, Whitburn's replacement (Archie Whitburn had decided to return to his first love, architecture).

Rose's work as an architectural draughtsman made sense of the intricate brickwork of the ziggurat which had undergone so many major changes of structure and design during the thousands of years that it dominated the region.

Excavation went on until 1934, the stimulus and almost constant excitement of archaeological discovery interspersed with new squabbles among academics and workforce that were due almost entirely to the intervention of Katharine. The burden on Woolley himself, of completing and recording the dig conscienciously while ministering to his wife's insistent demands, was great. But the rewards too were immense. In the final seasons of a dig which lasted for twelve seasons altogether, yet more astonishing relics were found. A pair of statues, which he called 'ram caught in thicket' represented a masterpiece of Sumerian art, made of gold, lapis lazuli, and white shell over a wooden core. The rams stood on their hind legs, forelegs caught in a thicket whose golden stems and flowers were in themselves of breathtaking beauty. The sight of them as they emerged from the earth 'was one to reward us for any amount of work', said Woolley. 'No such monument of Sumerian craftsmanship had ever before come into our hands.'

'Murder in Mesopotamia'

I fell in love with Ur, with its beauty in the evenings, the ziggurat standing up, faintly shadowed, and that wide area of sand with its lovely pale colours of apricot, rose, blue and mauve changing every minute . . . The lure of the past came up to grab me . . . The carefulness of lifting pots and objects from the soil filled me with a longing to be an archaeologist myself. How unfortunate it was, I thought, that I had always led such a frivolous life.

Agatha Christie, An Autobiography

What a scene Ur must have presented to the many visitors who came from far and wide year after year to be taken, if they were lucky by Woolley, if not by one of his assistants, up the stairway of the ziggurat, through the streets and market-places and palaces of this most antique of cities. The majority were wealthy Christians and Jews, anxious to see at first hand the gold-enriched tombs of third-millennium kings and queens, the putative birthplace of the patriarch Abraham about which they had read in their newspapers and magazines.

But there was more to Ur than its excavated remains, its history and allegory. In Woolley's time it was a living workplace. The work as it proceeded became a ballet of the desert, choreographed by Woolley and conducted by the remarkable Hamoudi. Hundreds of workmen in well-organized gangs laboured in the trenches, on the great palace walls, and in the distance, beyond the city limits, on the vast dynastic and prehistoric burial site which generations of citizens had turned into a mighty rubbish tip. As the men toiled, Hamoudi dominated from on high, always choosing a point where he could oversee his men, flapping his arms like an eagle, 'like a proud eagle

ready to swoop on his prey', cajoling, ridiculing, laughing, sympa-
thizing. 'To command,' said Hamoudi, 'a man must be loved and
feared.' He was a dynamo, recharged by Woolley at intervals, who
gave his energy to others out of astonishing loyalty and devotion to
his employer. Yet he never pushed a man too far. He had no
favourites among the workmen, most of whom came from the
marshy region on the other side of the river. All were treated alike
to his wit, his invective and his charm. And when the men tired he
would burst into song and suddenly take on the role of boatman as
he used his spade to make the movements of a punt-pole, and the
evening air resounded to the chants of the men as they swayed in
rhythmic imitation of a night journey through the marshes in their
long swift skiffs.

Hamoudi was once asked what accounted for the rare understanding between him and Woolley. The Arab replied simply, 'We have
broken much bread together.'

Another observer who arrived on the scene as the excavations
were drawing to a close was Mr C. F. Taylor, master at Clifton
College. He travelled with two friends, Matthews and Sanderson,
and he left in a daily journal a graphic account of the rail journey by
'sleeper' from Basra to Ur, 'bedclothes have a way of collecting into
a ball so that your middle is sweltering under blankets about 1 foot
deep while your toes and shoulders catch at the edge of a seat.' And
on to Woolley's Ur: '. . . we have already caught sight of the Ziggurat
almost red-roofed in the early light rising above what we afterwards
discovered were Woolley's dumps.' There was a rest house at the
station, presided over by a kindly old Indian, where a life-saving cup
of tea and English breakfast were provided. Woolley promised 'an
apology for a motor car' but it failed to turn up. The three men
walked along the rail track, about a mile and a half, in bitterly cold
weather.

> Woolley comes out of his house (built and paved with Sumerian
> and Babylonian bricks and roofed in traditional Sumerian
> fashion with matting, reeds, earth and mud) his monkey face
> rather tired and worried, for Mrs W. is ill, but very gracious
> and ready to take us off in a few minutes to see the work.

There was a description of the men at work, clearing chambers and
walls at the east corner of the ziggurat. Spades, with crossbars for
the digging foot to rest on, were in use, with army trenching tools
for more skilled work, and Taylor told how Hamoudi's men

sometimes varied the words of their songs as they chanted verses which began with lines such as, 'His (W's) eyes are on us even in London . . .' (and, in unison with working men everywhere) 'Our wages are less this week than last.'

> . . . we saw the variously dated walls enclosing the Ziggurat, the 'palm tree' column which disposes of the belief that the column was unknown in Mesopotamian architecture, the royal tombs, King Dungi's with his horse (after death) above, the altar with six channels before it, along which dribbled sweet-scented oils and then fell into the six saucer-like cavities in which they found wood ash, showing that they were for burning, the fine outer wall of King Dungi's building, the death pit . . . the 'flood' pit where they dug down through strata to a band of silt deposited by 'the' flood and to 'inhabited' strata below. W. picked up a piece of pre-Noah pottery and gave it to H. N. [Matthews] . . .

After lunch the architect A. E. F. Gott, Rose's successor, and the latest assistant, Murray Thriepland, took them to see Nebuchadnez-zar's temple and then to the top of the ziggurat, from where they could see only endless desert interrupted by the railway station and two distant mounds. They photographed the ziggurat, the brickwork 'of a fine yellow in the low rays of the sun', as the workmen went home from the day's labours, stopping on the way at the site house where Thriepland attended to their ailments – 'toothache, a sore toe, a boil on the nose'. There were bonuses for the men who brought small finds with them, 'a fragment of a diorite statue, a nail about 2 inches wide and 4 or 5 long inscribed with a builder's dedication, a piece of obsidian (from the Caucasus) and so on.'

Katharine's advent at Ur changed everything. From the first, her capricious and dominating personality threw the expedition into a state of perpetual, petty disagreement. She was an accomplished artist and it is an accepted fact that she quickly proved a useful member of the team. One of her earliest and most accomplished contributions was a bronze bust of Hamoudi. It was a fine study and showed that her artistic talent was both real and broadly based. She made excellent line-drawings of the tools and weapons found in the palaces, the tombs and ordinary houses of Ur. And she was included in just about every site photograph taken after the start of the 1927 season, disporting herself in carefully contrived poses that would have done justice to the pages of any fashion magazine, her shapely legs always prominently displayed.

Woolley himself was a changed man. His astonishing capacity for work – he still went to bed in the early hours of the morning after sorting through the day's finds and making notes on them, and keeping up to date with his mounting literary commissions – was inevitably affected by the demands of his determined wife. Yet he was loyal to her, not only in the first difficult months of marriage but for the rest of their life together, though she seldom compromised with him and was never to permit him entry to the marital bed. Her insistent demands would have taxed the resources of a saint. 'She needed a man to look after her, but was not intended for the physical side of matrimony,' Mallowan declared, adding that she was 'opinionated and Teutonic in overriding contrary opinion, ultra-sensitive and ready to take offence'. Even the Arab workmen, to whom all women were necessarily subordinate beings, were afraid of her. When Hamoudi was away, as was sometimes inevitably the case, they argued among themselves and engaged in bouts of tribal warfare. But the mere sight of Katharine Woolley was enough to send them scurrying for cover.

Mallowan, as one of the most junior members of the staff, was assigned the duties of camp medical officer among other menial tasks, before the arrival of Murray Thriepland as the 'junior'. Thus fell to him the responsibility of acting as chief masseur to Katharine, whose recurrent headaches ensured that he spent most of his time assuaging the alleged muscle pain that followed her attacks. Between times he had to apply leeches to her forehead, a doctor having prescribed a certain amount of blood-letting as a remedy for her 'head' trouble.

It was Mallowan, too, who noted the effect of her presence on Woolley himself. Always amiable and polite, and usually genial, Woolley was also capable of being a tyrant he said, the more so after his marriage, and if a senior member of the expedition staff made a suggestion which ran counter to his own ideas he would say invariably: 'The Trustees would never allow that.' Later in life Mallowan became a Trustee of the British Museum, an experience which convinced him utterly that the Trustees would not have 'given a damn', though he felt at the time that it would be indiscreet to say so. Woolley's studied politeness became even more pronounced when Katharine arrived on the scene. He still worked as hard and as long as in the past, but now even his mental and physical resources were sapped by her demanding, unequivocal presence. When he eventually reached his bed, sited in the room next to Katharine's, he was often too tired to be roused by a normal call for help. Since Katharine almost always needed attention in the night, it was arranged that a string should be tied to his big toe and fed to Katharine's room so that she could tug at it when his services were required. The nearest doctor was two hours' journey away in Nasiriya and as there was no telephone connection he was called only in the direst emergency.

After many a sleepless night, Woolley would be digging with the men half an hour after sunrise, the obligatory start to the working day. Mallowan modified his judgement: Leonard Woolley could be a tyrant, but he was 'fair and never asked of a member of his staff or workforce what he could not or would not do himself.' Then again, he said that both Woolley and his wife were snobs, and that to some extent they deserved each other. That was perhaps a harsh judgement on Woolley. Fastidious he certainly was, and he did not easily tolerate fools or ill-mannered companions. But the hauteur which he sometimes exhibited after his marriage was surely an attempt, however feeble in concept, to placate Katharine whose snobbery was so inveterate that she could hardly bring herself to speak to some of the most distinguished academics and statesmen of her day, though she got on well enough with wealthy visitors to the site to extract large donations from some of them to help finance a dig that had almost exhausted its sponsors.

Mallowan made one surprising claim. In commenting on Katharine's influence, he said that there was no room for any other woman on the site and that the Woolleys 'wisely saw to it that there never was one'. Surprising, because another woman who was to play a very important part indeed in Max Mallowan's life appeared soon after Katharine's advent as 'Mrs Woolley'.

The Early Dynastic death pit of Ur still stirred the public imagination when Agatha Christie arrived in Mesopotamia in the late autumn of 1928. Already famous for her detective novels and mystery writings, she had achieved international notoriety two years before when she disappeared with a suddenness and completeness which would have done justice to any of the characters of her detective stories. Her much publicized disappearance, and subsequent discovery at a hotel in Harrogate in the north of England, was soon followed by divorce proceedings against her husband Colonel Christie and it was while she waited for the decree to be made absolute that she decided to take a much needed holiday abroad. She booked a passage to the

West Indies. Then she read Woolley's latest article in the *Illustrated London News* telling of the death rituals and the spectacular finds of ancient art at 'Ur of the Chaldees'. She promptly cancelled her trip to the Carribbean and caught the Orient Express to Stamboul. Thence Baghdad, and the single-track rail ride to Ur.

Katharine had just finished reading Agatha's *The Murder of Roger Ackroyd*, and awaited her with open arms. The welcome was warm and sincere but it was short-lived. The 38-year-old Agatha's fame had not affected her. She was modest, retiring, and attractive for all the qualities that Katharine Woolley lacked. She observed the imperious Katharine with a writer's regard for detail, and at times she was positively in awe of her.

Woolley himself spent most of his time at this period sifting through the remains of the royal tombs and digging down to 'Ubaid' level beneath the 'Flood' deposit, excitedly classifying painted pottery of the early third millennium BC. There was little time for socializing but he liked Agatha on brief acquaintance. The visitor was impressed by the host whose articles she had devoured when they appeared in the press. And she soon began to form in her mind the outline of a plot for a future work based on this encounter.

Archie Whitburn, who at the time of Agatha's arrival was working at his reconstruction drawings of the palaces and graves, was able to show the visitor the sights, and it was he who later on crystallized in the writer's mind the image of Katharine as an ambitious wife who drove her archaeologist husband to murder. Woolley himself took her round the housing quarter and brought to life for her the neatly laid-out streets with their houses and schools and markets, scenes which, she agreed, would have been familiar to the youthful Abraham. Agatha wanted to be home by Christmas 1928 and she left Ur in October, pressed by the Woolleys to return the following year.

No sooner had she left than another important visitor arrived, Woolley's early mentor Aurel Stein. The explorer and archaeologist of India, Kashmir, Afghanistan and Turkestan, whose finds Woolley had classified in the British Museum some twenty years before, was now on the trail of Alexander the Great, diverting from Basra on his journey to Karachi to meet Woolley. After his four-day visit, he wrote to his friend 'Publius', Sir Percy Stafford Allen the President of Corpus Christi:

> All Woolley had to show me was full of interest from the big
> storied ziggurat down to the tombs he had succeeded in clearing

to a depth of over 30 ft. His work is thorough, capable and guided by an intuitive knowledge one expects in his case and he has fully deserved his rich harvests. All his results have been achieved with a minimum of staff.

Stein went on to Eridu, the place which according to Sumerian tradition stood before the Flood. Stein observed that it still awaited proper excavation. Perhaps with tongue in cheek, he added '. . . as it is some 15 miles away from water, Mrs Woolley suggested it might suit me . . .' He went on from there to join the Germans at Warka, ancient Uruk, and commented on their immaculate methods, adding: 'But somehow Woolley's improvisation and grasp of opportunities appeals more to my taste.'

Much of Woolley's time at this juncture was taken up by correspondence with Dr Hall who was preparing a long article for a new magazine, *Antiquity*, founded in 1927 by a man Woolley had come to know well, Stanhope Crawford, a genial bachelor who was quick to see the need for a professional journal which reflected twentieth-century progress in scientific exploration of the past. Crawford had worked in the Sudan with Reisner, and owed his archaeological training to Flinders Petrie. He came to regard Woolley as the great exemplar of the digger's craft. His first issue expressed the regret of antiquarians the world over at the fact that the celebrated 'dagger-grave', the richest of all Woolley's finds, had been left unfinished in the 1926–27 season, its treasure lying in confusion, flung into the shaft of the grave as it was filled by the gravediggers of 5000 years ago. 'Even now we have not reached the grave level proper, and may at any moment light upon something more important than anything yet discovered.'

Burrows had contracted jaundice in the 1926–27 season, and no sooner had he begun to recover from that debilitating condition than he was stricken with dysentery. He went to Philadelphia to convalesce and work on inscriptions, while Woolley was forced to cope with his own epigraphy, reading the ancient Akkadian inscriptions of the tablets and bricks with patent difficulty, aided by a powerful magnifying glass and a syllabary left behind by Burrows.

In a letter to Hall, Woolley had spoken of 'hundreds, perhaps thousands' of cuneiform documents. Hall corrected him for using 'an unduly loose expression'. He thought 'Perhaps hundreds' a better way of putting it. 'Implies less,' replied Woolley laconically, wearing a hat that would have looked perfectly harmonious in Fleet Street.

In much the same vein, Woolley wrote to the pedantic Hall in January 1927: 'Our tombs are remarkable. Burrows being away, I am not in a position to say anything really, but yesterday in a rich tomb we got a cylinder seal with an inscription which to my untutored eye looks devilish like the name of a prehistoric king of Ur! The tombs go back well beyond the first dynasty of Ur.' There had been rumours that the funds of the University of Pennsylvania were running low as the result of its immense outlay on this and other excavations in Egypt and Iraq, and that the Ur crew might have to curtail its current season while further funding was sought. The substantial donations Woolley had been able to squeeze from visiting royalty and industrialists had, however, helped to stave off the threat. 'Thank the Lord we shan't have to close down as early as I feared,' he told Hall. When the dig eventually closed for the 'hot season', Woolley was able to devote more time to the learned debates that were issuing from his discoveries.

The dating of the pre-dynastic finds was always contentious, as was the vexed use of the term 'Semitic' in defining the peoples and language of the region of Sumer and Akkad, and their Arab and Hebrew successors. One distinguished scholar, A. B. Cook, Reader in Classical Archaeology at Cambridge, had asserted in the *Cambridge Ancient History* that the word was safe only when used linguistically. Woolley pointed out that its use was essentially racial and that criticism had only arisen because of its 'very base use in racial denunciation'. Sir Arthur Keith the anthropologist had added his weight to Woolley's argument. He was working with Woolley and Hall on an account of the Ubaid period, and Woolley wrote:

> . . . if an authority like Keith chooses to go back to the racial term and pins it down to a particular semitic-speaking stock which he can isolate on anthropological grounds, I don't see that there can be any valid objection: after all, there must have been Semites or there would be no 'Semitic speech', and if he identifies them, well and good. Such arguments as Cooke [sic] advances are against the current abuse of the term, not against any use of it.

R. S. Cooke, Adviser to the Iraq Ministry of Pious Bequests, played an increasingly vital role in the affairs of the Ur expedition. In December 1927, Hall wrote to Woolley to say that Cooke was demanding the return of objects sent to London but claimed by Baghdad. 'Regards to Mrs Woolley . . . Have a good Christmas,' he added resignedly.

The 1928 season passed in the same flurry of activity and debate, excavation work in the daytime giving way to intense sifting, noting and writing work in the evenings, interrupted at intervals by the need to attend to Katharine's aches and pains and material needs. He had contributed long and detailed articles to the *Antiquaries Journal* on every season's work so far, he was now completing his book on the Sumerians for the Clarendon Press, writing regularly for *The Times* and the *Illustrated London News*, preparing a series of radio talks for the BBC, putting the finishing touches to his first draft of *Ur of the Chaldees*, and responding to Crawford's pleas for more and more articles for *Antiquity*. When assistants asked him how he found time for it all, he replied that writing was not a difficult task for him, 'more a relaxation'.

In the late summer of 1927 he and Katharine spent a fortnight in France where he relaxed while composing an illustrated article for Mee's *Encyclopaedia*. On the journey out for the start of the 1928 season he stopped off at Copenhagen with Katharine to deliver a lecture there. When he arrived at Beirut another illustrated talk had been arranged. In Baghdad he gave yet another full-scale lecture. The impact of the Ur discoveries was beginning to hit home. Everywhere he went now, talks and personal appearances were demanded. He was seldom unwilling, or unequal to the challenge. The importance of publicity was never lost on him. Archaeologists, he often remarked in defence of his promotional activities, never had enough money for their work.

Chronology came to the fore again in March 1928 when the date of the royal graves came under discussion in the professional press. 'The oldest is considered by Mr Woolley to belong to about 3,500 BC, and he regards this date as a conservative one,' wrote Crawford in *Antiquity*. More academic debate followed the next revelation in that journal. 'Most startling of all, grave 580 contains fragments of wrought iron.' Was it possible that the Iron Age, the most recent of the periods defined by metal usage in conventional archaeology, in fact preceded the Bronze Age; even the Copper or Chalcolithic Age? Argument in the academic world was intense. Hall, the erudite head of department at the British Museum, entered the fray on Woolley's side. So did the much respected A. H. Sayce of Oxford.

Woolley was impatient of criticism that his date for the royal necropolis was too early. '. . . the difference of a hundred years or so

Chronology of the Ancient World

Year	General	Rome	Greece	Palestine/Syria	Anatolia
4000	LATE NEOLITHIC	LATE NEOLITHIC	LATE NEOLITHIC	LATE NEOLITHIC	LATE NEOLITHIC
3500				Proto-historic CHALCOLITHIC	CHALCOLITHIC
				EARLY BRONZE	
3000			CHALCOLITHIC Early Minoan I Early Minoan II	Proto-urban Proto-Syrian	
2500			EARLY BRONZE Early Minoan III Middle Minoan I	Semitic speech	EARLY BRONZE
2000	EUROPEAN BRONZE AGE		MIDDLE BRONZE Middle Minoan II Proto-Palatial First Greeks Mycenaean shaft graves	MIDDLE BRONZE Disruption	Assyrians in Cappadocia Indo-Europeans MIDDLE BRONZE Old Hittite Kingdom Alalakh Yarim-Lim
1500	MID BRONZE EUROPE LATE BRONZE		LATE BRONZE Late Minoan I Late Minoan II Mid Mycenaean Late Minoan III Trojan war Sea Peoples	LATE BRONZE Hyksos Habiru Philistines	Hittite Empire Sea Peoples Phrygians
1000	ATLANTIC BRONZE IRON AGE EUROPE	Rome founded	IRON AGE Lycurgus of Sparta 1st Olympiad (776) Solon at Athens (550)	IRON AGE Israel, Homeric legends Solomon Assyrian invasion (722) Fall of Jerusalem (586) Exile	Cimmerians Urartu Caria Lydia Assyrian Achemenid (Persian)
500	Rome conquers Gaul	Etruscan tombs Gallic invasion Punic wars Conquest of Greece	Marathon Herodotus Alexander to India Roman	Sack of Jerusalem Ptolemaic/Seleucid Roman	Seleucid Roman
0		Triumvirate Empire Hadrian Goths Constantine		Herod Destruction of Jerusalem	
500					

Iran	Assyria	Sumer/Akkad/Babylon	Egypt	
		HASSUNA		4000
LATE NEOLITHIC	LATE NEOLITHIC	Harlaf		
			Amratian/Naqada I	
		Ubaid		
		LATE PREHISTORIC		
			Naqada II	
		Uruk	Gerzean	3500
CHALCOLITHIC	CHALCOLITHIC	First Writing	CHALCOLITHIC	
		CHALCOLITHIC		
		EARLY BRONZE		
EARLY BRONZE Susa				
Proto-Elamite		Jamdat Nasr		
	EARLY BRONZE	EARLY DYNASTIC/Sumer	EARLY DYNASTIC	3000
		First Dynasty Ur	Solar calendar	
		?Maskalumdug		
		?Mesannepadda		
		Gilgamesh	OLD KINGDOM	
Sumero-Elamite		Royal Graves of Ur	3rd Dynasty	
			Memphite/Cheops	2500
		Akkad/Sargon		
		Eudeg/Sumer revival		
	Old Assyria	Third Dynasty Ur		
	38 kings of unknown date	Ur-Nammu	FIRST INTERMEDIATE PERIOD	
	Shamsi-Adad I		7th Dynasty/Theban	2000
MIDDLE BRONZE	26 kings	Old Babylonian	MIDDLE KINGDOM	
		Hammurabi	11th Dynasty	
		Hittites	SECOND INTERMEDIATE PERIOD	
		Kassites	Hyksos 13th Dynasty	
			NEW KINGDOM	
			18th Dynasty	1500
		LATE BRONZE	Amarna period	
LATE BRONZE			Tutankhamen	
Choga Zanbil			Sea Peoples	
Middle Elamite	Tiglath-pileser I	2nd Dynasty of Isin	21st Dynasty	
Indo-Europeans		2nd Dynasty of Sealand		
IRON AGE		Elamite		1000
Neo-Elamite				
Median	Sargonid	Assyrian conquest	SAITE PERIOD	
Assyrian		Neo-Babylonian	26th Dynasty	
Cyrus/Pasargade	Destruction of Nineveh			
Darius/Persepolis	Persian rule	Persian rule (539)	Persian rule	
Achaememid			LATE PERIOD	500
Seleucid	Seleucid	Seleucid	Ptolemaic	
			27–31 Dynasties	
		Macedonian conquest		
Parthian	Parthian	Parthian	Roman	
			Cleopatra	0
Sassanian	Sassanian	Sassanian		
			Coptic ascendancy	
				500

in the dating of a grave matters little in view of what must have gone before, and cannot impair the claim of Mesopotamia to have led the way in the march of civilization in the Western world.' Hall agreed enthusiastically:

> Nothing like the recent discoveries at Ur has indeed been seen in a European museum since the appearance of Schliemann's finds at Mycenae, and no such rich find of gold objects has been made since the wealth of the discovery of Tutankhamen. Like Mycenae and Knossos, Mr Woolley's discoveries tell the archaeologist a very great deal that he did not know before. They may justly be claimed as the most important work of the kind now being carried on . . .

Hall thought the two museums and the two nations concerned should be congratulated on their harmonious partnership in 'the most important archaeological excavation in the world'.

> I stress this for I do not think that the great importance of Mr Woolley's finds is sufficiently realized. Not merely because they contain a lot of gold, as they do (and since gold of itself doth attract a journalist, this fact has received some public attention), but because they tell us so much that is new, which Tutankhamen, for all his splendour, did not.

He went on to recapitulate the most important of the discoveries so far.

> What Woolley and his helpers discovered last season is a necropolis of early graves, of three different periods, in three superimposed strata. This was found within the later *temenos* wall of the temple, but was no doubt originally outside the *temenos*, which was enlarged. The highest graves are of the time of the Akkadian Sargonide [*sic*] kings (c. 2700–2600 BC); the second series is of the first dynasty of Ur (c. 3100–2900 BC: Mr Woolley dates the tombs 'between 3200, or rather earlier, and 3100 BC'; the third, and lowest series, in Mr Woolley's opinion, dates well before the first dynasty, and is to be assigned the provisional date of 3500 BC.

There was clearly a difference over dates, which would enlarge as knowledge increased. Later scholarship would show that the Sargonid kings reigned from 2340–2195 BC. But as Woolley had said, what matter a hundred years or so in view of all that had gone before? The most interesting graves, said Hall, were those belonging to a period previously unknown from contemporary remains, although Langdon and Mackay at Kish were 'running them close'. The first dynasty burial site was already familiar from the contemporary temple remains which he and Woolley had excavated at al-Ubaid. But 'those at Ur have far transcended these in interest and in wealth'. A relief showing a chariot drawn by creatures called onogryphs, which Woolley identified as lions, caused disagreement. 'They have lions' feet and claws, certainly,' said Hall, 'but their hindquarters and tails are those of asses: nobody ever saw a lion with a sweeping, bushy tail like that. A lion's is like a pump handle. The heads may have been of lions, but may equally possibly have been of gryphons.' One way or another, a new creature had been invented. Then there was a detailed analysis of Woolley's description of burial practices in the early historical period: the clay coffin, the matting shroud and, between those methods a middle period of wickerwork coffins. In older graves, Woolley had noted signs of cremation, though as a rule only the heads were burnt. In some cases the fire had been made outside the grave proper, so that the bones were not even scorched. He thought it was a survival of an even earlier practice.

The bearing of Woolley's work on the current theory that Egypt was the centre from which all civilization sprang, east and west, was 'obvious' according to Hall. 'Our deductions cannot yet be pressed: we need further evidence which we hope will shortly be forthcoming.'

Sayce had no reservations when it came to Woolley's evidence of iron usage in the early third millennium, pointing out that at Kara Eyuk, ancient Kanish, in Cappadocia, cuneifom tablets had recorded a thriving Assyro-Babylonian trade in the Old Babylonian Period (c. 1910–1740 BC). Sayce suggested that the same tablets also showed that the metal mines of the Taurus, including iron-ore, were being actively worked by companies whose agents lived in Kanish. Their houses were filled with 'business letters, receipts, cheques and the like', recording the sale and purchase of iron and other objects. Sayce, working from imperfect translations, was somewhat awry with his 'facts'. Subsequent research showed that it was the Assyrians who worked the metal mines of the Taurus, and that their produce was chiefly tin.

All the same, the newly stimulated debate was exciting. Ur had begun to change the entire scholastic view of ancient civilization.

But revolutionary doctrines have a habit of running out of control. Ten years after the 'discovery' of iron at Ur, chemical analysis showed it to be meteoric in origin, no more significant than the iron used by Eskimos in their so-called 'Bone-Age', or by the neolithic forebears of the American Indians.

The 1928 summer vacation in England was an opportunity for the Woolleys to decide where they were going to live. Chelsea attracted Katharine and they rented a house in Chester Square, number 41a, for a few months. One of the wealthy visitors to Ur who had been charmed by Katharine into a sizeable donation, the travel magnate Sir Henry Lunn, had insisted that he should fix up a combined lecture and holiday visit to Switzerland, but the plan fell through. Instead, Sir Henry insisted in such 'generous and delightful manner' that they should occupy his flat in the Albany Hotel at Hastings for the summer, that most of Woolley's current business correspondence with the British and Philadelphia museums was conducted from that address. He had been listed as the main speaker at an Oriental Congress at Oxford in September and had arranged to travel back to the Middle East via Stockholm where a lecture had been booked for October, and America where a tour had been arranged by Pennsylvania University.

Gadd, now working as second assistant at the British Museum, was constantly being asked to arrange for more slides to be despatched to Woolley in different parts of the world. 'Gold helmet, bowls (fluted and wire-handle), silver-plate tumblers, lion's head from Queen's grave, Standard of Ur,' etc. Woolley's lists were a veritable catalogue of the Ur treasures. But he often had difficulty in obtaining even slides of the objects he needed for lecture purposes. Sidney Smith, by then Hall's principal assistant, could always find a reason for delaying the execution of Woolley's requests. Relations between the two men, never easy, became positively antagonistic. Hall intervened with good humour when he could in an effort to keep the peace. 'We are doing marvellously well . . . sick to death of gold headdresses but the other things are wonderful,' he told Woolley in December.

In a year of frenzied activity, Woolley's latest book, *The Sumerians*, was published at Oxford. It outlined the early habitations of northern Syria and the Upper Euphrates, inhabited long before the Gulf waters receded to their present limit in the fifth millennium; the alluvial plain from Baghdad to Qurnah (then at the head of the Gulf, and the reputed Garden of Eden) divided 'Semitic' Akkad in the north from Sumer in the south. He described the Sumerians, who called themselves 'black-heads', perhaps of Indo-Aryan stock, with their pictographic language of unknown origin, overwhelmed in the end by desert 'Semites' who were the forebears of the Bedouin though differing culturally from their Akkadian cousins. It was a picture that would be modified by further study, in geology and anthropology as well as archaeology – but it was sufficient for the moment.

He dedicated the book 'To My Wife'. The gesture was doubtless made with goodwill; certainly with no exaggerated devotion or suggestion of debt. The reviewer in *The Times* was more concerned with the inevitable parallel.

> However odious comparisons may be, it is not unreasonable to say that Tut-ankh-amen has yielded pride of place to Meskalam-dug for the moment; Egypt has receded into the background before Babylonia.

On her return to London, Agatha Christie bought herself a mews house in Chelsea, 22 Cresswell Place, and straight away wrote to the Woolleys inviting them to stay with her when they came back from Ur in May 1929, an invitation that was taken up. Agatha decided that she could never bring herself to 'like' Katharine Woolley but she tolerated her, perhaps accepting her guest's outrageous conduct as grist to her literary mill. Katharine, insensitive to any opposition or questioning of her own rightness, believed that Agatha liked her.

Leonard spent most of each day at the British Museum where hundreds more cuneiform-inscribed tablets, cylinder seals and sculptures had turned up from Ur. He and Katharine decided that they would make Chelsea their home between seasons and they left their rented house in Chester Square, taking a lease in St Leonard's Terrace, between the King's Road and Chelsea Embankment. Woolley enjoyed the implicit joke of his sainthood but Katharine was not happy with the house for long. On their next visit to London they found a residence she liked in Embankment Gardens, No 7. That remained their London address for several years.

In June, soon after moving to the new home, Leonard was invited by Madrid University to lecture on Ur. The Duke of Alba would take the chair. Katharine was at his side, looking appropriately regal. Freddie Cavendish-Bentinck had arranged it. Katharine found him 'delightful'. When Woolley returned to London he took

Agatha on a tour of the Ur exhibition at the British Museum. Her enthusiasm for archaeology had blossomed in exile. She felt that she owed a great debt to her friend Leonard.

When the Woolleys proposed that she should go back to Ur in the spring of 1930, Agatha agreed with alacrity. Katharine made no secret of the fact that she preferred to be surrounded by men and did not care to have other women on the site; but she also admitted to enjoying the reflected glory of Agatha's fame and the literary attention which she attracted. Agatha, for her part, was equivocal about Katharine. Reflecting in later life on the mercurial friendship which began at Ur, she wrote of the 'extraordinary' woman 'who was to become one of my great friends in the years to come'. Analysing Katharine's virtues and vices, she said 'People would declare that she was impossible, that they would have no more to do with her, that it was insupportable the way she treated you; and then, suddenly, once again they would be fascinated.' There can be no doubt of Katharine's attraction for the writer ever in search of new subjects and out-of-the-ordinary characters. 'Of one thing I am quite positive, and that is if one had to choose one woman to be a companion on a desert island, or some place where you would have no one else to entertain you, she would hold your interest as practically no one else could.' Agatha indexed her vices and merits. She was never banal, always stimulating, capable of 'insolent rudeness' and successful in the art of charming anyone she sought to attract.

Another woman who was to become famous as a traveller in the East, Freya Stark, was in Baghdad when the Woolleys passed through at the end of October 1929. Miss Stark was taking tea with Mrs Drower, the wife of the Legal Adviser to the Faisal Government. Afterwards she wrote: 'We just had tea when Mr and Mrs Woolley walked in. Mrs Woolley is remarkably fascinating, with something strange and possibly cruel about her: but quite irresistible I should imagine.'

Agatha returned for her second spell at Ur in March 1930. Just before her previous visit Mallowan had been taken ill with appendicitis and was recovering in Nasiriya where the operation was performed when Agatha appeared on the scene. Now he was perfectly fit and Katharine seconded him as Agatha's personal guide and attendant. Site work was running down, although a great deal more would be accomplished before they came to the end of the dig. There was much ado about the bed Agatha should occupy since rain was coming through the roof of the site house into one of the bedrooms. Agatha's version was credible.

'I think, Katharine,' said Len, 'that you and Agatha had better have the smaller room with the two dry beds, and we'll have the other.' 'I think,' said Katharine, 'that I really *must* have the larger room and the good bed. I won't sleep a wink if there is water dripping on my face.' Katharine, said Agatha, 'went firmly across to the delectable corner and placed her things on the bed.' Finally her finger pointed to Max who was given the wet bed.

After waking most mornings drenched from the night's downpour, Max Mallowan was delighted when told to take the Woolley's guest on a tour of the desert and the sights of Baghdad. Agatha was visibly nervous of the arrangement. She thought it an imposition on the young man and wondered if he would mind. He found her a 'most agreeable person', and was more than happy to take her under his wing.

They went off together to inspect the vast site of Nippur north of Ur which the University of Pennsylvania had been excavating on and off since John P. Peters, a professor of the Episcopal Divinity School at Philadelphia, went there in 1888 only to find himself and his team besieged by marauding tribesmen. Gertrude Bell had called it the most striking site she had ever seen. It took Agatha's breath away. Nippur was a centre of learning and of veneration of the gods, the legendary abode of Enlil, principal deity of Sumer. The couple went on to Diwaniya, where they were involuntary guests of the Political Officer, Ditchburn, who had been ordered to put them up by the High Commissioner much against his will. He was unsociable, and disliked archaeologists in particular. Max and Agatha got away as quickly as they could and went on to Nejef and Karbala, the holiest cities of the Shi'a Moslems. At Baghdad in March 1930 they were joined by the Woolleys at the home of a mutual friend, J. Ramsay Tainsh, Director of the Iraq State Railways. The Woolleys decided to travel with them to England by way of Syria and Greece, since Agatha had expressed a desire to see Delphi.

While sightseeing in Athens, Agatha suffered a fateful ankle injury, and Max decided to take her on to England ahead of their companions. On the way he proposed marriage, but she demurred, concerned about the reaction of the Woolleys. They seemed pleased, said Agatha. 'Certainly Len was pleased' (she was one of the very few people who ever called him 'Len'). As for Katharine 'it was always more difficult to tell.' She advised them to wait for 'at least two years'. Max in particular was determined to go through with it despite Katharine and despite the refusal of the Roman Catholic church to recognize the contract of a divorced woman. Both were Catholics. While they made up their minds, Max threw himself into work as Woolley's helper at the Museum. 'I have a suspicion that Katharine Woolley induced Len to make the work even heavier than it might have been: she was much annoyed with me for not postponing the marriage,' Agatha wrote. Leonard, it seems, was embarrassed. He called on Agatha and stuttered an apology about the difficulty of her living at Ur with Max. There was room only for archaeologists. People might think her appearance odd. He, as Agatha recalled, went on lamely in an embarrassing exchange with 'What I thought – what we thought – I mean, what Katharine – I mean, what we both thought . . .' 'Yes', said Agatha expectantly, ' – was that it might be better if you didn't come to Baghdad – now . . . I mean I don't know that the Trustees would think it a good idea.' Agatha had already made up her mind not to go to Ur with Max, though she could see no reason why she should not go to Baghdad at any time she chose. 'I think, Len, it is hardly for you to suggest to me where I should and should not travel in the Middle East.' 'Oh!, Oh, I do hope you don't mind. It was just that Katharine thought . . .'

They were eventually married in Edinburgh on 11 September. Agatha was forty, but gave her age as thirty-seven on the marriage certificate. Max, in a gentlemanly attempt to adjust the difference, gave his age as thirty-one. In fact, he was twenty-six. Max henceforth renounced the Catholic faith and the happiest of marriages was to last for 46 years, until Agatha's death in 1976.

'It's no good, I shall never have the proper Katharine-like Olympian attitude to the male sex,' Agatha remarked soon after her marriage. Max had been told by Woolley that he must be in Baghdad 'not a day later' than 15 October. The couple arranged to honeymoon in Greece en route to Baghdad, where they would meet up with the Woolleys. They went by the Orient Express and found bed-bugs in their sleeping compartment. They stayed in Venice and went on to Athens where Agatha was taken ill with ptomaine poisoning. Max told the doctor that unless his wife was deemed to be on her deathbed he would have to leave her and travel alone to Baghdad: to be late for his appointment with the Woolleys was unthinkable. The doctor, never having experienced the sharp edge of Katharine's tongue, replied that 'Only an Englishman could approach the matter with such total inhumanity.' The spectre of Katharine bestrode continents, however, and Max left his wife to recover in Athens and made for Baghdad, hoping that she would follow and stay at least a few days at Ur, whatever Katharine's objections. He arrived on time, only to find that the Woolleys had changed their plans without a word of explanation and would arrive a week later. He was to proceed to Ur and build a new wing to the expedition house. A hundred workmen were engaged and the job was completed to Max's specification in five days with a carefully planned guest-room for Agatha and a cramped bathroom for Katharine. When Katharine saw the new building she ordered the bathroom to be demolished and rebuilt to her requirements. Agatha, in any case, had gone back to London to write *Death in the Clouds* in which she told the story of an Englishman who deserted his sick wife in the cause of duty. The wound was still there, she said, but 'healing over'. She went back to Ur in the 1930–31 season, but only to pick up Max and return with him to England by way of Persia and the Soviet Union. The Mallowans would henceforth follow their own literary and archaeological paths.

An unexpected tribute came to Woolley in the 1930 season. The Poet Laureate of the day, Robert Bridges, had been the year before to see for himself the 'holocaust of treasure' of the royal cemetery and wrote his famous poem 'The Testament to Beauty', based on a conversation with Woolley:

> Who yesteryear sat down in Mesopotamy
> to dig out Abram's birthplace in the lorn grave-yard
> of Asian monarchies; – and low hummocks of dust
> betray where legendary cities lie entomb'd,
> Chaldaean Kish and Ur.

Woolley wrote to the poet from Ur on 18 February 1930:

> Dear Dr Bridges
> Though distance and the delays of the post have made me seem slow in doing so, I should like to say how proud I am at having our work here at Ur perpetuated in the 'Testament of Beauty': no other tribute paid to it can have been so palpable – '*Laetus sum*'!

He hoped Bridges would return the following summer to see the latest treasures.

The newly-wed Mallowans left Ur before the conclusion of one of the great archaeological expeditions of history, and much happened after their departure.

A procession of assistants, old and new, came and went to complete the work of the final years 1930–34: Winckworth and Cyrus Gordon as epigraphists, Railton, Ross Williamson and Murray Thriepland as general assistants, Rose, Richardson and Gott, architects.

As well as the harbour site of Nabonidus's buildings, the vast palaces of Ur-Nammu, Amar-Sin, and Shulgi lay exposed over many acres, along with the vaulted tombs of the latter kings, approached by stairs from upper structures and laid out around courtyards. Shulgi, towards the end of the expedition's work, was shown to have been a musician king who played a 30-stringed lyre called after Ur-Zababa, a monarch who established the royal weights and measures of ancient Sumer. Towering above it all the great ziggurat in rich red brick, each brick stamped with the name of Ur-Nammu, founder of the Third Dynasty, once crowned at the summit of its third stage by the shrine of Nanna the moon god, where mysterious rites and ceremonies took place, where the king at a sacred marriage ceremony engaged in ritual sex with a substitute for the goddess to the accompaniment of hymns of explicit imagery. And the royal cemetery, more than 2,000 graves marked out and examined, mostly dating from 2750–2450 BC, others full of the treasures of Sargonid art of the twenty-fourth century BC, and yet more brick tombs of the Third Dynasty of Ur.

'The sight of the Royal Cemetery when we were in full cry was amazing – and I recall that one of the royal tombs, which contained no less than 74 bodies buried alive at the bottom of the deep royal shaft, appeared, when exposed, to be a golden carpet ornamented with the beech leaf head-dresses of the ladies of the court, overlaid by silver harps and lyres which had played the funeral dirge to the end.'

In 1935 Agatha began writing one of her 'Poirot' stories based on her impressions of Mesopotamia and her first experience of an archaeological dig. Dr Leidner, drawn from Woolley, was the eminent archaeologist in charge. Archie Whitburn persuaded her to give the wife, in the shape of Katharine, the central role. Her portrait of Louise Leidner, a lady who demands and commands attention

from all around her and is eventually murdered by a blow from a
heavy object (found by Poirot to have been delivered by the husband)
was recognizable to everyone except Katharine.

'Lovely Louise'.
'Is she so very handsome then?' I asked.
'It's taking her at her own valuation. *She* thinks she is!'

Katharine always believed that she was represented by a minor
character named Emmott. The book, published in 1936, was dedicated to 'My many archaeological friends in Iraq and Syria.'

It would be for Max, when he himself had achieved renown as an
archaeologist after forty years in the field, to pronounce a last word
on Woolley's achievement at Ur.

'No other man alive, and no one today, could have coped with
this gigantic task as the finds poured in. The Antiquities Room was
filled to the brim; there was gold scattered under our beds ... The
masterly direction of this complicated operation is a tribute to
Woolley's capacity for organization ...' Then: 'Unfortunately,
Woolley tended to have preconceived ideas and was determined to
prove his finds were older than anything of the kind hitherto
discovered. In particular, he was bent on proving that the beginnings
of civilization in Mesopotamia were older than the beginnings in
Egypt, a misconception which led him and some of his colleagues
astray ... He preferred to play a lone hand and was reluctant to
consult authority, particularly when he had built up a chronological
framework which he considered to be satisfactory ...' But there was
fair excuse. At Ubaid, Uruk and other pre-historic sites, Sumerian
archaeology was pushing further back in time than, at that juncture,
any pre-dynastic level in Egypt had reached. But the levels at which
the conditions of civilized life could be said to exist were of
comparable date.

In the joint venture of the Ur excavation, it was Legrain, Burrows,
Cyrus Gordon, Smith and Gadd, and later scholars such as Oppenheim and Kramer in America, who set Ur and ancient Sumer in true
perspective, demonstrating linguistic, commercial and cultural ties
with other cities and states in that period when civilization began to
flower in Greece, Egypt and Western Asia. They would be the first
to admit that their work, and the world's understanding of the past,
would have been much less complete were it not for the monuments
and the thousands of cuneiform texts which Woolley rescued from

oblivion. It was the dating of early cylinder seals, demanding as they did a new understanding of ancient arts and crafts and practices, which put chronology on a sound footing. Woolley's actual discoveries were enhanced by imaginative reconstructions based on his understanding of architecture. Another great strength was his ability to provoke his assistants into subjecting conjecture to scientific examination. He discovered that Nabonidus installed his daughter as high priestess in a nunnery called E-gig-par close to the ziggurat. In a room of this ladies' residence was found a batch of clay discs which were schoolboys' exercise books of the 7th century BC. In a neighbouring room were texts and a diorite statue of Shulgi, some fourteen hundred years older than Nabonidus's daughter. And alongside, in the extinct language of the Sumerians, a museum label stated that the bricks of Bur-Sin, another king of the third millennium who died 'from the bite of a shoe', were copied from bricks found in the 'ruins of Ur', with the note 'which I saw and wrote out for the marvel of the beholders.' The excavator of these things gave the world a new vision of the first civilizations and of the prehistorical period. His 'observations missed nothing and his imagination grasped everything,' Mallowan wrote. And again: 'To his eternal credit is the written and graphic record which has put Babylonian chronology of the third millennium BC on soundly based lines. The fact is that both civilizations, Egyptian and Sumerian, developed more or less *pari passu*, in step, and that is what Woolley's own excavations have demonstrated.'

As for the Flood: 'Woolley's flood was in fact a deposit laid down at the end of the prehistoric period which goes by the name of Ubaid, in about 4000 BC, and therefore much too early to be related to the records of the Mesopotamian Flood, which are specifically associated with a king of Suruppak (Ut-napishtim) who flourished ... in about 2900 BC.' Most scholars believe that to have been the deluge of the Old Testament, traces of which were found at other southern sites. Nevertheless, 'there can be no question that he did indeed find the remains of a great flood, one of many which have ravaged Babylonia from time immemorial.'

One of the last recorded visits to the dig was that of Freya Stark in March 1933. She had already visited the Baghdad Museum. 'The Ur collection is really amazing – the sheer beauty of the gold work so remarkable.' A letter home told of the grand tour; how Woolley took her over 'Abraham's village', with its small, two-storeyed houses, narrow streets with corners rounded 'to make it easier for loaded mules':

> Mr Woolley said that now from clay tablets of bills, letters, etc., left about in the houses, they know the names and occupations of nearly every one of them. One was a school, with all the exercises left about, arithmetic, calligraphy, etc. Then we went to the Ziggurat. It is very impressive from its size and the three great stairs that run up in a triangle meeting at the top . . .

Woolley had estimated the population of Ur in its heyday at about 500,000. Miss Stark thought it strange that such a large place had no offices and few public buildings.

The American Sumerologist Samuel Noah Kramer was to write of 'the skill, care and imagination' with which Woolley excavated Ur (which the Sumerians themselves called 'Urim'). Kramer would also translate some of the most important legends of the Sumerians, and subject Woolley's finds to close scrutiny. The little temple of the goddess Ninhursag revealed by the Englishman provided us, he wrote, 'with a vivid picture of what one of the smaller provincial temples looked like in the middle of the third millennium,' and it proved beyond doubt 'that the so-called First Dynasty of Ur, which scholars had tended to look upon as legendary, actually did exist.' The American investigated the destructive power struggle between rulers of Kish, Uruk and Ur, in the third millennium period of King Meskalamdug and his near contemporaries Akalamdug and Mesannepadda. Woolley's kings did not appear in the Sumerian king list. Woolley thought his evidence pointed to the first two kings being older than the third. Kramer, finding that Mesannepadda, founder of the First Dynasty, was an older contemporary of Gilgamesh (the hero-king 'who probably reigned some time about 2600 BC'), decided that he, Mesannepadda, might have preceded the others. As for population, Woolley later modified his Ur estimate to '360,000 souls'. Kramer thought 200,000 nearer the mark. And Woolley's famous schools, their exercise books and essays intact, made for rumbustious commentaries in the later treatises of Kramer and others. Looking at the evidence of Woolley, Frankfort and the French at Mari, Kramer was constrained to say that their school essays showed 'how little human nature has really changed throughout the millenniums.' The ancient schoolboy was 'terribly afraid' of arriving late at school, 'lest his teacher cane him.' Then: 'In school he misbehaves and is caned . . . As for the teacher, his pay seems to have been as meagre then as it is now; at least, he is only too happy to make a "little extra" from the parents to eke out his earnings.'

Woolley believed emphatically to the end that his was the city of moon worship whence Abraham went forth to Harran, another city known for its moon worship, in the last decade or so of the third millennium. But of the patriarch himself, there was no trace, though many a cuneiform inscription was scrutinized in the belief that the name would turn up in a school exercise or a bill of sale or a legal or philosophical document. Woolley's city would surely have been Ur of the Chaldees when the book of Genesis came to be written in the Babylon of the Captivity in the 6th century BC. But the Old Testament scribes related events that were by then fifteen centuries old, and they would inevitably have thought of Ur as the Babylonian (or Chaldaean) city. Many archaeologists believe that Ur of the Persians, Kalat Shargat of the present day, Assyrian Assur (or Ashur), is a more plausible candidate. Ammianus Marcellinus, historian of the Roman campaign in Persia, spoke of Ur as the 'castle of the Persians', and said that Jovian's army retreated to within sight of it in 363 AD. He also said that it was close to Roman Hatra, Al Hadhr of the present. Others favour Urfah, to the north-west, which is close to Harran whence the last of the Assyrian kings sought refuge 1,400 years after Abraham.

Whether or not Woolley's Ur was the city of Genesis, its excavation opened a window on the ancient world which has enabled mankind to see the earliest civilized peoples going about their daily tasks with a clarity which no other archaeological investigation, before or since, has equalled.

Fame and Privation

One of the after-dinner anecdotes Woolley liked to tell about his time at Ur concerned a confrontation with a little old lady of Bath by the name of Miss Tanner. It happened when he went back to the spa city to sell Uplands after his father's death. As he made his way up Bathwick Hill towards the house, its tropical greenhouses gleaming in the sunlight, the grey-haired lady came up to him and said, 'Forgive me, aren't you Mr Woolley?'

'Yes madam.'

'I expect you have made a fine mess of that mound at Ur.'

'Forgive me madam, but what do you know of the mound at Ur?'

'Oh, I used to travel in Persia and Mesopotamia when I was a girl. My dragoman and I used to camp on the mound of Muqayyar. Of course it wasn't called Ur then.'

'Camp on it! Why madam, lions made their dens in it in those days.'

'I dare say,' said the lady as she walked away. His achievement and the fame that stemmed from it had been put into numbing perspective.

All the same, plaudits came in the lump. Doctorates were awarded by Dublin and St Andrews, his Oxford college made him an honorary fellow, the Royal Institute of British Architects made him an associate, artistic and scientific institutes the world over offered him lucrative lecture tours and appointments. The Athenaeum elected him to membership in time to provide the coveted 'Club' entry in Who's Who. His BBC lecture series of 1929 had come out in book form in the following year, reaffirming his belief that archaeology must resist overstatement of the significance of its discoveries. 'What is six thousand years in the life of the human race?' And what is that, he asked, in relation to geological time? Woolley's appeal as lecturer, broadcaster and raconteur lay in his rejection of pretension and vanity. He used the language of ordinary people and he liked to debunk himself as well as his subject when he sensed affectation. He was often introduced as 'the famous scholar', but he would tell his audience, 'I am not a scholar, I'm much too impatient for that. I'm just a simple digger-up of relics.' He was capable, though, of pretending to knowledge when it served his purpose. A fellow archaeologist, the American W. F. Albright who dug famously in Palestine, visited Ur at a time when Woolley was trying to impress on Hamoudi the need to find out the uses of objects. One small object defeated even Woolley's fertile imagination, however. Eventually, Albright came up with a plausible suggestion. Not knowing that Albright's Arabic was fluent, Woolley explained the purpose to Hamoudi in the foreman's native tongue, making out that it was his own idea, and not Albright's.

Woolley refused to allow archaeology to become stigmatized as a dry academic subject, glorified only now and again by spectacular discovery. He revered the past, but only to inform the present and light the way to the future. Addressing a City of London Vacation Course on education in 1930, he told a gathering of teachers and psychologists: 'The real value of archeology is that it is giving a new outlook on our own world.' Indeed, he saw continuity of past and present as the essential ingredient of progressive education. 'We see the same thought at work in 3000 BC as we see in the present . . . We see the same social problems being met in various ways . . .' People should go to museums not out of curiosity but in order to widen their outlook so that they could gain 'a quickening of understanding and a fresh interest in the lives they lead today.'

The final four seasons of the Ur excavations were essentially a winding-up process. In February 1930 Woolley had reported in *The Times* the sinking of a new shaft in the town site, to a depth of 56 feet below the level previously reached. In doing so he adopted the method used by the Germans at Assur, of making sure before abandoning a site that they had reached the lowest level of habitation, the point at which virgin soil made further discovery impossible. Woolley was now at a level which, he wrote, 'on a conservative estimate we date at 3200 BC', confirming previous calculations which 'have to deal with the very beginning of man's settlement here in the River Valley'. Painted objects, mostly with bird themes, were he thought connected with the religion of the race which 'inhabited Ur before the Flood'.

The Cambridge epigraphist C. P. T. Winckworth, who had joined the team that season in succession to Burrows, was to tell students in future years that Woolley did not for a moment believe that his famous 'flood level' had anything to do with Noah's flood, but that it was good for publicity. Not everyone at the time took that aspect of the Ur story seriously. Writing in *Antiquity*, Margaret E. Malim expressed a not uncommon mood of academic scepticism in an article entitled *Noah's Flood*. 'During the last two years,' she noted, 'the newspapers have more than once announced with a flourish of headlines that undoubted evidence of the great Flood had been discovered in Mesopotamia. The average reader felt quite excited.' Piecing together the evidence of geology, pottery and the Greek king lists, she dated Woolley's Genesis-cum-Mesopotamian Deluge at c 4250–4200 BC.

> The Flood drowned all the dwellers in the Valley of Euphrates, except the chief Shuruppak (Utanapishtim, Xisuthros or Noah) who escaped with his family and birds and beasts in the Ark.

Xisuthros, tenth king of Babylon in the Greek lists, was equated with Noah, tenth in descent from Adam. The god Cronos (analagous to Gilgamesh of the Assyrian scribes) had warned Xisuthros. Gilgamesh was the hero of the 'Flood' story in the version presented by George Smith of the British Museum in 1872 from tablet fragments in the Akkadian tongue. Thus Babylonian, Greek and Hebrew variants came together in a mythical rendering of what was probably a common enough event, a flood in the swampy pastures between the two rivers of Mesopotamia. What then of Woolley and his version?

> Mr Woolley sinks his shaft deeper and deeper, until workmen reach virgin soil. But Woolley persisted and found evidence of an earlier settlement. What was the explanation of this layer of clean, unstratified clay, which divided the later races from the early neolithic settlers with their flint tools and black-painted ware? Clearly it must have been the Great Flood.

After the Flood came the Sumerians, the First Dynasty of Kish was established, and during its long reign the inhabitants of Ur, having no system of scavenging, threw their rubbish over the city wall. Thus, over many generations of littermongering, there came about the great rubbish dump which Woolley bored through to reach the tell-tale water level.

It was an oblique, tongue-in-cheek and not entirely accurate, note of caution, but the satire was not lost on the pragmatic Woolley. He continued to speak, justifiably, of a Sumerian flood level. But he did not publicly propound its identity with the Genesis version after his return from Ur, though others, for one reason or another, continued to do so.

Archaeology became enmeshed with personal matters in the 1930s, to the point of obscuring the still important work going on at Ur. Ongoing rivalry with the bureaucratic Sidney Smith transformed academic drama into something close to theatrical farce. Winckworth had arrived at the site in 1930 while Smith was there as the temporary custodian of Gertrude Bell's old job, Director of Antiquities. Smith had decided to deal at first hand with growing nationalist complaints that the British and Americans at Ur and Kish were robbing the new Iraq of its legitimate heritage. Such complaints had begun to surface three years before. When writing to the British Museum on one occasion, Woolley had remarked that he was glad Hall 'liked the Sphinx' one of the prize objects of that year's work. But he added that the Iraqis were insisting that it was theirs and not the British Museum's. At an Oxford archaeological congress in the following year Woolley resisted the temptation to fuel a potentially dangerous fire. But his assistant from Carchemish days, Philip Guy, since employed by Garstang in Palestine, had no such inhibitions. He delivered a broadside against foreign countries that 'always wanted something for nothing' and formally proposed the motion: 'This Congress desires to bring home to the Governments of countries in the Near and Middle East the need for increasing the facilities granted to accredited excavators and for reducing to a minimum the formalities attendant on obtaining them.' Guy drew attention to the never-ending petty obstacles put in the way of the excavators. Things were to get worse, however, particularly after Smith's brief spell as adjudicator in dividing up the finds. In the thirties German influence had grown to something like its pre-war eminence, and the man who was shortly to take over as principal adviser to Faisal's government on archaeological matters was Dr Julius Jordan, a brilliant scholar and excellent musician who was violently anti-semitic and an incipient National Socialist. He was already causing trouble between the Baghdad and British Museums. Smith, who became Keeper of the Egyptian and Assyrian Department of the British Museum on the death of Dr Hall in 1930, had arrived in Baghdad to take up his new appointment the year before, and he

tended on the whole to believe the Germans and Iraqis when any
dispute arose which involved Woolley and his team. He visited Ur in
February 1930, before leaving for home. Woolley wrote to the still
incumbent Hall to announce with ill-concealed emphasis that he
proposed to depart the following day for the German site at Warka.
The new Keeper went home in a seething temper at the end of
February, to be followed by the Woolleys and the epigraphist
Winckworth in March.

On the way to England, Winckworth, lecturer in Assyriology at
Cambridge, asked Woolley if it would be possible for him to borrow
some of the cuneiform tablets which were on their way to the British
Museum, so that he could work on them during the summer
vacation. Woolley thought it an excellent idea.

The almost certain opposition of Smith caused him to take matters
into his own hands. On 2 December 1930 Woolley wrote cautiously
to his friend Gadd, now Smith's deputy at the British Museum,
referring in a matter-of-fact way to Winckworth's request. Gadd's
reply is not recorded, but whatever his advice was, it surely indicated
that Smith would never accede to the museum's tablets being loaned
to Cambridge. The story of what followed relies on subsequent
correspondence and on Winckworth's uncorroborated version of
events.

According to that account Woolley persuaded Max Mallowan to
join him and Winckworth in a 'raid' on the museum in June 1931.
The three men arrived in Winckworth's car – Woolley never learnt
to drive and disliked motor cars – and they were able to drive
straight through the south-west corner gate since Woolley and
Mallowan were, of course, well known to the porters and other
museum staff. They parked as close as possible to the basement
through which the heavy, unwieldy boxes of tablets would have to
be carried. Mallowan engaged the nearest attendant in conversation
and Woolley and Winckworth hurried off to collect the tablets.
Three boxes were duly placed on the back seat of the car and
covered with a rug. Mallowan bade the attendant farewell and the
three unsuspected academics sped off to Cambridge. They drove
straight to Winckworth's college, Christ's, deposited the tablets in
his rooms and went to dinner, their mission accomplished. Woolley
went home to Chelsea to pack his bags for a long-promised visit to
the University Museum at Philadelphia.

There the matter would have rested, were it not for the fact that
in the following month the Iraqi directorate of archaeology decided

to send an inspector to London to make a count of all the Ur objects, including tablets, in the British Museum's possession.

The Iraqi was on the way and attempts to contact Winckworth proved hopeless. In fact, Winckworth had gone on holiday. The 'Cambridge' tablets had been placed in the keeping of the University Library, the only institution at Cambridge which at that time had books to guide the scholar in translation, but Winckworth had retrieved the tablets before the vacation at the request of the librarian. He had left them in his house at Milton, a village just outside Cambridge, in the care of a daily housekeeper who had agreed to live in for the period of his absence. The lady had been told to guard the tablets with her life. Nobody must be allowed to touch them. Smith, frantic at the thought that his department might have to admit to the inspector that it had lost a large collection of tablets, and having discovered that the librarian had handed them back to Winckworth who, in turn, had disappeared, decided that the only course open to him was to threaten the librarian with legal proceedings if he failed to return them to the British Museum. The librarian thereupon went to Winckworth's home and demanded that the housekeeper hand over the objects. She refused. The librarian put his foot in the door to prevent her from closing it and the dutiful lady pushed him aside and telephoned the police. The horrified librarian turned on his heels and hurried to the nearest bus stop only to be met by a constable on the way. Having ascertained that he had found the culprit, the bemused policeman asked the librarian for his version of the story. That so much excitement and drama could ensue from the loss of a few clay tablets was clearly beyond the experience or understanding of the officer of the law. Still, he humoured the librarian and suggested that rather than make a further attempt to break into the house he should try to contact Winckworth. That he eventually succeeded in doing: Winckworth cut short his holiday and transported the tablets to London. The Iraqi inspector arrived, made only a cursory count of the objects and returned home completely satisfied; or so it seemed.

Woolley's action in lending the tablets to his epigraphist was a triumph of common sense over inflexible authority. But Smith would not allow him to forget that he had offended against the letter of the law.

In keeping with the entire affair, a letter from Sidney Smith to Woolley written four years after the event, dated 2 September 1935, appeared to suggest that Winckworth might actually have returned more tablets than he was loaned in the first place.

'Let me try to state the position as we see it in the department.' He set out the story as best he could. Winckworth had 'taken away' three boxes of tablets, 'never opened', on June 10th 'I think.' 'The Library handed back to Mr Edwards [I. E. S. Edwards, Egyptologist in the department] at the end of August 300 tablets and fragments.' No cross-check could, Smith thought, be satisfactorily made. All the returned tablets were of business documents and letters. There was not one grammatical text, yet it was grammatical texts that Winckworth was supposed to be working on. He went on:

> The position is this. We do not know, but I, at least, thought, that Winckworth had some grammatical texts at Cambridge. There is no proof that he had so many tablets as he returned. No one here has any distant recollection of the details. It is not obvious how you can check what Winckworth had. In your recollection, had Winckworth some grammatical texts at Cambridge?

Woolley's reply to Smith is not recorded, but correspondence on the subject went on into the following year, the dispute exacerbated by Woolley's decision to wage open war with the Iraqis over the matter of the share-out of antiquities.

When the 'Cambridge' story reached Mallowan's ears some years later he denied it vehemently, exclaiming that Woolley would not dream of such a thing. A favourite student of Smith's, Miss Munn-Rankin, when she heard the story said that she had been told a different version by Smith. Professor W. G. Lambert of Birmingham University, who was told it at first hand by Winckworth when a student at Cambridge, believes that his teacher was unlikely to have embellished the story, though the passage of the years may have given rise to some confusion as to time and sequence. In any case, Woolley had little regard for institutional rules. Throughout the rest of his academic life as lecturer at Cambridge University, Winckworth proudly showed students an inscribed brick from Ur mounted on the wall of his study, and in a dark-green set of cardboard drawers he kept several Ur tablets (perhaps the very texts that Smith sought). He told Lambert that Woolley had allowed him to keep them 'as a teaching officer of a public institution'. At the instigation of Professor Lambert, Winckworth's wife returned them to the British Museum after her husband's death.

Woolley had a close connection with a distinguished jeweller in London's Bond Street, Jack Ogden of the royal diamond merchants James R. Ogden, and he frequently sidestepped the museum's own laboratories by secreting jewellery and metal objects to his friend so that they could be mended or modified professionally. 'Faceted bead found among *old stuff* for Dr Woolley's evaluation' read one note for 1933 in the jeweller's writing. An instance was the dented helmet of Meskalamdug, the 'great wig of hammered and engraved gold' found in the grave of the prince of Ur in 1927. An Ogden craftsman took the dent out without anyone knowing before it went on display. Katharine Woolley was virtually a law unto herself when it came to the restoration of some of the most precious of the Ur finds. She fashioned the gold headdress of Queen Pu-abi from the gold ribbon removed from the soil of Ur, and modelled a new head for the queen from a contemporary female skull. She also restored many of the other prize finds from the royal graves and the great death pit. But Katharine was, in a manner of speaking, an official, if unpaid, employee.

The Birmingham City Museum contains a collection of cylinder seals gathered by Squadron Leader Harnett in Iraq between 1922 and 1927; five of the seals were from Ur, presented to him by Woolley. Many other visitors of the time came away with small gifts, probably duplicate tablets and seals in the main. At least one item, a large clay nail bearing an inscription and an official Ur designation, a 'U' number, is known to have come up for sale in an auction room. Members of Woolley's own family were given small and unimportant objects as keepsakes. Some may, of course, have been purchased from Iraqi traders who were never short of objects, both valuable and worthless, from the excavation sites. Some undoubtedly came from the official dig. Nothing of real value was ever given away, but Woolley liked to be generous and was quite willing to circumvent authority in order to see that his assistants had access to the materials they had helped to recover and interpret. It was not always as easy for him to obtain artifacts for his own use. Every now and again Woolley made an effort to establish at least a satisfactory working relationship with Smith, the man who had a final power of veto. On his return from Ur in 1934, Woolley engaged in his favourite pastime, angling, renting a picturesque house at Lechford in Hampshire called the Fishing Cottage. From there he wrote breezily to Smith, ending 'It's lovely down here, and work prospers.' He wanted to know whether Smith would enter the numbers of certain objects in the Ur files. Smith was not to be moved by friendly asides. He could only employ one clerk on such work. An attendant was away sick. Work on the catalogue would have to be delayed indefinitely. Woolley decided to play the same game, refusing to break his holiday to go to London for a meeting with Smith. Transparently, he avowed that he had to go to Bath for an urgent appointment with his doctor. No one who knew Woolley could recall a single day's illness in his working life and he hardly ever visited a physician.

The conclusion of the Ur excavations in 1934 and the publication of Volume II of *Ur Excavations* by the two museums, with the aid of a grant from the Carnegie Foundation, brought forth more public excitement and official adulation.

Antiquity referred to Dr Woolley's 'always lucid and often enthralling commentary', adding, in recognition of Katharine's overt role: 'British archaeologists have every reason to be proud of their post-war record at home and abroad; and everyone will congratulate Dr and Mrs Woolley on the successful conclusion of one episode in a great joint undertaking.' In the same issue, June 1934, E. A. Speiser of the University of Pennsylvania wrote of Woolley's 'splendid' and 'vivid' reports. In October, a young and promising archaeologist, Dr Mortimer Wheeler, wrote in *The Times* commending a forthcoming series of lectures of interest to 'a wide public' to be given by Dr Woolley at the Courtauld Institute in Portman Square. Woolley had been persuaded to give the talks, which concentrated on Sumerian art, by a 27 year-old Cambridge graduate named Anthony Blunt, who was closely associated with the Institute and whose urbane charm and views on art and many other topics appealed to Katharine in particular.

To the end of the Ur dig, Woolley's mastery of publicity kept archaeology on the boil. Newspaper readers and radio listeners were still agog with revelations such as were contained in his last big story, the discovery of an archive of schoolbooks, tradesmen's accounts, and love letters more than 4000 years old. From those cuneiform records, stored in thirty large packing cases in the British Museum cellars, said *The Times*, Mr Woolley 'hopes to find out who lived in each house, what they did for a living, and to make, in fact, a complete directory of the city.' School lessons in mathematics and literary composition were recorded in their entirety in clay exercise 'books'. Perhaps in anticipation of Woolley's argument that past and present are intimately bound together, a letter from a commercial traveller in 'a distant country' to an Ur moneylender, complained that five previous letters had remained unanswered.

On the way home in March 1934, Woolley had called at Tal Asmar, a site some 50 miles north of Baghdad where another of the great men of Middle East archaeology, Henry Frankfort of the University of Chicago, had unearthed a unique hoard of statues and other objects which were found to be contemporary with Woolley's finds from the Third Dynasty of Ur. The great temple of Ab-u found at Tal Asmar had, in fact, been inhabited from about 3000 BC until the end of the Sargonid period, about 2300 BC. The site was in the charge of two men of the new generation, Seton Lloyd and Thorkild Jacobsen. Both were to prove outstanding figures in Mesopotamian archaeology, and Woolley's meeting with Lloyd, another architect who had served his apprenticeship with Lutyens, was to give rise to a lasting friendship. Full of enthusiasm for the new link with his own early historic finds, Woolley wrote a long letter to *The Times* which was published in full and spilled over two pages. In it he both praised his famous contemporary and wagged an admonitory finger. Dr Frankfort's discoveries were 'of remarkable interest', but his methods were open to question. 'Dr Frankfort embarks on what he admits to be the most dangerous of archaeological speculations, the translation of the thickness of accumulated debris into terms of years.' Whenever such a course had been adopted in the past it had been condemned by later knowledge. After a long technical argument about the period of use of plano-convex bricks by Sumerian builders, an argument which must have been over the heads of a good many readers even of *The Times*, Woolley remarked that Frankfort's present estimate of 450 years was an improvement on his 'former views, but still seems too short'. His conclusion, polite but pedantic, went unchallenged: 'No positive chronology based on purely archaeological evidence can hope for general acceptance, but the sum of evidence available to date would imply that the plano-convex age ended earlier and lasted longer than Dr Frankfort allows on the strength of his discoveries at Tell Asmar.'

Neither Woolley nor the press had quite finished with Ur. Articles were to continue to appear on the 'City of Abraham' for some time to come, but it was an opportune moment for a fresh name to be put before the public. Tal Asmar and the work which Mallowan was doing in Iraq kept archaeology in the public eye while Woolley prepared for his next venture.

The closure of the Ur excavation had been advanced by the Iraqi propaganda war. In 1934, the Iraqis decided to amend the Antiquities Law drawn up by Gertrude Bell and the Iraqi Education Ministry eleven years earlier and subsequently approved by the League of Nations. In March 1935 Woolley brought the battle into the open. In a letter to *The Times* and in a major article in *Antiquity*, he accused the Iraqis of mounting a propaganda campaign as a prelude to the debate in the Baghdad Parliament, designed to show that under the existing law the country 'has been robbed' of treasures which were 'legally and morally hers' by concessions made to foreign museums. The curator of the Baghdad Museum, Abdul Rizaq Effendi, 'personally repeated to me the statement' made in the local press that Iraq had not received one half of one per cent of the actual finds. Yet, he said, the most recent division had taken place just a few days before, as the result of which 75 per cent of tablets and seal impressions went to Baghdad. Of 1296 objects remaining, the Department of Antiquities took 816, including all the best objects in each category. In 1932–33, Iraq took 302 out of 464 objects. The Iraqi proportion was not a half of one per cent, he pointed out; it was 63 and 65 per cent of those two divisions alone. He went on to catalogue some of the 'finest pieces' taken by Baghdad: the diorite statue of Entemena ('the best statue that we ever found'), the gold priestess, the mosaic of a milking scene from the al-Ubaid period, a gold *bulla* inscribed A-anni-padda ... etc. Then: 'Since 1929 ... when Mr Sidney Smith took in hand the organization of the Museum [in Baghdad]', division had been much less favourable to the joint expedition. In truth, the Antiquities Law as it stood was so severe that 'the wisdom, indeed the possibility, of carrying on excavations has been doubtful.' Woolley had fought a long battle on behalf of the two museums he represented, and he was dismayed to find that the man who most often dogged his efforts in dealing with the Iraqis was the Keeper of the very department of the British Museum which stood to gain most from a fair interpretation of the international law governing the sharing of antiquities.

The knighthood announced in the Birthday honours list of June 1935 confirmed Woolley's position among the elite of his profession, ranking him alongside the great men in whose shadow he had so far laboured, Sir Arthur Evans and Sir Matthew Flinders Petrie.

Recognition was welcome but it did not go to his head. The same cannot be said for Katharine. Her sense of superiority was reinforced by her husband's knighthood and her own entitlement. Woe betide anyone, within the family or without, who forgot from now on that she was 'Lady Woolley'. All Leonard's confidence and self-assurance were needed to prop up his defences against a wife whose dictatorial manner knew no bounds. His social life was circumscribed at every turn by her determination to select his friends and approve his movements. Protest was out of the question. The penalty of endless scenes of outraged vanity and feigned ill health was too great. His family was now cut off from him by decree, though he made secret visits to the Clifton home of his formidable sister Edith Laxton and her family of four children, usually when he was lecturing at Bath or Bristol. But when his godchild Margaret Laxton married, he was forbidden to send her a wedding present. Even those clandestine visits, pleasant interludes that they were, became painful reminders of what seems to have been a common Woolley attribute, inimical partnership. Edith, narrow-minded about many things and almost as selective as Katharine in her choice of friends, was hanging on to a turbulent marriage. She read nothing but the Bible and religious tracts, believing even the finest secular literature to be morally injurious. As wife and mother she found it hard to show affection to her children or husband. But for a few years after Leonard's return from Ur, Edith and the Laxton home provided sanctuary of a kind when the burden of marriage became unendurable.

Soon after the final return home, another and compelling reason came to light for his stoic acceptance of an impossible domestic situation. Katharine had always been surrounded by doctors. She was a walking catalogue of obscure ailments, but after the return to England she began to lose weight and to show symptoms of tiredness and weakness. Leonard persuaded her to go to a specialist for tests. She consulted a surgeon of great renown and pronounced opinions whose interest in the Ur excavations had brought him into the Woolley social circle. Sir Cecil Wakeley, consulting surgeon and senior lecturer in anatomy at King's College London, Grand Warden in Freemasonry of the United Grand Lodge of England, and President of the Bible League, diagnosed disseminated sclerosis. The nature of Katharine's illness was to remain a closely guarded secret for the rest of her life. She insisted that no one should know, and Woolley respected her wish.

The Woolley family records are thick with examples of Victorian priggery and do-goodery; examples which go some way towards explaining why sons and daughters alike were hopelessly inadequate in their personal relationships. One such example is provided by the family autograph book which was started by Leonard's grandmother Mary Pearce Woolley. Over the generations, family and friends had penned favourite sayings and pieces of verse in this leather-bound, gold-embossed volume. One such entry, dated 1815, consisted of a prudish answer to an advertisement for a wife which had appeared in the *Morning Chronicle*. A note in the writer's hand at the head of the verse insisted 'Not to be copied'. All through the pages there was much of Israel's journey 'o'er the desert sand', of 'weak men's temptations' and 'Sinning Man' and 'Jehovah's throne', of reproof, apology, pardon; much, too, of Homer and Horace (in grandmama's hand).

That book survived. A family diary, similarly bound, which came down from the grandparents, full of details of births and deaths, holidays and mild family scandal, was destroyed by Leonard and Edith after their father's death — burnt in one of those ceremonial bonfires of Victorian and Edwardian times which are the historian's and biographer's nightmare. Of the other surviving brothers and sisters, Kathleen still taught in Japan where she founded the Nippon Girl Guide movement and lived in the missionary bungalow she built for herself, returning to England every five years (up to the second World War when she was taken prisoner in the Far East). Even that grand old lady, kindly and intellectual, one of the earliest graduates of Somerville College, was ostracised by Katharine and had to meet Leonard in clandestine ways. Sister Rachel was of quite different make-up. Quarrelsome, argumentative and domineering, she gave up her teaching apointment in Jamaica to become head of a diocesan school in India. Like aunt Honoria, who came of the Boyle-Pearce side of the family and wore nun's habit, she was a classical scholar of forbidding severity. Harold, by then chaplain at Harrow school, where Leonard was able to pay a clandestine call, was in later years unable to extend the charitable demands of his religion to the daughter of his first marriage, Janetta. She had an illegitimate child and was disowned.

Only the elder brother Cathcart, still living among the Dyaks in Borneo, and sister Marjory, a jolly, extrovert woman who had no time for the moralizing tendencies of her family, seemed capable of throwing off the cloak of righteousness.

It is not difficult to picture the family scene when the question of divorce arose. Brothers and sisters threw up their hands in horror. In any case, Leonard's loyalty to Katharine, and his acceptance of her wilful behaviour (though it had little to do with her illness), was more easily acceded to once her serious malady was diagnosed.

To the world at large he still exhibited the old amiability and impishness, and the keen, unabrasive intellect which won immediate response. There was a natural modesty amounting almost to shyness. Despite success, he retained some touching reminders of that youthful poverty which was imposed by the need to provide for his family from a very modest income the moment he left university. As his finances improved, he gave high priority to helping his sister Edith educate and provide for his nephews and nieces; a practice which ended abruptly with his marriage. He had never dressed extravagantly but at the moment of worldly success he went up a grade and acquired a suit from the Fifty-Shilling Tailors. He remained a lifelong customer of that institution, unimpressed by the 'bespoke' dress sported by most of his friends and colleagues.

Among those who took to heart the dramatic headlines of the Ur dig, none was to prove more diligent in following them up than Queen Mary. Even before the official and royal recognition signified by the knighthood, there were invitations to the Palace, where King and Queen listened intently to Leonard's graphic tales of ancient history and his descriptions of the Ur finds and asked innumerable questions. The Queen demonstrated that she had followed events closely. Early in 1935 came the first of innumerable commands to accompany her on sightseeing tours of the British Museum, where many of the Ur treasures, lavishly restored, were now on display.

Other important, if less august, friendships came his way. Rudyard Kipling, whose interest in all the parishes of the Indian Empire had not neglected such outposts as Mesopotamia, was to become another interested follower of the Ur dig and its biblical associations.

When they met first, in February 1919, it was the follow-up to an acquaintanceship between the men's fathers. When George Woolley had visited the English Potteries to see friends at Wedgwood, Copeland and Minton in the last century, he had also called at the Nile Street pottery in Burslem (later Royal Doulton) where Lockwood Kipling was apprenticed as modeller and painter. At his first meeting with Leonard Woolley, Kipling was probably more interested in the younger man's experiences as a wartime captive of the Turks, living alongside the men of Kut whose catastrophe he had marked with the damning lines of 'Mesopotamia 1917', about the politicians who 'left them thriftily to die in their own dung'.

By the end of a war in which he lost his own son, Kipling showed open hostility to anyone guilty of diluting the imperial ardour. The famous author was engaged in protracted correspondence with Theodore Roosevelt at the time, castigating President Wilson for his supine attitude of forgiveness towards the 'Devil' in the shape of the defeated Central Powers; and at the same time he virtually instructed the editor of the *Morning Post*, with the support of the paper's proprietor Lady Bathurst, to oppose the Irish Treaty with full force. To meet a young man of academic distinction who had served throughout, been taken prisoner and lived alongside the heroic men of Kut was conversational bonus enough. To discover that Leonard was the brother of Harold, one of the heroes of Hill 60, a place name that was always on the tip of Kipling's tongue, was even more rewarding. Woolley's captivity had been inconvenient rather than strenuous, and he had spent most of his homecoming attending to an ailing father. None the less, he found a sympathetic listener to his tales of wartime adventure. Kipling and his wife Caroline were both ill at the time and were in Bath for the 'waters'. Woolley, a conventional man of his day with an orthodox appreciation of the essential merits of empire, was, roughly speaking, on Kipling's side. But he was less inclined to extreme opinion than the great writer who became one of his close friends. Kipling made no bones about his dislike of the Jews. Woolley disapproved of anti-semitism, as earlier academic debates showed, in its racial and scholastic manifestations.

It was a short but propitious meeting and, as Ur was revealed in all its splendour and antiquity, Kipling followed the press reports closely. A friendship ensued which was to last until the writer's death in 1936.

Writing had assumed a central role in Woolley's daily life. Fortunately, it was an occupation which he looked on as 'fun' rather than work.

Now he had the time to complete a work which would, in a sense, testify to his unshakeable belief in biblical history, though his own interpretations often differed from those of theological scholars of the day. His book *Abraham* was dedicated to Kipling.

Dear Kipling,
We discussed this book together while it was in the making. Now it is done, and I dedicate it in gratitude and affection to you to whom archaeologists and historians owe so much. Yours ever,
Leonard Woolley, December, 1935

Significantly, the book was subtitled 'Recent discoveries and Hebrew origins.' His friend 'Rud' placed Jews in much the same category as Irish and Indian nationalists. For Woolley, more interested in the battles of the Books of Moses than in the counter claims of Arabs and Zionists, here was an opportunity to apply the grace notes of biblical knowledge and insight to the basic archaeological score. More than that, it was his chance to underline his own claim to authority in the determination of biblical veracity, a matter in which the 'unveilers' of history were often at odds with scholastic tradition based on conventional theology and 'Higher Criticism'.

The categorical assertions of the past decade, the claim that 'this square' or 'that street' was where Abraham and his family shopped or went to school or lived, had given way to a robust frankness. Not a single tablet among the thousands examined bore the name Abraham, he admitted, though the tablets which survived were but a hundredth part of the number written in the twenty-five years or so that the patriarch might have spent at Ur. 'But if these Mesopotamian excavations have produced no record whatsoever of Abraham, have they, it might be asked, any real bearing on history? Is there any justification for speaking of Ur in a book which professes to deal with Abraham?' Indeed, could we be sure that the biblical reference to Abraham and Ur was trustworthy, and if so could we be sure that the Ur of the Old Testament was 'the city excavated by us in Mesopotamia?' Again, was there ever such a person as Abraham and, if so, 'can we know anything about him?' The questions presupposed an importance attaching to Abraham which demanded a critical examination of the Bible and of his own conclusions drawn from the Ur excavations.

> It is difficult to overrate the importance of Abraham. He is the founder and begetter of the Hebrew race which through good and ill report has played an incalculable part in the development of modern society. Three of the great religions of to-day, the Jewish, the Christian and the Moslem, look upon him as one of the chief prophets and witnesses to man's faith, the only one to be called the 'Friend of God'.

There was, of course, the difficulty of the antediluvian king-lists which worked their way through to the compilers of Genesis. Totting up one Sumerian account, eight legendary rulers reigned for a total of 241,200 years. Another account totalled 456,000 years for the same kings, but the figures were calculated in *sars*, or cycles of 360 years. Twenty-three kings of Kish accounted for 24,510 years 3 months and 3 days. The lives of the Israelite fathers seemed positively reasonable by comparison. With the appearance of Abraham, he noted, Genesis becomes personal and historical. The character of the Old Testament changes perceptibly. The mythology of the Creation and the Flood, the impossible chronologies and long genealogies, the origin of nations and the differences of national speech accounted for in the multifarious tongues of the Tower of Babel, suddenly give way to individual actors with definite form, their careers related with circumstantial detail and in natural sequence. 'We get at once the impression that the writer is dealing with times nearer his own, concerning which he is, as might be expected, better informed; he writes with authority, and what he wrote has by most people for many centuries been accepted as literally and indisputably true.'

There was a critical appraisal of the works of those 'pious conservatives', the editors or 'redactors'. He examined the differences of emphasis, of language and sentiment, of the three main versions of the Pentateuch, the 'Five books of Moses': the *Priests' Code*, composed during the Babylonian exile or soon after, c 535 BC; the *Jahivistic* version of 'prophetical' narrative in which God is always *Yahweh*, 'Jehovah' of the English Bible; and the *Elohist* version, where God becomes *Elohim*, deriving like the Jahivistic text from some time after the foundation of the Kingdom of David in about 1000 BC, probably combined into a single text before 750 BC. Thus, he posed the extreme argument of the humanists and anti-religious scholars. The biblical scribes and editors, so the argument went, worked between a thousand and fifteen hundred years after Abraham's departure from Ur, relying on oral tradition, 'religious propagandists who tried to commend their views by attributing them to the remote past of the nation'. Yet they, the scribes and editors, could not have had any knowledge of the doings of Abraham or of the legislation of Moses. Embellishment and alteration followed inevitably.

For the sceptics, the Bible had no historical foundations. For them, Abraham was 'merely the eponymous hero of his race, a mixed creature of mythology, poetry and folk-lore, given human shape and name with the idea of assuring the essential unity of a nation'. And what of the Hebrew accounts of the Creation and the Deluge? Were they not mere copies of the earlier myths and hero legends of the Sumerians and their semitic successors, recorded in the Babylonian cuneiform which the great archaeologists and linguistic scholars of the nineteenth century – Rawlinson, Hincks, Oppert, and others – had put at our disposal? And what of the Mosaic laws and commandments? Was there not a remarkable similarity between them and the Code of Hammurabi, king of Babylon in about 1910 BC, written on the great stone found by the Frenchman de Morgan at Persian Susa in 1902?

Such arguments had gathered strength in rationalist and humanist quarters since the publication of Darwin's *Origin of Species* in the 1860s. But now, Woolley insisted, archaeology had changed everything. Archaeology had come to the rescue of theology. Discoveries made 'during the last half century', had proved that there was no period in Hebrew history for which there was not contemporary written authority. The famous letters of Tal al-Amarna in Egypt, discovered accidentally by a peasant woman in 1887, contained correspondence of the 15th–14th centuries BC between the kings Amenophis III and IV (Akhnaten) and the princes of many lands, but chiefly Palestine, Phoenicia, and southern Syria. The cuneiform messages were written in Akkadian, the diplomatic language made universal in the second millennium by the power of Babylon, and they contained many typically Canaanite words, including a reference to the 'Habiru', which is generally accepted as the original form of Hebrew. And another Babylonian tablet found in southern Mesopotamia tells of 'Habiru' in that region during the reign of Rim-Sin, king of Larsa, soon after 1850 BC. Thus, a Hebrew tradition, capable of passing the biblical traditions from one generation to another, existed long before the Exodus, and almost certainly went back to the Patriarch Abraham himself, who is spoken of in Genesis xiv as 'the Hebrew'. But there was a discovery at Ur which Woolley found just as significant.

Below the floor of a Third-Dynasty temple, dated by Woolley to c 2300 BC, he had uncovered the foundations of an altar. They consisted of a square pit with three courses of rough limestone blocks, with a thick layer of burnt red earth above them. The Sumerian texts showed that the earth was burnt to purify the site. But Sumerian liturgy offered no hint of the use of unhewn stone in the making of a sacred altar. No parallel to the altar-base of Ur had been found elsewhere in Mesopotamia. But it was thoroughly in accord with Hebrew practice. Woolley quoted Exodus xx: 'And if thou wilt make me an altar of stone, thou shalt not build it of hewn stone: for if thou lift up thy tool upon it, thou hast polluted it.' And again (Genesis xxviii, 18) respecting Jacob's conversion of the rough stone at Bethel; (Genesis xxii, 9) Abraham's intended sacrifice of Isaac; (and Genesis xxxi) the stone at Gilead; all providing evidence that 'the presence of the Habiru or Hebrews in southern Mesopotamia affected even the ritual of the Sumerians.' He quoted his former assistant Cyril Gadd, author of *History and the Monuments of Ur*, in support of his contention that the Habiru and Hebrews were identical people who disappeared from sight at the time of Hammurabi, about 2000–1900 BC and migrated northward, the time and direction of Abraham's sojourn from Ur to Harran. There was a detailed examination of the rival claim of Urfa to be the biblical Ur. Most Bible maps had marked it so, believing that its proximity to Harran proved the matter. Woolley argued that the closeness of the cities would, in fact, have made the patriarchal journey 'rather ridiculous', a legend based on a move of a dozen miles or so. No, 'the Ur of Abraham is "Ur of the Chaldees", and at no time in its history could Urfa have been describes as a Chaldaean city.' The conveyors of oral tradition were merely designating the place with the name it was known by in their day, though to complicate the matter further, the Ur of Abraham ceased to exist in 1885 BC when its people revolted against Hammurabi's son Samsuiluna and burnt it to the ground, 600 years at least before the Chaldaeans made their appearance. The 'local colour' of Old Testament witness invested the bare bones of the story with historical flesh, 'real and knowable'. Yet:

> Direct evidence there is none. There is not and presumably there never will be available any secular record concerning the details of Abraham's life, and in the only cases where such would seem to be possible, the fourteenth chapter of Genesis, we have seen how difficult it is to establish any correlation. But indirect evidence is possible; the 'local colour' of the Abraham stories will be found a very fair criterion of truth.

Ingeniously, he invoked H. G. Wells' romance *The War of the Worlds* and Flaubert's *Salâmmbo* in support of an argument that strayed into romantic pastures, 'local colour' in either case being, as with Abraham's story in the Old Testament, the handmaid of truth.

Modern research, not least Woolley's own labours at Ur, demonstrated that the written record of those formative events in the history of mankind must be accepted 'as more or less contemporary, and therefore in its essence true'. He redressed a failure in earlier essays to stress the essential duality of the Abraham legend, the paternity of the Arab as well as the Jewish race through Ishmael, his son by Hagar the Egyptian woman. 'Ishmael was as truly a son of the house as was Isaac, so much so that when Sarah gave Hagar to Abraham to be his wife she could say, "it may be that I may obtain children by her" . . .' Perhaps the most important chapter, 'The Written Testimony', insists on vital links between the Hebrew chronology of the prehistoric period in the Bible and the Sumerian king lists which deal with prehistoric times. It could hardly be coincidental that Uta-Napishtim, hero of the first recorded Flood legend, was the tenth of the kings who reigned before the deluge, while Noah in the Hebrew version came in the tenth generation after Adam. 'It is quite likely that the early Hebrews, striving to bridge with a few names what they felt to have been vast spans of time, may have been influenced by the chronology of the King-Lists, which had been drawn up in writing and had been studied at Ur before Abraham's day.'

The appeal of Woolley's intensely argued essay was immediate and edition after edition was called for as Christian and Jew in Europe and America sought avidly for confirmation of religious belief. In contrast, his range was too wide and his method too popular for the academic world. On the whole, theological and archaeological scholars saw the book as shallow, 'out of touch with linguistic and literary problems', lacking in authority. Yet it must be said in Woolley's defence that whatever scholastic deficiencies may have been apparent at the time of publication remain substantially open and unanswered at the present day, while the book itself is still a principal source for all those writers who profitably maintain the thesis that 'archaeology proves the Bible'.

Kipling did not live to see the publication of *Abraham*, though he read the completed manuscript. The poet was secretly cremated at Golders Green Cemetery in January 1936, and his ashes interred at Westminster Abbey a few days later. Leonard and Katharine joined the literary elite in paying homage to a friend, while the body of King George lay in state in nearby Westminster Hall. As someone said, King and Trumpeter had gone together. A new era was ushered in.

Woolley and his sponsors decided that Ur had nothing further to offer. He was forty-two years old at the start of the Ur excavations. He was fifty-six when, in February 1936, he turned to Syria. On journeys to and fro he had made tentative probes of the coastal region around Antioch and he thought it promising.

Atchana and the Indus

In the autumn of 1934 Flinders Petrie and his caravan surveyed the coastal region of Syria north of the Orontes. Some months before they set out from England, Lady Petrie had published in the *Morning Post* a letter announcing a new fund, The Biblical Research Account, saying that prospects in Syria were favourable and that nothing except financial means stood in the way of an investigation of 'alluring problems'. Often at odds with fellow field archaeologists, and with the various official and semi-official bodies which gave permission and provided funds, Petrie was forced time and again to found his own institutions. Difficulties were usually overcome by his forceful personality and the resonance of his name in academic quarters, and by his wife's skill as a publicist and appeals organizer. In December the Petries were in Beirut and he applied for permission to dig to the French Inspector of Antiquities and the Joint Archaeological Committee of the British Academy, set up in 1918 at the Government's request to administer applications for exploration in the territories of the disbanded Ottoman Empire. In January 1935, Petrie himself wrote in *The Times* that he had found two suitable sites, 'ancient ports which would have been busy centres of trade plying from 3000 BC'. Money had come in from the public and he expected to start digging as soon as the rains ceased. He looked forward to 'a season of great promise in discovery'. At 81, the still active Petrie was the acknowledged grand master of archaeology, even though Sir Arthur Evans was two years his senior and was also still active. It was the more surprising, therefore, when the Joint Committee declined to recommend his application, telling him that North Syria was reserved for Sir Leonard Woolley who intended to dig there for the British Museum. Petrie was bitter and, according to his biographer, may have owed the summary dismissal of his application to the fact that he had said caustic things about 'incompetent' excavators in Syria in his recently published autobiography.

Whether or not Petrie was aware of it, Woolley was actively on the lookout for suitable sites in the same region. In the spring of 1935, armed with a commission from the British Museum 'to look for a new site to excavate', he made a quick visit to the Syrian coastline he had come to know so well in wartime twenty years before.

'I was convinced that the mouth of the river Orontes must have played a very important part in the overseas commerce of a land whose exposed and rocky coast so seldom affords a safe anchorage for ships', he wrote, 'the broad river winding through the flat alluvial plain . . . an ideal shelter for the small mercantile craft of the ancient world.' He was astonished when locals told him that there was no mound of any kind at the mouth of the river. But he found a track running between the modern customs sheds. It ran between low broken banks; on one side the ground sloped gently up to a domed white tomb. He saw fragments of pottery sticking out from the roadside bank and littering the slope leading to the tomb. The first fragment he picked up was too recent for his liking, a piece of an Athenian vase of the fifth century BC. Just beyond the tomb the ground broke away to become a low cliff, at its foot a dry wadi. The Orontes, he guessed, had once filled this now dry river bed. 'I felt sure that there had been a big mound here which the river had then swept away . . .' There was a local legend that floodwaters had once washed away all the crops and threatened the very tomb of the blessed Shaikh Yusuf, on the edge of the cliff, until that saint rose up in anger and rebuked the river, which then dutifully receded. It was the kind of far-fetched story which instantly appealed to Woolley, and he was not alone in embracing it: pilgrims journey to the shrine of Yusuf to the present day.

At any rate the path was cleared for Woolley to begin his next large-scale excavation. He applied to the French Inspector, his old friend from Carchemish days, M. Brosse, and was given instant permission to dig in the French mandated region between the Amq Plain and the Orontes Valley.

This time, circumstances and aims were very different from those which led him to Ur. Katharine was at his side from the first, and provision for her comfort and amenity took priority over all else. Unlike Ur, the site was mercifully not too far removed from civilized amenities. Aleppo was close enough by car and thus she was within reasonable travelling distance of Damascus and the Lebanon, where she could find suitable company among rich Americans and Europeans.

Ambition here was confined to the filling in of archaeological gaps rather than the making of earth-shaking discoveries, laying bare a great primary city or revealing biblical or classical analogues. It was the opposite, in fact; to find small, relatively unimportant places which would show how ordinary people lived in small urban settlements, away from the mainstream influences of administrators and art establishments; working backwards from the second milllennium BC to the third, to learn how the patterns of trade and communication between powerful cities and states imprinted themselves on the lives of unremarkable provincial communities.

Two sites were chosen on the mosquito-infested Amq Plain at the north-west tip of Syria. To the north, a line of low hills separate the plain from the great plateau which stretches from Aleppo to the Euphrates. South there drifts a sea of small hills, and to the west rise the high Amanus mountains whose extremities plunge into the Mediterranean just short of the Gulf of Alexandretta, a place of poignant memory for Woolley. From the east and north, two little rivers, the Afrin and the Kara-Su, feed into the plain to form a central lake and marshlands all around. And from the Lebanon in the south, the Orontes runs its chaotic course until it arrives at Antioch and finally reaches the sea at al-Mina, which means simply the 'harbour', just below Seleucia. At the neck of the Orontes, where it turns westward to run into the valley of Antioch, stood one of hundreds of mounds dotting the Amq plain, called Atchana, 'Thirsty Mound'. Woolley chose it, along with al-Mina on the coast, as the likeliest places to reward his digging.

For five war-interrupted years, helped by E. A. Lane, an assistant keeper at the Victoria and Albert Museum, A. E. F. Gott, his last architectural assistant at Ur, and Murray Thriepland, Woolley and his small team were to dig at the mound of Shaikh Yusuf at the jaw of the harbour, at Tal-Atchana and associated sites to the north. As in Carchemish days, there was a whiff of ulterior motive. Although the dig was to be conducted in the name of the British Museum, the Trustees decided, much to Woolley's regret, 'that the funds at the Museum's disposal did not warrant their financing an expedition whose commitments it was difficult to calculate and whose avowed purpose was admittedly speculative'. Fortunately, said Woolley, his old friend and military staff chief at Cairo, Neill Malcolm, came to the rescue and raised the necessary funds.

He worked with urgency, but mindful always that the augmenting of existing knowledge was the aim, rather than flamboyant discovery. He had chosen mounds which, from the evidence of potsherds lying on the surface, illustrated towns and villages going back to the Bronze Age. He hoped, though, to find evidence of occupation in the fourth millennium BC, thus taking the story back to pre-dynastic times, to the Chalcolithic period before bronze, when copper was the dominant metal, and beyond to the 'Pottery Neolithic' when all that can be known is evidenced in stone and clay, and calcified bone.

Hamoudi was still in command of the workforce, an old, tired man now, though he could still bark his orders from the hilltops and he willingly came over from his home at Jerablus to take charge of the fifty or so Syrian labourers employed at the start. But he needed the support of his sons, Yahia and Alawi, who had been apprenticed at Ur, the former being in charge of photography. For Hamoudi and Woolley, the Syrian excavation was the culmination of twenty years' uninterrupted friendship.

As with the Royal Cemetery at Ur, Woolley was guided by inspiration and guesswork in deciding precisely where to dig. Clearly Atchana lay on the main road between Aleppo and the Mediterranean. Most importantly, it was close to the entrance of the Orontes valley and therefore controlled the harbour at the mouth of the river. He surmised that it lay at a junction of the road with the north-south route linking Hittite and Syrian traders, and the east-west road along which the cedar wood of the Amanus forests made its way to the Euphrates and thence to the rich and treeless cities of Mesopotamia. If anyone wanted to command those routes in ancient times, he would need to station himself, said Woolley, 'precisely where the mound of Atchana stands'. At some time, he believed, the Amq plain must have been part of a kingdom, and Atchana was surely its royal city. In the event, the place was found not to go back to the earliest days of the Amq, 'not much before 3,000 BC', he thought.

As for al-Mina, all vestiges of the earliest settlement had been swept away by the river changing its course. All they found in the first three years of digging was evidence of Greco-Roman occupation in the period c 700 BC to 100 AD. It was a long way short of his declared starting point of 1200 BC. Again, Woolley resorted to inspirational method.

He recalled the words of Herodotus, that the Greek hero Amphilochus had built the city of Posideium on the Syrian coast, and that Amphilochus was the son of Amphiaraus, one of the Seven who

fought against Thebes. He must, therefore, have lived at the time of
the siege of Troy, about 1200 BC. Posideium, Woolley felt sure, must
be his port of al-Mina. He also believed that a small hill close to the
river and about three miles inland from al-Mina, must have been
related to the port. Brief inspection revealed heaps of potsherds. A
few trial trenches proved his reckoning correct. He had so far dug
down through ten strata, the lowest coinciding with about 700 BC.
The pottery of the inland mound, known as Sabouni in the present
day, represented all ten levels of al-Mina. Then they came to
Mycenaean sherds dating to the 13th and 12th centuries BC. Then
bowls decorated in white slip were recognized from Greek exploration to be of the 15th century. A cylinder seal took them back to the
18th century. Rubble and brick proved to be from the massive
enceinte wall of an acropolis which topped the hill. The rubble of
other buildings came to light at its foot. This, Woolley noted, was
the place where the merchants of al-Mina lived, the suburban retreat
of the well-to-do, though others doubtless had even more splendid
villas on other hills, some now covered with modern dwellings. The
harbour really had been in use from very early times. Sabouni stood
in relation to the port as did Athens to the Piraeus. Labourers,
fishermen, petty traders, lived at Posideium. The rich merchants
lived inland and came down daily to their work. Woolley had
revealed a Greek city of the time of Troy and had, in passing, made
an interesting link with ancient Greek tradition. Was it, perhaps, the
infamous Sea Peoples, invaders of Egypt and much of the Near East,
who destroyed al-Mina and its associated cities in the twelfth century
BC? Woolley thought it probable, and that the port was rebuilt soon
afterwards, chiefly to perpetuate trade with Greece.

Within a month of his arrival, Woolley contributed his first long
article to *The Times*, preparing the reader for riches to come.
Echoing a rhyme he had picked up from Agatha Christie he wrote of
'sitting upon one such lofty *tell*', counting the mounds surrounding
him, more than fifty in the immediate vicinity. Here, with so many
sites to choose from, he surveyed a region where Syro-Hittite
civilization flourished between 1200 and 600 BC. 'Obviously,' he
wrote, 'we may hope to find sculptured reliefs and inscriptions, but
for that we must have the good luck to hit upon a palace or a
temple.' He soon found inscriptions, though they were relatively
sparse. Mallowan was to tell students in years to come that despite
his protestation of modest ambition, what Woolley really hoped for
in his five years in the Orontes valley and on the Amq plain was

another royal necropolis. Whatever the truth of Mallowan's assertion, the Syrian dig held out no such grand prospect.

In May, Woolley took up some of the scholastic challenges of his
latest excavation in a letter to Sir Arthur Evans. The Ashmolean had
taken a minor part alongside the British Museum in sponsoring the
expedition in its early stages. Evans was back in Oxford where, after
Hogarth's death in 1927, Thurlow Leeds had become Keeper of the
Ashmolean:

> My dear Evans
>
> You will have seen my first report from here, but you would, I
> know, like to be told a bit more, so I'm sending information for
> you and Leeds.

He went on to tell Evans of the success of the harbour site. No other
such colony, Woolley asserted, had produced so much pottery, with
the possible exception of Egyptian Naukratis, '& it ranges from the
9th to the 4th centuries, always with first-class stuff – first-class but
hitherto mostly in fragments: even the great mainland sites are
hardly so productive.'

> But I've been much worried by our not getting the earlier things:
> we got to virgin soil with geometric wares & either that part of
> the town which was earlier has been swept away by the river
> (which is very winding) or the earlier port was elsewhere.

A settlement he had just discovered, with its acropolis on a natural
hill commanding river and plain, had produced pottery no earlier in
date than the 9th century BC. Disappointing, but further search
might, he thought, give them a port of earlier occupation. 'I think it
looks promising.' After just three-days work at Tal-Atchana inland
he had found pottery with distinctively Cretan (Minoan) and Hittite
decorative associations. A clay bull's head, Minoan or perhaps
Hittite, had been found, along with a magnificent bronze sword with
lunate handle, apparently plated with silver. He drew it for Evans's
information.

There was no epigraphist with Woolley this time. He had to send
the few tablets found so far back to the British Museum, and to
throw himself on the mercy of Sidney Smith. For a time the
arrangement worked well. The two men corresponded in good
humour, and Smith had already deciphered from one of the tablets

the name of the ancient city nowadays called Atchana. He had also found mention of the neighbouring Hurri peoples in the political archives. In May 1937, working on beyond the normal date for site closure in the Middle East, Woolley wrote to Smith thanking him for his recent letters, and their 'most welcome news'. As for the discovery of references to the Hurri as parties to a treaty with Atchana, it was 'very much to the point'. It could, he thought, have an important bearing on questions raised by the pottery of Atchana as well as being of historical value in itself. 'I'm inclined to think the Hurri broke the treaty and burnt Atchana (or Alalakh, if that's its name).' It was a friendly exchange, but there were signs of disagreement with complaints from Smith about the treatment of tablets before they were despatched to the museum and the taking of castings from soft Plasticine moulds.

The Woolleys spent the hot season at home in each of the three years of excavation between 1934 and 1937, and Katharine took hold of the social reins. In 1934, the close contact Woolley had maintained with his old army chief, Neill Malcolm, blossomed into the closest friendship of his married life. Now retired as Major-General Sir Neill Malcolm, and living at Carlisle Place, just round the corner from the Woolley's home in Chelsea, he had been a widower since 1930. He was a successful businessman, and still bore the scars of the several campaigns in which he had been seriously wounded since he first served in India in 1897. He was one of several private financiers of the Atchana excavation. He owned an attractive 'fishing' cottage called the Mill House at Swallowcliffe in Wiltshire to which he liked to retire when he needed a few days' relaxation and he regularly sought the company of the amusing raconteur and fellow angler he had first known as Lieutenant Woolley in Cairo. Neill was one of the few among her husband's acquaintances who could tolerate Katharine for any length of time.

In spite of Lady Woolley's vitriolic tongue, there were other friendships. The Mallowans called on them occasionally, and their visits were returned, but they were now immersed in Max's Syrian digs and Agatha was still wary of Katharine. Among other 'permitted' friends, the most likeable from Leonard's point of view was George Eumorfopoulos, rich and enthusiastic collector of Chinese ceramics and jades, who visited Ur in 1929, and made an immediate impression, not least perhaps because of regular and generous contributions to the excavation funds. He and his wife Julia lived a few doors from the Woolleys on Chelsea Embankment, and after Ur the two men often went to country-house sales together in search of pottery and fine art. A companion whose company both men found increasingly attractive was young Anthony Blunt, who was on the staff of the Warburg Institute in the University of London and about to be appointed deputy director of the Courtauld Institute. He often dined with the Woolleys, Malcolms and Eumorfopouloses in Chelsea, and conversation ranged widely across the worlds of art and archaeology.

Social life at Chelsea Embankment in the summer months embraced parties at which the 'acceptable' fraternity of old Middle East contacts joined with archaeologists and other scholars of the day. There seemed to be but one precondition, as far as Katharine was concerned, the possession of a peerage or at very least a knighthood, according to Freya Stark. She was one of the few exceptions to Katharine's rule of thumb, and attended such a party in December 1935. 'The party at the Woolleys was fun too,' she told her mother. Miss Stark found Lady Allenby 'charming', and the Storrs as much so. 'I met Lord Curzon's daughter whom I liked and the head of the Air Force and the Army (who sat next to me at dinner and I liked too).' The Woolleys 'admired the dress' of the young woman who was to succeed Gertrude Bell as the grande dame of the desert lands. Sir Ronald Storrs said 'nice things' to her. On another occasion, Miss Stark found that everyone present had a title, and left in disgust.

Katharine found both Blunt and Malcolm much to her liking. Unless ill health prevented her, she always accompanied Leonard and his old army chief to Wiltshire on their fishing trips. It was on one such occasion that they met the elderly widow, Lady Horner, better known by her maiden name Frances Graham, the author of *Time Remembered*. Her country home, Manor House at Mells in Frome, Somerset, was not too far from Malcolm's Wiltshire retreat and she often came over to the Mill to make up a foursome. And she introduced Malcolm and the Woolleys to her friend Sir Sydney Cockerell, who was at the centre of intellectual life in London and Cambridge in those days. Frances Graham had known all the leading lights of the pre-Raphaelite movement, and was responsible for the purchase, through the National Art Collections Fund, of many valuable paintings of the period for provincial 'friends of art galleries'. Back in 1904, she had written to Cockerell to tell him – 'I don't know that I know one woman in a thousand! But I really have known one or two men – of whom Burne-Jones was chief.'

Sydney Carlyle Cockerell was sixty-seven when they first met, but fascinating, especially to Katharine. Protégé of William Morris, secretary of the Kelmscott Press, Director of the Fitzwilliam Museum, literary executor to the scandalous poet Wilfrid Scawen Blunt, and confidant of George Bernard Shaw and the leading Fabians of the time, he was altogether an uncommon bird.

Leonard wrote to Cockerell on 25 October 1934, from 12 Royal Avenue, the latest in a procession of Chelsea homes rented and leased to please Katharine, a few hundred yards from the Embankment Gardens house and conveniently close to the King's Road. He explained that they would be unable to meet a week hence, on the 31st, as he, Woolley, had to be at the Museum. Katharine would be unable to make it either, to her regret, as she was not 'particularly well' and the doctors had insisted that she take things 'more easily'. Her visit must be postponed indefinitely. 'But why not come and stay with us when in town?'

By November, Leonard and Katharine were both 'delighted' to learn that Sydney was coming to town. Woolley offered his excuses for not turning up to join Cockerell at an 'Audit Dinner', but Katharine had neglected to pass on the invitation.

Katharine wrote to Cockerell on 1 July 1935: 'Dear Sir Sidney (she always addressed him formally and misspelt his name), *When* are you coming to stay a night here? We do so want to see you & I hear you are often in London.' Three days later, after Sydney had accepted the invitation:

Alas – the 12th we are pledged to the Ballet with a young friend – his long leave – but can you come another night?

The almost imploring invitations, alternating with sudden 'attacks' which at the last moment prevented their meeting, went on.

Katharine was obviously fascinated by the brilliant Cockerell. Clearly she saw in the worldly Fabian a new-found lease of life. But she played her customary coquettish game, enchanting the men around her with displays of open admiration and generosity of spirit at one moment, felling them with off-hand dismissal or verbal abuse the next; or taking cover when they responded, with the onset of any one of a legion of ailments.

It was in March 1936, just before departing for Syria, that Leonard resumed a correspondence which had begun to take on an air of farce. He wrote to thank Sydney for a recent letter to Katharine:

As a matter of fact you wouldn't have seen Katharine had you been in town, for she has had a chapter of accidents; first she fell down a flight of stairs and cracked a bone in her finger, as well as bruising herself badly, and then she collapsed with influenza & is still in bed. The main point now is to get her fit for our journey on March 16th.

Leonard gave Cockerell an Aleppo address at which they could be contacted. Katharine's inflamed interest would have to lie dormant for a few months more.

On 1 August 1936, Katharine wrote from the Queen's Gate Nursing Home in London, announcing her return from 'a glorious time in Aleppo', explaining that she had come back with a poisoned toe which necessitated her temporary residence in a medical institution. Freya Stark, who visited her in the nursing home at the beginning of July, was less than sympathetic. 'Yesterday I went to see Lady Woolley in a nursing home with a bad toe – much more fuss than I made over pneumonia I may say, but that is just how people are made.'

For Woolley, Mill House was the perfect summer retreat, with a stream nearby where he could fish to his heart's content, and enjoy occasional visits from friends who passed by. But his peace was disturbed by Sidney Smith who was working intermittently on the Atchana tablets. Leonard wrote often in 1936 and 1937 from Mill House. 'May I take it that you will undertake the publication of the tablets found this season?' he asked in September 1937. He suggested that *Iraq*, the journal of the British School of Archaeology in Iraq, might be a suitable place, 'a graceful act' towards the Gertrude Bell fund 'which gives us a subvention'. Smith doubted whether he personally could undertake the work. The strain of the Ur publication, 'which ought not to have been undertaken under the terms and in the way it was undertaken', was already proving too much for him. 'Publication is entirely your affair,' he wrote. 'Thanks very much,' responded Woolley. 'Of course you cannot commit the department for more than the present season – after all, we might overwhelm you with tablets next year!'

While Leonard kept up an uneasy rapport with Smith, Katharine wrote from Mill Cottage to Cockerell to describe an event which was remarkable even by her standards, though it indicated that her physical condition was seriously worsening:

But for you I doubt whether I would have arrived here – the
crowd at Waterloo on Friday was so vast that only the royal
procession of my ambulance could have got through – the
ambulance men were charming & one huge one carried me
from my bedroom to the ambulance as if I were a cinema star –
very flattering when one is used to the unskilled carriers who
stagger & gasp as if one weighed 50 tons . . .

'Why not come and visit us at the cottage?' she concluded. Cockerell
was wearying of the difficult lady. 'Dear Sir Sidney, I feared there
was little chance of luring you here,' she wrote on 5 August, two
days after the earlier letter. 'But it was worth a try!' Lady Horner
was with them in Wiltshire. Cockerell was staying with the Siegfried
Sassoons.

By September Katharine fancied a change of scene and they went
to stay with unnamed friends in Gloucestershire. In October they
arrived back at Royal Avenue to find an invitation to lunch with the
Cockerells on the 20th. Cockerell came to stay in the meantime. His
wife 'Freza' (Florence) had been having headaches and Katharine
sympathized. The promised lunch was to be at the Cockerell's home
outside Cambridge. 'Perhaps we can take you to the Fitzwilliam
afterwards,' Katharine suggested. She added that an insect bite on
her knee had subsided and that she was practically well again, 'and
did so enjoy your visit.'

An enjoyable week-end in Cambridge was to signal a virtual end
to socializing in England. Pleasant, warm summers in the late thirties
evaporated with the onrush of academic tasks awaiting Leonard,
and the intervention of ominous political events in the world at
large.

At the start of the 1938 season in Syria, Woolley was trying to mend
his epigraphic fences. On 13 March he wrote to Smith from Atchana
to tell him that he had completed nine days' profitable work which
had produced twenty tablets. 'Wish you were here to tell us what
they are all about'. On 17 May he sent to London three packing
cases of inscribed tablets.

Not only had digging revealed a substantial palace of considerable
age; the tablets had begun to throw up the names of likely rulers, or
perhaps conquerors. In August 1938, summering again at Mill
Cottage, Woolley sent Smith a draft report on Atchana for publication in the *Antiquaries' Journal* and a suggestion of '1475 BC as a
round date for the destruction of the Palace'. Smith retorted:

The tablets do not prove anything about the date of destruction of the palace save that the event had to be later than Shamshsha-tar [named as a king of the region in the inscriptions, the son of Niqmepa]. Niqmepa's son may for all we know have reigned a long time.

Smith would try to get something ready for the *Antiquaries' Journal*.

Later excavations would show that the chief interest of al-Mina lay in its trade with ancient Greece; a trade which was broken off when the inland capital it served was destroyed. But a detailed investigation of that city would have to wait. In 1938 another architect, Ralph Lavers, arrived in place of Gott, and a year later Colonel Burn of the India Army and the assistant Peter Olland took day-to-day charge while Woolley considered another task of topical importance.

Work was to go on until the late spring of 1939, when threat of war forced a halt. As at Ur, it was the peripatetic Freya Stark who was among the last to visit the Atchana site, and she caught a rare glimpse of Katharine more or less at ease with the world. 'I got out to Atchana and found Katharine Woolley very friendly and all cheerful and was kept for the whole day and allowed to wash pots . . . with Katharine making a fearful to-do over the Altounians who came to grief over her washing. I do like her in many ways, but she is quite conscienceless in what she says of people.'

While working in Syria, Woolley had met many old colleagues and friends from centres of learning in Europe and America as they made their way to and from the archaeological sites of the Near East. There was always special delight for Woolley in the appearance of Max and Agatha. Mallowan was a leading light in the British School of Archaeology in Iraq, founded as a memorial to Gertrude Bell in 1932. Together with Agatha, he returned to Iraq in 1932 to work at Nineveh and in 1934, while Woolley was preparing his Syrian expedition, they asked if they might 'borrow' Hamoudi. They were on their way to conduct a survey of the Habur Valley, since they too were looking for new sites to attack. Their comings and goings provided an opportunity for pleasant and rewarding meet-ings, social and archaeological, at the start and tail ends of the digging seasons. Agatha was writing her play *Akhnaton* in 1936, and there was much ado over evening drinks in Aleppo about the character of the young heretic king who built Egyptian Amarna as a centre of monotheistic worship in the fourteenth century BC, and whose workmen's township Woolley had uncovered in 1921–22.

But there was a more immediate topic of conversation. In 1932, Max had been working for Campbell Thompson in the latter's last year at Nineveh, and he made a deep sounding in the area of the Ishtar temple which had been left incompletely explored by Layard back in the nineteenth century. At a considerable depth he encountered a distinctive pottery which was identified by the name of the mound at which it was first discovered by Baron Max von Oppenheim in the early 1900s, Tal Halaf. Woolley and Lawrence had remarked on similar pottery at Carchemish, the best examples being of egg-shell thickness, with a smooth burnished surface and decorated with sophisticated geometrical patterns in lustrous red and black. From the great depth at which it was found at Nineveh, such pottery must have been of marked antiquity but little could be said at that time of its precise date or origin. Woolley was to find fragments in the Amq district which suggested that very early residents of that region had acquired Halaf pottery, probably from traders in search of wood, and had made clumsy copies of it. The Amq peoples, whoever they were, seemed to be adaptable. Further digging would reveal wares which, though copies of Halaf, were difficult to distinguish from the original. Though neither Woolley nor Mallowan knew it at the time, their joint discoveries were linking the very earliest known trade routes of Anatolia, northern Syria and Iraq, and taking history back to the verge of the Neolithic period. Now, Indian discoveries added to the jig-saw of language, trade and culture which seemed to bring the Persian Gulf and the Aegean, and the great river valleys and deltas of Western Asia and Africa, into an unsuspected unity of development. It was a fascinating time for archaeologists, but a time threatened by gathering war clouds and dramatic political events. Iraq, in particular, was increasingly enmeshed in the schemes of the Third Reich. Julius Jordan was the dominating force in archaeology, and Mallowan was astonished to discover that so educated a man could have fallen so completely for the nonsense of *Mein Kampf* and its perpetrator. Woolley, the great man of Iraqui excavation a decade before, never ventured across the Euphrates after British authority declined and German influence became paramount. He preferred to work with the French whose writ still ran in Syria and with whom he had a good rapport.

*

By late 1937, a new challenge had intervened to absorb Woolley's
boundless energy. The Government of India wanted him to take
over as the country's archaeological adviser, following the retirement of Sir John Marshall who had held the post of Director-
General of Archaeology in Calcutta since 1902. Woolley was
interested but would not commit himself. He did not like the idea
of an official appointment or staff job. He was stubbornly freelance
by nature and hated committees. He would look at the problem
and report.

In its press statement of 15 June 1938 announcing Woolley's
acceptance of the invitation from Lord Linlithgow, the Viceroy, the
India Office set out the matters to be investigated. They were
principally: to decide on the most promising areas for further
exploration; to decide on the methods and agencies most likely to
give speedy and fruitful results, allowing for the participation of
universities and other non-official bodies as well as government
agencies; and to propose the training methods, and the backgrounds
and ages of recruits most likely to ensure the best results.

It was 35 years, the statement pointed out, since Lord Curzon
when Viceroy instituted the Survey of India with a central directorate
and appointed the classical scholar Sir John Marshall Director-
General of Archaeology. When Sir John had retired in 1931, over
3,000 monuments had been excavated or restored and were being
cared for by the Survey Department. The 'epoch-making excavations' at Taxila, Harappa and Mohenjo-daro had yielded finds of
the greatest importance. But there was a hint of the difficulties which
the administration had encountered since Sir John's withdrawal.
'Indian members of the Survey – its headship is now in Indian hands
– have shown themselves both eager and fit to carry on the great
work of unveiling the hidden past of their Motherland. But it is
appropriate that the work should be reviewed by so great an
authority as Sir Leonard Woolley.'

The tribute to Woolley cloaked sensitive nationalist feelings, and
some disaffection on both sides since the distinguished Sir John
Marshall's office had been taken over by his Indian subordinate, Rai
Bahadur Daya Sahni.

The Woolleys left for India on 26 October, their departure duly
noted by The Times' social diary. The tour of inspection lasted just
three months, in which time he covered the entire sub-continent with
the same unhurried despatch that caused so much wonderment to
visitors to his own archaeological sites. He was ever on the move,

yet never apparently in a hurry. Long days spent in interminable, leisurely meetings, or inspecting sites or travelling great distances in crowded trains, were interspersed with late nights spent in reading reports and writing notes. There was little time for socializing in the course of a non-stop tour, though there was of course the mandatory call at Lutyens' glistening New Delhi to meet the Linlithgows. Katharine was helpful to Leonard in his work, relatively free from health problems apart from the inevitable attacks of migraine, and affable enough in her dealings with their hosts, Indian and British.

The unfortunate Bahadur Daya Sahni, who had done sterling work at Harappa, one of two great Indus Valley sites, had inherited an unenviable legacy. Marshall had achieved great things despite Delhi's notorious bureaucracy. He had easy access to a succession of viceroys and their advisers, and was well funded by government. But the archaeological committee of the Survey was unimaginative and generally uncooperative. As soon as Daya Sahni took over as Director-General in 1931 the world trade depression hit India with hurricane force. Massive cuts were made in the budget at just the time when Indian archaeology was put on the map by the discovery of Chalcolithic (Copper) Age burial sites at Harappa and Mohenjo-daro, and at Nal in Baluchistan. International attention centred on third millennium cylinder seals, similar to those of Mesopotamia, which had been found among the more plentiful square stamp seals of the Indus Valley. The name Indo-Sumerian had been adopted as a provisional code for their identification. The effect of the budget cuts had been 'stunning' and the department was on the verge of breakdown when Bahadur Daya Sahni resigned in 1935. He was succeeded by Marshall's assistant at Mohenjo-daro, Mr K. N. Dikshit, a year before Woolley came on the scene. Woolley spoke to both men, and was shown round the principal sites by them. He was grateful for the courtesy he was shown, and for such hospitality as his busy schedule allowed, but he was irritated by the deliberation of the Indian field archaeologists. After his own trials over the years in seeking adequate funds and prompt payment in the field, he might have been expected to show fellow-feeling for the beleaguered Indians. But he found the new Director-General and his colleagues lacking in zeal and without a coherent plan.

After journeys from Karachi to Lahore (partly by spotter-plane), on to the Tibetan frontier and across to the North-West Frontier and the Indus Valley, he and Katharine returned to Delhi in early

December. They travelled to Ceylon by way of Bombay and Madras in order to catch the boat home at the end of the month. By the time they arrived in England, Woolley had completed a devastating report for Lord Zetland, the Secretary of State for India.

War, Art and Vita Nova

Despite war cries and preparations for the issuing of his India report, he went off to Syria in February 1939 immersed in Atchana and the prospect of more significant discoveries. He was able to send Sidney Smith a large batch of tablets soon after he arrived. He had seen enough to know that he had identified the earliest of the provincial capitals of the Amq plain, and a name, probably a monarch's. Smith reported back – 'Your tablet impressions do not I fear give any exact date. Only one gives a certain royal name, that of a king of Yamhad.' That ruler, Yarim-Lim, was mentioned in the tablets of another vitally important Syrian site, Mari, which the French were excavating. Dossin, the French archaeologist, had said that Yamhad was the principality in which Aleppo lay in ancient times. More tablets enabled Smith to expand on his own unenthusiastic assessment.

When Woolley arrived home in June, peace still hung in the balance. In the event, there was just time enough to prepare a report on Atchana for *The Times*, to inform the reader that he had unearthed an ancient city there which was called Alalakh in its own day.

The limelight fell on the India report which he finished while staying with Malcolm at Mill Cottage.

Lord Zetland had prepared the ground in April with a talk to the annual conference of the India Society at Burlington House in which he spoke of the importance of cultural values rather than political disputation in assessing Britain's role in India 'at the bar of history'. When Lord Linlithgow had informed him that he would welcome a visit from an archaeologist of 'world-wide renown', he had, he said, 'no hesitation in extending an invitation to Sir Leonard Woolley'. He added: 'That scholar has written a report of the highest interest containing suggestions for the future work of the [Survey] department.'

On 13 July, the report took up almost an entire page of *The Times* and about the same amount of space in the *Morning Post*. It was the main story in every Indian newspaper. In *The Times* it dwarfed a leading article and readers' letters defending Mr Chamberlain's policy of 'appeasement'.

'In the opinion of no less an authority than Sir Leonard Woolley,' said the newspaper, the Archaeological Survey of India 'has lacked in recent years a coherent plan, though opportunity exists, for filling the gap of 2,000 years in our established knowledge of prehistoric India.'

There had admittedly been difficulties in the way of fruitful development, and Woolley praised the progress made under Sir John Marshall's aegis, particularly at Mohenjo-daro, Harappa and Taxila, in spite of bureaucratic difficulties. But since 1931, everything had changed. It was 35 years since Lord Curzon had established the Survey, and even allowing for achievements under Marshall between 1902 and 1931, the story was still a sorry one. Perhaps there was unconscious comparison with his own work at Ur and in Egypt and Syria, where there was always a need for stringent housekeeping.

> The Department has been starved financially and more money must be spent if its work of exploration is to be put upon a proper basis, that is a fact which cannot be gainsaid. But a mere increase of the grant unaccompanied by other charges would actually do more harm than good, for the truth is that the Department is altogether lacking in men trained for the work which they have to do.

He had encountered plenty of enthusiasm among the all-Indian staff, and intelligence enough. What was lacking was experience and proper training.

After describing his visits to the main archaeological sites in the north and setting out the chief discoveries at the Indus Valley sites, and at Taxila in the North-West Frontier province, he wrote: '. . . of the cultural history of India not even the skeleton exists. There is nothing to show how the Indus culture came into being and between its end and the Asoka [Buddhist] period . . . there is a gap of some 2,000 years of blank ignorance.' Even for those periods which may be called 'historical', the sequence of history was quite unknown. The position in the south of India was worse than in the north. He suggested radical changes in the structure and methods of the Survey Department. He laid down the determining factors in choosing an archaeological site. There should be no more of those 'small, sporadic and haphazard' excavations which had so dissipated the department's resources to date. There should be a distinction drawn between one man's duties and another's. Up to the present everyone had been expected to be a 'superman'. Specialization was essential. So was the appointment of a temporary executive adviser. Woolley had an idea of the person most suited to that function but he named no one in the report. In any case, the need for decision in the matter was overtaken by political events.

The debate continued none the less. The wide-ranging commission to put Indian archaeology on the right track marked a departure for Woolley. He had always been a field man. He admired the patient scholarship of the epigraphists and glyptographic experts who made sense of the primordial languages and cylinder and stamp seals which revealed so much of art and everyday life, but he was happy to rely on their skills for detailed information, reserving his own energies for the actual pursuit of antiquity beneath the earth. He preferred the sharp end of the business, and was accustomed to the criticism, the ridicule even, of the 'desk-bound'. He had a passionate contempt for the committee mentality, and, as the Cambridge tablets episode of 1931 showed, he was quite capable of cutting through red tape if it got in the way of efficiency or fair play. Now he had consented to be a one-man committee of adjudication, telling others how they should do their jobs, and where. There can be no doubt that he enjoyed his new role, but equally, he was embarrassed by it. Having done as he was asked he let it be known to the India Office that the man he favoured for the job when the time came was his young friend 'Rik' Wheeler. It was a favour that Wheeler would repay within three years, by writing from Africa where he was serving with the army, to Sir Alfred Clapham, Secretary of the Antiquaries' Society, suggesting the urgent need for a supremo to protect Europe's art heritage. The message reached Churchill who immediately suggested that Woolley should handle the job from within the War Office. For the moment, both tasks lay in the future. Mortimer Wheeler was ten years Woolley's junior. He had proved himself at St Albans and other British sites and had shown himself to be a good organizer and a brilliant, if somewhat histrionic lecturer.

Woolley's report revolutionized the archaeology of India in the long run, but he hardly ever referred to his role. Neither did he claim credit for what happened. He was a little shamefaced about taking on his peeping-tom role.

His embarrassment was not lessened by the fact that while he was
in India, his path crossed that of the old 'sage' Sir Aurel Stein. Stein
was both teacher and man of action revered by the Indians, Moslem
and Hindu, as one who lived and taught among them, and uncovered
a significant part of that history which Woolley found sketchy at
best, and non-existent for a period of 2,000 years. Indian politicians
turned to Stein instantly to defend their reputations. And he obliged.
He too was embarrassed. Woolley had been his pupil and his host,
they admired and liked each other. But Stein needed the help of the
Archaeology Department at the time in connection with a plan to
publish a large collection of important paintings, and his determination to defend the department may not have been untinged by the
thought that he was the obvious candidate anyway for the task of
assessing its worth. In any case, his Indian friends implored him to
speak out and the task had to be faced. Dikshit, still Director-
General of the department, wanted 'a powerful voice' to represent
his own and his colleagues' case. Stein obliged with a statement
which had many of the qualities of Woolley's own report, especially
when it damned with faint praise:

> W's report is a remarkable piece of work in many ways,
> considering the short time during which he had to make
> observations all over this vast continent and his naturally
> inadequate knowledge of Indian conditions. Many of his
> remarks are just, some of his criticisms less so. The main fact he
> could scarcely be expected to dwell on in print, viz. that while
> Marshall worked under all the difficulties inherent in bureau-
> cratic mentality, administrative machine and want of an
> example of state-aided research in archaeology at home etc., he
> did achieve great things; but he could not create foundations
> sound enough to assure safe and satisfactory progress under
> much weakened and less well-prepared successors. Complete
> 'Indianization' is now practically achieved. History will judge
> whether it will be of benefit to India.

Whatever the urgency, the wholesale reorganization demanded by
Woolley's report would have to be set aside while more pressing
issues were dealt with. Within two months of its publication the
world was at war.

In his sixtieth year and in demand by several universities who would
gladly offer him chairs, Woolley had no need to go to war for a

second time in twenty-five years. As in 1914, however, he was determined to serve, though he was saved the need for a personal decision by the arrival of call-up papers under the emergency regulations. On 4 September 1939 he was re-commissioned with the acting rank of Captain and posted as a GS03 to the Intelligence Division at the War Office.

The secret-service branch of the military, in which he had worked with distinction last time, was the obvious choice. Even so, he decided that a week-end's fishing at Mill Cottage with Neill Malcolm might inspire his first military boss to make a last gesture of help in securing a useful job. Now seventy, Malcolm had spent the past two years in Europe as Britain's High Commissioner for Refugees, helping the 'aliens', and particularly the Jews of Austria and the Sudetenland, to escape Hitler's clutches. He was still remembered in the army as an heroic figure of the North-West Frontier campaigns, the Boer War and the first Great War, and he still had influence at the War Office. But neither he nor anyone else could do much to prod Whitehall into taking intelligence seriously in 1939. The old Military Intelligence Directorate had been disbanded in the 1920s, at a time when all espionage and counter-espionage activity was political and commercial in nature, and concerned primarily with undermining the Bolsheviks. Many of the younger men who were to serve in the intelligence services had been disillusioned by ill-concealed sympathy in high places for Franco's Falangists in the Spanish Civil War, and less openly perhaps for Herr Hitler.

Military Intelligence as such had come to an end in 1929 when the occupation of Germany ceased and the British flag was hauled down at Wiesbaden. Even the Army Intelligence Corps, the basic training school which gave Woolley his initial instruction in 1914, was defunct. A card-index system which originated in 1916 in Whitehall Place had contained the names of hundreds of spies, agents and contacts in every part of the world. When the man who was to resurrect the Intelligence Corps, Major Gerald Templer, went to the War Office in 1937 he found that most of the cards had disappeared. Of the few that remained, lying pathetically in a single box, most represented people who were untraceable or long since dead.

The only sections of the old Military Intelligence Directorate to have survived the 'appeasement' years were MI5 and MI6, the counter-intelligence and 'special' intelligence services which since

1916 had become almalgams of army and civilian interests, respec-
tively under Home and Foreign Office control.

For Woolley, as for many of his contemporaries, the Second Great
War was to start off even more dismally than its predecessor.

In the nearly catastrophic first year of 'phoney' war, frantic efforts
were made by the army staff to create the basis of a workable
intelligence organization. The DMI (Director of Military Intelligence) was Maj-General Freddie Beaumont-Nesbitt (Eton, Sandhurst
and Grenadier Guards), who had been deputy director of a barely
functioning office since arriving in Whitehall Place from Paris, where
he was military attaché, in 1938. Beaumont-Nesbitt's deputy, Briga-
dier Van Cutsem, took a particular interest in the section to which
Woolley was assigned, Mediterranean and Middle East.

Woolley's first work entailed the creation of an internal advisory
service, involving the keeping of a day book in which every significant Middle East event was recorded and commented on. In a year
of re-organization and precious little real activity, however, Woolley
busied himself with the preparation of a 'secret report' on Middle
East strategy, containing information gained from friendly embas-
sies on the comings and goings of Arab, Turk and Balkan politicians and emissaries. Between times, he still gave talks on art and
archaeology.

Almost before he had had opportunity to try on his new uniform,
he had been asked to deliver the Sir George Birdwood memorial
lecture at the Royal Society of Arts in December. He decided on a
condensed account of all the exploration sites of India, and demonstrated that he had not been blind to the architecture of the country
during his visit – to differences in Dravidian and Moghul building –
or to the Indus sites. Taxila, which Marshall had revealed to the
world in 1922, acquired its name he told his audience, from 'the
Graecized form of the Indian *Iakshasila*, coined first by the soldiers
of Alexander'. Taxila had been ruled by Greeks and Darius's
Persians, and after them Scythians and Parthians, Kushans, and
White Huns. No city of antiquity had changed hands so many times,
yet the city which Marshall's team found, along with the city on
whose remains it was built, had been destroyed ages before the army
of Alexander arrived on the scene. Marshall's city which stood in
the fourth century BC was the topmost of three cities on the Bhir
Mound close to the North-West Frontier. Woolley made handsome
use of material from the speeches and writings of Marshall, but he
conveyed it with all his customary dialectical skill.

While he settled in at Whitehall Place, Leonard heard of the death of his closest friend of recent years, George Eumorfopoulos, who had suffered an agonizing decline in the past few months. The philanthropist who had helped out financially at Atchana (through Neill Malcolm), and whose Chinese porcelain and jade collections were among the finest in the world, died just before Christmas of that year, unaware that war had been declared. Woolley was asked to write a *Times* obituary of one of the few friends who had won Katharine's full approval and thus made social life in Royal Avenue more endurable. He recalled his friend's air journey to Baghdad in 1929, and his visit to Ur where he spent four days. '. . . we never had a more enthusiastic visitor; it was an experience to which he always looked back with keen pleasure, and we with a pleasure no less keen.' The Eumorfopoulos collections had been presented to the British and V&A Museums before his death and future generations would forever associate his name with them. Woolley's appreciation recalled the many interesting people he had met at 'the treasure house on Chelsea Embankment'. He would always remember it 'as a hospitality unlike any other in the world because it came from those two loving personalities, George and Julia Eumorfopoulos.'

Among the fraternity of art lovers and connoisseurs Woolley had met at the Eumorfopouloses' home, the man whose company he enjoyed most, the urbane, enthusiastic Anthony Blunt, was at army HQ in Paris with counter-intelligence at the end of 1939. He returned with the retreating army to the arcane world of MI 5 in London and was a welcome visitor at the house in Royal Avenue. Despite blackout and blitz, war enhanced the social life of the Woolleys. Their parties, designed chiefly to keep Katharine happy, became a familiar feature of the Chelsea scene.

Another old acquaintance who enlivened the first few months of war was Richard Meinertzhagen, Beatrice Webb's nephew. One of the most colourful of Woolley's intelligence colleagues from the First World War, and another Chelsea neighbour, Meinertzhagen was drafted into the staff offices the day after Woolley. If the two ex-Cairo men had a common bond, it was Lawrence, about whom they had different, and sometimes contradictory, opinions. Meinertz-hagen, who as Allenby's field intelligence chief in 1917 was Law-rence's senior in the Syrian campaign, thought him effeminate and a liar, though he came to modify his judgement. Woolley took an altogether humorous view. He and Lawrence had enjoyed some lively experiences as young men, sometimes wandering together among the natives of Syria and Anatolia dressed in their Oxford college blazers, brandishing revolvers and engaging in open warfare with Arabs, Kurds, Turks and Germans. Woolley liked to relate those distant adventures just as much as had Lawrence, and with as much inclination to garnish the facts. Neither Woolley nor Meinertzhagen believed for a moment that there was more than a skeleton of truth in Ned's heroic tales of the desert war, but it all made for amusing conversation at the Athenaeum and Travellers', where they sometimes lunched together.

Events began to move with more purpose in 1940. Maj-General Davidson succeeded Beaumont-Nesbitt, and there were wholesale changes to the staff organization. The reappearance of Anthony Blunt was particularly pleasing to Woolley. He had published a book on Poussin's drawings just before the declaration of war and he gave the Woolleys a signed copy. Talk turned inevitably to art and to the danger of Europe's artistic treasures falling into the hands of Nazi leaders or being destroyed by bombing. The shared interest of the two men in matters of art and antiquity undoubtedly drew them together. But there was never a closeness of friendship. Indeed, it was Katharine who was most drawn to the 'charming' Blunt. His overt homosexuality is unlikely to have escaped Woolley's notice, or his opprobrium. Blunt's contact in MI6, Kim Philby, was also known to Woolley. Kim's famous father, Harry St John Philby, had served in Mesopotamia before going off to Transjordan, and finally to Saudi Arabia between the wars. Woolley had met Philby in the East and in England, and like most of those who had occasion to deal with him, he found 'Hajji' Philby's assumption of pre-eminence in the Arab lands both laughable and irritating. Nonetheless, Woolley took to his son, who would recall after his defection to the Soviet Union that, at the time the three of them were together in Military Intelligence, Blunt tried to persuade MI5 to offer Woolley a job.

Churchill, according to Philby, refused to countenance the move, perhaps having other tasks in mind for him.

Another dinner guest of the early war period was Laurence Kirwan, Secretary of the Royal Geographical Society and a fellow officer in Middle East 'Intelligence'. He was dining with Katharine and Leonard in Chelsea on the night of the first great blitz when London appeared to go up in flames and everyone dived for the nearest cover. Katharine, her physical condition much worsened now, was as formidable as ever in discussion or debate, but unaffected it seemed by the efforts of the Luftwaffe.

An outsider who called on Woolley in his WO 'dungeon' when he was involved with Middle East matters, was a young and aspiring film producer named Roy Boulting. More than forty years after the event, Boulting recalled their meeting. Commissioned from Sandhurst into the Yorkshire Hussars, he was attached to the Royal Armoured Corps. His regiment was sent to the Middle East soon after hostilities started but he was held back for special training at Catterick. While he was there, someone at the War Office heard that he had some film-making experience and he was sent to join the Army Film Unit. In 1942, when the British army fell back at al-Alamein, one flank resting on the coast, the other on the al-Quattara depression, Boulting sensed his opportunity. He suspected that an important battle might be about to start and asked the War Office for expert advice. He was sent to see Woolley at Whitehall Place:

> . . . there he was in the very bowels of the earth underneath the War Office, established in a small room, memorializing on paper the day-to-day events in the Middle East. I can see him now, a quiet, small silver-haired figure, bespectacled and infinitely courteous. I must have seemed – as indeed I was – an extremely callow youth. It was Sir Leonard who explained to me the implications of a further defeat at Al Alamein; the Middle East overrun, the oil denied us, and a linking up of Axis forces, which at that time were thrusting down through the Crimea. With great kindness, he gave me access to his official daily journal, and thereby enabled me to understand to a much greater extent the possibilities that lay beyond either victory or defeat. For me, it was a tutorial: a relationship of student to teather . . . Out of his assistance, perception and guidance came *Desert Victory*. I quite liked that, and felt that at least one had made some small contribution to the prosecution of the war.

Boulting added a postscript to his recollection of Woolley. 'Beyond these exchanges between youth and age; the elaborations, explanations and hypotheses thrown from one to another across his desk, there is nothing. We never met socially, never had a meal together; I did not know where he lived, or who with. But I remember him gratefully as someone who, like most men of distinction and eminence in their field, was prepared to accept brash youth with kindness and understanding.'

Soon after Boulting's visit Woolley was transferred to a new directorate, Public Relations, under the control of Sir James Grigg, Permanent Under-Secretary at the War Office. He was upgraded to General Staff Officer grade 2, and given the temporary rank of Major.

The new work was not demanding. Some of his colleagues spent a large part of the war in amiable contemplation of such issues as euthanasia, eugenetics and the merits of hexametric verse. Some could not type and chewed pencils endlessly, hardly ever putting them to paper. Nearly all went off to their clubs for lunch, the Travellers' being the most popular. A few of the 'country' wallahs favoured Whitehall pubs. The new regime deprived Woolley of one lunchtime companion, Meinertzhagen, who was pensioned off to spend the rest of the war in command of a unit of the Home Guard.

The tedium of work was relieved by extraneous calls on his services. He was still in demand as a lecturer and despite the daily calamities of the war there were occasional requests from *The Times* for archaeological articles to lighten the daily burden of disaster. But it was his preoccupation with the problem of preserving art treasures which led to his largest and most important role in the war.

Mortimer Wheeler was prominent among those who expressed increasing concern at the time with the fate of Europe's art, a term which embraced buildings, monuments, archives and excavation sites in Britain and abroad. From 1941 onward, Woolley was in regular communication on the subject with Wheeler, and with Crawford and Sir Charles Speers, the Chairman of the Institute of Archaeology in London. He started to organize a card-index of monuments and fine arts collections, so that in the event of loss or war damage, the records could be easily traced for restoration purposes. In the period when a German invasion was expected at any moment and Britain's cities were under almost constant air bombardment, it seemed an urgent task, at least to Woolley and Wheeler and their like.

It was a concern shared by the British and American governments, and Prime Minister Churchill began to take a personal interest in Woolley's work. A year later he was transferred to yet another staff department, this time the Civil Affairs Directorate under another Permanent Under-Secretary, Sir Frank Bovenschen (with Maj-General Kirby in executive charge), billeted at the Victoria Hotel in Northumberland Avenue, not far from Army HQ but distant enough to ensure a good deal of independence.

Before taking up the latest appointment, he completed his essay on 'Mediterranean Strategy' which he had been asked to undertake in the first place by General Smuts in the first days of war. The document was sent to all naval and military commanding officers in the Middle East theatre, marked 'Secret. To be kept under lock and key when not in use.'

It began with a résumé of great power involvement in the area from the time of the first Crusade, with a preamble which must have caused its readers, not least the Prime Minister, some amusement: 'Yet these disasters in the field and desertion by their allies never once gave rise to mention of the word "peace". Such was the spirit of the people that the Chief of the State was met by a popular demonstration of all ranks and thanked for not giving up hope for his Country. *Livy XXII LX1 15.*'

The report went on:

He [Smuts] put his finger at once on Japan as one of the two dangers threatening the Empire, but dealt at most length with the question of the Mediterranean. He pointed out that with the fall of France and the expulsion of British forces from the Continent, Europe must cease to be the theatre of war upon a big scale. Great Britain, now a vast fortress, should be able, provided that the Navy kept the seas open and America could be a base for supplies, to weather the strain and in time wear down the German power until it cracked and crashed . . . To save the Empire and Commonwealth it was, therefore, necessary to hold Africa south of the Equator at all costs . . .'

Having conveyed General Smuts' views on overall war strategy, Woolley got down to the brass tacks of fighting the enemy under headings such as 'Effort to save French Colonies', 'Foreign Fleets', 'Threat to Egypt', 'Question of Evacuation'.

Dealing with the Balkans, he gave details of meetings at Berchtesgaden between Hitler and Hungary's Teleki and Czaky, and the Bulgarian and Slovak President and Premier. All the familiar Balkan disputes had been ironed out 'in submission to Hitler'. As for Egypt and the Arab world, German agents were spreading the word that British imperialism and the Zionists were hand-in-glove, that Hitler was the sworn enemy of the Jews and therefore the natural ally of the Arab peoples. Rashid Ali in Baghdad had been in contact with German agents from the outbreak of hostilities. Operations in Syria and Iraq were designed to outflank the Allies as Rommel built up his

Afrika Corps. Alexander's offensive in Libya was the only possible
course for the Allies up to 1943. Churchill's visit to Washington in
June of the previous year had resulted in an agreement with
Roosevelt to restore the pre-war *status quo*. Allied control of the
entire North African coast was the indispensable condition of an
attack on Sicily. It was a highly political approach, and front-line
commanders faced with immediate problems of waging war might
have wondered what harm would befall the cause if the document
fell into enemy hands.

Within a year of the events outlined in Woolley's guide to the
strategic importance of Africa, an armada had set out from Malta
and the Tunisian ports to ferry an army across the Sicilian narrows.
That was a development which was to present Woolley with his
most significant wartime challenge.

His new work in Civil Affairs entailed continued co-operation
with the Military Intelligence Directorate. His brief was to work
with the reformed and now active – if sometimes flawed – intelligence branches such as the Special Intelligence Service and Special
Operations, to keep watch on the most sensitive and tempting of all
wartime loot. It was suspected that the Nazi leaders had ransacked
some of the most important museums and galleries of Europe. Italy,
occupied by the Germans and veritable treasure-house of European
painting and sculpture, was especially vulnerable. Even where theft
was not the problem, destruction was an ever-present threat and the
Allied armies had to be made aware of the danger. With all the
immense problems of waging war, and at a time when the possibility
of losing the struggle can never have been far from his mind,
Churchill called Woolley to Downing Street and Chequers on three
occasions in 1943 to brief him on the progress of his work. If the
Prime Minister's concern made Woolley's task easier as far as official
co-operation went, there remained the difficulty of obtaining reliable
information on criminal acts which often involved highly placed and
well protected individuals. Access to the most secret agencies on the
Allied side, including American army Intelligence, became essential.
Agents were despatched to the Continent, briefed by Woolley on the
pictures, sculptures and archaeological treasures most likely to find
hiding places in disused mineshafts and Swiss bank vaults, and on
the most likely beneficiaries. More reliable sources of information
became vitally necessary.

The new job had great appeal for Katharine. She had been a
reluctant bystander in the first three years of war. Now, despite her

disability, she insisted that she would make an ideal secretary for her husband in his new job. The War Office caved in and she was installed in his office at Northumberland Avenue.

On the home front, Osbert Crawford was useful. He still nursed his brainchild *Antiquity* at his Southampton office, with blithe disregard of German air attacks. He was a life-long photographer and historian of ancient monuments in Britain and on the Continent, and he was able to supply Woolley with very useful records. Remarkably, he still had correspondents in Europe who often kept in touch by way of the Red Cross. On several occasions he sought Woolley's help in avoiding the censor in order to keep track of informants in France. In short, he was a one-man secret service and Woolley found him helpful enough to justify several trips to his lair on the south coast.

More important in the wider sense was Woolley's friendship with Rik Wheeler. The amusing, theatrical and erudite Wheeler did not meet with universal approval in archaeological circles. But Woolley liked him and, as it happened, the two men had a long-standing bond of service with the same regiment in the First World War, the Royal Field Artillery. As a young man, Wheeler had served with distinction in Europe and at the onset of hostilities in 1939 was a Lieutenant-Colonel in the Territorial Army. He was on the staff of the Royal Commission on Historical Monuments in 1913, and in 1939 was appointed a commissioner of the same body. In a sense, he had assumed seniority over the older Woolley in matters of arts rehabilitation. Until 1943, when he raised a gunners' brigade to fight with the 8th Army in North Africa and the 10th Corps in Italy, he worked closely with Woolley in Northumberland Avenue.

Wheeler's biographer, Jacquetta Hawkes, later remarked on one attribute he shared with Woolley, a grasp of the importance of publicity as a necessary adjunct to fund-raising. Digging at Roman Isca on the Usk estuary, Wheeler made full use of local folklore which identified the well-preserved oval amphitheatre with King Arthur's Round Table. Wheeler was accused of 'shameless exploitation' of an unfounded legend. Miss Hawkes refused to jump to Wheeler's defence, preferring instead to cast the culprit in a familiar mould: 'The accusation is true, but Wheeler's action was hardly more shameless than the use made of largely irrelevant Biblical associations by excavators in the Near East, particularly ... by Leonard Woolley of Noah's Flood at Ur.' Another outstanding archaeologist who was also delighted to be asked to help at the same time was the Secretary of the Institute of Archaeology, Miss Kathleen Kenyon, formidable daughter of the British Museum's director and herself destined to become one of the leading field workers of her profession.

With the expert help of his British colleagues, and his agents abroad, Woolley built up an incomparable record of the world's most important treasures, together with files on those paintings and sculptures known to have been concealed by friendly governments and agents, or stolen or damaged by occupying forces.

His responsibility embraced more than art, however. Europe's major archives were a constant cause of concern to the British and American authorities. Royal archives, in particular, often contained secret and sensitive communications between members of surviving royal families, many of whom were interrelated. For Woolley, the royal records were perhaps an even bigger headache than art treasures. Important politicians had asked him to help in 1941 when the Italians first published accusations of vandalism by British troops in North Africa, but he was otherwise engaged then and could only give informal advice. In 1942, America became involved through the revelation by refugees of German theft and vandalism in Poland running into millions of dollars. By 1943, newspapers in Britain and America carried articles describing wholesale destruction by German troops in Italy, including the burning down of the Royal Library in Naples, with the destruction of 200,000 volumes as well as Greek and Roman papyri from Herculaneum. Italy became the centre of attention. The time had come for action and in January of that year the USA took the lead with the setting up of an *ad hoc* committee based at Harvard. The university there took on the extraordinary task of listing all buildings of artistic or historical importance in every European country. With an office in New York, the committee produced its famous series of 'Frick' maps, with important monuments shown on them and details in the margins. There was also a manual somewhat optimistically offering the troops advice on 'first aid' to damaged buildings and artifacts. In June 1943, a group of museum directors in Britain was so concerned that it put out an urgent call for the protection of monuments in Italy. The War Ministry decided that it had better grasp the nettle and set up an Archaeological Advisory Branch of the Army Staff within Civil Affairs, with 'minimum strength'. No one could claim that the new office's staffing was extravagant. It consisted, according to army records, of 'Major Sir Leonard Woolley, Lady Woolley his secretary, and a clerk.' In due time the advisory branch became the Monuments and Fine Arts Sub-Commission, 'extended to include archives'. Woolley devised its motto, adapted from Pericles' *Funeral Oration* – 'We protect the arts at the lowest possible cost.' The appointment was not gazetted until October when Woolley was named Archaeological Adviser to the Directorate of Civil Affairs, upgraded to GSO 1 and given the rank of Lieutenant-Colonel.

With the new job came a change of lifestyle. In the first four years of war he had kept up the house in Royal Avenue and Katharine had weathered the Luftwaffe storm with surprising stoicism. Her physical condition had deteriorated markedly. There were still the incessant migraine attacks, the same determination to have things her own way, but the war itself seemed if anything to improve her spirits. Leonard's social life was made easier by the exigencies of war. His work demanded contact with many colleagues and friends with whom he had lost touch during the married years. Not even Katharine could countermand the instructions of the Prime Minister or the Chief of Staff, and so a new freedom accompanied the henpecked husband's wartime labours.

There were still demands on his professional services. In 1942 he was awarded the Huxley Memorial Medal and was called on by the Royal Anthropological Institute to deliver its annual Huxley Memorial Lecture. He chose 'Syria as a Cultural Link in the Ancient World' as his subject, highlighting the work of the Frenchman Claude Schaeffer in revealing the ancient royal city of Ugarit at Ras Shamra in the north of Syria. As it happened, Dr Schaeffer was serving as a corvette captain with the Free French forces in England, and he was in the audience to hear tribute paid to his work by a British archaeologist whose achievements he believed to be 'preeminent in their age'. Needless to say, Woolley also surveyed his own work in Syria, at Atchana and al-Mina; and he ignored the sillier manifestations of wartime nationalism by praising the work of the Germans at the Hittite capital of Boghazkoi in Anatolia.

There was a great deal of administration to cope with, too. The British Museum was still inundated with correspondence from students and scholars, religious sects and ordinary museum-goers about the Ur discoveries, and most of it was forwarded to Woolley for answer by Sidney Smith, who now combined the Professorship of Near Eastern Archaeology at London University with his museum duties. An actress wrote from the Isle of Wight demanding an exact description of Queen Pu-abi's headdress so that she could wear a replica on stage. Such tasks, dealt with conscientiously, were something of a distraction at the high point of war.

From October 1943, at Churchill's instigation, Woolley and Katharine moved to a splendid new address. With advancement and the need for secrecy in his work, he was given one of the apartments in the Dorchester Hotel in Park Lane which were reserved for senior officials who had to entertain important (sometimes clandestine) visitors and who were likely to be summoned to Downing Street at any moment by a notoriously impatient Prime Minister.

A month or two earlier, in August 1943, Roosevelt had approved the setting up of an American Commission for the Protection and Salvage of Artistic and Historic Monuments in Europe, commonly called the Roberts Commission after its chairman, the Hon Owen J. Roberts of the Supreme Court. The commission was told that it must co-operate with the School of Military Government at Charlottesville, Virginia, and 'with learned men brought in from universities and museums'. With American presidential weight behind it the Commission made a confident bid to take over the whole European art-preservation commitment, sending a 'blueprint' for action to the War Office through the US Embassy in London. The threat of civilian eggheads interfering in areas of military operations terrified the generals. Woolley was instructed to co-operate with the Americans but to ensure that only military personnel, working through the Civil Affairs branch of the General Staff, should be allowed to operate in the war zones.

In organizational terms, Woolley was left to his own devices. His immediate task was to find a band of men – no women were permitted – from the ranks of museum curators, archaeologists, art historians and other academics (but not art or antiques dealers) who possessed the knowledge necessary to track down missing works and who were brave enough to work, if necessary, behind enemy lines and in a world that could be dangerous enough even in peacetime. The job specification was simple enough. Potential recruits must be 'tough, able to speak the language of the country in which they will work, and must not appear soft or dilettante.' The countries involved stretched from Burma and Indo-China within the South-East Asia Command to Scandinavia and the Mediterranean theatres of war.

It took the best part of a year to find a suitably qualified corps of 'art experts'. Work was accelerated by German propaganda which claimed in nightly broadcasts that the 'thieves and Jews of Anglo-American imperialism' were busily removing the art treasures of the world to the British Museum, the Metropolitan in New York, and even to private collections. On 1 October 1943, German radio spoke of the director in charge as 'a well-known gangster'. A later broadcaster spoke of 'the Jewish art dealer Pimpernel'. On the same day, Rome radio announced that ships had left Sicily for London with precious works of art aboard, 'some of which will go to the British Museum, some to private collections.'

The vituperative words of the German and Italian broadcasters may seem far-fetched in retrospect. At the time, there were many people on the Continent, and not a few in Britain and America, who were very willing to believe them. Equally, the British press was happy to return the compliment with hair-raising reports of German vandalism and Italian perfidy.

As new urgency came to invigorate his workdays, Woolley's domestic life took on an extra responsibility. Katharine became almost totally confined to a wheelchair. He had to wheel her to the office every morning, through the park from the Dorchester to Northumberland Avenue.

On 16 March 1944, the newspaper *Völkischer Beobachter* carried a report which told of 'wild competition between the English and American Jew art dealers whose agents are bidding against each other to get out of southern Italy anything of any interest at all.' A few weeks later German Home Service radio announced that 'a new batch of Jewish art dealers had arrived in southern Italy from the USA.' By then, many of Woolley's men had accomplished remarkable feats of discovery, restitution and repair. And the American Commission's very active force had joined them in Italy and elsewhere. Woolley had raided the great academic institutions and archives of the world to find his recruits. In the end, he was able to find forty-eight men capable of speaking the necessary languages, having enough knowledge of the arts, and capable of covert work. Several were recommended to him by the intelligence sections representing territories such as Germany and Italy which posed special problems. Personnel came from the Ashmolean, the British Museum, the British Schools in Rome and Athens, the Fitzwilliam, the Tate Gallery, the V & A, the Slade School, the Public Record Office. Several Far Eastern officers came from the Indian and Burmese civil services. Lt-Col Archey, director of the Auckland Institute, looked after the entire South-East Asia area, recruiting his own assistants locally and saving many pagodas, monasteries and Buddhist monuments from destruction, and pursuing such precious stolen records as the Burmese 'Palm-leaf' manuscript. Major Balfour, a tutor at King's College, Cambridge, was sent to Belgium and France and was killed on active service. Lt-Col Casson, Reader in Classical Archaeology at Oxford, was assigned to Greece and was killed in an air accident while carrying out his work.

The Italian colonies of North Africa, and the campaign against Europe's 'soft underbelly', remained Woolley's chief preoccupation throughout 1943–4. He wrote:

> For the Fascist Government, the Italian colonies in North Africa were the symbol of the promise of the re-birth of the ancient Roman Empire.

They had, he said, exploited to the full the classical remains of Cyrenaica and Tripolitania – Cyrene, Lepcis Magna and Sabratha – pouring out money 'lavishly on excavation and restoration'. To the Italian Fascist, such places 'symbolized the glories of his traditional ancestry'. Wavell's forces had occupied Cyrene on 3 February 1941. The subsequent Greek campaign caused the British to withdraw, however, and the Italians returned to claim widespread vandalism by British troops. A pamphlet was issued detailing the damage, for which Australians were held chiefly to blame, and showing pictures of smashed treasures. When British troops returned and Woolley's officer inspected the scene, it was found that the evidence had been falsified. Statues broken in antiquity had been taken from workshops where they were being built up from fragments after excavation and photographed lying on the ground as if the 'invaders' had smashed them. All the same, enemy propaganda was effective enough to impress Churchill who insisted before Alamein that Woolley should send a deputy with Montgomery's army to ensure that there was 'no repetition'.

Woolley wrote: 'Among the first to enter Tripoli was Lt-Col Mortimer Wheeler, Director of the London Museum.' He had been asked to take charge of the ancient sites there with one of Woolley's officers, Major J. B. Ward Perkins, as his assistant.

As battles raged across Roman sites in Libya and Tripolitania, the even more pregnant question of Sicily came to the fore. Churchill's deep sense of history seemed to focus on Sicily. It was, as James Mann, Keeper of the Wallace Collection, wrote at the time, 'the very hearth of Classical, Christian, and Renaissance culture'. Woolley was to answer for the preservation of its treasures.

In the event, Roman sites in North Africa were damaged and scorched by gunfire, but none was harmed irreparably. The Italians had removed the principal treasures of Lepcis Magna before battle was joined. But it was only the intervention of Mortimer Wheeler, serving with the Eighth Army, that prevented wholesale destruction at Lepcis and Tripoli. He cordoned off the ruins, posted guards round them, and made a group of Italian prisoners responsible for their safety. A British officer used the Roman amphitheatre at Tunis as the stage from which to make the official announcement of victory to the troops. While Wheeler was fighting with the Eighth Army in 1943, a written Parliamentary question was put to the War Minister about damage to archaeological treasures. The Minister replied that when British forces advanced into Libya in 1942 'immediate steps were taken' to preserve monuments which might come into British possession. Wheeler accused him of being misinformed; '. . . not to put too fine a point on it, his office had been guilty of communicating an impudent lie.' When Wheeler moved on with the army and Ward Perkins, who was injured, was sent to Cairo, Woolley asked for Wing-Commander Max Mallowan, working with Air Force Intelligence, to take their place with the North African force. He was told that Mallowan could not be released for the task. Woolley was forced to go out to Tripoli himself to fill the gap in the autumn of 1944. Eventually Major Geddes Hyslop RE, an architect from the British School in Rome, took charge there, followed by Major Haynes whose pre-war work was in the Greek and Roman Department of the British Museum. The treasures of Cyrenaica and Tripoli were consigned safely to their care.

Sicily was spared much of the destruction that had been feared, but valuable Renaissance paintings, stored in what were thought to be safe places, were destroyed.

There was, of course, a vested archaeological interest in the preservation of important sites. In August 1943 a conference at the Institute of Archaeology had discussed the problems that bomb and shell damage would pose when the war was over. Surveys would have to be carried out over vast areas, from bomb-blasted Britain to the equally devastated industrial regions of Germany, from the Mediterranean to the Far East. John Linton Myres, who had occupied the Wykeham chair of ancient history between the wars and remained in close contact with Woolley over the years, spoke of the need for first-aid to badly damaged sites in Sicily, while bomb damage might actually reveal profitable places for future digging in Tunis, Tripoli and Cyrenaica. Myres thought it 'the State's duty to protect the records of archaeological discoveries and prevent their exploitation'. He also thought that future research should be state aided. It was a view that brought him into conflict with one of archaeology's most remarkable – if not always most amenable – women, Dr Margaret Murray. That pupil–disciple of Petrie (eventually his successor at University College), was fiercely independent and opposed to state intervention in archaeology or anything else. 'What I want,' she told the conference, 'is the amateur, the person who will do the work for the love of it.' Margaret Murray lived to be a hundred and one, to burn some of the most important notebooks of her demi-god Petrie, and to promote the virtues of individualism and amateur enthusiasm to her last breath. Woolley's summing up was diplomatic. He agreed with Dr Murray that it was not desirable to involve the Treasury directly in the work of archaeological investigation. On the other hand, it had to be admitted that British and American excavations, carried out by individuals or learned bodies, were at a disadvantage compared with the government-supported expeditions of Germany and France. Perhaps his mind flicked back to his youthful days in Italy, when he had so admired government-sponsored work there. Perhaps the status accorded French and German archaeologists suggested that state sponsorship should be endured if not welcomed. The setting up of an international body was proposed, to represent archaeologists in the post-war period. Margaret Murray would have none of it, but the resolution was carried. Woolley escaped the lady's wrath, rushing away before the conference ended.

With the advance into Italy itself during 1944, there were fears of wholesale destruction which were realized at Monte Cassino and other places where military demands took precedence over art conservation. The opposition of army commanders to Civil Affairs intervention made it necessary for Woolley to work at a distance. Much of the work at this time was covert, involving co-operation with MI6, SIS and Special Operations. The most vital work involved the theft by high-ranking German officers of paintings worth millions of dollars from the galleries of Naples and Florence. A Fine Arts and Archives Sub-commission was formed to provide cover for the intelligence men whose job was to track down the paintings. In some cases Woolley's office had been able to record the banks they had been deposited with, and others were known to have been hidden in the Brenner tunnel. By the end of the war, most had been recovered and were hanging again in the Neapolitan and Florentine museums. The records of how these and other thefts were traced in war, and precisely how the works were recovered, were never made public.

Italy was by no means the only place of concern as far as art and antique treasures were concerned. Holland, repository of some of the world's most important paintings, had spawned a thriving industry in counterfeit in the war years, spurred on by the search for bargains by members of the occupying forces. Many paintings and artifacts had been stolen in France. And the incursion of Soviet troops into Eastern Europe had posed a special problem. By the end of 1944, it was suspected that the eastern ally was removing such treasures as Schliemann's Trojan finds from the State Museum at Berlin. Such matters fell into the lap of Woolley's Civil Affairs branch as the world turned its attention to Hiroshima and the atom bomb. Their resolution would be a long-drawn-out business. A start was made, however, in 1944.

From January of that year German radio had been making almost daily accusations about the American and British Commissions representing Jewish buyers of the New York and London salerooms. On 4 May, Churchill wrote a letter to the Secretary of State for War announcing that he had appointed Mr Macmillan to chair a committee responsible for 'restitution and compensation for works of art wantonly destroyed by the enemy'. Woolley had a new political chief, but he now had to answer directly to a Monuments, Fine Arts and Archives Panel under the chairmanship of Sir Robert Abdy and containing the names of directors of all major galleries and museums. Essentially a political committee, it was represented at Supreme Allied Headquarters. In March, the Chief Administrative Officer at the War Office. Maj-General J. H. Robertson, had sent guidelines to all commanders stressing the need to protect monuments and works of art. When in doubt, they should contact Woolley's office at Civil Affairs. Woolley wanted to ensure that knowledgeable officers under his aegis were on the spot, especially in connection with the work of uncovering hidden 'repositories' to which Robertson's letter had drawn attention. There was much talk of Himmler's and Goering's 'hoards', and it was believed that Hitler himself planned to annexe the entire Alphonse Rothschild Collection (a suspicion supported by the discovery of an inventory of that collection when Allied troops reached Berchtesgaden in 1945).

With the invasion of Europe, Woolley was asked to provide a British contingent to work with the Americans. He made an attempt to have Blunt transferred to his staff. On 17 April 1944, he wrote to Colonel C. E. D. Bridge at 12 Army Group, pleading with him to use his influence to obtain Blunt's release. 'The officer I would prefer and could most strongly recommend as a capable man, a first-rate German speaker, and out of the top drawer as an art historian, is Major Anthony Blunt, now serving with MI5. I have spoken to Major Blunt, who promised to make strong representations to his CO but did not hold out much hope that he would be released.' Blunt himself seemed keen, but the directorate of MI5 refused to agree to the move. It has been suggested that he was needed for another task in Germany connected with the royal archive at Schloss Friedrichshof, allegedly containing sensitive correspondence between Queen Victoria and her daughter 'Vicky', wife of the Emperor of Germany. Such a task would, in any case, have come under Woolley's control in the ordinary course of events, but it was subsequently alleged that 'the Palace' took the matter into its own hands. Blunt appears to have had other highly secret tasks to perform in Paris, though according to the then deputy director of counter-intelligence at SHAEF and later head of MI5, Goldsmith White, he did have a role, initially, as an art historian. Eventually, Woolley chose Major Ellis Waterhouse for the tasks he had intended to assign to Blunt in France and Germany. As it happened, Ellis Kirkham Waterhouse was well known to both men. He had been at Marlborough school with Blunt, and was a graduate of New College. Woolley had known him as librarian of the British School in Rome up to 1936 – where Blunt and Guy Burgess called 'to talk politics' – when he returned to London to catalogue pictures for the Royal Academy. He had worked for MI6, chiefly in the Middle East, for much of the war. Someone, perhaps Blunt, had recommended the Marxist historian Kligender for 'Woolley's outfit' and it fell to Waterhouse to tell that candidate that the War Office was unlikely to subscribe to a civilian appointee, preferring men from 'various military organizations'. Woolley was perfectly happy with Waterhouse, who was to become Slade Professor at Oxford after the war, and in his official report commended his work highly.

Crawford had worked patiently with Woolley's help to keep contact with friends in France and Holland. Woolley wrote to him from the War Office on 13 November 1944 in an attempt to help his clandestine work, carefully avoiding mention of the subject of Crawford's enquiries.

Hotel Victoria,
Northumberland Avenue, WC2
C. A. 20(b)

Dear Crawford
I think that you can now write freely to France (passing the censor, of course) and get a reply. As to a visit, that is, I gather, more difficult: theoretically there is civilian traffic but only where the journey is important for the war effort. But if you are satisfied with writing and doubtful of the post, I could send a letter on for you (again subject to censor) through our Fine Arts liaison in Paris. As for the young lady. No. We aren't an agency for such! and we don't ourselves employ women. She certainly would not be allowed to go out there.
Yours sincerely,
Leonard Woolley, Lt-Colonel.

The letter was written after the liberation of France. Europe was opening up again, but there were still constraints on Crawford's enterprising freelance work.

Woolley's second war was a good deal more comfortable than the first. The Dorchester Hotel, maintaining a life-style of some elegance even in war and despite bombs and austerity, made the final two years of European conflict very endurable. He was busy, of course, often working late into the night at Northumberland Avenue. Katharine was in her element. She had always expected to be waited on by those around her, both men and women, and hotel life suited her admirably. It was, nonetheless, a lonely existence. She had understood Leonard's archaeological work and in her way had helped him. She enjoyed being on site, so long as she was the centre of attention and the focal point of activity. She had contributed solidly to the report on the Archaeological Survey of India, and when talking to the Mallowans and others had insisted that it was of joint authorship, a claim to which some of the report's more critical passages lent credence. Her husband had learnt that it was easier to indulge her than to protest or argue. He allowed her pride of place in most things. When in 1937 H. A. L. Fisher, the Warden of New College, was given the Order of Merit, he received hundreds of congratulatory messages which he kept in an album. One of the messages read 'Our warm congratulations, Katharine and Leonard Woolley.' She always had priority. In the end, most people tired of her tantrums, but her fascinating manner – which Agatha Christie and Freya Stark found irresistible – occasionally compensated for the waspish tongue so that friendship endured. But few could stay the course. There was a brief social excursion with a friend of Fisher's, the ultra right-wing Evelyn Wrench, Chairman of the Over-Seas League and President of the London Library. That too ended with embarrassment and ill-feeling. Old friends and acquaintances from the academic world, from diplomacy, the army, travelling companions and helpers from Carchemish, Egypt, Ur and Atchana, gathered at parties in Royal Avenue. Usually they came but once.

Leonard's entire life during the twenty years of marriage had been circumscribed by her wishes. Her incomparable snobbery had deprived him of many friendships and of contact with his family. Yet, in a way, he had come to be fond of the iron-willed creature who dominated his domestic existence. If he had any reservations, he kept them to himself while she lived. For her part, she maintained her own strange brand of loyalty to her husband.

Katharine performed her unique role to the last, entrancing even as she wasted away, insufferable even as those around her tried to find excuse in her sickness and her transparent loneliness.

Throughout the summer of 1945 she was wheeled each day to the office. She seems to have been a capable secretary, though she was in great pain and movement was difficult. There was, especially towards the end, a visibly brave side to her which perhaps explained Woolley's endless patience and willingness to give way to her. She continued to type long reports and letters and to look after his business arrangements as the postponed pursuits of peace began to assert themselves and the war dragged to its close. Penguin Books decided to bring out *Ur of the Chaldees* in paperback. On 19 October Nicholas Pevsner, the general editor, wrote to ask him 'How do you want your name and title to appear on the King Penguin?'

'Large and bold', Woolley replied. He had begun to think of archaeology again, even as his men in Europe and Asia pursued some of the richest and frailest spoils of war. While coping with a long-distance inventory of Europe's art treasures, a matter which increasingly concerned Churchill, he was in correspondence with Alan Wace and the Palestine Exploration Fund about the dereliction of some of the sites that had been hurriedly abandoned at the outbreak of war.

Katharine took a particular interest in one offshoot of his work, that of helping academics and artists who were in danger from the Nazis to find refuge in America and Canada, as she had helped Ukrainian refugees in 1919. The few who could be given special help could not be named for fear of attracting enemy attention or stirring up an uncontrollable demand. But one or two came to light from surviving letters. One of the last Woolley was able to help was Dr Jaroslaw Pasternak, who had spent the war in Bonn.

As the year 1945 progressed Katharine began to show signs of fatal decline. She had cried wolf so often that Leonard tended at first to disregard her complaints. But he knew that her condition was one of gradual and inevitable deterioration. By the autumn she was under constant medical attention. By early November her breathing had become difficult and she was obviously very ill, but she would not go into hospital. Sir Cecil Wakeley was in regular attendance.

On Wednesday 7 November Woolley arrived at the Dorchester late from his work at the office. Katharine sat with him for a few minutes and then announced that she would retire to bed early. As she left the room, she remarked in her unequivocal way, 'Leonard, I shall die this night.' He seldom doubted that she meant what she said.

When he looked into her room next morning she lay peaceful and unmoving in her bed. She had died in the early morning of Thursday 8 November, at the age of 58. Wakeley listed the multiple causes of death: bronchopneumonia, cardiac failure and disseminated sclerosis. She was buried at the town of Bishopthorpe in Yorkshire. The Archbishop of York conducted the service which was attended, so far as anyone knew, only by her husband and a single friend on her side, Mrs Margaret Smyth, with her son Robin. It was an eerily lonely end.

The Mallowans called at the Dorchester the day after Katharine's death to pay their last respects to the woman who perhaps found her only substantial reality as one of Agatha's characters. Woolley described to them the last hours with Katharine.

A few days after the funeral, Woolley wrote to Crawford to tell him that he had sent some letters off to France, 'through official channels', and hoping his friend would 'get the stuff'. He also wrote 'Many thanks for your sympathy. It is a hard blow; & apart from my personal loss the work suffers much by the going away of a most inspirational helper. She loved our archaeological work.' It was doubtless a sincere sentiment. In her will, made only a month before she died, Katharine left just over £41,000 mostly inherited from her first husband. She left £8000 in trust to Somerville, the Oxford college she had inhabited for two unfruitful years in her youth, for the establishment of a 'Katharine and Leonard Woolley Scholarship or Fellowship for archaeological work'. She specified that the bequest should apply to work in the 'Near or Middle East, in the Mediterranean generally or in the Far East'. She left a few articles of furniture to Mrs Smyth, and a painting of the Wylye Valley by William Nicholson to 'my husband for his use and enjoyment during his life and thereafter to the Ashmolean Museum'. All her private papers were to be destroyed.

The simultaneous end of war and marriage in his sixty-sixth year opened up for Leonard the prospect of a new lease of life.

'A bird let out of its cage'

He was still in uniform when he buried the woman who had been at the centre of his life in the most active and productive years.

In 1945, in his sixty-fifth year, a new life called, and it demanded a change of scene.

First, though, a few Civil Affairs matters had to be cleared up, and permission obtained from the Turks to restart work at Atchana. One of his last letters from the War Office was addressed to Sir Laurence Kirwan, now returned to the Royal Geographical Society as Secretary and Director. Woolley had been elected a fellow of the Society a year earlier, in February 1945, on the proposal of Sir George Clark the President of the British Academy and Provost of Oriel. On 8 January 1946 he delivered a lecture at the Society's headquarters in Kensington Gore, stressing the close connection between geographical and archaeological research, and pointing to the area of his pre-war excavations in the Orontes Valley, now, in the post-war dispensation, the Turkish Hatay, as a good example of the interconnection of the two disciplines in determining ancient trade routes. It was on the day after the lecture that he struck what he supposed to be a hot iron, writing to Kirwan to ask if the Society would help fund the Syrian excavations which he was proposing to return to almost immediately. His estimate of first-year costs was £4,000. The British Museum would be contributing part of that outlay, but the Trustees were 'scarcely in a position to put down such a sum'.

There was also a scribbled note to Crawford among his clearing-up mail from the Victoria Hotel, telling his old friend that some correspondence had been forwarded to France. 'I leave tomorrow [14 February 1946] for N. Africa and Turkey, so you'll excuse writing.' In the meantime, he had made a hurried trip to Germany. He was preparing an official report on the work of his Civil Affairs section and he needed to obtain information on reported losses of

paintings and archaeological treasures from galleries and museums
in Berlin, and to try to assess the immense losses resulting from the
British bombardment of Dresden. On 20 January he told Kirwan
that he had arrived back from Germany the previous evening and
would be sending him a handwritten report on the geographical
aspects of the Syrian dig – ie. 'the trade routes between the
Mediterranean and the Middle East . . . from the 3rd century BC to
about 1780 BC.' On 30 January, Kirwan wrote to inform him that
the Research Committee of the RGS had agreed to denote £100
towards the expenses of the forthcoming excavations.

In North Africa he sped by official car along the desert roads
which the British and German armies had contested, visiting the
Roman sites of Apollonia, Cyrene and Lepcis Magna, preparing a
brief report on damage and the possibility of resuming archaeological work. At Ankara he had friendly talks with politicians and some
of the young Turkish archaeologists who had worked with him
before the war. The Turks now controlled the entire Amq Plain in
which his excavations were concentrated, and no objection was
raised to his resumption of the dig. He could start work there
whenever he liked.

The appeal of field work had not deserted him. He went back to
an England in the grasp of austerity to don civilian clothes, find
himself a permanent home and seek the extra funds needed to enable
him to dig once more at Atchana. He finally relinquished his
commission on 29 April 1946, carrying into civilian life the honorary
rank of Lieutenant-Colonel.

He had rented out the house in Royal Avenue when he and
Katharine moved into the Dorchester Hotel. It had become available
again early in 1946 and he used it as a *pied à terre*, but he felt an
urgent need to cut himself off from the artificial life which marriage
and fidelity to Katharine's wishes had led him to. In June 1946 he
took a train to Ashford in Kent and wandered through the gentle
countryside of England's 'garden' in search of a possible home. As if
drawn by instinct, he alighted on a fine old converted mill at Great
Chart, only a mile or two from Ashford.

Worten Mill had a long history, which Woolley was soon familiar
with. It had once been part of Court Wurtin, the property of Thomas
de Wurtin under Henry IV, and of many a de Wurtin before him. It
was later known as Worting (or Wortin) Farm. The river Stour,
which had once turned the wheels of the corn mill, ran through the
building. A small, unoccupied cottage belonging to the property

stood on the other side of the bridge which spanned the river. The rooms were not large but spacious enough for his library of some 2,000 volumes and his ever-growing collection of pictures and sculptures. Across fields leading from the old mill towards the village of Hothfield was the parsonage or rectory and the parish church of St Mary. Ecclesiastically speaking, Hothfield is part of the diocese of Canterbury, and in 1946 its newly inducted rector was the Rev Leonard Saunders Chamberlen MC.

After the noise and bustle of wartime London, the death of Katharine and the austerity of the first year of peace, there must have been an almost unnatural calm about the charming white mill house in its quiet rural surroundings. With his wife's estate to come and his own earning capacity at a high point, there were no great financial restraints on him; and in any case his needs were modest. He was free once more to entertain friends and family and there were two or three spare bedrooms. Worten Mill answered perfectly to his needs and he bought it in July, within a month of first setting eyes on it.

His first social call was on the Rev. Chamberlen. He was warmly received. Chamberlen was somewhat younger than Woolley, and he knew of his brother Harold whose military exploits were still renowned in church circles and provided common ground at their first meeting. The rector was interested in biblical history, of course, but not especially in archaeology, though he knew of Sir Leonard's reputation. His wife, on the other hand, seemed to be passionately interested in the visitor's work and in his fame as an archaeologist. She was in her late thirties, with vivid red hair and spectacles which she wore quaintly on the end of her nose. But despite physical characteristics which might seem slightly eccentric at a distance, she was attractive to men. Woolley was perhaps flattered by her intelligent interest in his work. He got along well with her and her husband and made it clear at their first meeting that he would attend church as often as he could. He was soon a familiar and prominent member of the congregation, and much in demand as a lay preacher. He was also a regular and popular guest at the rectory. His brilliant conversation made him the centre of attention in a household with familiar signs of matriarchal authority. If he noticed anything at all unusual, it was perhaps the Rev. Chamberlen's unkempt appearance, and the fact that his wife contradicted him at every turn. Woolley might have been expected to sense warning signals. As it was, he saw nothing but growing attraction in the diminutive red-head who dominated her husband while neglecting his welfare.

As the summer of 1946 progressed, Woolley's social life centred more and more on the rectory, and he began to invite Mrs Chamberlen to the Mill. A complicating factor in his friendship with the couple developed out of his search for domestic help. He had come to know the young woman who did part-time work at the rectory, Mrs Waters, and wondered if she might be prepared to help out. At first Mrs Waters was reluctant. Her own husband had just returned from the army and wanted to resume his pre-war work as a gardener. Perhaps they could be persuaded jointly to look after the house and the garden? Eventually Mrs Waters agreed. She insisted, though, on continuing to help out at the rectory. Betty Waters was a good-looking and self-assured young woman and the unfortunate Chamberlen had come to rely on her practical good sense and her willingness to make-good and mend. She joked with him about his odd socks and his untidy appearance.

By the autumn, the Waters were established at Worten Mill, at the beginning of an association that was to last almost to the end of Woolley's days, an association which Betty Waters and her husband would look back on as the best years of their lives. At that juncture, though, the young woman who would look after Woolley more as a devoted daughter than a servant, could not bring herself to warn him of the danger he was in. She knew Mrs Chamberlen well and did not approve of her free-and-easy relationships. She knew of repeated affairs conducted under the nose of a weak and compliant husband. Lilian Margaret Chamberlen was in some respects an uncanny reawakening of Katharine; intelligent, articulate, fascinating and forceful. Like Katharine too, she had an instinctive ability to beguile and captivate men. But unlike Katharine, who feared men in proximity and always withdrew at the last moment, she was predatory and decisive. She wove a seductive web. Woolley, in the wake of a marriage which, by his own admission to his sister Edith was unconsummated to the end, was easy prey. It was not long before he became hopelessly and dangerously entangled.

Mrs Chamberlen had discovered a famous, interesting, and – to all appearances – wealthy man; and, even more to the point, a widower. The conquest of Leonard Woolley did not, all the same, deter her from pursuing existing friendships, often entertaining her men friends at the vicarage and with her husband's knowledge. Talk in the village was rife and Woolley's vulnerability was obvious

– to all except himself. Betty Waters put it aptly. He was, she said, 'like a bird let out of its cage'.

Imminent disaster was averted by the need to return to Atchana in February 1947. The months spent in Mrs Chamberlen's company, his domestic needs now cared for by a couple he trusted and liked, had given him the freedom he yearned for. It was a rejuvenated Leonard Woolley who went off for Stamboul and the excavation sites on the Amq Plain at the beginning of 1947.

Agatha and Max Mallowan visited Worten Mill just before he departed. Agatha saw him off with a rendering of lines she had already practised on him; lines which had buzzed in her mind in pre-war days as she trudged at her husband's side through Iraq and Syria. *A-Sitting on a Tell* was written as an introduction to a book which portrayed her 'other' life in archaeology, a life which had lasted, so far, for seventeen happy years. She called it *Come, Tell Me How You Live*. Leonard can scarcely have failed to see part of himself – as well as Max – in Agatha's 'Lewis Carroll' mirror. 'Who are you, sir?' and 'For what is it you look?'

> He said: 'I look for aged pots
>   Of prehistoric days,
> And then I measure them in lots
>   And lots of different ways.
> And then (like you) I start to write,
>   My words are twice as long
> As yours, and far more erudite.
>   They prove my colleagues wrong!'

She pursued in verse the record of five thousand years and exclaimed, 'Come, tell me how you live! And when, and where, and why?'

One reason for the Mallowans' visit was a wish to put an end to the running battle with Sidney Smith. Sidney had stayed with Max and Agatha at Greenway House and they agreed that the visit was 'most enjoyable'. Max had recently followed Smith as Professor of Archaeology at London and had taken on the directorship of the British School of Archaeology in Iraq. He found no difficulty with Smith, who now occupied the London chair of Ancient Semitic Languages, and he found the irascible Keeper of the Egyptian and Assyrian Department generally helpful. Perhaps Leonard should try to reach an understanding? Woolley was as convinced as ever that no effort on his part could calm the ruffled waters.

He arrived at Aleppo in February 1947, having stopped off at Istanbul on the way. His pre-war assistants were no longer available, but he was fortunate in obtaining the voluntary services of a young man for whom he quickly developed a high regard, William Brice, a geographer by training but a keen and proficient archaeologist by inclination. Three able Turkish archaeologists also joined him; Dr Bahadir Alkim of the University of Istanbul, Dr Tahsin Ozguc from Ankara University, and Bey Ahmet Donmez of the country's office of antiquities.

As for Woolley's eternal problem, finance, the ability of old friends from the days of Ur to help out had faded with war, age and reduced circumstances. George Eumorfopoulos had gone. Neill Malcolm and his family, the Countess Buxton, Evans, Maxwell, H. J. Oppenheim, the connoisseur Percival David, and old hands from the Mesopotamian administration, had helped out with contributions to the dig in the 1930s. Private funds were out of the question now. Before the war, the Victoria and Albert Museum had added to the British Museum's largesse. So had the Ashmolean, as well as rich individuals. The British Museum agreed to finance the 1947 season but after that Woolley would be on his own. The Royal Geographical Society's contribution could hardly sustain a large-scale excavation which had several more years to run. He was forced to appeal to the Government, and to his surprise and delight the Treasury agreed to finance the 1948-49 seasons: he resumed work in earnest.

Woolley had already established that Atchana's first occupants had been relative latecomers of the early Bronze Age, a little after 3000 BC (or Jamdat Nasr in Mesopotamian terms). The earlier occupations indicated by pottery finds at Shaikh Yusuf and al Mina must, he decided, relate to the late Neolithic.

When the site closed down in 1939, he had been seeking evidence of that earlier period and of Bronze Age habitations on the Amq plain which followed the tentative occupation of the Jamdat Nasr period. But he had found only suspicious gaps in what he expected to be a story of succeeding levels of community life. Now he sought to fill the gaps in the historical period.

Without Katharine to impose her demands on the digging community, the excavations went on apace and Woolley was able to sleep soundly as well as to work his customary long day – still from five in the morning until after midnight.

It was not until the second post-war year at Atchana that he made a significant breakthrough. Before setting out for Syria in 1947 he had written a second article for the *Journal of the Society of Antiquaries*, bringing up to date the story of the Atchana finds. He sent a draft to Sidney Smith who had transcribed the Akkadian inscriptions of the few tablets that had so far come to the surface, asking him if he would care to comment. Smith thanked him for the thought but added disobligingly 'I am at the moment so much occupied that I do not think it would be right for me to take the mss just now.' Perhaps he would be able to help a month or so hence, when he hoped to have more free time.

At the end of the 1947 season, Brice decided to go off on a tour of Anatolia. In August, Woolley wrote to John Linton Myres, by then retired to a Fellowship of New College, telling him he had had no news of Brice since he started his 'expedition'. He added, 'Such a nice fellow & should be really good.' Four days after writing to Myres he heard from Brice, 'Arrived Van – end of our journey.' Brice agreed to continue to help, but by then Myres, who was chairman of the British School at Athens, had recommended to Woolley another assistant, Sinclair Hood.

Arriving back at Atchana in March 1948, Woolley was approached by a grinning workman who said that he had something for which he expected 'big bakhsheesh'. From his knotted handkerchief he produced a few broken pieces of pottery which his brother, who had worked before the war for an American expedition at nearby Tal-Tayinat, declared to be 'important'. Woolley recognized it as Halaf ware, and asked the workman to take him to the place where he had found it. 'Naturally, I had to pay,' said Woolley, without disclosing how much. Thus he began to dig at the place known to local Arabs and Kurds as Tal ash-Shaikh. Hamoudi's sons Yahia and Alawi were now in charge of the workforce. The men dug quickly through the rubbish heaps which marked twelve successive levels of occupation, each cultural layer clearly identifiable by its pottery and artifacts, and covering in all about 350-500 years of occupation in the late prehistoric period, perhaps from 4200-3700 BC, or even earlier. At the lowest level, on the flat surface of the Amq plain, the occupants were still in the Stone Age. Their pottery was black-bodied and undercoated. They were a poor community, using stone implements, while their successors, who first imported and then copied the Halaf and Ubaid wares, had begun to use copper implements.

They soon came to virgin soil. Tal ash-Shaikh provided a contin-
uous history of a small insignificant village from its foundation at
the time when its inhabitants settled to raise livestock and grow
vegetables and make their crude pots, to their copper-using Chalcolithic successors. A few metal implements on the surface of the
mound suggested that the region had seen later occupation in the
time of bronze implements and writing, but that would have been
hundreds of years after the last of the Chalcolithic inhabitants. There
was no link with Atchana, his main site, and there was an unexplained gap of perhaps 500 years from the last copper-using inhabitants to the early Bronze Age. It was in the following season that the
last of his assistants, Sinclair Hood, came to the rescue.

He had picked up a few pottery sherds on a small mound called
Tabara al Akrad, the 'Kurd's Hillock', which were immediately
recognized as characteristic of ware first found at a Palestinian
mound called Khirbet Kerak. The site lay about a twenty-minute
walk to the east of Atchana. When Hood came to him with this
latest discovery, Woolley gave his young assistant instant permission
to excavate the mound himself. It was the kind of responsibility and
experience that Sinclair Hood sought, and he remarked on the
'generosity of spirit' with which his chief allowed him to take charge.

Excavators in Palestine had found that the same pottery appeared
at other sites, usually above a stratum where buildings had been
destroyed by fire. It was generally agreed that it was foreign ware,
probably from Anatolia. On the Amq plain, such pottery was found
by Woolley and others on dozens of sites, and at Tal Akrad it was
discovered at four successive building levels. In the Russian Caucasus, excavators were finding similar pottery, thick, sometimes red,
sometimes black, or with a combination of black and red body clays,
highly burnished and with painted geometrical decoration. In the
Caucasus the Khirbet Kerak ware was common, going back in time
to Neolithic levels. Strangely, in each of the royal tombs of the
Hittites which had been excavated at Alajahuyuk in Cappodocia, a
single characteristic piece of the ware was found. Those tombs dated
from about 2000 BC, when the pottery in question was no longer in
general use by the Hittites, so that the examples in the royal tombs
must have had a special, probably ritual, significance. But after 2000
BC, the Hittites were still using pottery-making techniques which
derived from the southern Caucasus. From such deductions, from
analogies drawn across all the known urbanized regions of the
ancient world from the third and fourth millennia BC, Woolley

constructed a picture of the early migrations which brought the first inhabitants of Mesopotamia and Syria from their mountain fastness in the north.

'In the latter part of the fourth millennium before Christ events of which we know nothing at all – perhaps through drought and famine, perhaps invasion by some stronger tribe – drove them from their country and forced them to seek a home elsewhere.' He drew as best he could a picture of the prehistoric migration, starting in the late Neolithic, across the mountains and rivers of Western Asia to established Chalcolithic cultures in Anatolia and in the fertile valley of the Amq. These precursors of the Hittites, he wrote, faced the same problems as confronted the Hebrews in the Land of Promise, and they ousted the inhabitants from their primitive homes, took over the new territory and lived there for many generations, until they in turn were put to the sword by invaders from the east. Only two roads of escape were open to them, one leading south and the other west. Some went through Syria and Palestine, slaughtering the inhabitants as they went, for they were warlike people; others went across the Amanus mountains back to Anatolia where they set up a powerful kingdom and laid the foundations of the Hittite empire. 'For in the Khirbet Kerak people we must recognize the ancestors of the Hittites.' The Old Testament, never far from Woolley's thoughts, described the Hittites as being settled in Palestine before the arrival of Abraham in about 2000 BC, long before the Hittite empire came into being. Until then, the Old Testament assertion had been regarded by most archaeologists as anachronous, introduced into the narrative by later scribes. But, if Woolley's people of the Amq plain were Hittites, their survivors would 'certainly' have been living in Palestine in the patriarchal age. As for the Anatolian Hittites, it had long been accepted that they were of Caucasian stock. Work at Tabara had gone a long way towards solving the 'vexed question' of Hittite origins.

The official account of the Tal ash-Shaikh excavation was never published. Woolley decided that it should be given to a Turkish academic journal and the material necessary for a full report was handed to his Turkish assistants. But it never appeared in print. Sinclair Hood was able to record fully his work at Tabara al Akrad, however. He paid tribute not only to Woolley for allowing him to carry out the work, but to the Turks, led by Bey Ruhi Tekhan, director of the Antioch Museum. As for the significance of the work, carried out at record speed by a team of ten men under Alawi:

The interest of this site lies not only in the very full picture it gives of the Khirbet Kerak Culture in the Amq plain, but also in the fact that it fills the gap between the Chalcolithic of Tell Esh Sheikh and the Bronze Age of Atchana, while the material from the pre-Khirbet Kerak levels provides useful additional evidence for correlating contemporary cultures in Mesopotamia and Palestine.

Woolley's scenario suggested an altogether new explanation of the origins and importance of the Hittites.

In my opinion there is only one interpretation of the evidence . . . I do not imagine that it will prove at once acceptable to all scholars who have put forward different theories as to the origin of the Hittites, but I feel fairly certain that it must be broadly speaking true.

Further digging at Atchana revealed new aspects of the rise of civilization on the Amq plain. The old Tabara 'proto-Hittites' lived in primitive villages, leading the lives of simple agricultural folk and practising their warlike arts. Already, the pottery first produced in the pre-historic period before 3000 BC had been perfected, and from about 2800 to 1800 BC the shapes and patterns of these sophisticated wares were virtually unchanged. Woolley could not resist the modern parallel of the Willow pattern which, astonishingly, had persisted in England for more than 150 years. But 'will it endure for a thousand years?' he asked. As for the 'obstinate conservatism' of the potters of the Amq, he could think of no like case.

In the early Bronze Age, a new conquering people settled and built a city which came to be called Alalakh, and among the first of their buildings was a temple dedicated to their god. The site was to be occupied for a further 2000 years, and during that time the temple was rebuilt fifteen times, in different styles and dedicated to different gods.

What Woolley described as the 'temple' was, in fact, a giant altar or worshipping structure; a cube of solid brickwork, about sixteen feet square and thirteen feet high, with pointed timber roof. It was carefully preserved as an essential part of the next temple, projecting through the tiled floor of the subsequent building which was erected in the Uruk period, about 3000 BC. Against the north-west face of the cube he found a thick deposit of ashes, animal bones and potsherds. They must, he thought, be the remains of sacrificial rituals. Then came a more mysterious find. Digging beneath the pavement in the courtyard of the earlier temple, Woolley's workmen came upon a vast square pit, its upper part brick-lined, which continued down to virgin soil. Investigation showed that as soon as the first inhabitants of Atchana had dug this shaft they filled it in again, not with bones and earth but with huge boulders, with a packing of smaller stones between them. The largest of the stones weighed more than three tons and they must have been transported over several miles of the plain, for there were no such stones close to Atchana. After filling the shaft so laboriously, workmen had laid floor tiles over it and then constructed on the tile surface a free-standing brickwork structure with a low doorway at its centre. The door was, however, plastered over so as to be completely hidden. One end of the structure covered the exact position of the shaft. The brick superstructure, which Woolley called a 'mastaba' by loose analogy with early Egyptian tombs, and the shaft with which it was associated, clearly had something to do with worship, but more than that it was impossible to say.

In October 1947, Woolley had written in the *Illustrated London News* of the discovery of the 'Lost City' of Alalakh and its king:

> We found, though we could not fully excavate, a royal tomb of the eighteenth century BC. Attached to the palace of King Yarim-Lim was a chapel, sacked and burnt by the rebellious populace, which contained numerous objects, including a won-derfully fine stone portrait-head of a king, probably Yarim-Lim himself. Believing it to be a funerary chapel, I dug down under the floor and found the walls of a burnt building filled with and enveloped in a solid mass of mud brickwork ... Still we dug down. The building rested directly on another [the 'mastaba' of earlier temples] ... by now we were digging 14 feet below water-level, the sides of the shaft mere mud, fell in constantly, work became really dangerous, and when our pumps broke and no others could be obtained, we were scarcely sorry to close the season, although the cremation urn of King Yarim-Lim prob-ably only lay a few feet further down. But if we failed to open the tomb, we have learnt a great deal about the burial rites of a Hittite king.

Woolley eventually dug through seventeen levels to reach the pre-historic period at Atchana. It was, however, at a much later level that he made the most spectacular discovery of his investigation of the Amq region. Working at no great depth, he was able to extend the digging work over a large area, and thus to uncover a royal palace, together with the later version of the temple which had stood already for a thousand years, and the city gate. Archaeologically speaking the most important finds of the final season, 1949, were the court and temple archives with their hordes of cuneiform-inscribed tablets. All the tablets – merely a small surviving part of the original archive – fell within the reigns of three kings, Hammurabi, Yarim-Lim, and Niqme-epukh. Yarim-Lim was the ruler of Yamhad, a kingdom whose capital was Aleppo, and he was the contemporary of Hammurabi, the great law-giving king of Babylon. Most of the documents related to Yarim-Lim, covering a period roughly from 1792 to 1750 BC. It was from these records that Woolley was able to draw a graphic picture of the 18th century BC province of Alalakh for public consumption, and at the same time to spark off another dispute with Smith. But perversely, their argument was to end in an act of academic co-operation which proved as fruitful as it was remarkable.

Yarim-Lim seems from the records to have died before Hammurabi's thirtieth birthday, and from that his reign could be dated as c. 1780-1765 BC. Before that time, this far northern region of Syria appears to have been under Egyptian influence, but the collapse of the Twelfth Dynasty left the field open to petty kingdoms. Alalakh passed into the hands of a shadowy figure, Abban, who was the father of another Hammurabi, king of Yamhad (or Aleppo indifferently), and grandfather of Yarim-Lim. Abban settled Alalakh not on his son, Hammurabi, but on his grandson Yarim-Lim. On his father's death, the latter succeeded to the entire realm. His importance could be gathered from an intelligence document, surely one of the earliest secret service communications, found at another Syrian mound, Mari, excavated by the French. It was sent to the king of Mari, Zimri-Lim, by one of his agents, and told of the support enjoyed by the several sovereigns of the region. Hammurabi of Babylon enjoyed the support of about ten or fifteen kings, he said. The other great power of Mesopotamia in those days, Rim-Sin of Larsa, had about the same royal following. But Yarim-Lim of Yamhad had at least twenty kingly vassals. Yarim-Lim seemed to be able to play off one power against another while keeping his own territory, and his own purse, intact.

As soon as Smith saw Woolley's dates for Yarim-Lim and Hammurabi, he saw another opportunity to deprecate Woolley's work, remarking that Professor Albright in America had put forward a different and more plausible chronology, giving Hammurabi of Babylon's reign as 1728–1686 BC. Woolley argued that those dates were inconsistent with the evidence of Atchana. Smith, though respected for his learning and great authority, was not renowned in academic quarters for compromise. In this dispute, however, he seems for once to have maintained a balance in argument. He was to show that both Albright and Woolley were correct in disputing existing chronology, which showed a variation of some 200 years in vital dates. Smith eventually constructed a new chronology based on his translation of Woolley's Alalakh tablets, which brought down the accepted date of Hammurabi of the First Dynasty of Babylon by a considerable distance.

If the 'Lost Kingdom' lacked the drama of the royal death pit at Ur, it nonetheless marked the high point of public interest in archaeology after the war years, and re-established Woolley's reputation among a new generation not yet consumed by the excitement of the space age. The distant past was still a matter of public interest and Woolley, now the most eminent figure among the few survivors of the prodigal inter-war years of discovery, described how the king had been placed in his burial chamber on a bed of clean clay, and then covered with the mixed soil full of broken prehistoric pottery which the excavators found when they dug the great pit: '. . . the dead king was no ephemeral creature of yesterday, but was divinely appointed from the beginning, and he lay by rights not in common earth, but under the ashes of Alalakh's remotest past.' The Syrian dig had, after all, produced a king of importance, and a palace of sorts.

Sinclair Hood, the last of Woolley's field assistants, always remembered the generosity of the man who gave him his first professional opportunity. Educated at Harrow and Magdalen College, Oxford, Hood had been a student at the British School in Athens (an institution of which he was later to become director) when he was recommended to Woolley. As a schoolboy, Hood had heard Woolley lecture on Ur and he never forgot the experience. Gordon Childe and Garstang, as well as Myres, had mentioned him favourably to Woolley. Though work on the Amq plain was running down when they met at Ankara in 1948, the younger man realized that it was an appointment of the utmost importance to his career. His boyhood impression was confirmed the moment he met Woolley.

'He was a very remarkable man. He had great charisma. My first impression when I met him in the old British Institute of Archaeology at Ankara was his kind smile and how extraordinarily young he looked for a man of his age. He was a wonderful organizer of an excavation, and a brilliant raconteur. At lunch and especially dinner on the excavation he would talk of his experiences and never repeat himself.' Hood found his first field director 'an essentially modest man' and he believed that beneath the surface he had 'a great veneration for Sidney Smith'. That observation perhaps explained much. If Woolley had a streak of vanity, it showed itself, Hood thought, in his determination to work at the drawing board on his own plans and surveys, even when very capable architectural assistants were on hand. 'He was proud of his accuracy as a surveyor and planner,' Hood noted. Max Mallowan made the same observation.

Woolley rescued the head of the statue of Yarim-Lim, a magnificent portrait by the standards of any age, along with a horde of pottery, seals, figures and other objects which marked the passage of people and trade through a forgotten outpost of the world over a period of four thousand years.

The dedication of his paperback book on Alalakh to Major-General Sir Neill Malcolm ('but for whom there would have been no digging at Atchana'), paid tribute to one of the most enduring of Woolley's friendships. He was one of the few who endured Katharine's sharp tongue and returned for more. But if Katharine had determined Woolley's associations and friendships for the past twenty years, Lilian Chamberlen determined them now. By the time the Atchana excavations came to an end, Woolley's personal life had passed through a tropical storm.

When he arrived back at Worten Mill in the early summer of 1947, Lilian Chamberlen was more or less installed in his house. She had lived in the rectory in his absence but she seems to have made it clear to her husband that the affair with Woolley was permanent. Chamberlen had been prepared to accept the younger men as relatively harmless invaders of his domestic life. Woolley, more or less contemporary, famous and intellectually his superior, was a threat of a different kind. For his part, Woolley was apparently no less indifferent than the wife to popular opinion. He sometimes stayed overnight at the rectory with open disregard of the opinions of local people with whom he mixed in church and out of doors. Even when a solicitor's letter announced that the Rev. Chamberlen proposed to take divorce proceedings, a relationship which was so potentially damaging to his own reputation went on unabated. Woolley's behaviour was rash in the extreme. He took Mrs Chamberlen away with him and they stayed together at hotels. Almost as soon as he arrived home, early in May 1949, he took her to the Malcolms' place in Wiltshire. Freya Stark was nearby at Bradford-on-Avon and she called at Swallowcliffe and observed 'Len Woolley . . . looked much plumper and less worried: he seemed to think of a month or two on the incense route with great interest.' Half jokingly, she and Woolley had talked of a journey together to Arabia, presumably the Yemen or Oman, to be financed by the Royal Geographical Society. There was no mention of Mrs Chamberlen.

A private matter became a public scandal and the press became interested. In the hope of forestalling predictable Sunday newspaper headlines, the family and friends intervened. Harold Woolley pleaded with his brother not to break up the marriage of a respected fellow-clergyman, and became angry when Leonard virtually told him to mind his own business. Agatha and Max remonstrated. Edith, whose own marriage had recently ended in bitterness, understood; but she implored her brother to be sensible. Betty Waters, still in some awe of her new employer, wanted to warn him of the dangerous course he was embarking on. 'I knew the danger. But nothing would stop him,' she said, 'he was like a young man, infatuated.'

On 17 December 1947, Mr Commissioner Tyndale in the Divorce Court granted a decree nisi to Chamberlen, on the grounds of his wife's adultery with Sir Leonard Woolley. Inevitably, punitive costs were awarded against Woolley.

The unfortunate Chamberlen, described by Betty Waters as 'a weak and neglected man', who had allowed his wife every imaginable freedom until she and Woolley took the deliberate step of making their affair public knowledge, went off to Woodbridge in Suffolk. By the time of the court hearing Woolley and Lilian had left Great Chard too. They had bought a large house called New Hall at Small Dole near Henfield in Sussex. The Waters went with them, but Betty asked Woolley if she and her husband could live in separate accommodation. She did not approve of the arrangement and made no secret of her attitude. As it happened, the seven-bedroom house had a separate wing in which the housekeeper and her husband were able to live, well removed from a situation which was set to plumb even greater depths of indiscretion.

Woolley had been compelled to leave the Alalakh excavations

earlier than usual in order to attend the court proceedings. He and
Lilian Chamberlen arrived at New Hall just before Christmas 1947.
Soon after, the second act of a bizarre drama began to unfold. Mrs
Chamberlen's son was attending Dartmouth Naval College and
during the summer holidays he had taken home a young tutor to
Worten Mill. As soon as they were settled at Small Dole, the young
man appeared on the scene. Almost immediately, a *ménage à trois*
was established. For Woolley, the position could hardly have been
more humiliating. It was made worse by Mrs Chamberlen's boy-
friend assuming an air of authority in the house. Soon after they
moved in, Lilian wanted some of the rooms redecorated. Contractors
were called in and before long they were addressing the young man
as 'Sir Leonard'. They assumed that he was the head of the house.
Betty Waters, indignantly loyal to her employer, 'put them right', as
she recalled.

The effort to escape his self-imposed condition was to cost
Woolley dear. Mrs Chamberlen would not give up the younger man,
neither would she release Woolley without threat of more scandal
and, if forced to it, further action in the courts. If he was to free
himself from what had become an intolerable burden, he would
have to make a generous financial settlement. Within a year of
moving to New Hall he sold the house and prepared to move to a
rented home in Dorset. He found Mrs Chamberlen a house at
Rustington on the Sussex coast, where she lived with the younger
man. He drew up an annuity (reflected in his will) which made
adequate provision for Lilian for the rest of her life. In three years
he had thrown away the savings of a successful professional career
and his wife's fortune, leaving himself with enough to provide a
modest annual income based on the presumption that he would live
to the age of eighty.

If proof were needed of Woolley's resilience, of his ability to work
under the most searing of personal circumstances, it surely showed
itself at this time. While he twisted and turned to escape the web he
had entered with such cavalier irresponsibility, he worked as hard as
ever. He went back and forth to Atchana, wrote articles for the
Antiquaries' Journal, the *Illustrated London News* and *The Times*,
worked with Brice on the preparation of the final Alalakh report,
corresponded extensively with Smith, Gadd and Barnett at the British
Museum and with the Philadelphia Museum, wrote copiously to
Myres, Crawford, and others, and prepared an account of the work
of his department at the War Office on 'Art Treasures in War'. At

the beginning of the affair, in October 1946, while he still wrestled with the wartime destruction of European art works and sought funds for the return to Alalakh, he took time off to write a letter to *The Times* advocating the pre-emptive bombing of recalcitrant tribes in Waziristan, quoting in support of his argument the words of a tribal leader in the South Arabian Hadhramaut who, after the handing out of similar punishment in 1937, wrote to the British Resident, 'You did well to bomb us, and we thank you. If we had given in before, people would have said we were cowards.'

At the end of 1948 he moved, with the Waters still in attendance, to Sedgehill Manor near Shaftesbury. It was a large manor house, originally Elizabethan, which had been renovated in the present century when a wing had been added to it. There were five bedrooms and a large lounge which was turned into a billiards room.

Tranquillity had come at last, in his seventieth year.

The Last Rites

In May 1949 Woolley went on a pilgrimage to Oxford which must have struck a mixed chord of irony and nostalgia. He was invited to give that year's James Bryce Memorial Lecture at Katharine's old college, Somerville, providing an opportunity to discuss with the college governors the purpose for which Katharine's £8,000 bequest should be used.

The theme of his lecture, Middle East Archaeology, embraced the work of French, German, American and British contemporaries, as well as his own excavations in Egypt, Mesopotamia and Syria. In the generation before his, he said, archaeology meant essentially 'classical archaeology'. The work he and his contemporaries performed made the Middle East the centre of discovery and attention. Much of the lecture was devoted to a tribute to the Rev. Archibald H. Sayce, who had died soon after his visit to Woolley at Ur. Oxford's renowned and controversial professor of philology had always had what Woolley regarded as the right kind of questioning approach. His 'curious and restless intellect set no limit to its catholicity,' he said. 'He was in advance of his time; a fatal error in the world of scholarship.' His 'willingness to conjecture' and to be proved wrong, had a strong appeal for Woolley, as did his unshakeable Christian conviction.

Woolley was not on the surface the obvious choice to give a lecture commemorating James Bryce, the politician and historian who wrote *The American Commonwealth*, became regius professor of civil law at Oxford and who was for many years associated with the Liberal Party. Woolley mistrusted the political animal. For politicians, the admission of error was tantamount to confession of weakness. He believed omniscience to be the province of God. As Sinclair Hood remarked in reflecting on his old chief, Woolley took pleasure in admitting that he was wrong. He sometimes seemed to go out of his way to say, almost as an aside, 'Yes, I was quite wrong about that.' It was a trait which must have mystified Sidney Smith, who seldom if ever admitted to being in error. It also made Woolley an academic outsider. Corporations and institutions, especially political bodies and universities, are disturbed by people who regard error and frailty as perfectly normal human qualities.

One of the last attempts to persuade him to serve on a committee was made in November 1946 when Kirwan at the Royal Geographical Society tried to talk him into one of those attractive sinecures which proliferated under the banner of UNESCO. 'There are a number of such bodies,' Kirwan wrote, 'on the arts, on museums, on libraries, and so on.' Although the British Academy functioned as 'a National Co-operating Body', and dealt among other things with archaeology, he felt that the Social Sciences Committee of UNESCO, on which he, Kirwan, represented the RGS, should have an archaeologist member. 'There are only four or five meetings a year,' he said; it was four or five meetings too many for Woolley's liking, and he declined the invitation.

Never in the whole of his career, even at a time when he was probably the most sought-after archaeologist in the world, did he seriously consider acceptance of an academic post or a place on a committee. For him the freedom to say what he half-believed was paramount.

The same elements of make-up and reasoning may have accounted for his remarkable ability to throw off the consequences of rash behaviour in private life. The publicity which accompanied the Chamberlen divorce seemed hardly to affect him, and certainly did nothing to curtail his output of work. When he moved to Sedgehill Manor, the whole matter had become a burden of the past. Court costs, damages and the settlement with Lilian had cost him the modest fortune which he had accumulated through hard work and success, and his inheritance. It was a small price to pay for his new-found independence. Betty Waters, whose family came to regard him as a friend rather than employer, was not a woman to be deceived easily, and she had suffered enough setbacks in life not to make sentimental or over-charitable assessments of the people about her. She worked for him for fourteen years, and she summed him up nearly thirty years after his death; 'He was a truly wonderful man and he would have made a wonderful father – and a very good priest. Life and energy and goodness seemed to emanate from him. He was kind, and he had no affectation. But he was hopeless with women. He simply did not understand them.'

His niece, Edith's daughter, Margaret, was just as forthright. All
the Woolleys of that generation were, in her view, unbalanced in
their family and marital relationships, a characteristic which she
attributed to a 'morally inflexible, narrowly religious upbringing'.
Margaret had seen the generation of her grandparents through the
unblinkered eyes of childhood. As a young woman she had observed
the generation of her mother, of Leonard and his brothers and
sisters, as marriages and family relationships collapsed one after
another. Could the premature death of their mother have been a
contributory cause? A selfish and self-absorbed father doubtless
added to the formative influences which determined the adult lives
of his offspring. Whatever the causes – and psychoanalysts would
almost certainly see 'Oedipus' or 'Phaeton' complexes hidden
beneath layers of over-zealousness and emotional inadequacy – there
was not a single succesful marriage or lasting relationship in a
generation where intellect abounded and there was much achievement and good work to boast of. Edith's daughter, unimpressed by
psychological explanations, saw at work in the life of Uncle Leonard
the influences that had also brought her mother's tempestuous
marriage and her own early life to ruin. His unfulfilled marriage, his
feeble submission to his wife's demands, his unbalanced approach to
'the other woman' and an exaggerated deference to the opposite sex
in general – all were attributed by her to the intensity of indoctrina-
tion in childhood. Of the entire family, she remarked; 'None were
capable of showing love, or simple affection, even towards their own
children.'

Whatever the foundation for that belief, Leonard Woolley discovered the family relationship he so patently needed with Betty and
Alfred Waters and their children at Sedgehill Manor.

The only outward expression of the religious conviction he carried
through life, the only certainty he ever expressed, was a quietly
assured belief in God and the Christian faith. He did not share the
pioneering zeal with which his sisters, in particular, carried religion
to the four corners of the world. In the aftermath of recent disasters
he resumed his everyday life without fuss, rancour or self-pity. At
Shaftesbury he again became a regular churchgoer, a familiar sight
as he made a lively way across the fields to Sunday service. The
Waters, being Roman Catholics, went to a more distant church and
Woolley always ordered a car to take and fetch them. In reply to
Betty Waters' efforts to persuade him to have a motor-car, he said

that he preferred to walk. 'Anyway, I would only be tempted to go to places I have no desire to see.'

Soon after they moved to Shaftesbury, Betty had her first child. Woolley's concern for her when he visited the maternity home was so apparent that the nursing sister asked with amusement, 'Who is the expectant father?' He was there with a pram for the child on the day it was born.

Angling and travelling to country house sales in search of pictures and antiques occupied most days, but there was still work. The Atchana excavations did not come to an end until after he had moved. He was always at his desk by early morning, breaking off every now and again for a game of billiards, calling Alfred Waters from the garden to resume where they had left off an hour or two before.

As the Waters' two sons grew up, he took them with him on fishing trips and for country walks. Long years spent in the deserts of the Near East had given him a familiarity with delicacies not much sought after in England, such as edible fungi. He taught the Waters boys how to recognize the safe varieties, and whenever he was expecting guests he would ensure that Betty included a rare fungus of some kind in the dish.

There were occasional house parties, but Woolley did not like to entertain in the mass. He preferred to have one or two visitors, with good conversation over a meal and a glass or two of wine. Not all his guests were as keen as their host on the strangely-shaped and coloured 'mushrooms'. Most of the friends of his own generation were too old or frail to make the journey to Shaftesbury, but a few stalwarts came regularly. Sedgehill Manor was convenient for the Mallowans motoring to and from Greenway House in Devon. Of all his old acquaintances, Betty Waters liked Agatha most. 'A dear' was her uncomplicated description. Neill Malcolm turned up at intervals, though when Woolley moved to Shaftesbury he was eighty, and suffering more acutely than ever from his multiple war wounds. The Julian Huxleys, whom he had known in London during the war – though Lady Huxley, Juliette, could not take to Katharine – became the closest of his friends of the later years. They turned up at Sedgehill Manor whenever Julian could escape from his post-war involvement with UNESCO and his world-wide commitments as a lecturer. George Boscawen and his wife, Lord and Lady Falmouth, came up from Cornwall every now and again to renew a friendship which originated at Ur and was reinforced in the billiards room of the Athenaeum.

Perhaps the visitor whose company he found most congenial was Mortimer Wheeler, now basking in the limelight of the Indus Valley civilization which he had begun to unravel since being appointed Director-General to the India Archaeological Survey at Woolley's instigation in 1944. Wheeler had married for the third time in 1945, and his new wife, Margaret, was prepared to play a listening role while the loquacious archaeologists talked and argued for hours on end. But even in the company of so animated a man as Rik Wheeler, it was Woolley who did most of the talking. Lady Wheeler remembered him as 'a wonderful host and most brilliant conversationalist'. The talk cascaded; ancient history, Ur and Alalakh, the Indus Valley and the still sought-after outposts of the ancient world, claret vintages and the culinary merits of fungi, the early days with Lawrence at Carchemish, war and 'intelligence', old acquaintances and, in Woolley's case, old captors, the Turks, whom he counted now among the best of his friends. According to Margaret Wheeler, there were 'fascinating tales about Lawrence'. When they differed and argued, it was with good humour and much laughter. 'I had two gods, Leonard and Rik, and I still have,' Margaret Wheeler announced with a familiar certainty, forty years on from the days when she visited Sedgehill.

Woolley's assistants at Atchana, Brice and Hood, made the journey too. William Brice was still working with him on the Atchana-Alalakh report. Such visitors had to travel by train to Semley Halt, the railway station which was about a mile from the manor, and walk the rest of the way. In bad weather he would send a car for them.

He seldom made use of the local taxi-cab service. He still went to London occasionally, to the British Museum chiefly, and travelled far and wide to give lectures. As soon as he moved to Shaftesbury he made a point of establishing good relations with the railway authorities, using some of the artifice of his excavation days to keep the district stationmaster sweet. Long-distance travel meant a journey to Exeter to catch the express train. Once, early on, he was directed to the wrong platform and the train went without him. He immediately contacted the stationmaster, proffered his card and congratulated the official on the efficiency of his service, expressing his regret that on this one occasion service had fallen below its customary high standard. 'Leave it to me, Sir Leonard,' said the stationmaster. The train was halted at the next station on the line and a car provided to rush Woolley to meet it. Later on, fast trains passing through Semley Halt stopped there to pick him up whenever he wanted to go to London. When he came home from London or some more distant place, he would usually obtain a lift from the local coal merchant whose lorry was always parked at Semley Halt. 'Going my way?' He would arrive home, to the surprise of neighbours, in earnest conversation with the coalman.

The first local dignitary to seek out the famous archaeologist who had come to live in the district was Teulon Porter, the crippled Secretary of the Shaftesbury Society. Porter was a memorable figure, tall and with a gammy leg, who raced round the district on a powerful motor cycle, dressed in goggles and an old-fashioned leather helmet. He was a keen student of the 'Saxon town perched on a hill' and was delighted to find that Sir Leonard shared his interest. Soon the digger of Ur was hard at work on an unpaid archaeological exercise at Sedgehill, keenly observed by Teulon Porter. Woolley had found a triangular site close to his home at Sedgehill which he labelled 'prehistoric' and quickly trenched with the help of a gang of 'labourers' recruited from the local grammar school. With limited time and no resources, he was only able to go down a few feet, working spasmodically, reaching a medieval level thick with sherds of 13th century 'scratch' ware. Surviving correspondence in the Shaftesbury museum suggests that Woolley intended to continue the excavation, but that lack of time and trained labour probably conspired to cut it short when two trenches had been dug and some interesting pottery salvaged. A notice in the museum commemorates a lecture at the Shaftesbury Town Hall on the evening of Wednesday 6 April 1949, 'A Talk illustrated by slides, by Sir Charles Leonard Woolley F.S.A, D.Litt, L.L.D, A.R.I.B.A, on Digging Up History'.

Teulon Porter persuaded Woolley to write the memoirs which were to be his last excursion into popular writing. *As I Seem to Remember*, a witty and sometimes skittish account of wartime adventures, of secret service work and archaeological asides, was destined to be published posthumously by the Shaftesbury Society in conjunction with Allen and Unwin. It was an immediate success.

Another local family, the Warburtons, embraced Woolley with devotion and friendship in his last years. Captain Warburton was managing director of an engineering company and helped his new neighbour to cope with the financial problems which had become an increasing cause of concern. The parish church (remarkably, St Katharine's), inevitably became the social centre of Leonard's semi-retirement, and he was soon active in its work as church warden and lay preacher.

He was always poorly dressed and would never give in to Betty Waters' pleas that he buy himself a new suit. Dressed in ruffled coat and pullover, usually with fishing tackle to hand, he became a familiar sight in the neighbourhood.

The Waters and their two sons became the focus of his new life. Though Harold and sister Edith visited him occasionally, and Edith's daughter Margaret kept in touch, there was little other contact with his own family. Betty would sometimes take one of his books off the library shelf when she was tidying up and Woolley would find her sprawled on the floor reading, her duster cast aside. When he caught her she would hurriedly grasp the duster and pretend that she had been working. 'Come on, sit down and I'll tell you about it,' he would say, and she sat and listened spellbound.

Though increasing deafness and the enjoyable social life he discovered at Sedgehill militated against the hard working routine into which he had settled over the years, there was still plenty to do. Indeed, one of the biggest intellectual challenges of his life greeted his seventy-eighth year. In the heady atmosphere of post-war togetherness, the United Nations Educational, Scientific and Cultural Organization harnessed a majestic gathering of international scholars to no less a task than the recording of the history of the development of the human mind. Orient and occident were to receive equal representation. Political barriers, marked at that time not by simplistic terms such as 'east' and 'west' or 'Iron Curtain' but by the philosophical divisions of Marxism and Capitalism, were to be ignored. During 1947 and 1948, Julian Huxley as director-general called up a galaxy of historians, scientists, poets and artists, anthropologists and divines, to draft a plan for a 'cultural and scientific history of mankind', for submission to the General Council. Huxley was already in correspondence with Woolley about the origins of the written word in Mesopotamia during the 'Uruk' period. Anticipating the kind of philosophical argument that awaited him, Woolley remarked that before the written word, stamp seals were used to mark objects as a sign of ownership. He went on: 'It's a pleasant comment on the Marxist theory of prehistoric communism that man was jealously hallmarking his private possessions as early as the Chalcolithic age'.

The Communist world at first viewed the project with suspicion and refused to co-operate. In 1952 a draft plan was circulated. Not until 1954, however, was the Commission ready to put it into effect with a proposal for a quarterly *Journal of World History* and a massive, multi-tome *History of Mankind*. The first volume, covering 'Prehistory and the Beginnings of Civilization', was to be written in two parts by Jacquetta Hawkes (Mrs J. B. Priestley) and Professor Henry Frankfort. The latter died in 1954, however, before work could start, and at Julian Huxley's suggestion, Woolley was invited to write the second part of the first volume.

On 15 August 1954, Woolley wrote to Huxley in reply to an unofficial invitation.

> My dear Julian
> ... The idea of the History certainly does appeal to me (though whether I'm competent to tackle the job is another matter) & I wrote to Jacquetta & told her that I might undertake it provided that I do not have to drop my essential duty of putting the remaining Ur volumes through the press ... I'm really sorry that Frankfort could not do it – he'd have been much better than I, though his writings are not easy to read; but he had the right sort of mind. He is a very serious loss ...
> Yours ever, Leonard.

By decree, the work was to be of the 'highest intellectual standing'. Those who were about to embark on it were enjoined by UNESCO's International Commission to do so 'in a spirit of serene and dispassionate objectivity'. All texts were to be submitted for approval to the National Committees of member states. On top of that stultifying requirement it was decided to appoint an editor of the English texts, in which language all volumes would eventually be published. It was little short of a miracle that anything ever appeared in print. Undeterred, Woolley set to work in 1958 on a task that would take him to his last breath.

He was still in demand as a lecturer. Invitations to be the guest of honour at dinner parties still poured in. But most were turned down now, largely on account of his increasing deafness. He had taken the chair in November 1950 at the Royal Society of Arts when Mortimer Wheeler lectured on Archaeology in India; but it was a rare concession, made to please an old friend. As for giving talks and lectures, he commented 'The students *will* shout at me. I hate being shouted at as if I were deaf.' There were more honours. In 1955 he made his last journey to the USA, to his old hunting ground in Philadelphia where they presented him with the University's highest award for archaeological field work, the Lucy Wharton Drexel Medal. The Americans were surprised to find that the 'grand old man' they had expected was still as young-looking and impish as ever, dwarfed by the large men and women among his hosts but very much the centre of attention. In the same year, his popular account of Alalakh, *History Unearthed*, was published. At the close of 1956 he opened the magnificent exhibition staged by the British Museum to mark the Silver Jubilee of the British School of Archaeology in Iraq, formed in 1932 as a memorial to Gertrude Bell and initially financed by her bequest. Woolley had never played an active part in the School's administrative work, but he had contributed much to the resurrection of Iraq's ancient past and he was the obvious choice to open the exhibition. Max Mallowan, who had by then been the School's director for some years, remarked characteristically that 'only a moron could fail to be roused' by it. On the same occasion, a distinguished member of the British Museum staff asked Mallowan about the state of relations between Woolley and Smith. 'They could not be worse,' Mallowan replied.

Sidney Smith was destined to outlive Woolley by almost twenty years, and it was not until a moment before the former's death that a final, tragi-comic postscript was written to mark their abrasive relationship. Professor Smith was ninety years old, diabetic and in fading health when the archaeologist Duncan Noble interviewed him on the subject of Woolley, who by then had been dead for nineteen years. Dr Noble was asked not to make notes of the interview because of the Professor's age and infirmity, and the distraction that note-taking might cause. Noble's recollections were put to paper as soon as he reached home after leaving Smith. The emeritus professor spoke of the poor digging standards which prevailed at Carchemish, under the regimes of Hogarth, Campbell Thompson and Woolley. Then, his memory playing tricks which were obvious to the interviewer, he explained that 'Campbell Thompson had dug at Ur before the war,' that 'Hall was going to get the dig' but died before he could be appointed; that Woolley was given the job much as a last resort, 'it wasn't easy to find someone who would take on a dig in the Middle East.' In fact, 'C. T.' had dug after the war with the aid of troops, and Hall, who also dug briefly at Ur and al-Ubaid in 1919, died in 1930 when the excavation of Ur was almost completed. No one but Woolley was remotely considered by Pennsylvania, the chief contributor to the Ur funds. Smith was at pains to assure Noble that he, Smith, was not Woolley's enemy, that on the contrary he 'respected' and 'admired' him. 'Woolley had very fine judgement in his own subject,' he said. He emphasized Woolley's most pronounced achievement, 'how he explained the significance of things and how very good his excavation methods were ... better than the French, Germans, and Americans, because he explained the context in which things were found, and therefore their significance.' Woolley's imaginative survey of the walls of Ur had turned out to be 'absolutely right'. But there was a reverse side to Smith's coin. Many of the clay tablets of Mesopotamia were found inscribed but in an unbaked and therefore fragile state. Woolley, he said, had laid claim to 'inventing' a process by which, thousands of years after they had been left in their virgin state, they could be baked so that their inscriptions could be impressed on to wet cylinders and preserved for all time. But he had not invented the method; it had been used for a long time at the British Museum. In fact, Woolley claimed no more than to have 'devised' a method of preservation by careful firing. Report served the old man ill when he recounted stories of Woolley's capture at sea in the first war. 'Please do not publish this,' he asked, afraid that the story might 'make Woolley look foolish.' He then related an anecdote which Woolley himself had told often, an exaggeration of the true circumstances of capture, but intended to amuse, that when the yacht *Zaida* went down, he was wearing field boots and spurs. Smith thought it indicative of Woolley's overweening pride. 'The Turks were amazed' when he was washed ashore and they found him in full officer's regalia. Woolley related many colourful versions of an event which he always claimed was a 'holiday' cruise, but which was almost certainly connected with a secret mission to land agents near to Alexandretta. Official files give little away. But what is quite clear is that the crew were not washed ashore. They were rescued by a Turkish vessel after being in the water for some four hours, and if any of the officers were wearing boots and spurs when they entered the water, they quickly removed them. As for Woolley's personal life and behaviour, Smith saw nothing but foolishness and lack of judgement. Contrary to all other known impressions, Smith considered Woolley to be neither humorous nor prepossessing. He spoke of his lack of height and his 'curious wrinkled face'. His affairs with women 'had to be hushed up'. He spoke of a woman singer Woolley 'knocked about town with' before he met Katharine, 'a quite worthless person' who 'refused to marry him'. Whoever the lady may have been – if she existed outside Smith's imagination – Woolley cannot have spent much time with her. He did not reach England from Turkish PoW camp until December 1918, when he was preoccupied with family affairs and the acquisition of a new home for his father. He was back at Carchemish, still in uniform, in the spring of 1919. And Smith did not return to the British Museum until 1919. He could have known little of Woolley's activities before Ur and Katharine claimed him. 'He had no judgement over women,' said Smith. Others, who knew both men, have said that neither was notably proficient in that respect. Smith was correct in his assertion that from the moment Woolley married Katharine 'he was completely her slave.' But it is clear that Smith's memory was too much at fault for any serious store to be put by his professional recollections. He spoke disparagingly of 'Woolley's Syrian adventure', with reference to the dig at Atchana. It is perhaps significant that one of Smith's most important contributions to his own field of archaeological scholarship was his publication 'Alalakh and Chronology', based on a study of Woolley's Atchana tablets. The significance of Alalakh was being reassessed by archaeologists in the 1980s, and Woolley's neglected Syrian discoveries were being seen anew, along with other Syrian and Anatolian excavations, as subjects of primary scholastic importance.

Smith and Woolley never met in retirement. Indeed, it is said that none of Smith's former colleagues ever went near him in his last years. But he pleaded with those who proposed to write the life of his great contemporary, that they should deal only with his work and ignore his private life. Other archaeologists were to make the same request in later years. Such well-meaning people seem not to understand, as Woolley would all too clearly have understood, that weakness of the flesh – though it may not be an admirable quality – is not exactly an uncommon human defect, and is entirely compatible with creative and scientific achievement of the most exceptional kind.

Mrs Smith was still alive when Noble went to see her husband, and she said afterwards that it had made the Professor 'happy'. He felt forgotten and neglected and was 'delighted that someone had come to him for his views'. Left in a state of excitement by Dr Noble's questions, and reminded painfully of a long dispute based on a concoction of mutual admiration, jealousy, frustration and stubborn pride, Smith forgot to take his insulin. He retired to bed never to awaken.

In 1957, Volume IV of the British Museum/University of Pennsylvania reports on Ur was published. Professor Seton Lloyd, reviewing it in *Antiquity*, chaffed that it had 'come of age prenatally', having been made ready for publication by Woolley twenty-one years earlier. Another award came at the same time. In 1957 London University awarded him the Flinders Petrie Medal, an honour in which he was in succession to Aurel Stein, Arthur Evans, the Abbé Breuil, J. D. Beazley, Mortimer Wheeler and A. B. Wace.

Now seventy-eight, he still looked and felt an active, no more than middle aged figure, though he had begun to experience the first annoying twitches of advancing years. Much to his own surprise, he had become the sage of archaeology. Great and famous contemporaries who had dominated the scene for so long were mostly dead and gone, victims of age or war. He was more or less a lone giant of the past when he took on what was to prove his last, and in some ways most exacting task, the UNESCO book.

The new literary role was the culmination of all his past writings and he took it very seriously, submitting sections of the text for individual and committee approval as he went along. In 1955, the Soviet Union and the Peoples' Republics of Czechoslovakia, Hungary and Poland decided to support the project, and so a new layer of academicians was imposed on the existing international committee consisting of some thirty distinguished scholars under the president, Julian Huxley, and six vice-presidents. Almost every observation made by the writers from then on was to be subjected to searching, and often irritating, Marxist analysis.

The Beginnings of Civilization presented Woolley with a golden opportunity to range over the enthusiasms of a lifetime, from that youthful penchant for China and central Asia expressed in his student correspondence with Aurel Stein to the early Greek history which unfolded at the time of his first job as assistant at the Ashmolean, and the later, all-absorbing preoccupations with Egypt, Mesopotamia, Syria and Anatolia. Despite all the frustrations and restrictions of a committee-bound task, he took it on with characteristic verve at the moment when a deep organic disorder began to effect his health and physical vitality. He had been lucky. Hardly a day's illness had intervened in a life of exceptional achievement and remarkable productiveness. As the work progressed, a sickness which he at first attributed to the inevitable ravages of time began to diminish his strength. Will and intellect remained intact, though, and he wrote for long hours every day for months on end. When he had completed the day's work he dealt with the correspondence associated with the book, sending off chunks of text to the Egyptologist Sir Alan Gardiner, to C. J. Gadd on Sumerian linguistic matters, Van de Waerden of Zurich on mathematical and astronomical questions; to Professor Diakonoff in Leningrad and the Sinologist Vasilyev in Moscow, Bodenheimer in Jerusalem, Yabuuchi and Kaizuka in Japan, Parrot, Casal and Caquot in Paris, Shui Chien Tung on the Chinese calendar, and on almost anything to the editor of the English edition Professor Ralph E. Turner at Yale. When answers and criticisms came back, it was often necessary to write again with more questions, sometimes in disagreement. He was conscious of straying outside the strict realm of his proven competence, pleading in defence that 'the voice is Jacob's voice, but the hands are the hands of Esau.'

His method of covering all the early civilizations within social, economic, scientific and cultural contexts, enabled him to give due weight to the interplay of language and custom across the millennia of the ancient world's rise and decline. Following on from Jacquetta Hawkes's Part I (his work when published began at page 359), he was able to launch into a graphic account of the Urban Revolution of the Bronze Age in which the Neolithic hunter-gatherers formed the first village settlements, gradually growing in size and social organization, first into townships and finally into agglomerations called by an 'untranslatable word', *cities*. So, by way of social structure, he deals in turn with the evolving fabrics of each of the ancient civilizations, under 'Techniques, Arts and Crafts'. Predictably, it was in the chapters concerned with the applied and decorative arts, music and literature that he seemed most at home, tracing method and mechanical principle back to primitive agricultural and building experience.

Julian and Juliette Huxley spent many a week-end at Sedgehill in the first two years of work on the book. Archaeology had become one of the famous scientist's passions in later life. In November 1955, he was able to return Chapter VI to Woolley with a few 'ventured' suggestions. Later there were 'helpful criticisms' of the chapter on 'Languages and Writing Systems'. There was also much ado with Jacquetta Hawkes, as well as the panel of editors. Soon the inevitable committee circulars were carrying multiple requests and suggestions across continents. The task was rapidly getting out of hand.

Woolley's basic interests and assumptions had changed little since those lonely youthful journeys to the Whitechapel Gallery when he first experienced the full force of visual things. For him, arts and crafts represented the logical chapter headings of life. More immediate human concerns like agriculture and building were simply manifestations of craft techniques. In his expansive work for UNESCO he reverses the customary procedures, and the result is always interesting, and often amusing. Editorial notes at the end of each chapter contain many a cryptic note from the distinguished Marxist contributors, notably Professor Diakonoff, who fought a running battle with the author. From the Bronze Age through the Urbanization of Society to Social Structure, the debate raged between the orthodox Western and the Marxist extremes of interpretation. Woolley included every exchange in his chapter notes, turning what might have been a very dull debate into a fascinating intellectual duel.

This was, of course, the period of the famous Lysenko controversy and feeling in the West against the rigid and often bizarre methods of 'Stalinist' scholarship, even among Marxist intellectuals, ran high. Commenting on the Russian academics in particular, he wrote:

My Russian commentators, to whose help I am indebted, have urged that my readers should be acquainted with the different views existing among modern scholars of the important question of the process of development of mankind and, especially, with the point of view of Marxist philosophy, which directly opposes the theory that 'human history is no more than a kaleidoscopic change of whimsical patterns with no inner consistency and no principle in their development'.

He proceeded to summarize the Marxist view, from primitive, communal, pre-class society, through the urbanization stage and the growth of property ownership by individuals to the development of technical knowledge and the advent of the non-slave worker in feudal society, explaining: 'Since the whole purpose of this book is to trace man's progress it obviously does not regard history as a "kaleidoscopic change of whimsical patterns"; but none the less do I find it impossible to fit the stages of progress in general to the Procrustean bed of what my Marxist friend terms "the law of social development". In my view "the different local varieties following

from the specific conditions of time and place" [quoting Diakonoff]
rule out any such conformity.'

> Slavery was, of course, a usual feature of ancient society, but in
> the different societies the importance of the part played by it
> varied very greatly; thus, in Egypt, civilization attained its zenith
> in the Sixth Dynasty, but not until the Eighteenth Dynasty did
> the institution become a considerable element of Egyptian
> society; there is no evidence to show that the city states of Tyre
> and Sidon were based on slave ownership. Again, the 'law of
> social development' whereby a 'feudal' stage resulted from
> slavery with the development of technical knowledge cannot be
> of universal application, if only because not all ancient civiliza-
> tions passed through the feudal stage. The Marxist view seems
> to me to lay upon slavery a quite unwarranted emphasis . . . for
> an organized society the function of the governing class was,
> and was generally recognized to be, as essential as that of the
> farm labourer, and the smooth running of the state and its
> defence against external enemies was in the interests of all
> classes alike . . . I have purposely avoided the use of the term
> 'slave-holding society' because I wished to avoid the term's
> implications: the detailed discussion will perhaps justify me, but
> it [chapter 'The Social Structure'] was written objectively and
> not in support of any theory.

Again Diakonoff was permitted the last word:

> Sir Leonard Woolley seems to misunderstand me when arguing
> that 'not all civilizations passed through the feudal stage'. In my
> opinion *no* ancient civilization had reached the feudal stage (in
> the Marxist sense of the word 'feudal' as quoted by Sir Leonard
> above) . . . A class division was no doubt necessary for the
> progress of society in ancient times, but nevertheless, in those
> times as well as in all others, no one would drudge in order to
> ensure a safe and prosperous life for the governing class, unless
> forced to do so, be the governing class never so important for
> the progress of civilization. The state is necessary for the
> 'smooth running' of class-society, not because it defends society
> against external enemies.

As for music and literature, Woolley stressed the growing importance
which those subjects assumed in his own life with the introductory

quotation 'Give me the making of people's songs and I care not who makes their laws.'

It was in the passage on the Hebrews in the chapter 'Religious Beliefs and Practices', that Woolley came to the crux of his own belief; to a synthesis of his implicit faith and his worldly experience. It brought him to confrontation with both Marxist and traditional Hebrew scholarship.

In recapitulation of his thesis in *Ur of the Chaldees* and *Abraham*, he stressed the importance of the worship of the moon god at Harran and Ur, capitals of the earthly realm where Nanna was king, as the homes of the family from which the Hebrew nation claimed descent. The Jews became aware that their forefathers 'worshipped strange gods beyond the river'. Legend and tradition came together in the old-wives' tale that Terah was by trade a maker of images; but if legend could be cast aside, tradition was vindicated by the fact that Terah was the Hurrian name of the Moon god who was worshipped at Harran (Nannar of Ur). Hebrew religion was, therefore, rooted in that of Sumer. As for the precise date of Abraham's residence at Ur, he was in no doubt that the Larsa period, c.2000–1800 BC, was close enough. That, as he noted in his exploration of Ur, was the time when the cult of the family god reached its climax, when every house had its own domestic chapel 'beneath whose pavement lay the graves of the family's forebears and when family worship filled the void left in man's religious consciousness by the growing exclusiveness of temple ritual and by Nannar's failure to protect his kingdom against foreign enemies'. Abraham's removal from Ur to Harran would have made no difference theologically. The moon god was lord of both places. The Hurrian law prevailing at Harran made the possession of figures of the family god (the *teraphim* of Genesis) a claim to primogeniture. It was only when he arrived in 'barbarous' Palestine that the first step was taken leading to the isolation of the Hebrews as a 'peculiar people'. The proposal to sacrifice his first-born, Isaac, was, said Woolley, an unwilling concession to local practice in the region the patriarch wandered through as a pastoralist with his flocks, where there were no temples of the sort he was accustomed to, only crude and unfamiliar 'high places'. The town-bred family of Terah had a supreme contempt for the barbarous peoples of Canaan. The intended sacrifice of his son apart, the civilized traditions of Ur were such as to make him reject the demands of Canaanite ritual.

It was all too much for Diakonoff who accused his 'friend' of making no distiction between history and myth, that 'thinking that Abraham was historical' he had no right to disregard other well-founded opinion. Furthermore, 'all Soviet scholars will insist on such opinions being brought to the notice of the reader.' Woolley based his interpretation of biblical events on tradition, 'as distinguished from myth'. The extreme views of Soviet scholars were, he said, simply based on Marxist principles, which were formulated when the Higher Criticism was in fashion. 'I do not hold that the Hebrew tradition is impeccable, but am convinced that it has an historical basis. Abraham I believe to be a conflation of at least two (and probably three) historical individuals ...' The evidence for his argument was, he said, to be found in his book *Abraham*. Woolley's defence was questioned by Turner. 'Sir Leonard Woolley has dated Abraham ... by reference to the Old Testament record and has supported this by identifying the word *Habiru* in use at that time, as a reference to the Hebrews. He concluded that the god whom Abraham took with him was an unnamed family deity and that his god became the Hebrew Yahweh. At present this construction remains a hypothesis not accepted by all scholars.'

It was the same story when he came to Moses and the Exodus. Interestingly, Woolley made no criticism of the Bible's famous omission of the names of the Pharaohs of the Oppression and the Exodus, information which would have made it possible to date both events with certainty, and would have been more concrete than a good deal of the legend attaching to the expulsion and tortuous journey of the Israelites. 'Prof. Diakonoff has challenged my treatment of Moses as a historical character in the same way as he has challenged that of Abraham.' Again Woolley retorted that he believed there to be a 'a basis of truth in the tradition', though imagination had coloured the incidents and perhaps, 'in some cases', invented them. The part played by the Mosaic tradition, whatever may be said of it, was too important to be ignored. Diakonoff maintained that Moses was 'a figment of the Hebrew imagination'. In that case, replied Woolley, it was 'an astonishing feat'. Even so, he had treated Moses as a symbol, 'without insisting on his historical character as an individual, citing those incidents which, perhaps in a poetic form, throw light upon religious ideas.' His Russian critic pointed out artfully that the golden calf was an image of a male animal and could hardly, as was suggested, have been made in honour of the goddess Hathor. Woolley thought the redactor of Exodus at fault for using a masculine word which was simply a 'mistake in the 600-year-old oral tradition'. Diakonoff accused him of simply 'accepting a miracle without comment', offering an 'uncritical and quite unhistorical narrative'. 'I was not,' replied the author, but he was quite sure that the narrative would present no difficulty to most of his readers.

In 1957, unable to cope any more with the financial worry that had increased with age and the loss of earning capacity – and the loss of most of his savings in the Chamberlen business – Woolley decided to move from Sedgehill Manor. It was a hard decision. It meant that he would have to leave behind the Waters family who had been his mainstay for more than ten happy years. It also meant abandoning the home he had come to regard as his first real anchorage, with its finely proportioned rooms housing his large collection of pictures, pottery 'gewgaws' and furniture, its circular library on the first floor overlooking the croquet lawn, the spacious billiard room and the organized chaos of the study. Family and friends had become familiar with the house and the journey to Semley Halt. His god-daughter Margaret recalled visits with her mother when she was allowed to try her hand at the alluring baize-covered table, in between interminable bouts of a 'special' variety of billiards – picked up at the Athenaeum – which Uncle Leonard inflicted on Alf Waters day in and day out. According to Betty Waters, 'he had lost the will to live'. He made no secret of his belief that if he survived for many more years he would run out of money. His worries were exaggerated. His annuity assured him of £2000 a year for another two years, his book royalties still made a useful contribution to his living expenses, and he still had savings sufficient to guarantee survival for a few years.

Captain Warburton and his American wife offered an attractive solution. They suggested taking a house together and sharing the cost of running it, so that Woolley would have to pay only for his modest share of space and amenities. In fact, Warburton's company bought the property, Kingsworthy Court, near Winchester in Hampshire. Woolley made provision for the Waters, paying a year's rent on Sedgehill Court so that they could continue to live there whether or not they took other employment. Despite age and work Woolley visited the family until he was no longer capable of the journey. He saw to it that they wanted for nothing while he was alive.

The new house was spacious, with a large drawing room and conveniently designed library and billiards room. The Warburtons and their friends became the hub of a new social life, though the Huxleys made the journey to Winchester now and again. He continued to work with all his customary vigour and dedication, but the zest for life had begun to go, along with some of his closest friends. Malcolm had died in 1953, Crawford in 1957 as he moved to Winchester.

Early in 1957 he was able to write to Huxley asking him to look at the last chapter of his History. 'After I had finished the first ten chapters there came a long commentary from our "Soviet historian" friends complaining that I had wholly failed to do justice (a) to the Russian archaeological discoveries and (b) to the important cultures of the USSR area; and had also neglected the pre-history of Europe.' The accusations were, he said, 'perfectly true'. He had expected criticism, 'especially from British archaeologists'. He could not please everyone. 'I have said . . . what I wanted to say.' With the glint that still showed in his ageing eye, 'I'm just going to write to Juliette, on non-technical subjects!'

The eleventh and last chapter of the book, 'The Limits of Civilization in the Bronze Age', was completed by summer, and the editorial comments of the panel of experts assembled. Then came the almost inevitable *coup* of the academic committee. Professor Carneiro, president of the Bureau of the International Commission responsible for the book, announced on 4 November 1957 that several committee members had raised questions about illustrations, particularly maps, and that others, new to the committee, wanted to approve chapters which had already passed through the bureaucratic machine. A 'decision of the Bureau' demanded that other authors should be allowed to interpolate passages of their own where they disagreed with the author, and to alter the text as they saw fit. And it required Woolley's compliance. He replied indignantly: 'That Decision . . . is not a revision of the Bureau's previous statements, but a reversal of them, amounting, in the circumstances to a breach of contract. I absolutely refuse to accept it.' Finally, 'I would ask you, therefore, my dear Professor, to give me your official assurance that the Decision recorded . . . (and) revised on 4th November 1957, is null and void. Failing such assurance I shall have to take legal steps to prevent publication by UNESCO of any part of my text or any version of it; which, of course, I should do with deep regret.' Writing to Huxley, he blamed Professor Ralph Turner for 'pulling a sharp one' with the Committee because he, Woolley, had resisted some of his criticisms.

Huxley supported Woolley, as did other author-editors to whom copies of his letter were circulated. Carneiro and Turner climbed down and the book went through for publication substantially unchanged.

Soon after the resolution of his last academic squabble, rapid physical decline set in. At the end of January 1958 he wrote to Juliette Huxley to tell her that he had collapsed at home in the New Year and woke up in hospital, with all his teeth removed, 'looking like a pug-dog with mumps', and covered in black bruises. He discharged himself after two days, refused an ambulance and instead took a train to Gillingham in Kent, spent the night in an hotel and went to an auction sale next morning. He found nothing of interest but the psychological effect was, he said, 'nicely calculated'. He felt fit enough to give notice to his Swedish housemaid who had proved hopeless at her work. He went on working, and declining, for a further year.

Huxley brought his weight to bear and the Committee was finally abolished in 1959, and an adviser appointed for each separate volume of the series. In April 1959, he told Woolley: 'Everyone was filled with admiration for the way in which you had run ahead and revised your part so that it is practically ready for publication.'

When it was published three years later, the UNESCO book bore the editorial note that its author had died before all the work on it was complete, and that the comments submitted by scholars, together with Woolley's notes on their comments and those of Professor Turner, had been entrusted to Professor Jean Leclant of Strasbourg University. In fact, during the long period of gestation and birth seven of the original panel of scholars, apart from Woolley himself, had died.

His last rewards came in the final months. After Sir John Myres' death in 1959, a memorial lecturership was established at New College and he was invited to fill the post. He was elected an Honorary Fellow in November. Soon after the Society of Antiquaries awarded him its gold medal for his work at Ur and Atchana. It was too late for him to accept or even acknowledge the honour.

He collapsed at Kingsworthy Court in early February 1960. He was too sick to be cared for at home and was taken to a private nursing home at 16 Fitzroy Square in London. Teulon Porter and his wife accompanied him to London and were at his bedside day and night for the first few days. By 14 February Woolley was too ill to speak and they left. His last conscious act was to write a cheque for the Waters in the presence of the Huxleys. It arrived on the day of his death with a note from Juliette. Harold Woolley was also at the bedside, and as the executor of the will he asked for a final codicil to be read in which it was agreed that all the bequests previously made by Woolley of works of art and artifacts to the National Art Collections Fund, the Ashmolean, New College, his old school St John's, and his sister Edith, were revoked. Any objects could be sold by the Trustees in order to provide such cash as might be required to meet legacies and the demands of the estate. Woolley was unable to sign the documents with his name and made his mark, two crosses. The document was witnessed by his solicitor, John Wyndham Stanton, and the matron of the nursing home, Janet M. Miles. In the final throes, he compounded the folly of his father in permitting his valuable art collection to be sold off, if necessary without expert evaluation, to pay for death duties and bequests. Not all his art purchases had been as adroit as he thought. None the less, his collection contained many Turners which he had bought back after the sale of his father's property and before Turner's true value in the market place had been established. Ironically, although almost all his drawings, paintings and artifacts were left to the Ashmolean, few were ever to go there, but many were to find their way after a quarter of a century to the Birmingham City Museum and Art Gallery. In the meantime, they had been in private hands, most of them acquired through the principal executor, the Rev. Harold Woolley.

Freya Stark wrote from Italy on 6 March to her friend 'Jock' Murray, the publisher of Albermarle Street. 'What a spate of friends and even acquaintances *dying*,' she wrote, 'Len Woolley, Ernest Barker, George Trevelyan . . .' In fact, Woolley had died on 20 February 1960 at the age of seventy-nine. The cause was given as general abdominal carcinomatosis, or cancer of the abdominal tract.

Cremation was at Golders Green on the 24th. Of the family, only Harold and Edith were present at the service. The Huxleys were there, along with Sir Basil Blackwell and Lady Bonham-Carter (whose husband Edgar had been Acting High Commissioner when Woolley first went to post-war Iraq), representatives of the British Museum and Pennsylvania University, Oxford University, St John's College, the Royal Asiatic Society, the Royal Geographical Society. Of the survivors of Ur, Archie Whitburn and Cyril Gadd were there. The Mallowans were unable to attend. At a memorial service on 14 March held at St Martin-in-the-Fields, Agatha and Max were present along with the firmament of archaeology. Every British School of Archaeology from Ankara to Jerusalem was represented, as were the great museums and universities with which he had been associated. Entire memorial editions of academic journals were devoted to him in which Max Mallowan in particular and the new generation in the mass paid homage to the old master who had retained his boyish image to the last.

Huxley wrote in his *Memories* of the last years at Sedgehill, where he enjoyed a 'happy old age, after a marriage which brought him little joy'.

> In the mornings he would show us his collection of pictures. These were almost all salvaged from obscure sales in country places, where, for a few shillings, he had bought some forgotten drawing or painting and lovingly restored it. Among the junk, he had secured some fine Ruskin water-colours, good Varleys and Cotmans, a small Breughel, a delightful Angelica Kaufmann, and many others ... Gentle and unassuming, he was a truly remarkable man, his archaeological work of first-class importance, his honesty in acknowledging his few mistakes striking. He was that rare creature – a man at peace with himself.

As I Seem to Remember, edited by Teulon Porter, the last of his close friends, came out within a few months of his death and in reviewing it for *Antiquity*, Mortimer Wheeler wrote:

> Leonard Woolley enjoyed living and, when the time came, died without regret. His work was done; he had corrected his last proofs, and on his death bed he had been awarded a Gold Medal. His life as a whole has been astonishingly like one of his own stories ... In his lifetime Woolley scarcely received the academic recognition that was his undoubted merit. He was too good, it seemed, to be true. The confident but always acutely experimental intelligence underlying the remarkable discoveries which again and again advertised his achievement was too often of a kind that escaped the easy comprehension of his cloistered critics. In this unimportant sense he suffered from success.

Chapter Notes

Legend for source notes and bibliography:
BL British Library
BM British Museum
Bodl. Bodleian Library, Oxford
ILN Illustrated London News
IO India Office Library and Records (British Library)
JRAS Journal of the Royal Asiatic Society
WAA Western Asiatic Archive, British Museum
GR Greek and Roman Archive, British Museum

Chapter 1 *Inheritance*: pages 7–25

Family background: General Registry; family records, Mrs Margaret Witton and Mr Warren Laxton; G. H. Woolley, *Sometimes a Soldier*. **Early school years and impressions of Bethnal Green**: Dr Duncan Noble and Mrs Witton; Rev. G. H. Woolley in *Sometimes a Soldier*. *Observer*, 31 August 1919, sent to Edith by Dr Waugh (father of Evelyn and Alec), friend and physician of Laxtons at Midsomer Norton, Somerset. **St John's School**: Mr M. E. C. Comer to author, 12 October 1987; Old Johnian Society records and *The Johnian*. **Oxford**: Bodleian correspondence, Ms Eng Lett, c. 346 folios 44–5, Ashmolean Museum records, Spooner: Woolley, *Dead Towns and Living Men*. Hogarth and Evans: *Ashmolean Reports*, 1889–1910; Ronaldson: *Drawings of New College Oxford*, introduced by C. Leonard Woolley, Blackwell 1906. **Robert Burton and Haverfield**: Bodleian Acc. Ms Top Oxon c. 152. **Craster**: Woolley in *Spadework*. **Hall** and **Chirol**: Winstone, *Gertrude Bell* and *The Illicit Adventure passim*. Hogarth in Asia Minor: BM GR. **Lawrence** and **Woolley**: Mrs Witton to author, Woolley, *Spadework* and *I Seem to Remember*, Thurlow Leeds, *Letters*. Campbell Thompson: Mallowan, *Memoirs*. **Resignation** from Ashmolean: Ashmol. *Report* 1907. **Karanog/Meroë**: Woolley, *Dead Towns and Living Men*, chapter 1. D. Randall MacIver and C. L. Woolley: Reports of the Eckley B. Coxe Jr expedition, vol i Areika (1909), vols iii–v Karanog, vol vii Behen; F. Ll. Griffith, *ibid*, vol vi, *Meroitic Inscriptions*. **Italy**: Woolley, *Dead Towns*, chapter 2. **Stein**: Bodleian, MS Stein 112, fols 108–14. **Carnarvon**: *ibid*, Woolley to Stein from Highclere.

Chapter 2 *'Mound of Many Riddles'* pages 26–48

Spadework, p. 66ff; British Museum Correspondence, Western Asiatic Archive (WAA), diary of Carchemish excavations from 13 March 1911 to 1914. *The Times*, 9, Oct 1911, R. Campbell Thompson. *Illustrated London News*, 24 Jan 1914, D. G. Hogarth. Lawrence with Petrie: Drower, *Flinders Petrie*, p. 319f. R. Campbell Thompson: *A Pilgrim's Script*, 1915, and Mallowan, *Memoirs*.

A. E. Henderson and **Hogarth**, 1904: BM GR; original lease. Mr Patrick Henderson, British Museum concession at Jerablus and early digging: BM WAA, 1911. **Funding of dig**: BM WAA, Hogarth to Kenyon 13–20 May 1911; Hogarth to Fitzmaurice, Pears, Ramsay, *ibid*, 20 May 1911; and Fisher, *Fear God and Dread Nought*, Cape 1952. See also Jeremy Wilson's *Lawrence of Arabia*, p. 100, which became available as I was compiling these notes; funding by Mr Walter Morrison, MP for Plymouth (1861–74). **Hamoudi at Carchemish**: Woolley, *Dead Towns* etc. **Dahum at Carchemish**: *ibid*; Lawrence, *Letters*, p. 103ff; Wilson, *op. cit.*, p. 94ff. **Woolley on Lawrence**: *Lawrence by His Friends*, p. 72. Gertrude Bell: her *Letters*, 1927, p. 252; and Andrae, *Mitteilungen der Deutschen Orient-Gesellschaft* (Babylon 10 March 1911), and *Lebenserinnerungen eines Ausgraebers*. **Hamoudi and Dahum in England**, July 1913: Woolley, *Dead Towns and Living Men*; Lawrence, *Letters*; Mrs Corbett Winder to author, 22 April 1989; Wilson, *op. cit.*, p. 125. **Woolley and Lawrence at Aleppo and Beirut**: Ceram, *Gods, Graves and Scholars* p. 212. **Lawrence and Dahum**: Woolley in *T. E. Lawrence by His Friends*. Wilson, *op. cit.*, (p. 128), asks why Woolley included these 'allegations' in his essay, and concludes that Woolley was being disingenuous. In fact, Woolley was simply responding to the widespread belief that Lawrence had homosexual tendencies. The argument would hardly seem worth pursuing in today's climate, although it is significant that a present-day novelist, Martin Booth, makes use of an 'accepted' sexual relationship between James Elroy Flecker and Lawrence in his book *Dreaming of Samarkand*; but Mr Wilson's attitude is odd. When Leeds and Lawrence treat Woolley as a subject of mirth, and patronize his 'passionate belief in his own connoisseurship' and his 'encroachment into the deeper recesses of historical and archaeological research' (p. 129), it is all jolly witty acceptable stuff. But when Woolley loyally defends his ex-assistant, posthumously, against a widespread suspicion, encouraged by Lawrence's own writings, of homosexuality, he (Woolley) is charged with making scandalous 'allegations'. **Lawrence's river excursions, Kurds and gun running**: see Wilson, *op. cit.*, p. 945 and notes pp. 1155–6. *Author's note*: the Lawrence documents embargoed until the year 2000 in the Bodleian collection but made available to Mr Wilson are generally disappointing, but there is one important exception. On p. 945 he publishes as Appendix II a report by the American Vice-Consul at Beirut, F. Willoughby Smith, date 9.12.1912, based on evidence given by Lawrence and Woolley, and submitted by the latter, which arose out of the murder of the Kurdish leader Ibrahim Pasha by the Young Turks following their victory in 1908. In 1911, Lawrence on a visit to Harran, over 100 miles due east of Carchemish, was shown a collection of some 10,000 Martini rifles in the Crusader castle there which were to be used by Kurds in a revenge attack on the Turks. But 'something bigger' was afoot. The American referred to a planned Arab uprising under a leadership encompassing the Khedive of Egypt, the Sharif of Mecca, the Senussi, and Ibn Rashid. In all essentials, the information gathered by Lawrence and Woolley confirmed the report of Captain Shakespear (Shakespear to Cox 8 April 1911, Foreign Office Diary 29 May 1911, FO371/1249 and India Office L/P&S/7/248) of a conspiracy of Arab rulers, except for one essential, the omission of Ibn Saud, who according to Shakespear was being asked to lead the uprising, but whose inclination was to be guided by Britain. Willoughby Smith spoke of meeting the Sharif of Mecca 'who appears to lack qualities of leader' though 'his brother is a stronger man'. Wilson in parenthesis p. 948: 'has probably confused Sherif Hussein with one of his sons, Feisal or Abdullah, whom he could have met in Turkey'. It is much more likely that the American knew what he was saying, and that he meant precisely the Sharif's brother, Nasr bin Ali, who remained in Constantinople as a member of the Upper House of Parliament after Husain bin Ali was sent to Mecca by the Young Turks in 1908. If Wilson's thesis is right, that neither Lawrence nor Woolley, nor Hogarth to whom they reported, was engaged in any kind of secret activity before the war, the sceptic might be forgiven for wondering why the two young archaeologists at the outset of their respective careers concerned themselves with such politically arcane matters, and why that document was concealed for so long.

Sinai expedition: *Wilderness of Zin*, intro by Kenyon. The reader can gain a more balanced picture of life at Carchemish by reference to chapters 6 and 7 of Mr Wilson's *Lawrence of Arabia*. In turning to the source notes on those chapters, in which Wilson makes several gratuitous references to my own 'evidence', the reader may care to note that he makes no reference to Hogarth's correspondence with Gerald Fitzmaurice, embassy dragoman and hub of all things secret in Constantinople (BM WAA files), gives no evidence for his assertion that the money came entirely from Walter Morrison 'a wealthy businessman' who is well-known for his support of Petrie in Egypt, see Drower pp. 295, 332 (though he refers to a letter from Hogarth to Kenyon questioning whether the latter knew the benefactor's identity, without actually naming him), ignores the evidence of other perfectly respectable authorities quoted in my *Illicit Adventure* and *The Diaries of Parker Pasha*, and dismisses my attempts to put the Lawrence business into some kind of perspective as 'valueless'. He places the efforts of other writers such as Richard Aldington and Desmond Stewart in the same category.

Chapter 3 *In the footsteps of Moses* pages 49–58

Young: *The Independent Arab*, p. 14ff. Woolley and Lawrence: *The Wilderness of Zin*. Lawrence: His *Letters* 26.12.1913 *et seq*. Woolley: *As I Seem to Remember*, p. 88ff. Hogarth: *Carchemish* Part I, British Museum, 1914. *Quarterly Reports* of Palestine Exploration Fund, 1914.

Lawrence, Woolley and Flecker: TEL *Letters*; and see Wilson, *op. cit.* BM WAA Lawrence to Hogarth, Oct 1913–Jan 1914 re progress of German railway, Flecker, Gregori, etc. Leeds: *Letters from TEL*, 4–23 April 1914. **Routes of Woolley and Lawrence and Gertrude Bell**: Winstone, *Illicit Adventure* p. 107ff, but *note*; I have changed Woolley's dialogue in places and added facts derived from other sources to make it more meaningful to the general reader. I also note that Mr Wilson, *op. cit.*, pp. 999–1000 describes as 'astonishing' my claim that Lawrence and Gertrude Bell had an 'undoubted meeting' at Kalat Ziza on 5 January 1914, when the latter was on a mission to Hail in Central Arabia. I made no such assertion. I merely stated the known movements of 'Gertie' and her 'Beloved Boy' at the time and deduced that they in all probability met. Miss Bell was detained at the Hijaz rail terminus of Ziza for nine days at the beginning of January 1914, allegedly waiting for permission to move on. Woolley and Lawrence travelled along the Hijaz rail link on the 5th *(Wilderness of Zin)*. According to my account taken from their admittedly obscure timetable, they went on to Gaza arriving there on the 6th. Jeremy Wilson says that Lawrence was in Gezer, 'an archaeological site many miles distant' on that day. Gezer is about 20 miles north-west of Jerusalem on the rail link from Deraa to Gaza (via Jerusalem). Digging there had ceased in 1909 (PEF records) but Lawrence could easily have visited the site on the journey from Ziza. As for the photograph of 'Lawrence in Howaitat dress' which Wilson finds 'preposterous', it was Mr Nigel Dennis, the *Sunday Telegraph* reviewer of my *Gertrude Bell*, who first insisted on the identification. Most observers, though not all, seem to agree with him. If it is Lawrence, the photo can only have been a joke. (It must be remembered that Lawrence was unknown to the world at large at that time.) Wilson's description of the subsequent meeting of Lawrence and Gertrude Bell at the Hogarths' place (p. 147), taken from a letter written by Hogarth to Woolley (6 July 1914), is an interesting sidelight. Neither Lawrence's nor Miss Bell's letters, as far as I can see, make mention of the meeting. **Hogarth at Carchemish**: Lawrence to Leeds 4–23 April 1914.

Chapter 4 *Secret Service* pages 59–80

Lawrence and Woolley, *Wilderness of Zin*; Woolley, *As I Seem to Remember*, p. 88ff; Lawrence, *Letters* and *Letters to Leeds*; Gertrude Bell, *Letters*; Winstone, *Illicit Adventure*, p. 143ff and notes; Official History of the War, MacMunn and Falls, *Military Operations in Egypt and Palestine to June 1917*; Moberly, *The Campaign in Mesopotamia*.

Cairo: Lawrence to Leeds 24.12.14 Lawrence and Woolley at Staff HQ: Lawrence to Leeds, 9.3.1915, and *ibid.* **Hogarth's role** 1914–15. Hogarth and Myres in Athens: Mackenzie, *First Athenian Memories*, p. 254ff. And see Wilson, *Lawrence of Arabia*, note p. 1008, 'The historian H. A. L. Fisher, whose brother was a senior naval officer,' apropos Hogarth's recruitment. The 'senior naval officer' brother of the Warden of New College was 'Number One', the First Sea Lord. Perhaps the truth of such matters will be revealed when Hogarth's long-promised biography appears and his papers are made available. In the meantime, I am confident of my own thesis. **Aubrey Herbert in Cairo**: Fitzherbert, *The Man Who Was Greenmantle*. p. 142ff. **Cairo**: Lawrence, *Letters* and *Letters to E. T. Leeds*, 24.12.14. **Woolley on Lawrence**: *Lawrence by His Friends*, p. 78ff. **Port Said**: notes in Winstone, *op. cit.*, p. 432ff; Weldon, *Hard Lying*, and Benn, *In the Side Shows*. **Arab Bureau**: *ibid*, and in particular FO882 in Public Record Office, *Arabian Report* and *Arab Bulletin* in India Office Library. **Gertrude Bell**, *ibid*, and her *Letters* (some unpublished, see author's *Gertrude Bell*). **Geoffrey Harold Woolley**, national press (22 April 1915 *et seq*), and see his *Sometimes a Soldier*.

Chapter 5 *Prisoner of War*, pages 81–97

Family correspondence: Woolley and others, *Kastamuni to Kedos*; Keeling, *Adventures in Turkey and Russia*; Barber, *Besieged in Kut and After*; Sandes, *In Kut and Captivity*. Note: *Mastik* is a potent drink in Turkish; *Ekmek* is bread.

Chapter 6 *Return to Archaeology*, pages 98–113

BM Corr. WAA, 1919–1922. Family records.

Demobilization: WO records (Mrs Witton).
Inexpedient for Lawrence to go out: BM WAA, Woolley to Kenyon, 26. xi. 19, and Kenyon to Woolley 6 Dec. 1919. **Conditions at Jerablus**: Jeremy Wilson, *op. cit.*, p. 544 says Woolley there 'at the end of 1918'. Unlikely the war with Turkey did not end until 31 October, when PoW's picked up by RN ships for repatriation. But he did, as Wilson suggests, find that half the old work force had perished from typhus during 1916.
Financial report 1919–20: BM WAA Woolley to Kenyon, 24 January 1920; and K to W, 18 Feb. Woolley to Lawrence re Carchemish, French and Turks, from Consulate-General Beirut: Bodleian Ms Res. d. 60, 17.i.21. **Damage to King's Gate and Carchemish reliefs**: Woolley/Kenyon, BM WAA 21. xii. 19/19.i.20. Guy: *ibid*. Digging resumes: BM WAA, 21 March 1920. **French and Turks at Carchemish**: *ibid*. **Certificate to Haj Wahi**: Woolley to Kenyon, 9 April. **Carchemish valediction**: *Spadework*, 77ff. **Purchase of 'Uplands'**: Statement by Meade-King & Co in BM WAA, 1920 (no date); and Mrs Witton to author, 9.10.1988. **Family life at Uplands**: Mrs Witton to author. **Ordination of Rev. G. H. Woolley** at Coventry Cathedral: *Times*, 20 December 1920. **Assistants**: BM WAA Woolley to E. Stanley Hall, Architectural Association, 22.vi.21. **Digging at Amarna**: Woolley to Kenyon, 30 Nov 1921. 'Indefinitely postponed': *ibid*, Woolley to Kenyon, 28 Dec 1921. Philadelphia, *ibid*. **Close down**: *ibid*, 31 Jan 1922. Egypt: *The Times*, 14 July 1920. General J. G. Maxwell, President EES, 'Tell El-Amarna', appeal for funds. **Amarna**: ILN, 6 May 1922; Woolley, Excavations at Tell al Amarna, 'Workmen's Model Dwellings of Three-thousand Years Ago'; and *ibid*, 16 Dec 1922, 'The Heretic Pharaoh's Prime Minister

and His House'. Woolley's version of events and his renderings of Egyptian
names have been retained, even though they have been drastically revised
by modern scholars. See also Aldred, *Akhenaten*, p. 202ff – Valley Tomb
No 55, evidence showing that plaster casts 'unearthed by Leonard Woolley
at the *maru* temple ... in the southern precincts at Amarna in 1922 and
... ignored ever since', helped the Russian Perepelkin to show that the
temple was built principally for Akhenaten's 'other Queen', Kiya, not for
Nefertiti 'as the British excavators had believed'. And *ibid*, p. 288ff,
'fragments of monuments excavated by Woolley in the *Maru*-aten show
that the sunshade temple there had also been taken from Kiya and bestowed
upon Meritaten [the King's eldest daughter].'

Chapter 7, *Ur of the Chaldees*, Pages 114–126

Robert H. Dyson Jr, 'Archival Glimpses of the Ur Expedition in the Years
1920 to 1926', documents from Archive of the University Museum of
Pennsylvania, Philadelphia, in *Expedition*, vol 20, number 1, Fall 1977. Sir
Max Mallowan, *ibid*, 'Recollections of Sir C. Leonard Woolley'. P.R.S.
Moorey, *ibid*, 'What do we know about the people buried in the Royal
Cemetery?'. Samuel Noah Kramer, *ibid*, 'The Ur Excavations and Sumerian
Literature'. Gertrude Bell, *The Letters of*. Mallowan and Wiseman (eds),
'Ur in Retrospect', in *Iraq*, vol xxii, 1960. Moorey, *Ur 'of the Chaldees'*,
Hall, *A Season's work at Ur*. Kramer, *The Sumerians*. Oppenheim, *Ancient
Mesopotamia*. *The Times*, Dec 1922–April 1932. Woolley, Ur Excavation
reports in *Antiquaries' Journal*, October 1923–October 1934; Woolley and
others, British Museum reports for the joint Museums. Education chief:
Lionel Smith. John G. Taylor (incorrectly 'J. E.' Taylor in Woolley and
most other sources): Woolley in *Abraham*, p. 161f.

Cuneiform and the languages of Sumer, Akkad and Elam: apart from
published sources, I am indebted particularly to Dr Irving Finkel of the
British Museum for his patience in guiding me through these prickly
thickets.
   Art, history and dating from the cylinders and cylinder seals: likewise,
my thanks to Dr Dominique Collon of the BM whose *First Impression* was
my guide.
   Invasion of Ur site, November 1922, by Muntafiq tribesmen: see
Woolley, *Spadework*, p. 91–2. Ubaid and Eridu: Hall, *A Season's Work at
Ur*, and ILN, 1.4.22; and Hall, *Ibid*, 'BM Excavations in Babylonia, 1919'
(Preliminary excavations at Tal Muqayyar [Ur], Tal Abu Shahrain [Eridu],
Tal al Obaid] Feb 1919–May 1919). Also, Woolley, *op. cit.*, p. 91ff.
Woolley's belief in precedence of Sumererian cities: Mallowan, *Iraq* XXII,
p. 9ff. Zigurrat: Woolley, *The Sumerians*, p. 61–67, and ILN 25 Oct 1924.
Carter, Petrie, Evans, Wace: *The Times* and *Illustrated London News*,
1922–26. **Flood**: see Edmond Sollberger, *The Babylonian Legend of the
Flood*, BM Publications, 1971. Miss Bell, J. M. Wilson: her *Letters*, 1
March 1923, Bell, 'wonderful finds': *ibid*, 9 Jan 1924. **Flood and king lists**,
chronology of city states: see Moorey, *op. cit.*, p. 32ff. At al-Ubaid: Bell,

op. cit., 6 March 1924, and Woolley, 'Tel el Obaid', ILN, 25.4.25. **Ziggurat and 3rd Dynasty of Ur**; ILN 25 April 1925; *note*: 3rd Dynasty now dated 2112–2004 BC; **Woolley's chronology** no longer accepted. Kurigalzu I, c 1390; Kurigalzu II, c 1343. Marshall and others: ILN, 13.11.1922, Marshall, Taxila, 'Where Greeks once Ruled in India'; *ibid*, 9.12.22 Tutankhamen; *ibid*, 1 March 1923, Wace, 'Stained with Agamemnon's Blood?', dagger from Mycenae; *ibid*, 27.2.26, Marshall, Mohenjo-Daro. **Moon-God**: Woolley, *ibid*, 18.4.25 and 25.4.25.

Chapter 8, *Treasures of Mesopotamia*, pages 127–139

Main sources as for chapter 7.

Workmen: Moorey, Ur *'of the Chaldees'*, p. 52, and Mallowan, *Iraq* XXII. **Woolley and Hamoudi**: Mallowan, *ibid*, p. 2f. **Constitution**: 10 July 1924. **Bell and Lionel Smith** at Ur: Bell, *Letters*, February 1924 *et seq*, and Mallowan, *op. cit.*, p. 11. Bell, Langdon at Kish. Bell, *op. cit.*, Jan 22, 1924, *et seq.*, Goddess 'Bau' or 'Baba'. Sidney Smith, Gadd, RAF: Woolley to Hall, BM WAA, 13–29 February 1924. **Katharine Keeling**, *née* Menke: Official Registry; Mallowan, *Memoirs*; Somerville College records; Mrs Keeling in Baghdad, Mrs Ailsa Corbett Winder to author. **Colonel Keeling**: *The Times*, 23 Sept 1919 (report dated Cairo, 21 Sept); death certificate issued at Cairo by Acting Vice Consul Edgar Grout, Application No. PSR 4642 B. Certificate issued under the Registration (Special Provisions) Act of 1957, Army Officers Records of War Deaths 1914–1921, given at the General Register Office London under seal, 12 May 1988, Application No. PSR G10650. I am indebted to Mrs Henrietta McCall for her help in researching this subject. England: BM WAA, 31 July 1924 *et seq*. Legrain: Dyson, *Expedition*, 10 Sept 1924 *et seq*. Ur 1925: BM Woolley to Hall, 3 Feb 1925 *et seq*, and Philadelphia, Legrain and Woolley to Gordon, 3 Jan 1925 *et seq*. Mallowan: *Memoirs*. **Death of Gertrude Bell**: Winstone, *op. cit*; *note*: In one of her last letters to her family, dated 2 June 1926, she wrote of being concerned at the size of the antiquities job she had undertaken, and at no longer having J. M. Wilson to help her, but 'I feel bound to fulfil the undertakings I gave when, at my instance, the Iraq Govt. allowed excavations to be begun 4 years ago.'

Chapter 9, *Marriage, Pu-abi and the Flood*, pages 140–156

Main sources as for chapters 7 and 8.

Carter's exchanges: *The Times* 27/7/25. **Lecture**: *The Times*, 23 May 1925. **Bath and Rev. Woolley**: Mrs Witton to author. **Disposal of collections**: Last Will and Testament of George Herbert Woolley, dated 3 March 1921. Codicil, filed 'on or shortly after 3rd March 1921', reads – 'My trustees shall in all cases sell each of my collections such as my "Arundel Collection" "Turner Collection" "Rembrandt Etchings" and "Bartolozzi Prints" en bloc.' **Woolley as guide**: Mallowan, *Memoirs*, p. 34ff, and *Iraq* XXII.

Andrae: BM WAA, Woolley to Hall, 12 Dec 1926. **Herzfeld**: *ibid*, Woolley to Hall, 25 July 1927. **Marston**: Professor W. G. Lambert to author, and see Marston, *The Bible Comes Alive*. **Ur correspondence with Gordon**: Philadelphia Museum files. See Dyson, *Expedition*, 8 July 1926 *et seq*.

Marriage: Mrs Witton, and Mr and Mrs Waters to author, recorded conversations during 1987–89. **Royal graves**: Woolley in *Ur of the Chaldees*, Benn, 1929, pp. 13ff, 83ff, and *Ur Excavations*, vol II, 1934; Moorey, *Ur 'of the Chaldees'*, p. 51ff, and *Expedition*, p. 924ff; BM WAA, Woolley to Hall, 15 Jan 1927 *et seq*. **Graves of king and queen**: Moorey, *Ur*, p. 62ff. '. . . rites of human sacrifice': ibid, p. 74ff; Woolley, ILN, 23 June 1927. **Ur gold**: Anon, ILN, 26.11.1927, 'A Miracle of Goldwork 5500 Years Old', and Woolley, ILN, 'The Gold Wig of Mes-Kalam-Dug, 2000 years earlier than Tutankhamen'; and *ibid* 3.3.1928, and 'Wholesale Human Sacrifice', 23.6.1928. **Staff at Ur**: Mallowan, *op. cit.*, p. 38ff. **Flood**: Moorey, *op. cit*, p. 24ff. **Ur and Sumerian life**: Woolley, *Abraham*, p. 61ff.

Chapter 10, 'Murder in Mesopotamia, pages 157–180

Ur general: BM WAA, 26.12.1927–15.9.1933. Mallowan, *Memoirs*, and *Iraq* XXII. Woolley, *Ur of the Chaldees*, *The Sumerians*, *Digging Up the Past* (based on a series of six radio broadcasts), and *Ur Excavations vol II*. *Antiquity*, Vol 1 Number 1 (March 1927) – Vol Number 30 (June 1934). Gadd, *History and Momuments of Ur*. Kramer, *The Sumerians*.

Wooley on Shub-ad's headdress, Sumerian art, human sacrifice and 'Scientific Treasure Hunting' in ILN 11.8.1928, 26.1.1929, 21.9.1929. **Woolley, Langdon, Hertzfeld and others in Iraq**: Bell, unpublished letters 9.3.1923, 28.10.25, 13.1.26 (University of Newcastle-upon-Tyne). Typescript of Journal of Mr C. F. Taylor in papers of Sir Christopher Cox, New College Library, beginning 'Christmas Eve 1932'; Mss (dated 1931) in library of Clifton College. **Stein**: Mirsky, *Sir Aurel Stein*. **R. S. Cooke**: A. T. Wilson in *Loyalties, Mesopotamia* (OUP 1931), Gertrude Bell, *Letters, passim*; Cooke succeeded Bell as Director of Antiquities, until 1929 when Sidney Smith took over for a year, succeeded. **Dates of Sargonid graves** in *Antiquity* Vol 2, Number 5 (2340–2195 BC now generally accepted). **Sayce**: *Antiquity* Vol 2, Number 6. **Sir Henry Lunn**: Woolley to J. L. Hammond, 16 May 1928, from 41a Chester Square, Bodleian Ms Hammond 21, Fol 133. **Agatha Christie, Max Mallowan and the Woolleys**: Mallowan's *Memoirs*; Mrs Rosalind Hicks to author, 11 August 1988–5 February 1989; Christie, *Murder in Mesopotamia*, and *An Autobiography*; and Keating, *Agatha Christie, First Lady of Crime*, and Morgan, *Agatha Christie*, and Sanders and Lovallo, *The Agatha Christie Companion*. **Review** of *The Sumerians*, *The Times*, 1 Feb 1929. **Madrid**: *The Times*, 20 June 1929. **Cavendish-Bentinck**, a life Trustee of the British Museum. **Freya Stark**: her *Letters* II from 30 Oct 1929, and *Beyond the Euphrates* from 28 Oct 1929. Baghdad 1930: Stark, *Letters*, and Mrs Corbett Winder to author, April 1989. **Agatha's bed**: An *Autobiography*, p. 420ff. **Nippur**, *ibid*; and Winstone, *Uncovering the Ancient World*, p. 203. **Marriage of**

Max and Agatha: see Morgan, *op cit.*, p. 187ff. Bridges: Bodleian, Dep. Bridges 14, fol. 43. **Woolley and Flood**: Mallowan, *Memoirs*; Malim, 'Noah's Flood' in *Antiquity* Vol 5 Number 17, 1931; Ceram, *op. cit.*, p. 32; and see *Cambridge Ancient History* Vol 1 Part 1 (CUP 1970). **Ur schoolbooks** etc; Woolley quoted in *The Times*, 14 May 1931; and Kramer *op. cit.*, p. 240f. **'Chaldaean' Ur**: see author's *Uncovering the Ancient World*, p. 312f. Sumerian King List, Kramer *op. cit.*, Appendix E.

Chapter 11, *Fame and Privation*, pages 181–200

Anecdotes and background: Family records, Mrs Witton and Mrs Waters, Mr Warren Laxton, in conversation and correspondence with author. **Ur general**: BM WAA 17 July 1934–14 July 1936; BBC talks: see Woolley, *Digging Up the Past* (introd). **Woolley as archaeologist**: Mr Sinclair Hood to author, August 1988; Woolley, *op. cit.*, p. 120ff; and Professors Seton Lloyd and W. G. Lambert to author, July–October 1988. Lecture, City of London: *The Times*, 7.8.1930. **Ur in the Ubaid period** and Woolley's 'Flood': Mallowan, *Memoirs*; Woolley, ILN 25 April 1925, 'Tell el Obaid'; *Antiquity* Vol V Number 18, 1931; Moorey, *Ur 'of the Chaldees'*, p. 32ff; Ceram, *Gods, Graves and Scholars*, p. 328ff. **Guy**: became director of Palestine Museum 1926 and head of British School in Jerusalem, see Drower, *Flinders Petrie*, **Woolley, Mallowan and Winckworth**: Professor Lambert to author, 1 July 1988; BM WAA 2 Sept 1935. Ogden: BM WAA 1933 (n/d). **Ogden's and Woolley's private enterprise**: BM WAA, undated; and Professor Lambert to author. **Birmingham City Museum**: Professor Lambert to author, and correspondence Mr Richard Lockett, Assistant Director of Curatorial Services, with author, 17 November 1988. **Small gifts**: ref to Sotheby's and Christie's catalogues reveals many items over the years which have come on to the market from the private collections of civil and military personnel in Iraq. **Wheeler** and **Courtauld Inst**: *The Times*, 11 October 1934. **Smith**: BM WAA, 10 Aug 1934–2 Sept 1935. *Antiquity*: Vol VIII, No 30. **Frankfort** and **Tal Asmar**: Woolley in *The Times*, 20 April 1934. **Antiquities Law**: *Antiquity* vol IX No 33, March 1935 (abbreviated from Woolley in *The Times*). **Knighthood**: *The Times*, 3 June 1935. **Marriage and family attitudes**: Mrs Witton to author. **Kipling**; Woolley, *Abraham*, and Birkenhead, *Rudyard Kipling*. 'Racial elements in Sumerian Art': Lecture by Woolley (3 April 1936) reprinted in Journal of Royal Society of Arts LXXXIV. **Antediluvian king lists and Genesis**: Woolley, *Sumerians*, p. 21ff; Ceram, *op. cit*, p. 216ff. **Amarna tablets**: see Cyril Aldred, *Akhenaten, A New Study*, and F. J. Giles, *Ikhanaton, Legend and History*, London 1970. **'Lacking in authority'**: Mallowan, in 'Sir C. Leonard Woolley', DNB.

Chapter 12, *Atchana and the Indus*, pages 201–216

Petrie: Drower, *Sir Flinders Petrie*, p. 398ff. **Woolley in Syria**: Woolley, *A Forgotten Kingdom*, and *Alalakh* (An account of excavations at Tell

Atchana in the Hatay, 1937–49, Report No 18, Society of Antiquities); BM WAA, 3 March 1936–26 May 1939.

The Times: 24.3.1936. Letter to Evans: 14 May 1936, Ashmolean Museum, internal records. Freya Stark: *Letters III.* **Cockerell**: BL MSS 52769 (783B); and Lady Horner, Violet Meynell (ed.) Friends of a Lifetime: Letters to Sydney Carlyle Cockerell, p. 374ff. **Brief report on excavations in Syria to end of 1937**: *The Times*, 22 Jan 1938. **Halaf pottery and period**: See John Curtis (ed.), *Fifty Years of Mesopotamian Discovery*, p. 30, and Woolley, *Forgotten Kingdom*, p. 25ff. **German influence**: Mallowan, *Memoirs*. **Woolley and India**: India Papers of 2nd Marquess of Zetland, Secretary of State for India, India Library and Records (British Library) MSS Eur. D. 609; *The Times*, 16 June 1938, 25 April 1939, 13 July 1939, 4 Dec 1939.

Chapter 13, *War, Art and Vita Nova*, pages 217–242

The Times, 25 April 1939, Syria: *ibid*, 3 August 1939. **Woolley and Smith**: BM WAA May 1939. **Lord Zetland**: Report on Archaeological Survey of India: IO, Zetland Papers. **Wheeler**: Hawkes, *Mortimer Wheeler*, p. 227. **Aurel Stein**: Mirsky, *Sir Aurel Stein*, p. 523ff. **Birdwood memorial lecture**: *The Times*, Dec 4, 1939; and Marshall in ILN, 13.11.22, 'Where Greeks Once Ruled in India'. **War service**: Army Lists: Ministry of Defence Library records; Sir Laurence Kirwan, past Director and Secretary of the Royal Geographical Society to author, 9 October 1988; Woolley, *Mediterranean Strategy, 1939–43*, compiled from official documents, BL Mss X. 705/262, and *A Record of the Work Done by the Military Authorities for the Protection of the Treasures of Art and History in War Areas*, War Office 1947, HMSO 1947 (2/6d); *The Times*, 6 Nov 1943, 2 Aug 1944, 22 Nov 1924, 3 Jan 1945, 19 April 1945; ILN, 9 July 1945, 8 Aug 1945. **Blunt and MI5**: see Costello, *Mask of Treachery*, p. 443f; *The Times*, 13 Oct 1988. **Eumorfopoulos**: *The Times*, 22 Dec 1939, Sir Leonard Woolley and 'A friend'. **Boulting**: Letter to Dr Duncan Noble, 14 Jan 1982. **Crawford**: Bodl. Mss Crawford, Letters of Sir Leonard Woolley to O. G. S. Crawford, 1944–?, 1956. **Hawkes on Wheeler**: see *Mortimer Wheeler*, p. 96. Huxley Memorial lecture at Royal Anthropological Institute, 1942; Dr Shaeffer and Ugarit: typescript *Woolley, Huxley Mem. Lecture* in Bodleian library. **Conference, Institute of Archaeology**: *The Times*, 9 Aug 1943. James Mann: *The Times*, 13 Jan 1944. **Wheeler**: Hawkes, *op, cit.*, p. 219. **Waterhouse**: see Costello, *op, cit.*, and Woolley, *Record of Work Done . . .* **Crawford**: Bodl. Mss Crawford. Fisher: Bodl. Ms Fisher 74, fol. 130. **Death of Lady Woolley**: *The Times*, 10 November 1945; funeral, *ibid*, 12 Nov; and 30 Jan 1946, her estate valued at £41,966,6s,7d.

Chapter 14, *'A bird let out of its cage'*, pages 243–259

Correspondence, BM WAA, 1 Sept 1945–7 Jan 1947; Crawford, Bodl, q.v; Kirwan, Royal Geographical Society files, 9 Jan–8 Nov 1946. Mrs Witton and Mrs Waters to author, correspondence and interviews, March–October 1988. Mallowan, *Memoirs*.

Atchana, post-war; Sinclair Hood to author, August 1988; William C. Brice to author, 20 Jan 1989; Hood, *Anatolian Studies*, Vol 1, No 1, 'Excavations at Tabara el Akrad, 1948–49'; Woolley, *A Forgotten Kingdom*, and *Alalakh*. **Myres**: Bodl. Ms Myres 42, folios 26–40. Woolley's dates, as with all chronology of his period, subject to modification in the light of modern scholarship; where I have qualified Woolley's findings I have used Brinkman's Mesopotamian chronology in Oppenheim, *Ancient Mesopotamia*, otherwise British Museum sources, but I have not attempted to correct all Woolley's dates some of which are still disputed. ILN, 25 October 1947. **Decree nisi**: *The Times*, 18 Dec 1947. **Waziristan**: *The Times*, 5 October 1946.

Chapter 15, *The Last Rites*, pages 260–281

Katharine and Bryce Memorial Lecture: Miss Pauline Adams, Librarian and Archivist, Somerville College, to author, 28 September. **Views on Woolley**; Sinclair Hood, Kirwan, Mrs Waters; corresp. and conversations with author, cited above, Chapter 14. *Note*: Crawford, Bodl. Mss 21, folio 44, appeared to be proposing a dig in Eritrea in 1947, in collaboration with Woolley, who suggested that he contact the War Office for approval and 'Larry Kirwan of RGS' for financial support. **Brice**: according to his own recollection, Mr Brice visited Woolley at Worten Mill (letter to author 20.1.89). **Shaftesbury and Teulon Porter**: Introd. to Woolley, *As I Seem to Remember*, and Mr Tony Innes, Shaftesbury and District Historical Society, to Mrs Witton, 17 Nov 1988 and subsequent telephone conversation with author. *Alalakh publication*, 1947–49; BM WAA 7 Jan 1947–28 Dec 1949. **UNESCO** and *History of Mankind*: Julian Huxley Papers, Rice University, 26 March 1949–28 April 1959; and Woolley's notes on correspondence with other experts. **Wheeler lecture**: 'Lessons of Taxila and Harappa', *The Times*, 22 Nov, 1950. **In America** (Philadelphia): Robert H. Dyson Jr in *Expedition*, Vol 20, No 1, and Professor Edith Porada to author. **BM Anniversary Exhibition**, 1956; Introd. to Curtis, *Fifty Years of Mesopotamian Discovery*. **Mallowan on Woolley and Smith**: related by Mr Terence Mitchell to author. **Interview with Sidney Smith**, notes committed to memory by Dr Duncan Noble, 12 June 1979, and recorded later same day. **Ur Report**: Seton Lloyd, *Antiquity*, Vol 31 1957. **Warburtons and Woolley**: Mrs Witton and Mrs Waters to author. **Death of Crawford** and other archaeologists: *Antiquity*, Vol 30, No 118, June 1956, and Bodl, Crawford Mss 54, folio 221; Woolley's last note to Crawford, dated 26 Sept 1956, a 'Caveat' on Wheeler's article in June issue headed 'The First Towns?', was set in type but was squeezed out by news of the death of Gordon Childe. A few days later, 28 November, Crawford himself died. **Carneiro and Committee**: Woolley to Carneiro, President of the Bureau, from Kingsworthy Court, 19 Nov 1957 and 2 Dec 1957, and to Huxley 29, ix.58. **Hospital** (at Basingstoke), letter to Lady (Juliette) Huxley, 31.i.58. **Myres**

Memorial Lectureship: *The Times*, 10 Nov 1959. **Woolley's bequests:** Last Will and Testament dated 6 September 1956, witnessed by Mr and Mrs Teulon Porter, and codicil providing for Mr and Mrs Waters, dated 14 Jan 1957, witnessed by the Teulon Porters; and second codicil, dated 15 February 1960, signed with his mark. **Birmingham City Council Museums and Art Gallery:** Mr Richard Lockett to author, 17 November 1988; *Turner Prints:* 'The Museum and Art Gallery purchased a number of 'Turner prints which had belonged to Woolley, a first group in 1975 and a second group in 1987. However, we only have it on the authority of one of the intervening owners that the first lot of prints came from the Woolley collection ... The second parcel had passed through the same hands ... *Archaeology:* The archaeology department has a considerable amount of material from Woolley's excavations at Ur including cuneiform tablets and watercolours made by Louise Perkins for publication as colour plates in the excavation reports. There are in addition a few pots from excavations at Tell Atchana.' The only recorded accessions to the Ashmolean collections are pottery pieces, chiefly Greek and Roman, see *Annual Report* of Museum for 1960, On 6 June 1989, a number of inscribed bricks and tablets, seals and works of art from the Uruk, Jamdat Nasr, Old Babylonian, and Ur III periods, were sold at Christie's, Freya Stark, *Letters*, 6 March 1960 to John Grey Murray, from Asolo. **Funeral service:** *The Times*, 25 February 1960. **Memorial service:** *The Times*, 15 March 1960. Julian Huxley, *Memories*, Vol II (Allen & Unwin 1973).

Bibliography

ALDRED, Cyril: *Akhenaten and Nefertiti*, Thames and Hudson 1973
—*Akhenaten King of Egypt*, Thames and Hudson 1988
ANDRAE, Walter: *Lebenserinnerungen eines Ausgraebers*, Berlin, 1961
BARBER, C.H.: *Besieged in Kut and After*, Blackwood, 1917
BELL, Gertrude (*ed* Lady Bell): *The Letters of Gertrude Bell*, Benn, 1927
BENN, Captain Wedgwood: *In the Side Shows*, Hodder & Stoughton, 1919
BIRKENHEAD, Lord: *Rudyard Kipling, Weidenfeld & Nicolson*, 1978
CARTER, Howard: *The Tomb of Tutankhamen*, Century 1983
—and MACE, A.C.: *The Discovery of the Tomb of Tutankhamen*, Dover 1977
CERAM, C.W. [Merak]: *Gods, Graves and Scholars*, trans. from *Goetter, Gräber und Gelehrte*, Hamburg-Stuttgart 1949; Gollancz 1952, Pelican 1974
CHRISTIE, Agatha: *Murder in Mesopotamia*, Collins, 1936; Fontana 1985
—*An Autobiography*, Collins, 1977
CHRISTIE (Mallowan) Agatha: *Come Tell Me How You Live*, Collins 1946; repr 1975
COLLON, Dominique: *First Impressions*, British Museum Publications 1987
CORBETT, Sir Julian: *Naval Operatons, 1914–18 War*, Vol. 3 the Mesopotamian Campaign, Official History, HMSO 1920–33
COSTELLO, John: *Mask of Treachery*, Collins, 1988
DROWER, Margaret S.: *Flinders Petrie*, Gollancz 1985
FALLS, Cyril: *Military Operations in Egypt and Palestine from June 1917*, Official History, HMSO 1920–33
GADD, C. J.: *History and Monuments of Ur*, Chatto and Windus 1929
HALL, H.R.: *A Season's Work at UR*, Methuen 1930
HAWKES, Jacquetta (ed.): *The World of the Past*, Thames and Hudson 1963
—*Mortimer Wheeler*, Weidenfeld 1982
HAYTER, William: *Spooner*, W. H. Allen 1977
HENNIG, Richard: *Die deutschen Bahnbauten in der Turkei*, Leipzig 1915

HONOUR, Alan Edward: *Treasures under the Sand*, Kingwood 1968

KEATING, H. R. F. (ed): *Agatha Christie, First Lady of Crime*, Weidenfeld and Nicolson 1977

KEELING, E. H.: *Adventures in Turkey and Russia*, Murray 1924

KELLER, Werner: (trans. Neil), *The Bible as History*, Book Club Associates 1956

KING, L. W.: *A History of Sumer and Akkad*, Chatto and Windus 1910

KRAMER, Samuel Noah: *The Sumerians*, University of Chicago Press 1963

LAWRENCE, T. E.: *Seven Pillars of Wisdom*, Cape 1935; Penguin 1962

—(ed Garnett), *The Letters of T. E. Lawrence*, Cape 1938

—(ed A. W. Lawrence), *T. E. Lawrence by His Friends*, Cape 1937

LEEDS, E. T.: *T. E. Lawrence: Letters to E. T. Leeds*, Whittington Press 1988

LLOYD, Seton: *Foundation in the Dust*, Introduction by Sir Leonard Woolley, OUP 1947

—*The Archaeology of Mesopotamia*, Thames and Hudson 1978

MACKENZIE, Compton: *First Athenian Memories*, Cassell, 1931

MACMUNN, G., and FALLS, Cyril: *Military Operations in Egypt and Palestine from Outbreak of War to June 1917*, Official History, HMSO 1920–33

MALLOWAN, Sir Max: *Mallowan's Memoirs*, Collins 1977

MARSTON, Sir Charles: *The Bible Comes Alive*, Eyre and Spottiswoode 1937

MEYNELL, Violet (ed): *Friends of a Lifetime: Letters to Sydney Carlyle Cockerell*, London 1940

—*The Best of Friends*, London 1956

MIRSKY, Jeannette: *Sir Aurel Stein*, Chicago 1977

MOBERLY, T.: *The Campaign in Mesopotamia*, Official History, HMSO 1920–33

MOORTGAT. A.: *The Art of Ancient Mesopotamia*, London 1969

MORGAN, Janet: *Agatha Christie*, Collins 1984

NEWBOLT, Sir Henry: *Naval Operations, 1914–18 War*, Vols. 4–5 Mesopotamia, Official History, HMSO 1920–33

OATES, D. and J.: *The Rise of Civilization*, Oxford 1976

OATES, J.: *Babylon*, London 1979

OPPENHEIM, A. Leo: (ed. Reiner) *Ancient Mesopotamia*, Chicago 1977

—*Letters from Mesopotamia*, Chicago 1968

POSTGATE, J. N.: *The First Empires*, Oxford 1977

ROUX, G. *Ancient Iraq*, Pelican 1986

SAGGS, H. W. F.: *The Greatness that was Babylon*, London 1962

SANDERS, Dennis, and LOVALLO, Len: *The Agatha Christie Companion*, W H Allen 1985

SANDES, E. W.: *In Kut and Captivity*, John Murray 1919

STARK, Freya: *Beyond Euphrates, Autobiography* (1928–33), Century 1951

—*Letters*, ed. Lucy Moorhead, 1976

STROMMENGER (Nagel), E, and HIRMER, M., *The Art of Ancient Mesopotamia*, London, 1964

VAN DE MIEROP, Marc: *Sumerian Administrative Documents*, Yale 1987

WELDON, L. B.: *Hard Lying*, Jenkins 1925

WILSON, Sir A. T.: *Loyalties: Mesopotamia 1914–17*, OUP 1930

—*Mesopotamia 1917–20: A Clash of Loyalties*, OUP 1931

WILSON, Jeremy: *T. E. Lawrence*, Heinemann 1989

WINSTONE, H. V. F.: *Gertrude Bell*, Cape 1976

—*The Illicit Adventure*, Cape 1982

—*The Diaries of Parker Pasha*, Quartet 1983

—*Uncovering the Ancient World*, Constable 1985

WOOLLEY, Sir C. Leonard: *Dead Towns and Living Men*, Milford 1920; with additional chapters, Cape 1932; revised and enlarged, Lutterworth 1954

—(ed) *From Kastamuni to Kedos*, Blackwell 1921

—*The Sumerians*, Oxford 1928

—*The Excavations at Ur and the Hebrew Records*, Allen & Unwin 1929

—*Digging up the Past*, Benn, 1930/1973; Penguin 1937/1960

—*Ur of the Chaldees, A record of seven years of excavation*, Benn 1929; new edition, Faber & Faber 1934; Penguin 1938; enlarged edition, Benn 1950; French edition, Paris 1938; Russian, Moscow 1961: Revised and updated as *Ur 'of the Chaldees'* (ed.) P. R. S. Moorey, Herbert Press 1982

—*Excavations at Ur, A record of twelve years' work*, Benn 1954; Barnes and Noble, New York, 1963

—*The Development of Sumerian Art*, Faber & Faber 1935

—*Abraham*, Faber & Faber, 1936

—*Ur: The First Phases*, Penguin, 1946

—*Middle East Archaeology*, Oxford, 1949

—*Spadework*, Lutterworth, 1953

—*A Forgotten Kingdom*, Penguin, 1953; revised, Max Parrish, 1959

—*History Unearthed*, Ernest Benn, 1958

—*Mesopotamia and the Middle East* (printed in Holland in 'Art of the World' series, No 7), 1961; and *Mesopotamien und Vorder Asien*, in 'Kunst der Welt', trans. L. Voelker, Holle, Baden-Baden, 1961

—*The Young Archaeologist*, illus. Sorrell, Edinburgh 1961

—*As I Seem to Remember*, Allen & Unwin for the Shaftesbury and District Society & Museum, 1962

—*The Beginnings of Civilization*, Vol One, Part II of History of Mankind, UNESCO/Allen & Unwin, 1963

WOOLLEY, Rev. G. H.: *A Journey to Palestine*, Oxford, 1935

—*Sometimes a Soldier*, Benn, 1963

WOOLLEY, Katharine: *Adventure Calls*, John Murray 1929

YOUNG, Major Sir Hubert: *The Independent Arab*, John Murray, 1933

SPECIALIST PUBLICATIONS
WOOLLEY C. L.: *Karanog; the town*, Philadelphia, 1909
—and MacIVER, D. R., Areika, Philadelphia 1909 (with chapter on
  Meroitic inscriptions by F. Ll. Griffith, and Foreword by Eckley B. Coxe
  Jr)
—and McIVER, D. R. Buhen, Philadelphia 1911
—and LAWRENCE, T. E., *The Wilderness of Zin*, Palestine Exploration
  Fund, 1915; with intro by Sir Frederic Kenyon, Cape, 1936
—and PEET, Thomas Eric, *The City of Akhenaten*, EES, 1923 (with
  chapters by B. Gunn and P. L. O. Guy)

CARCHEMISH EXCAVATIONS
Report on the Excavations at Djerablis conducted by C. L. Woolley and T.
  E. Lawrence, with introduction by Sir F. G. Kenyon:
Part 1 *Introduction* by D. G. Hogarth, 1914
Part 2 *The Town Defences* by C. L. Woolley, 1921
Part 3 *The Excavations in the Inner Town* by Sir Leonard Woolley, and
  The Hittite Inscriptions by R. D. Barnett, 1952

UR EXCAVATIONS
Antiquaries Journal: Journal of the Royal Society of Antiquaries
Vol III, No 4 October 1923
Vol IV, No 4 October 1924
Vol V, No 1 January 1925
Vol V, No 4 October 1925
Vol VI, No 4 October 1926
Vol VII, No 4 October 1927
Vol VIII, No 1 January 1928
Vol VIII, No 4 October 1928
Vol IX, No 4 October 1929
Vol X, No 4 October 1930
Vol XI, No 4 October 1931
Vol XII, No 4 October 1932
Vol XIII, No 4 October 1933
Vol XIV, No 4 October 1934
Volumes published jointly by the Trustees of the British Museum and the
  Museum of the University of Pennsylvania
Vol I, *Al 'Ubaid*, by C. L. Woolley and H. R. Hall, with chapters by C. J.
  Gadd and Sir Arthur Keith, 1927
Vol II, *The Royal Cemetery* by Woolley with chapters by E. R. Burrows
  SJ, Sir Arthur Keith, L. Legrain and H. J. Plenderleith, 1934
Vol III, *Archaic Seal Impressions* by L. Legrain, with note by Sir Leonard
  Wolley, 1936
Vol IV, *The Early Periods* by C. L. Woolley, 1955

Vol V, *The Ziggurat and its Surroundings* by C. L. Woolley, 1939

Vol VI, *The Ur III Period* by C. L. Woolley, 1974

Vol VII, *The Larsa Period* by C. L. Woolley, with contributions by M. E. L. Mallowan, 1976

Vol VIII, *The Kassite Period* by C. L. Woolley, edited by T. C. Mitchell, 1965

Vol IX, *The Neo-Babylonian and Persian Period*, by C. L. Woolley with contributions by M. E. L. Mallowan, 1962

Vol X, *Seal Cylinders* by L. Legrain, with introduction by Sir Leonard Woolley, 1951

TEXTS

Vol I, *Royal Inscriptions* by C. J. Gadd and L. Legrain, 1928

Vol II, *Archaic Texts* by E. Burrows, 1935

Vol III, *Business Documents of Third Dynasty of Ur* by L. Legrain, 1937/47

Vol IV, *Business Documents of Neo-Babylonian Period* by H. H. Figulla, 1949

Vol V, *Letters and Documents of Old Babylonian Period* by H. H. Figulla and W. J. Martin, 1953

Vol VI, *Literary Texts* by C. J. Gadd, S. N. Kramer and A. Shaffer, 1963–

Vol VII, *Middle Babylonian Legal Documents and Other Texts* by O. R. Gurney, 1974

Vol VIII, *Royal Inscriptions* Part II by E. Sollberger, 1965

Vol IX, *Economic Texts from the Third Dynasty* by D. Loding, 1976

Antiquities of Ur: Introduction to temporary exhibit of joint excavations of British Museum and Philadelphia University Museums, 1930

'Excavations at Ur, 1931–32 Expedition', *Journal of the University Museum of the University of Pennsylvania*, Vol 23, no 3, 1933

EXCAVATIONS AT ATCHANA-ALALAKH

HOOD, Sinclair: *Anatolian Studies*, Vol 1, Excavations at Tabara el Akrad, 1948–49

WOOLLEY, Sir Leonard: *Alalakh*. An account of excavations at Tell Atchana in the Hatay, 1937–1949. Contributions by C. J. Gadd and R. D. Barnett, *Report No 18*, Society of Antiquaries, 1955

—*Classification des céramiques antiques* No 2; Classification of the Pottery of Central and Northern Syria, 1922

MILITARY

Mediterranean Strategy, 1939–43; a typescript by Woolley

Protection of Art Treasures in War, A Report on Work of Military Authorities, War Office, 1947

MEMORIAL

Obit. *The Times*, 22 Feb 1960, Mallowan; JRAS 1960; *Sumer* 16 (1960); *Syria* 37 (1960), A. Parrot.

Iraq, vol XXII (1960), *Ur in Retrospect*, in Memory of Sir Leonard Woolley edited by M. E. L. Mallowan and D. J. Wiseman, British School of Archaeology in Iraq

Expedition, vol 20, Number 1, Fall 1977, *Recollections of C. Leonard Woolley* by Sir Max Mallowan; *Archival Glimpses of the Ur Expedition in the Years 1920 to 1926* selected by Robert H. Dyson Jr; *What do we know about the people buried in the Royal Cemetery?* by P. R. .S. Moorey; *The Ur Excavations and Sumerian Literature* by Samuel Noah Kramer.

Index

Note: Letters and words in square brackets indicate alternative spelling or rendering in Arabic and ancient languages. Except in a few instances recorded in the text, Woolley's dates and proper names have been preserved even though they are mostly superseded. They are shown in correct or alternative versions in the index. The reader is particularly recommended to refer to the index for dates of principal Mesopotamian rulers, which are taken from Professor J. A. Brinkman's lists in Oppenheim's *Ancient Mesopotamia*, and Professor S. N. Kramer's *The Sumerians*.

Isca, 229
Isis worship, 22
Ismailiya, 74
Israelites, 49ff
Istanbul, *see* Turkey
Italy, 23
Izmir, 91, 96f

Jabal Musa (Mount of Moses), 52
Jabal Tih, 52
Jaffa, 50, 68ff
Jamaica, 193
Jamal Pasha, Ahmad, 72, 77f
Jamdat Nasr, period, 155, 248
Japan, 145, 193
Jaussen, Père A., 50
Jeane d'Arc, warship, 76
Je[u]bail, 68
Jenkins, Capt RNR, 69
Jerab[a]lus, *see* Carchemish
Jeremiah, prophet, 104
Jews, *see* Semites
Johnian, The, 15f
Jones, Lt A. B., 88
Jordan, Julius, 184, 213
Jovian[us], Flavius, 180

Kadeis, Ain (Kadesh), 51
K[q]aimak[q]am, provincial governor,
    passim
Kalat Shargat, *see* Assur
Karbala, 173
Karchi, 162, 215
Kara Eyuk (Kanish), 169
Karanog, 21
Kara-Su, river, 203
Kashmir, 24, 162
Kastamuni, 81ff
Keble College, Oxford, 15
Kedos (Geddos), 91ff
Keeling, Col B. E. F., 131f, 140
Keeling, Lt E. H., 90
Keeling, Katharine Elizabeth, *see* Lady
    Woolley
Keith, Sir Arthur, 164
Kelly, Christine, 4
Kelmscott Press, 209
Kemal, Mustafa (Ataturk), 102, 107,
    110
Kenyon, Sir Frederic, 23, 37, 40f, 47,
    54, 100ff, 120, 131, 133ff, 142ff
Kenyon, Dame Kathleen, 230
Khalasa, 51

Khalil bin Ibrahim, 38
Khalil Pasha, 82
Khazel, Al, brothers, 70ff
Khirbet Kerak, pottery, 250ff
King Arthur, legend, 229
King, Leonard, 98
King lists (ancient), 123, 183, 196, 200
King's College, Cambridge, 234
King's College, London, 192
Kingsworthy Court, residence, 277
Kipling, Caroline, 195
Kipling, Lockwood, 194
Kipling, Rudyard, 5, 194ff
Kirby, Maj-Gen S. W., 226
Kirwan, Sir Laurence, 224, 243f, 261
Kish, 123, 126, 179, 183, 184
Kitchener, Field Marshal Lord, of
    Khartoum, 14, 50, 54, 59
Kligender, Professor, 238
Knesevich, A. and Emil, 51
Knossos, *see* Crete
Knowles, W. H., 18
Kock, Frau, 29, 38
Koldewey, Professor R., 33
Korosko, 22
Ko[u]ntilla, 52
Ko[u]ssaima, 51
Kramer, Professor Samuel Noah, 177
Kressenstein, Gen Kress von, 79
Kurds, 38, 44ff, 57, 100
Kuri-galzu I, King, (c. 1400 BC), 125
Kurnub, tal, 52
Kushan, 222
Kut al-Amara, 73, 82, 194
Kuwait, 53

Lacy, Lt R. S. 95
Lady Margaret Hall, Oxford, 19
Lahore, 215
Lake Van, 108
Lambert, Professor W. G., 4, 187
Lane, E. A., 203
Langdon, Professor Stephen, 123, 129,
    169
Lascaux, wall paintings, 140
Lavers, Ralph, 212
Lawrence, Professor, A. W., 44, 119
Lawrence, Thomas Edward, 4, 20, 23,
    26, 30, 34ff, 44ff, 49ff, 57, 59ff, 78,
    98, 101, 115, 223; Woolley's views
    on, 33, 64f
Laxton, Edith (*née* Woolley), 7, 10, 60,